An Introduction to Journalism

An Introduction to Journalism

Essential techniques and background knowledge

Richard Rudin
Trevor Ibbotson

AMSTERDAM BOSTON HEIDELBERG LONDON NEW YORK OXFORD
PARIS SAN DIEGO SAN FRANCISCO SINGAPORE SYDNEY TOKYO

Focal Press
An imprint of Elsevier Science
Linacre House, Jordan Hill, Oxford OX2 8DP
200 Wheeler Road, Burlington, MA 01803

First published 2002
Reprinted 2003

British Library Cataloguing in Publication Data
A catalogue record for this book is available from the British Library

Library of Congress Cataloguing in Publication Data
A catalogue record for this book is available from the Library of Congress

ISBN 0 240 51634 6

For information on all Focal Press publications visit our website at:
www.focalpress.com

Composition by Genesis Typesetting, Rochester, Kent
Printed and bound in Great Britain

Contents

Contents

About the authors

Richard Rudin

Richard initially trained and practised as a newspaper journalist through the National Council for the Training of Journalists' (NCTJ) scheme, on weekly and evening newspapers. He then turned to radio journalism, initially in the commercial sector, reporting on many stories of national importance for Independent Radio News, as well as presenting major news programmes. He gained broader radio, as well as initial television experience, with the British Forces' Broadcasting Network in Germany. On returning to the UK Richard held senior editorial, production and presentation roles on major BBC and commercial stations, gaining an Open University honours degree and teaching qualification along the way – later adding an M.A. in mass communications from the University of Leicester.

His first lecturing and tutoring work was with the City and Guilds Media Techniques Certificate: Journalism and Radio and this led to a full-time post as a journalism lecturer at Liverpool Community College, teaching on City and Guilds, NCTJ, NVQ and postgraduate journalism courses, as well as setting exams in media for BTEC. He then became a senior lecturer in journalism at Liverpool John Moores University, where he teaches a variety of subjects at both undergraduate and postgraduate level. He remains a close observer of, and participant in, journalism and the media, including contributions to BBC Radio 4's media discussion programme *The Message* and articles for *RADIO Magazine*, as well as wide-ranging external examining, consultation and research.

Further details at: www.richardrudin.com

Trevor Ibbotson

Trevor is an independent media consultant, lecturer, media producer and writer. He is Chief Examiner, Specialist Media Advisor and External Verifier for the City and Guilds Diploma and Certificates in Media Techniques. From 1995 to 2001 he was Chief Examiner for GNVQ Media: Communication and Production for the OCR awarding body. Since 1997 he has been an External Moderator of OCN Schemes in Radio, Journalism and Television for the South of England Open College Network, University of Brighton. He has been closely involved with national curriculum development in vocational media qualifications and has worked extensively as a consultant for QCA and the former NCVQ. In 2001, on behalf of the City and Guilds, he was instrumental in mapping their existing and new vocational media schemes to the occupational standards laid down by Skillset, the National Training Organization for TV, radio, film, video and interactive media and The Publishing National Training Organization for newspaper and periodical journalism. He has over 30 years lecturing experience in further and higher education and has worked on City and Guilds, BTEC, NCTJ, BCTJ and degree-level courses as well as organizing and delivering short training courses in communication skills and media production. Trevor is keenly interested in community service broadcasting and has contributed to RSLs such as ETFM and Tube Radio at Thames Valley University, as well as delivering radio training for Horizon 'On Air' Transnational Refugee Projects in West London. In 2001, in conjunction with CSV Training Wales, he helped set up City and Guilds validation and assessment for Gem TV, part of the Gemini Trust, which is training young people in television production in Ethiopia.

Introduction

The idea for this book took hold many years ago. Like a lot of good ideas it occurred to several people in different parts of the country at about the same time. Many of these people were tutors and lecturers on the City and Guilds Media Techniques Certificate: Journalism and Radio. This course, which has recently been revised and upgraded to become The City and Guilds Diploma in Media Techniques, had already been running for many years across the UK, the Irish Republic and overseas and provides an excellent grounding in journalism and media production. As well as practical skills in print and broadcast journalism, students on this course are also required to pass an exam in media history, public administration, law, organization and professional practices within the industry. The City and Guilds' syllabus overlapped with many other respected and well established journalism and media courses and the burgeoning number of journalism degrees. There seemed to be no suitable book on the market that 'did the job' as an introductory and comprehensive core text.

True, there were a number of excellent books on journalism practice in different media, some of which had a little theory and background to the respective sectors of the industry; others were superb on the general background and theory but did not cover the full range of practice in all the main journalism media.

'As no one else has written the book we need, why don't we write it ourselves?' asked our tutors. It was thought important that, as the book needed to have broad appeal and content, at least two authors with different backgrounds should be involved. The job fell to Trevor Ibbotson, Chief Examiner of the City and Guilds vocational Media schemes and Richard Rudin, who had wide experience in industry and further and higher education.

The authors approached the task with due humility: this is not intended to replace the many excellent texts and other sources on the different topics but rather inspire the reader to further investigate and further develop their knowledge and practice in some or all of the areas covered.

In fact, the scope of the book presented the authors' greatest challenge. The City and Guilds' emphases on print and radio journalism production, media industry and history, law and government (central, devolved and local) are reflected in the length of the chapters devoted to those topics. Television and online journalism are also closely examined, as is freelance journalism – a hugely significant sector. The regulatory framework and vital health and safety matters are also included.

The approach throughout the book is to be 'journalism centred': all topics are related to the interests and concerns of journalists and journalism. Each chapter concludes with suggested activities for tutors, students and trainees, as well as an extensive list of *Sources and resources* so that tutors, students and trainees can further study and investigate each topic.

As well as those studying for and training in journalism it is hoped the book will be of use to those already successfully employed in the media – and not just as journalists – who need to check on certain aspects that affect their work, such as the law or the workings of different levels of government.

Although the material and outlook of the book is focused on the UK it is hoped that readers in many other countries will find much in the book that is relevant and useful.

The book could not have been completed without detailed feedback – at various stages of its development – from an 'ad hoc' team of educators and trainers from a wide range of institutions and organizations, who checked the content of individual chapters both for accuracy and relevance to their courses' requirements. Special thanks are due to Professor John Herbert of Staffordshire University – who is also a prolific author for Focal Press; Tim Crook of Goldsmiths University College; Pete Whitehouse and Sue Green of City of Wolverhampton College; Colin Farmery, Scott Tobin and Clare Marczak of St Vincent College, Gosport; Mike Ward of the University of Central Lancashire; Sue Farringdon, David McBurney and Paul Richards of CSV Media, and Sandy Felton of Liverpool Community College who not only contributed to the 'freelance' section and reviewed some of the first drafts of key chapters, but read through the whole, completed, manuscript. The authors are immensely grateful to the generous, supportive and detailed comments, corrections and amendments from these dedicated and inspirational educators and trainers.

Many more people engaged in both education and industry gave advice, suggestions and otherwise provided vital co-operation in the research, writing and photography for the book, including Steve Bone, Chief Reporter at *The News*, Portsmouth, for professional advice and permission to use his stories; Steve Harrison and his team at Trinity Digital Media in Liverpool; freelance journalists Mike Hally, Martin Kelner and Penny Kiley; News Editor Ruby Williams and her team at BBC Radio Merseyside and Robin Collins of Keylink Communications in Kirkby, Merseyside.

A number of organizations, from the National Union of Journalists to government departments, provided up-to-date information and clarification of matters when there appeared to be contradictions or ambiguities in published material. Naturally though any inaccuracies, inconsistencies and omissions, emphases and opinions, are the responsibility of the authors.

The whole project has been overseen by Beth Howard, Commissioning Editor at Focal Press, who dealt with her two 'charges' with extraordinary tact, diplomacy, imagination and thoroughness; providing encouragement and motivation whilst not being afraid to act firmly and decisively when a particular problem or issue appeared to be incapable of resolution!

Richard would also like to thank his employers, Liverpool John Moores University, for supporting his work on this project, especially Professor Roger Webster, Director of the School of Media, Critical and Creative Arts. Colleagues and students – past and present – in the School's Journalism Department have provided much inspiration and motivation.

Finally, part-time authors cannot hope to complete their projects without the support and understanding of their families, who grin and bear it when domestic duties are abandoned and weekends and holidays taken up with THE BOOK! So, final and special thanks and gratitude to Lynda, Alison and David.

1 Background and issues

Introduction

Journalism covers a huge range of output across all media and is recognizable as a form of communication in almost every country of the world. It is estimated that 80 per cent of adults in Britain read at least one national newspaper regularly and 75 per cent read a Sunday newspaper (McNair, 1999: 19). Most people rely on journalism for surveillance – to inform them about what is going on in the world. Clearly very few have direct experience of events and, just as importantly, they need to know what has not happened – if, when they wake and hear the breakfast-time bulletin leading on a relatively 'unexciting' story, they can be satisfied that 'nothing much' has happened overnight. Journalism also has an important influence in their views and attitudes.

Most people cite television as their most important source of news (*ibid.*) even if, as we have seen, audiences for the main TV news programmes have apparently declined in recent years. As will be argued in Chapter 7, radio remains an important source of news for most people, with almost all stations carrying a regular news service, and has a unique strength as well as some limitations as a news media. Then, of course, there are hundreds of local and regional newspapers, periodicals of all kinds and, increasingly important, online/Internet services (Peak and Fisher, 2002).

All of these outlets require journalists. Journalism is an expanding profession and, judged from the numbers of applicants to university, college and training courses, an ever more desirable career. Because of the diversity in both employers and types of journalism employment it is hard to determine precise numbers employed as journalists. The National Union of Journalists (NUJ) – the main journalism trades union in the UK – had around 25 000 paid-up members in 2001 but union membership varies widely in different sectors. For reasons that will be explored in Chapter 9 freelance journalists are more likely to feel the need of union membership than are employees and the BBC's continued recognition of the union means that broadcasting has a relatively high proportion of union membership. However, the NUJ believes that the magazine and online sectors are relatively under-represented. NUJ membership in 2001 by sector in rounded figures is as in Figure 1.1.

Freelance	6000
Provincial newspapers	5000
Broadcasting	4800
National newspapers	3200
Magazines	2800
PR	1600
Books	1100
News agencies	500
Online	50

Source: NUJ.

Figure 1.1

What kind of people are journalists?

The most detailed survey into the make-up and background of journalists in the UK was carried out by Delano and Henningham (1995). It showed that journalism is predominantly practised by white people, mostly (75 per cent) male, on average in their young middle age or late youth (mid to late 30s, but females being significantly younger on average than males). The figures supplied by the NUJ indicate that since this survey broadcasting in particular has seen a sharp rise in the proportion of females. About two-thirds of all journalists were married and just under half were brought up in the Church of England. Further analysis by the authors into the background, attitudes and motivations of British journalists (Henningham and Delano, 1998: 145) indicated that nearly one-quarter had decided they wanted to pursue a career in journalism by the age of 14 and fully two-thirds by 19. The largest proportion – 23 per cent – became journalists because of their writing skills. This is emphasized by the choice of the increasing numbers of journalists who are graduates: 48 per cent of journalists' degrees were in the arts, science was the discipline of just 5 per cent and commerce/business only 3 per cent (*ibid*: 149). Only 14 per cent said they had an 'intrinsic interest' in news and current affairs and just 2 per cent were motivated by a desire to influence public life.

A clear majority intended voting Labour at the next election, only 6 per cent being Conservative voters. This presents an interesting variance between the political allegiance of the national press at that time and that of the journalists. Clearly not every journalist at that time believed everything they wrote! This statistic also gives credence to complaints by the Conservative Party that most journalists are unsympathetic to their views. The gap between Labour- and Conservative-supporting journalists is likely to have widened still further since then, if it has followed the change in general public support for those parties. Furthermore, this may have implications not just for reporting of party politics as such but for the overall attitudes and sets of assumptions made by journalists. The journalists generally took liberal positions on a range of social, economic and moral issues (*ibid*: 151). The reason for this is probably not so much that journalists become 'corrupted' by being in the journalistic trade but more that journalism disproportionately attracts those who are suspicious of the establishment, are more likely to be personalities who question the 'status quo' and may be hostile to those holding and controlling wealth, as well as being more 'relaxed' than most in the population about moral/social issues. As we shall see in the section on the history of the press this is not a new phenomenon: political radicalism and constitutional change has been linked with the development of journalism.

Nearly 70 per cent of journalists in the 1995 survey had attended university or college – far more than the national average – and the proportion of graduates has increased still further since then. Journalism is now overwhelmingly a graduate profession: a huge change on the position 20 years earlier when Richard Rudin began his career!

The Delano and Henningham survey indicated that almost all journalists felt their job entailed delivering information to the public as quickly as possible; nearly 90 per cent put a high value on scrutinizing government claims and statements and almost as many in providing analysis and interpretation of complex problems. Over half thought it important to give 'ordinary people' a chance to express views on public affairs and almost half thought the provision of entertainment was an important part of their function.

Heroes or villains?

The image of the journalist – like others in the public eye such as doctors and police officers – has varied widely through different periods of time and amongst different sectors of the population. Many people seem to hold contradictory views about journalists: applauded when they uncover wrongdoing, fighting bureaucracy and tackle powerful, corrupt figures on behalf of the 'common person' – often putting themselves at risk of physical harm or harassment by the authorities; derided and condemned when they appear to have grossly invaded people's privacy or been rude, aggressive or devious.

The question of trust seems crucial here: if the public don't believe what they read, see and hear from the journalistic media, then the whole basis of journalism would seem to be undermined. As it will be argued in other chapters in this book, for journalists credibility is everything. Yet a pan-European survey by the TV Strategy Group reported in the *Press Gazette* (20 November 1998) showed that journalists had the lowest 'trust rating', not only over Europe but also when compared with audiences and readers in the USA. Of the different sectors, magazine journalists came off worst – only 28 per cent of readers said they believed or partially believed news reported in magazines. Across Europe radio was shown to be the most trusted medium.

Not surprisingly this survey, which reinforced others in the same vein (the same article also quoted a British Social Attitude Survey that found just 15 per cent of national newspaper readers trusted journalists in this sector to pursue the truth above getting a good story), offended many UK journalists. *The Guardian*'s editor Alan Rusbridger listed a whole range of cases in which journalists had played a positive, even heroic, role in exposing government propaganda and secrecy over vital issues of public interest, political sleaze, cover-ups and corruption in industry and public services, and in publishing miscarriages of justice – resulting in the release of those who had been wrongfully convicted. Not surprisingly Rusbridger was hurt and a little peeved by such surveys. He told the Guild of Editors 'If you had any official agency like that, they would be heroes. It would be a hailed and respected organisation. And yet we in the press are unhailed, unrespected, untrusted' (Reeves, 1998).

The heroic status of journalists was enhanced by the reporting of the war in Afghanistan from October 2001. Correspondents from the western media endured great hardship as well as enormous danger – seven western journalists were killed in the first few weeks of the war – to bring the story to their readers and audiences. The value of independent journalism was easily recognized at a time when the western allies – chiefly the USA and UK – and the Taliban regime were making contradictory claims about the conduct and effects of the conflict. The reporting seemed to have had an effect on the development of the war itself – the BBC's World Affairs Editor John Simpson even claimed that the BBC had liberated Kabul! (A few days later though he explained that what he had meant to say was that the population *heard* of their liberation first from the BBC (BBC, 2001). The use of new technology, especially the satellite videophone, which enabled 'live' pictures and reports to be broadcast, was a significant factor in the reporting.

There can be no doubt that those in government and other powerful institutions believe journalism has a powerful – perhaps crucial – influence on society, on attitudes, values and loyalties. The phenomenon of 'spin doctors' (see Chapter 11 on central government) testifies that politicians believe that seizing the news agenda – what gets reported and what does not, as well as the way those stories are reported – is a vital job of government.

Journalists are often criticized for becoming too closely involved with their subjects, of becoming part of the establishment, even involved in a conspiracy with the various elites in society – politicians, celebrities of all kinds, business leaders, Royalty, etc. One claim close to most journalists' hearts is that they are distinct from other groups in that they retain their independence, distance and detachment. Although they may have to strike 'deals' with (often) highly paid, highly influential, insistent and even bullying PR types, agents and the rest of the 'cast of characters', journalists should always remember they are working for their audience.

What is journalism?

It is sometimes suggested that any communication of information or the relaying of 'real' events is journalism. This is certainly wrong. For example, the broadcasting of proceedings in Parliament, unvarnished and unadorned by any form of editing or commentary, is not journalism – it is merely the relaying of an event. The publication or broadcasting of football results is not journalism, it is merely information. As we shall see in Chapter 13, this concept is important when it comes to the question of copyright. Journalism involves the sifting and editing of information, comments and events into a form that is recognizably different from the pure form in which they first occurred. Journalism is about putting events, ideas, information and controversies into context. It is about selection and presentation. Above all, perhaps, it is about the assessment of the validity, truthfulness or representativeness of actions or comments.

News is a noun clearly linked with journalism – and therefore a good starting point for analysing the whole concept of journalism.

What is news?

The usual definition of news is something that is 'new, interesting and true'. But that definition is not sufficient to categorize journalism and becomes progressively more problematic.

New is the least difficult; there is unlikely to be an argument over whether something has just or recently happened.

Interesting is a little bit more difficult because the obvious question arises 'interesting to whom?'. Our interest in a story is likely to be determined partly by where we live and by our economic and social position. Nevertheless, there will probably be broad agreement about some stories. For example, it is unlikely that anyone would seriously argue that the fact that hundreds of jumbo jets took off, flew and landed without incident is not news, whereas a jumbo jet that crashes with the loss of hundreds of lives lost is news.

Even so, why is it that only a tiny fraction of the billions of events that happen in the world each day that might pass the basic criteria – and would certainly be 'new' and 'interesting' to at least the direct participants in the 'story' – do not make it into even the local media, with even fewer making it to national and international news media? Academics Galtung and Ruge (van Ginneken, 1998: 28–29) have suggested there are 11 factors that influence whether an event is regarded as news and, if so, what importance is given to it (Figure 1.2).

But what is *true*? As anyone who has been involved either as a participant or professional in a road traffic accident knows, almost everyone involved in has a different perspective and account of what happened. Presuming they are not lying – saying something they know to be untrue – we can see that all their accounts are 'true' and yet all different. The job of the journalist is to assess those different accounts and to try to find a coherent, concise and objective account of what happened. This, of course, presumes that the journalist has no bias or direct involvement in the story or its participants or for any other

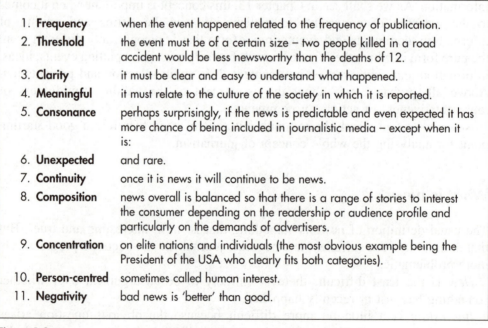

1. Frequency	when the event happened related to the frequency of publication.
2. Threshold	the event must be of a certain size – two people killed in a road accident would be less newsworthy than the deaths of 12.
3. Clarity	it must be clear and easy to understand what happened.
4. Meaningful	it must relate to the culture of the society in which it is reported.
5. Consonance	perhaps surprisingly, if the news is predictable and even expected it has more chance of being included in journalistic media – except when it is:
6. Unexpected	and rare.
7. Continuity	once it is news it will continue to be news.
8. Composition	news overall is balanced so that there is a range of stories to interest the consumer depending on the readership or audience profile and particularly on the demands of advertisers.
9. Concentration	on elite nations and individuals (the most obvious example being the President of the USA who clearly fits both categories).
10. Person-centred	sometimes called human interest.
11. Negativity	bad news is 'better' than good.

Figure 1.2

reason maybe less than objective. Indeed, as we shall see, the whole notion of journalists being impartial and objective, even if they genuinely wish to be so, is highly contentious.

Influences on journalism

As well as the factors identified by Galtung and Ruge, there are many important – often decisive – influences that affect both process and product. Most scholars and commentators agree that the chief influences are:

- *Ownership and control*. Most journalistic output is subject to the influence of the political, economic and ideology of a relatively few powerful companies and organizations. Journalists are likely to have their work 'amended' to fit in with these interests and, even if starting off with high ideals, operate 'self-censorship' in order to gain promotion and favour with the 'bosses'.
- *Financial*: linked to the above. The amount of money devoted to journalism will – at least in capitalist enterprises – be limited in order to produce maximum profitability. Journalism is still a relatively expensive, labour-intensive, operation. The need to produce a profit and/or meet audience targets is clearly a major influence in the form and content of journalism output.
- *Time, space and technology*. All journalism has to be produced to an immovable deadline: this inevitably means that work often has to be published or broadcast in a less than 'perfect' state and before facts and other material can be properly checked. Journalism has to be cut to fit in with the space or time available. As we've seen in the Galtung and Ruge analysis there is a concentration on elite nations and individuals. There is a practical as well as an ideological reason for this – pictures and reports are more likely to be available from and about rich industrialized countries, so a disaster in the USA, for example, is likely to receive more coverage than one in, for example, a remote part of the Indian sub-continent *partly* because there is more likely to be material available from the former. Television, in particular, 'needs' moving pictures. Linked with these limitations are:
- *Bureaucratic and work routines*. Journalists have to fit in with pre-ordained and usually inflexible requirements of newsrooms. Copy, audio and pictures have to be ready for a set time and in a set form and this requires fairly inflexible organization and procedures.

Journalism is about more than reporting 'news'

One of the main claims about journalism is that it has an important watchdog role: journalists are the eyes and ears of the public and help ensure that people, particularly those in public life, are acting properly and honestly. Whereas few people will have the time or interest to attend meetings of law courts, councils and other public bodies, the journalist's presence at such meetings ensures that business is conducted correctly and fairly. Furthermore, it is claimed that it is the knowledge that journalists are present and will check on how decisions are made that 'encourages' anyone who might be thinking of acting improperly to at least think again.

If we decide that journalism does not have to be all 'serious' or 'hard' news but can also be light, entertaining and about relatively obscure matters – or at least those that are of interest to only a small minority of people – then any definition must eschew defining journalism simply as news. Otherwise, we have to ask: what are all those people labouring away on magazines about small reptiles or particular types of antiques or indeed writing gossip items about celebrities if they are not journalists involved in something called journalism? Nor should any definition be specific to any type or types of media: someone working on an online service is as much a journalist as one working for a national newspaper, provided the work meets our broad definition, which is described in Figure 1.3.

Note the 'defined audience'. Journalism is all about producing a product – sometimes discussed as commodification – and is a social construction, which is formed and limited by the dominant ideology of a society: a set of views and ideas that are presumed to be 'normal' and 'common sense'. As in the production of any item, those manufacturing and producing it must know who is going to want that product. The audience – meant here to encompass viewers, readers, listeners, Web surfers, etc. – may be large or small, in a small geographical area

---

1. Selecting, assessing and editing information.
2. Describing events, which are of legitimate public interest or which are entertaining/non-serious, but are interesting to a defined audience.
3. Probing and testing claims and statements – especially those of authority figures (political, social, economic elites).
4. Acting as a 'watchdog' for the public benefit and investigating issues of concern and claims of wrong-doing that appear to be against the public interest.
5. Provide outlets for, and stimulating comment and opinion.

ALL:

6. Presented in an engaging way and appropriate to the medium of transmission.

Figure 1.3

or worldwide. But whatever the intended audience and whatever medium or media is used, journalism is a disciplined process having the end result always in mind.

The bit about 'interesting' is important too – we've already seen the importance of this adjective in relation to defining 'news' but it must be presented in such a way as to interest the audience – whether that is football fans, eminent surgeons, antique lovers, etc. Failure to recognize and meet this principle is the way to the bankruptcy court and the unemployment line.

The watchdog role is discussed above, but note the introduction of the idea of matters that are in the public interest: exactly what this public interest is (as opposed to what interests the public). This is one of the liveliest areas of debate in journalism today and is discussed further below in relation to privacy.

Finally, the medium (of transmission) may or may not be the message – but it is important. If a story is written for a newspaper it should be very different from the way it is presented for radio, TV, online, etc. As we shall see in this book, although there is a great deal of talk of convergence, different media do have different requirements and conventions and require different techniques. Multimedia presentations of a story require multimedia approaches and techniques.

Serious versus non-serious journalism

Central to much of the debates about the news media in the UK today is the concern over dumbing down and the apparent dominance of trivial, non-serious journalism at the expense of 'serious' matters – the latter is often described as journalism of the public sphere. Debates about the role and function of journalism have been going on for centuries but probably became more pressing and contentious at the end of the eighteenth and beginning of the nineteenth centuries, for it was this period that saw the development of democratic ideas, most obviously connected to the widening of the electoral franchise (the numbers and types of people eligible to vote) and with it the development of party politics. It was argued that if more of the population were to be given the vote then they needed both information and discussion of public issues to enable them to make a rational choice. Certainly, twenty-first century news media see this as very much their role: most obviously this tasks the form of leader, or comment/opinion columns in newspapers and in *Question Time*-type programmes on the radio and television. Because of the requirement on broadcasting to be fair and impartial, these media tend to be more facilitators of the debate: they set up the programmes that allow others to debate the issues, presided over by a neutral chairperson. The print media, having none of these restrictions, offer their own views (naturally these are nearly always those of the proprietors, senior editorial staff, or both).

Classifying types of journalism

There have been various attempts at classifying the news media, most commonly in the newspaper sector, between tabloid and broadsheet – which technically refer to the physical size of the newspapers but has been equated to the seriousness and depth of news coverage; tabloid equated with down-market, mostly trivia-led news and 'broadsheet' being serious newspapers, sometimes described even more contentiously as the 'quality press'. This has been refined to include 'mid-market' tabloid newspapers on one hand and the 'red tops' (so called because of the red mast-head) as the least serious/most trivial. 'Tabloid' is often used as a piece of short-hand to describe other journalistic media.

Other typologies or classifications have divided newspapers – and some other journalistic media – between elite and non-elite, as the readerships or audiences of the former are mainly those in the higher socio-demographic categories in society. Another related and often interchangeable classification is based on 'high' 'middle' and 'low' brow, based on the intellectual level at which the journalism is aimed.

←———————— Most complex		Least complex ————————→		
1	**2**	**3**	**4**	**5**
Daily Telegraph/ Sunday Telegraph; The Times/Sunday Times; The Independent/ Independent on Sunday; The Guardian; The Observer; Sunday Business	The Scotsman; daily morning paid-for regional press	Daily Mail/Mail on Sunday; Express/ Sunday Express; paid-for regional evening/regional Sunday press; paid-for weekly newspapers	The Sun; Mirror/ Sunday Mirror; News of the World; The People; daily regional free-sheets; weekly free-sheets	Daily Star; The Sport/ Sunday Sport
The Economist; The Spectator; New Statesman	The Week; Radio Times	Woman's Own	Hello!	What's on TV
Newsnight (BBC 2); Channel 4 News; The World Tonight (BBC Radio 4)	10 O'Clock News (BBC 1); Today (BBC Radio 4)	6 O'Clock News (BBC 1); News at Ten (ITV); Sky News; Five Live Breakfast (BBC Radio 5 Live); BBC local radio news	Channel 5 News; local commercial and national commercial Virgin and talkSport radio news	Big Breakfast news (Channel 4)

Figure 1.4 Levels of complexity of journalistic media/products

Figure 1.4 synthesizes these various approaches into a classification based on complexity: what level of education – particularly vocabulary – is required to easily understand what is being presented? What level of knowledge is assumed or required to understand it? How much of the reader's attention is needed in order to absorb its contents? What is the depth, breadth and range of material covered? What proportion of the output could be described as belonging to the public sphere? By considering these factors a five-tier classification is possible, ranging from 1: highest complexity, to 5: lowest complexity. Clearly, where a range of titles and/or output is described in one category (e.g., daily morning paid-for regional press) the level given is an average for that sector: individual examples could well be one category either side of that given. Although the second row gives examples of periodicals, in general these are so varied and specialist that is impossible to make even broad generalizations.

Future of journalism: issues and developments

Around the turn of the twenty-first century there was much excited talk about information technology, especially the Internet, leading journalism – and the media generally – into a brave new world in which the customer, citizen or consumer would be king: access to news and current affairs of all kinds would be available to all, any time, anywhere. Media companies large and small invested massively in the technology, many fearful that if they didn't they would be left behind. Linked to this was the prospect of converging technologies, making the concept of 'TV', 'computer' and 'telephone' redundant: new or adapted devices would do everything in the one box.

Then, just as the millennium began there was the phenomenon of the 'burst of the dot com bubble': the stock market, investment fund-holders and financial institutions suddenly lost confidence in new companies that had borrowed huge amounts of money but had no assets – or profits. Many went bust. At the same time older, established media companies also cut back on their investment in new technology, leaving hundreds redundant. The death of newspapers – so often predicted in the past with the arrival of each new medium – proved once again to have been exaggerated. If anything the online versions of newspapers appear to have stimulated readership of 'hard copies'.

Round-the-clock digital television news channels – whether operated by the established organizations such as BBC and ITN or by more recent arrivals – attracted a tiny fraction of the total TV audience. Digital radio (DAB), which offered round-the-clock news radio services for the first time in most parts of the UK had an even slower take-up, but audiences to old-fashioned analogue services – whether listened to via a conventional set or a modem – provided an enjoyable accompaniment to Web 'surfing'. RAJAR audience figures released in August 2001 suggested that, for the first time in at least three decades, radio listening exceeded TV viewing (RAJAR, 2001). News availability through WAP mobile phones appeared to offer novelty but not much more.

The Internet and the World Wide Web have, though, been extraordinary phenomena that have greatly changed the ways in which many people work and use their leisure time. Undoubtedly they are also extremely useful tools for the journalist, especially in researching stories. But almost everyone who has used the Internet has experienced great frustration in trying to find the news and information they want. The very lack of regulation and control, one of the main attractions of the Internet, is also one of its weaknesses. The most popular sites for news and information have turned out to be those operated by the oldest and most trusted media organizations, notably the BBC. The business of journalism – sifting, assessing, editing and summarizing – is as much valued in the Internet age as it was in the eighteenth century.

In the meantime many people who had hoped the Internet would ensure that many more 'voices', opinions and perspectives would break through into people's consciousness have been sorely disappointed. Although some 'Web-only' news services have broken stories and provided a refreshingly different perspective on events, in general the new media has resulted in a consolidation in the power and influence of the 'old' media organizations.

The impact of new technology on journalism and journalists' working practices has been enormous: multimedia and multi-skilling are the buzz-words that require and enable journalists to produce work across a number of media and to be technically proficient in those media. Digital technology has 'freed' journalists from reliance on a complex production process involving many different craft skills: increasingly journalists have direct production and editorial control of their material. But the demands of a 24-hour non-stop news world are voracious and many journalists complain that they have to cut corners in order to produce material for many outlets and that this leads to a superficial quality to their work; that they are increasingly tied to the news-desk or studio and unable to get out and find out the 'real' news. The danger of this is that journalists increasingly have to take official statements and information at face value – they don't have time to question or probe what is really going on. Purdey (2000) suggests that there is now a sharp divide between the ethos and approach of BBC and commercial radio journalists, with implications for journalists' training, recruitment and work practices in the two sectors.

Linked to this is that many journalists are becoming more like *news processors*: small newsrooms in local newspapers and commercial radio stations in particular rarely *break* news apart from stories picked up from the 'calls' to the emergency services: fires, crimes and road accidents. They are not primary news gatherers: they recycle news from local and national agencies, with perhaps the occasional report picked up from press releases from local councils and the like. It is rare in these news media to read or hear authority figures being vigorously questioned: instead a bland sound bite, giving the no doubt media-trained official chance to give the approved 'line' or 'spin' on the story, goes out unchallenged.

An even more fundamental and significant question has arisen as to whether all this extra news availability has led to the public becoming better informed or engaged in thinking about, discussing and participating in public affairs and the democratic process. Electoral turn-out in the 2001 general election was the lowest since the establishment of the universal adult franchise (see Chapter 11). A concept has arisen of the *information rich* and *information poor*. There has been much concern that an increasing minority, especially amongst the young, are 'managing' to avoid any engagement with serious journalism – this at a time when, at least when judged by examination success and university attendance, the population has never been so well educated. Far from the news media and education developing in tandem (as this chapter has argued happened during the age of enlightenment) the two elements now seem to be pulling apart.

In tandem with this there seems to be an increasing gap in both the public and in journalism between the serious and the non-serious; the latter becoming obsessed by trivia, celebrity-dominated gossip and titillation, fed by a con-sumerist ideology. However, the terrorist attacks on the USA in September 2001 and the events that followed led to a major shift in the editorial focus of many news outlets, particularly in the 'red top' tabloid press. These newspapers returned to more traditional types of journalism, concentrating on telling the audience what was going on in this major and disturbing and many-faceted 'story'. There was evidence of increased investment in traditional journalistic activities, particularly in foreign correspondents – a number of whom put themselves in great danger. Just at the moment when it seemed that much British 'tabloid' journalism was in danger of being smothered in a sea of increasingly trivial stories – many based around the antics of 'characters' on 'reality' TV game shows – popular, accessible but nevertheless serious-minded journalism was making a come-back. As *Daily Mirror* editor Piers Morgan told the Society of Editors:

> I hear Mirror secretaries talking of anthrax not EastEnders, Bin Laden not Robbie Williams, the terrain of Northern Afghanistan not their next holiday in Crete . . . There is a sudden and prolonged hunger for serious news and information (Preston, 2001).

Whether this reversion to more serious, public-sphere journalism by the *Mirror* and other tabloid newspapers is a temporary phenomenon or a more permanent, fundamental shift in journalistic values will only become clear after some months, if not years have elapsed since 11 September 2001.

Suggested activities

1 Construct your own definition of a journalist.
2 Using a questionnaire, do a mini survey of journalists at your local newspaper
   or radio station: do they seem to fit with the Delano and Henningham findings?
   (You'll need to be both tactful and discrete in how you do this!)
3 Study the Galtung and Ruge criteria of what makes news and apply them to an
   edition of a national newspaper or a television news broadcast – do these criteria
   seem to be justified in your example?
4 Use the same material to assess how objective is the coverage of a controversial
   topic.
5 Using the 'complexity' table (Figure 1.4) take three examples of different types
   of national newspapers and do a rough analysis of the editorial space devoted
   to serious/public sphere journalism and non-serious/trivial material.
6 Spend a day at your local newspaper: try to analyse what the main influences
   are on the journalists' work, e.g., work routines, deadlines, commercial/
   advertising influences, understanding of readers' needs/demands, legal/ethical
   considerations.
7 Using the information in this chapter and from the Sources and resources
   section below construct a chronology/timeline of the important developments in
   press and broadcast journalism in the UK.
8 Using the 'search' facilities on major news sites, investigate a current issue/
   controversy concerning journalistic regulation and/or ethics.
9 Find a news/feature story about the news media that portrays a journalist (or set
   of journalists) in the heroic mode (fearless, campaigning), and one that portrays
   them as villains (prying, immoral, insensitive). What are the underlying
   assumptions about what journalists and journalism 'could' or 'should' be?
10 Hold a debate on the proposition: 'journalists have a unique role in shaping the
   public's attitudes and values'.

Sources and resources

Allan, S. (1997) 'News and the public sphere – towards a history of objectivity and
   impartiality'. In: Bromley, M. and O'Malley, T. (eds) *A Journalism Reader*.
   London: Routledge.
BBC (2001) BBC News – TV and Radio (online) 'Excited' Simpson regrets Kabul
   claims. 18 November 2001. http://news.bbc.co.uk/hi/english/entertainment/tv_
   and_radio/newsid_1662000/1662979.stm (accessed 25 November 2001).
Branston, G. and Stafford, R. (1996) *The Media Student's Book*. London: Routledge.
CRCA (2001) http://www.crca.co.uk/rajarQ22001_pr.htm (accessed 28 August
   2001).
Crook, T. (1998) *International Radio Journalism*. London: Routledge.

Curran, J. and Seaton, J. (1997) *Power Without Responsibility – the press and broadcasting in Britain*. London: Routledge.

Delano, A. and Henningham, J. (1995) *The News Breed – a report on British journalists in the 1990s*. London: The London Institute.

Franklin, B. (1997) *Newszak & News Media*. London: Arnold.

Hall, J. (2001) *Online Journalism – a critical primer*. London: Pluto Press.

Hendy, D. (2000) *Radio in the Global Age*. Cambridge: Polity Press.

Henningham, J. and Delano, D. (1998) 'The British journalist'. In: Weaver, D., *The Global Journalist*. Cresskill NJ: Hampton Press.

Herbert, J. (2000) *Journalism in the Digital Age: theory and practice for broadcast, print and on-line media*. Oxford: Focal Press.

Herbert, J. (2001) *Practising Global Journalism – exploring reporting issues worldwide*. Oxford: Focal Press.

MacGregor, B. (1997) *Live, Direct and Biased? Making television news in the satellite age*. London: Arnold.

McNair, B. (1998) *The Sociology of Journalism*. London: Arnold.

McNair, B. (1999) *Journalism and Democracy*. London: Routledge.

National Union of Journalists. http://www.nuj.org.uk (accessed 31 May 2001).

Peak, S. (ed.) (2002) *The Guardian Media Guide 2003*. London: Atlantic Books.

Pilger, J. (1998) *Hidden Agendas*. London: Vintage.

Press Complaints Commission (PCC). http://www.pcc.org.uk (accessed 28 August 2001).

Preston, P. (2001) 'Seeing the light is one way to eclipse the Sun'. *The Observer*, 28 October 2001.

Purdey, H. (2000) 'Radio journalism training and the future of radio news in the UK'. *Journalism – Theory, Practice and Criticism*, 1(3): 329–352. London: Sage.

RAJAR (2001) http://www.rajar.co.uk (accessed 5 September 2001).

Randall, D. (2000) *The Universal Journalist* (2nd edition). London: Pluto Press.

Reeves, I. (1998) 'Trust me, I'm a journalist'. *The Guardian*, 20 November 1998.

Spark, D. (1999) *Investigative Reporting – a study in technique*. Oxford: Focal Press.

Ursell, G. (2001) 'Dumbing down or shaping up? New technologies, new media, new journalism'. *Journalism – Theory, Practice and Criticism*, 2(2): 175–196. London: Sage.

van Ginneken, J. (1998) *Understanding Global News – a critical introduction*. London: Sage.

Other recommended Web sites

CAR Park UK (Computer-Assisted Reporting and research resources for journalism in the United Kingdom from Focal Press author Alan Rawlinson): http://www.rawlinson.co.uk

Columbia Journalism Review (from Columbia University's Graduate School of Journalism, described as 'America's premiere media monitor', is particularly good on ownership and control of news media): http://www.cjr.org

Hold the Front Page (site for and about regional UK journalists, with the background to many journalism issues): http://www.holdthefrontpage.co.uk/index.htm

International Federation of Journalists (described as the world's largest journalists' organization, discusses many current journalism issues): http://www.ifj.org/index-html

Thunderbird (produced by the Journalism School of the University of British Columbia, Canada: has many relevant articles about current journalism issues): http://www.journalism.ubc.ca/thunderbird.html

USC Annenberg Online Journalism Review: http://ascweb.usc.edu/home.php

2 History and development

- Introduction
- History of journalism: the print medium
- The growing importance of journalism
- Technology and the battle between trades unions and management
- The battle over press regulation
- History of journalism: the broadcast medium
- Meanwhile, back with the 'wireless' . . .
- Journalism on the Internet
- Common threads in the history of UK journalism
- Suggested activities
- Sources and resources

Introduction

This chapter contains a condensed – and necessarily selective – account of the way journalism has developed. It considers political, economic and technological factors, as well as how the nature of each medium has affected the editorial, production and presentation aspects of journalism. Taken with the discussion in Chapter 1 this should provide the reader with a broad overview of the development of journalism and the main issues that have caused public debate about the role and function of journalism in society.

History of journalism: the print medium

Printing presses existed in China thousands of years ago, mechanical means of printing in the western world can be traced back to the 1450s and the first Gutenberg Bible. This process created the possibility of accounts of events developing from the spoken to the written word. The first period in which there is solid evidence that printed accounts of events were made available to a mass public is during the English Civil War in the mid-seventeenth century.

It is not entirely clear when a first publication that can be termed a newspaper was first published but most historians agree that it was probably in the 1620s in

Italy and Germany. Until 1694 anyone in England who wanted to publish first had to get a licence from the state. In addition, anyone who criticized someone in authority, whether the criticism was justified or based on truth, was liable to imprisonment. These laws were not changed until the end of the eighteenth century.

The abolition of the Star Chamber in England in 1641 allowed some press freedom and the same year saw the first publication of reports of parliamentary proceedings. The English Civil War provided the need for both information and propaganda by the competing Royalists and Parliamentarians, each of which produced their own news sheets. Unfortunately, victory for the Parliamentarians resulted in the reintroduction by Oliver Cromwell in 1655 of a strict licensing system for newspapers, and even – after the restoration of the monarchy – a new Printing Act in 1662, which contained stringent controls on the press. The *London Gazette*, founded in February 1666, has survived through the ages and is now the world's oldest surviving periodical. The first daily paper in England was the *Daily Courant*, which began publishing in 1702.

From its beginnings, journalism was seen by the establishment as a threat to its existence, or at the very least those holding power in society were alarmed that their actions might be challenged and that this would have unforeseen consequences. Indeed, the idea of the masses having access to information and ideas terrified those at the top of society. The conflict between journalists and the elites has a long and unbroken record in the UK and in almost every other country. Furthermore, the long and often bloody struggle for journalism and journalists to obtain independence and freedom of action from the state has run side by side in the battles for the rights and freedoms of 'ordinary people'.

The authorities had a major weapon at their disposal to try and avoid unwelcome criticism: taxation, which was imposed on both the price of newspapers and, most crucially, advertisements. These taxes were introduced in 1712 and were savagely increased in 1815 to four pence per sheet – a huge amount in those days. It was thought that if the state could make sure that newspapers were not affordable for most people there was no danger of the masses becoming sullied by ideas and information that might make them dissatisfied or even rebellious. The remainder of the seventeenth century and beginning of the eighteenth century saw a number of advances and retreats in the notion of press freedom, as Parliament relaxed controls and then in a panic – no doubt caused by unwelcome radical writings – reintroduced clampdowns.

Despite this, the number of titles grew nationwide, in both type and day of publication, including Sundays – the *Sunday Times* began in October 1822. Other significant and familiar titles that began in this period include *The Manchester Guardian* (1821) – the 'Manchester' was dropped from its title in 1959 when it moved its base to London – which is one of the most significant publications in the history of British newspapers, with a famously liberal stance and run by a trust set up by the family of the newspaper's first and most famous editor, C.P. Scott; the (*Evening*) *Standard* in 1827; *Punch* (1841); *The Times* (1843); *Economist* and *News of the World* (1843).

The first provincial newspaper is thought to have been the *Norwich Post*, first published in 1701. This was the first in a number of such titles, including ones in Edinburgh and Aberdeen – the *Aberdeen Press and Journal* (1747) is the oldest surviving Scottish newspaper.

Periodicals also flourished in this period including *The Spectator*, which survives to this day and was first published in 1711.

Alongside the struggle for freedom of expression was the battle for economic independence. For this reason, many historians of the press have argued that a number of other social and economic factors had to come together before journalism of the sort we know today was able to develop. Roy Porter believes there was a strong link between journalism and education for the masses. Looking at the example of just one provincial paper, the *Salisbury Journal* (founded 1736), he notes that along with

> news local and national, it dished up a minestrone of events, announce-
> ments, books, features ... In all around 200 teachers in seventy-eight
> Wessex towns inserted ads in the *Journal* in its first thirty-four years, a
> good proportion of which were brand new schools, showing that the press
> and education worked hand in hand to galvanize minds, and bringing out
> Johnson's dictum that 'knowledge is diffused among our people by the
> news-papers' (Porter, 2000: 78).

The link between the age of enlightenment – sometimes called the age of reason, as it was the period in which scientific knowledge helped to free people from religious dogma and challenged the widespread belief that one's place in society was divinely ordered – and journalism is fundamental. Not only did the age allow rational discussion of the physical and natural world, it provided social space for the discussion of public affairs.

But if society needed journalism to help its evolution, journalism certainly needed society to make sure that the masses were educated: most obviously in literacy – there is clearly no point in producing a printed form of journalism if most people are unable to read it! Literacy among ordinary people is in fact a relatively recent development in the UK. Until the Industrial Revolution the political elites saw little point in spending time and money in educating the masses. But with the rise of factories and the mass movement from the countryside to the new cities, it became necessary for the workers to be able to understand some quite complex instructions on the machinery they were required to handle. This concentration of people into small geographic areas made the distribution of newspapers and other publications so much easier. Added to that, the development of mass transportation – especially the railways – allowed the rapid and mass distribution of newspapers from the printing presses to the bulk of the population within a matter of hours. In this way, the idea that news should be reasonably up-to-date took hold.

Most social historians also believe that the mass consumerism and development of the middle classes in the nineteenth century provided the right economic, political and cultural background for the development of mass produced newspapers. The cover price of newspapers was never enough to ensure a profitable business; it was advertising that achieved this.

The nineteenth century, though, also saw the flourishing of a sector known as the radical press. The people behind the publications in this sector felt that the concessions made by the elites to the notions of free expression did not go nearly far enough. By (so far as possible) avoiding taxes and legal restrictions they put themselves technically and spiritually outside 'polite' society and the establishment. In addition, as running newspapers became a profitable business just like any other capitalist enterprise, they felt that the owners of such businesses were never likely to allow the expression of ideas that might damage their interests.

The middle of the nineteenth century saw a huge increase in the number of daily produced newspapers, most of them produced by and for a particular locality. Most of them were also openly supportive – indeed many cases funded – by one of the main political parties. They were also broadly pro-establishment and helped a rather disparate people – who had suffered enormous dislocation in their social and geographical placement – into a unified population with common values. This was particularly important in establishing the idea that the British Empire was a 'good thing'. This period also saw the development of two distinct types of national newspaper: the popular and the serious, the latter being characterized by *The Times*, which was generally regarded as an important 'newspaper of record' with an emphasis on political affairs at home and abroad.

The idea that a news *agency* could be formed to supply a number of publications and thereby reduce the cost of each newspaper having to employ journalists to cover all types of story in all areas of the globe took hold in 1851 when the Reuters news agency opened in London.

The 1850s, though, saw the most significant changes so far as newspapers were concerned when the dreaded taxes were abolished – the advertisement tax going in 1853 and the Stamp Act two years later – which allowed the publication of cheap, mass circulation newspapers. This period also saw the development of newspaper design of the sort that is still familiar today.

The turn of the century saw the launch of some of the most influential, mass circulation newspapers, many of which survive to this day. These include the *Daily Mail* (1896), *Daily Express* (1900), *Daily Mirror* (1903), *Daily Sketch* (1909 – which merged with the *Daily Mail* in 1971; the re-launched paper going tabloid in the process), *Daily Herald* (1911 – the first newspaper to sell two million copies).

The emergence of the journalist as a distinct category of employment, requiring specific skills and even training, resulted in the National Union of Journalists being founded in 1907.

By the end of the nineteenth century popular, daily, national newspapers owned by one or other of the so-called press barons came to dominate journalism. Moreover, many of the press barons also owned leading regional and local newspapers. The big five newspaper companies increased their domination of local newspapers in the period between the First and Second World Wars and this led to a reduction of choice with many major cities having only one local and/or a daily evening newspaper, with the combined circulation of such newspapers remaining almost static.

The growing importance of journalism

Journalism was not just seen as being the mouthpiece and servant of a political party or class but would act in the interests of a wider audience. The conflict between politically motivated and very wealthy proprietors and the more independent-minded editors and other journalists is a continuing theme of newspaper politics to this day.

The period after the Second World War saw increasing concentration of ownership by three leading publishers. Furthermore, in the 1970s and 1980s newspapers increasingly became part of companies that had many interests other than newspapers.

Other post-Second World War developments in the press worth noting include the move by the *Manchester Guardian* to London in 1959 and dropping 'Manchester' from its title; the launch of the first of the Sunday colour magazines in the *Sunday Times* in 1962; the purchase of *The Times* by Canadian Roy Thomson (who already owned the *Sunday Times*) in 1966 and the somewhat belated introduction of news – rather than all advertisements – on the front page of that paper; the purchase of the *News of the World* by Rupert Murdoch in 1969, with Murdoch launching *The Sun* as a tabloid newspaper in the same year.

The 1990s saw greater consolidation both in ownership and the number of titles of newspapers. *Today* ceased publication in 1995, the *Observer* was bought by the Guardian Media Group in 1993 and the *Independent* ceased to live up to its title by being bought by one, then another, major media group within a few years. The *Telegraph* titles, which were bought by Canadian millionaire Conrad Black in 1985, became the first to fully embrace the Internet with the launch of the *Electronic Telegraph* in 1994. Meanwhile the growth of free newspapers in the provinces led to a free daily newspaper, the *Metro*, being launched in London in 1999.

Technology and the battle between trades unions and management

Technology, always an important factor in the mass media, made a significant development in 1844 when the first story written from news that had been transmitted by telegraph was printed in *The Times*. The importance of the telegraph in the development of what we now recognize as news journalism can hardly be overestimated: it allowed reports to be transmitted with minimal delay from almost anywhere in the world. Because telegraphs were charged according to the number of words, such reports needed to be kept as brief and succinct as possible, leading to a more objective, factual style. The technology therefore affected the journalism – an example of *technological determinism*.

The development of technology that allowed photographs to be published in newspapers transformed the look and scope of many publications. The *Illustrated London News* probably takes the accolade for first using photographs when, in March 1889, it had photos of the Cambridge and Oxford boat crews. Although there were developments in printing presses and newspaper production, there was remarkably little in the way of significant development in the national press for some 100 years.

It was provincial newspapers who, in the 1960s, led the way in the introduction of new Web Offset technology (nothing to do with the World Wide Web!) and direct input by journalists. This was in stark contrast to the antiquated printing processes of the national newspapers in Fleet Street. The printing unions there had refused to allow the new technology because they rightly feared it would result in job losses and the end of lucrative and – many would say excessive – overtime, particularly on the production of the Sunday newspapers that became notorious for practices such as drawing full wages for non-existent employees. The vast majority of printers earned far more than most of the journalists and it was not uncommon for printers to earn hundreds of pounds for a single Saturday night shift.

Conflict between management and unions came to a head in 1978 when, after numerous and lightning stoppages by the print unions and a refusal by union leaders to guarantee continuous publication, the publication of both *The Times* and the *Sunday Times* was suspended for 11 months.

This dispute was the beginning of the end for the power of the print unions and the costly and inefficient 'hot metal' printing production of national newspapers. In 1980 the *Mail on Sunday* was launched and became the first photo-composed national newspaper in the country. This was a year before Rupert Murdoch had bought both *The Times* and *Sunday Times* and was enviously eyeing a provincial newspaper owner, Eddie Shah, who broke the printing unions' stranglehold on his *Messenger* titles and, in the teeth of violent opposition, moved to new up-to-date printing plants.

Murdoch was greatly helped in his plans by the curtailing of union power in successive Acts of Parliament introduced by the governments of Margaret Thatcher. This culminated in the forced move of all Murdoch's national papers to a new plant in Wapping. An era was rapidly coming to a close as other national newspapers in turn moved from their famous Fleet Street premises to new sites in London's Docklands. The breaking of the unions and the introduction of new technology was used to introduce new titles and, for a time, it did seem that the political and economic climate of the 1980s really would 'let a thousand flowers bloom' as, in that same epoch-making year of 1986, Eddie Shah launched a new national colour newspaper, *Today*; a serious broadsheet national newspaper *The Independent* launched in October; and a remarkably trivial, comic-like tabloid, *Sunday Sport*, first published a month before. Trying not to be outdone, Murdoch's rival proprietor, Robert Maxwell, attempted to introduce a 24-hour newspaper, the *London Daily News*, in 1987, but this lasted for less than six months. Two other newspapers survived for only short periods: an attempt at a tabloid popular investigative left-wing newspaper, the *News on Sunday*, lasted for just a few months and heavy-weight *Sunday Correspondent*, which was hit by the start of the *Independent on Sunday* four months after its September 1989 launch, and despite a re-launch as a 'quality tabloid' in July 1990, lasted for just a year.

The battle over press regulation

Concern about the state of the British press, particularly the small number of owners and the political influence that it was thought they bought to their publications, resulted in the first Royal Commission on the press in 1947. However, the government, like many before and since, was very reluctant to bring in statutory controls as they knew there would be fierce opposition to any such moves – not least in the newspapers themselves – with claims that there had been a return to government censorship and other restrictions on the free press. There is an additional problem for those seeking to 'control' press journalists – and indeed those working in other sectors: unlike other professions such as doctors and solicitors, the UK has never had a single set of qualifications through examination or other means which need to be acquired before someone could practise as a journalist or gain increased responsibility; nor is there a body that could disqualify or 'strike off' journalists who breach codes of conduct. Anyone can describe themselves as a journalist and seek journalistic work. This raises the question as to whether journalism in the UK can be properly regarded as a profession – a trade or craft might be a better description. Suggestions that a common, mandatory and legally enforced system be introduced have always been resisted on the grounds that journalists who cause trouble to the government or other powerful interests might have 'trumped up' charges brought against them, and that it might even lead to the creation of 'state approved journalists' – an idea abhorrent to anyone who believes in free, independent, journalism.

Self-regulation was deemed to be the answer to widespread public concern about the 'excesses' of some journalists and the General Council of the Press was formed in 1953. This became the Press Council in 1964 (following a second Royal Commission on the press) and, after a warning from a then-government minister David Mellor that the press was 'drinking in the last chance saloon', the Press Complaints Commission in 1991 (see Chapter 14).

The seemingly obsessive interest in the private lives of celebrities and of politicians led to increasing unease and criticism of the methods and conduct of the national tabloid newspapers. The newspapers had successfully fought off any attempts to re-introduce direct, statutory or state control of their output. As we've seen, from the middle of the eighteenth century all governments had, with the exception of wartime, accepted the concept and reality of a 'free press'. This means that newspapers are subject only to the general laws of the land and that there are no specific laws or statutory regulations that apply to them. There is no special censorship or licensing of print journalism. Instead, the press maintained that it could regulate itself. This argument was helped by the fact that the UK has never had a privacy law as such. Furthermore, the press argued, with much justification, that Britain was already one of the most secretive countries in the world and had some of the most draconian libel laws and that very often the only way of finding out the truth was to use methods that on the face of it seemed unacceptable – long-lens photography, secret microphones and transmitters, deception, interception of mail and phone calls, and the like. When the press went over what was the normally accepted boundaries of acceptable behaviour it claimed that it was doing so in the public interest. The controversy of what is in the public interest – as distinct from what really interests the public – is a very live one.

The Press Complaints Commission attempted to reassure and pacify politicians and public that it could keep its own house in order by developing codes of conduct and guidelines that newspapers would voluntarily adhere to. A series of sex scandals involving ministers in the then-Tory government helped to further aggravate the strained relationship between at least some sections of the press and the government of the day.

History of journalism: the broadcast medium

Twentieth-century new technology meant new possibilities and outlets for journalism. The use of radio for broadcasting (as opposed to one-to-one communications) allowed the spoken word to again become prominent in the communication of ideas, events and controversies. Each new technological development used for journalism had to establish its right to communicate ideas that were uncomfortable to those in authority. But with broadcasting the authorities had a ready-made excuse for limiting the number of outlets and for strictly controlling the content on them. This was – and is – due to the fact that whilst there is theoretically a limitless amount of paper allowing any one to set up and run a newspaper or magazine, the number of frequencies is strictly limited. Just as in the early days of the press those wishing to start a newspaper were required to gain a licence from the state and to prove that they were responsible citizens, so it was with radio and later TV. In Britain's case, an equivalent of the old newspaper Stamp Duty was imposed on radio, then television, receivers.

The monopoly position of the BBC provided the BBC's first General Manager (and later Director-General) John (later Lord) Reith with an extraordinary, perhaps unique, opportunity to fashion an ethos for this new and powerful medium that matched his personal creed. Reith believed 'the wireless' should certainly not be debased by becoming a means of selling goods and services, but first and foremost be a tool to help improve the cultural and intellectual life of the nation. He believed that by making available all that was best and finest in culture the masses could be elevated from their ignorant and often brutal lives.

The imposition of Reith's high-minded principles – though imperious and patronizing by the standards of the twenty-first century – were hugely important as they established in Britain, and through its Empire to many other countries and societies, that broadcasting should have a strong *public service* element. An ideology developed that broadcasting should be run neither directly by the state, nor for commercial purposes.

Even when commercially funded TV and later radio was permitted, the ethos of Public Service Broadcasting (PSB) became entrenched.

Significantly, Reith also believed that broadcasting should be free from state control and he had a fine balancing act to demonstrate this independence but not alarm and anger those in the Cabinet of the then-Prime Minister Stanley Baldwin, who were deeply suspicious of this power being out of their control and wished to take over the BBC. The crunch came during the General Strike of May 1926. This is the first and so far only time in Britain's history when all the country's workers were called out on strike. Winston Churchill demanded the government take over the BBC. Reith managed to persuade Baldwin to make the running of the Company (as it still was then) a personal matter of trust. However, Reith refused what would now be called a 'right of reply' to the leader of the Trades Union Congress and later argued that as the government must be presumed to be on the side of the people, and the BBC was on the side of the people, then the BBC must be for the government! Nevertheless, by keeping the government out of the BBC Reith achieved a victory of enormous importance in the history and culture of British broadcasting.

After some four years of experimentation with a commercially funded, non-profit-making monopoly, the BBC was turned into a public service corporation along the lines of the Post Office. Furthermore, unlike for the print medium, the government not only appointed the corporation's governors but retained the ultimate power to take over broadcasting in times of crisis. 'The wireless' also had the potential for great good or evil. Never before had dictators had such an effective medium for propagating their beliefs and policies – a fact ruthlessly and effectively deployed by the leaders of Nazi Germany and other fascist states. But it could also be force for the good in improving understanding and tolerance; understanding between different nations was an especially important aspect in the build up of tensions in Europe in the 1930s (indeed, the English translation of the BBC's motto is: *Nation shall speak peace unto nation*). To this end in 1932 Reith established the BBC's Empire Service, forerunner of the World Service (funded separately from the BBC's domestic services through a grant from the Foreign Office) with an impressive reputation for fair and accurate journalism.

The BBC established itself perhaps for all time as the nation's most important news provider during the Second World War. Reith, who resigned before the outbreak of war, had been a reluctant convert to the idea of news being an important feature of the new medium; he did not employ journalists of his own and the newspaper companies persuaded the news agencies to impose an embargo so that news agency copy could not be broadcast until the evening – i.e., after the news had already been published in that morning's newspapers!

Clearly this cosy agreement could not survive a world war for which the radio was uniquely equipped to bring up to-to-date information about the conduct of the war often taking place many hundreds of miles away, as well as uniting the nation in a common cause.

After the Second World War, though, the BBC was seen by many as out of touch and stuffy, and in need of direct competition. This was provided not through radio – whose audiences by then were by any measure enormous – but through the new medium of television. The legislation brought in by the Conservative government in the early 1950s specified that the new commercially funded service should have a common provider of national and international news, operated as a non-profit-making joint concern by the new regional companies that had been awarded franchises to broadcast to specific areas of the UK.

Independent Television News (ITN) decided to model its service less on the BBC's – which at that time was to all intents and purposes a radio news bulletin embellished by a few pictures and graphics – but on US and Australian commercial networks. In particular the decision was reached to make a feature of the news readers – or news*casters* as ITN termed them – who, it was decided should, unlike their BBC counterparts, be established and credible journalists.

The second great innovation was the use of new lightweight film cameras that were capable of recording synchronized sound. This style of television news proved to be an immediate hit with the fast-increasing audience for television and the BBC found that its hitherto almost unchallenged hold on the public's affections was being usurped by this new rival. It wasn't just in the field of straight news that the ITV service demonstrated innovation and vigour. It developed a stream of current affairs programmes that had a sharpness and investigative quality that the BBC's equivalents certainly lacked. Moreover, ITN and ITV completely undermined the deferential attitude of the BBC to politicians and other members of the establishment. ITN was the first British broadcaster to dispense with the courteous and almost submissive style of interviews with such people and it openly challenged the highly restrictive laws on the coverage of controversial issues and of elections. Just as the radical press had embarrassed the establishment and exposed unreasonable restrictions on free speech in the nineteenth century, legal challenges by ITN, especially over election coverage, and of matters before Parliament (for over 10 years broadcasters were forbidden to broadcast comment on any matter due to come before Parliament in the next 14 days) resulted in the overturn of some of the laws and regulations that then governed broadcast news in the UK.

Perhaps just as importantly, because of its monopoly of commercial broadcasting and the huge popularity of television, ITV was extremely profitable and its franchise-holders' subscriptions to ITN, based on population coverage and advertising revenue, ensured that the commercial news organization was extremely well funded. It was able therefore to commit itself to expensive news coverage and investigative documentaries. The 1960s and 1970s are sometimes seen as the golden age for investigative journalism. The BBC by then had also dropped its deferential approach and nervousness about upsetting authority and broadcast many controversial and anti-establishment programmes – not only news and current affairs but also in drama and comedy. During the same period national newspapers such as the *Sunday Times* also published a number of significant investigations and exposés. For those who believe in fearless and independent news and current affairs the 1980s had a mixed record. On the one hand, the Conservative government's introduction of Channel 4 as a non-profit-making, commercially funded service with programmes mostly produced by independent companies saw a flowering of new and challenging programmes by relatively small and non-establishment production companies. ITN won the contract to supply the channel's news coverage and Channel 4 News became the first, and to date only, daily hour-long news and current affairs programme on terrestrial channels. However, the 1980s also saw UK broadcasters in conflict with the government, which made a number of attempts to muzzle and intimidate journalists and their managers. The end of the decade saw the start of Direct Satellite Broadcasting, which heralded a true revolution in British broadcasting.

For commercial broadcasting, though, the biggest changes since the introduction of commercial TV in 1955 and commercial radio in 1973 came with the 1990 Broadcasting Act. This ended the concept of franchises for radio and TV companies and replaced them with licences, offered, in the case of ITV and new national commercial stations, on the basis of a 'blind auction'. This approach viewed licences as a valuable commercial asset and therefore, rather than offering these scarce resources to those companies that, in the opinion of the great and good in the authorities offered the best range and quality of programmes, the winners were those who – having passed a so-called quality threshold – offered the most money. Alongside this process was a replacement of the hitherto very much hands-on control and regulation by the Independent Broadcasting Authority (IBA) with a 'light touch' regulator – Independent Television Commission (ITC) for commercial television, and a Radio Authority. Although a number of positive programme requirements were included even in this new, more relaxed system – including the requirement by ITV companies to provide high quality news and current affairs in peak viewing times – there can be no doubt that throughout the decade there was a reduction in factual output, at the expense of ratings-grabbing and often cheaper light entertainment fare, especially at peak times. This caused much heart-searching and public debate. Many politicians and pundits declared that a very important part of the nation's culture – even its social fabric – was being lost.

Meanwhile, back with the 'wireless' . . .

For commercial radio, changes during the 1990s were, if anything, even more fundamental. After the 1990 Act the stations were no longer officially public service broadcasters. They were increasingly entertainment-led services that had no legal requirement as such to provide news and current affairs. However, companies were awarded licences in competition with others at the local and regional level partly on the basis of their commitment to 'meaningful speech'. The national and international news provider, Independent Radio News (IRN), which had been modelled on ITN as a jointly owned non-profit-making news supplier, lost its statutory monopoly and became a service for profit, funded by advertising slots sold around peak-time bulletins.

The net result of these changes for most commercial stations – particularly the larger services based in the big cities, many of which had hitherto provided a strong range and depth of news and current affairs programming – was that their newsrooms were slashed to the bare minimum needed for an hourly, superficial, news summary.

The introduction of national commercial radio – more than 50 years after the start of BBC radio – resulted in a daily news programme on commercial radio (on Classic FM) being heard nationwide for the first time.

Like other accounts in this chapter this is necessarily a generalized analysis and it should be noted that a number of stations both large and small bucked this overall trend. Indeed, at the beginning of the twenty-first century there were some signs that a number of stations had decided to increase news staffing levels and improve their factual output.

For the first time outside London a rolling news radio service – the Digital News Network – was available on digital radio multiplexes in four English regions from September 2001.

During the 1990s the BBC invested heavily in its news and current affairs provision for its local stations, which became, first and foremost, providers of news and current affairs material. Specialist reporters were appointed in each region, working to both local radio and regional TV and indeed the new job title of most of the news staff was 'broadcast journalist' – overtly requiring them to work across the corporation's radio, TV and Teletext/online services.

In the meantime a national rolling news and sports radio network – Radio 5 Live – drawing extensively on local radio input, established respectable audience figures and, for a BBC speech network, was produced on a modest budget.

Journalism on the Internet

The last few years of the twentieth century saw the rapidly expanding development of journalism on the Internet and the World Wide Web. Jim Hall (2001: 16) estimates that by the middle of the first decade of the twenty-first century more people in the developed world will get their news from the Internet than from a daily newspaper. Clearly this represents a major historic development. However, as discussed in Chapter 1, the early hopes that the 'level playing field' of access to the Web (anyone with access to a computer, modem and some basic software can construct and 'upload' Web pages as easily as a multinational corporation) would lead to an explosion in the number and variety of journalistic 'voices' and perspectives, have only been partly realized.

Common threads in the history of UK journalism

Radio, and later TV, in the twentieth century also had to fend off attempts by the print medium to prevent the new technologies from competing for attention and advertising revenues.

Each new medium has met with resistance both from those in power and from the older media – the Internet being the most recent example. However, unlike broadcasting, the authorities could not pretend that with this latest medium there was some sort of physical limit on the number of outlets and thereby justifying control and licensing. Indeed, it was the complete absence of any ability to control the output of the Internet that caused the authorities so much panic. Whatever they may claim, those in power are always fearful and suspicious of forms of communication to the masses that they cannot control. At the end of the twentieth century the governments in Britain and a number of other countries used the excuse (or legitimate reason, depending on your point of view) of the Internet being used for pornography, terrorism and other highly undesirable purposes, to initiate some control and monitoring of the new medium.

Another common thread in the history of media and journalism is that each new development has been welcomed initially by those who feel marginalized or ignored by the established media as a way of ensuring that new and different perspectives are made available in the public domain. Such hopes have nearly always been dashed as each new media becomes 'colonized' by the same powerful companies and interests.

There are also parallels in the UK's history with other countries in modern times, particularly perhaps Russia and Eastern Europe. It must also be recognized that an account of the history of journalism that describes an heroic struggle between the forces of the powerful and the elites against a free expression and the rights of ordinary people, is itself recognizable as an ideology and it is possible to describe these developments in other ways.

Suggested activities

1 Construct a time-line (chronology) of the major developments in journalism from the last part of the seventeenth century to the present day.
2 Research the history of a major media institution (e.g., the BBC, *The Guardian*, CNN). What have been the major factors in its development? What have been the tensions and difficulties in its development? Is it possible to define its journalistic ethos?
3 Investigate the history of one of the local media outlets, e.g., the local newspaper, commercial or BBC radio station, news agency or 'stand alone' Internet organization.
4 Draw up a list of some of the common factors in the development of different journalistic media; e.g., the press, radio, TV, Internet. Pay special attention to the influences of government, other political and economic factors, ownership and control, regulation, technology.
5 Organize and hold a debate around the issue of the 'freedom of the press'.

Sources and resources

BBC (history of the Corporation): http://www.bbc.co.uk/thenandnowhistory/ index.shtml (accessed 28 May 2001).

British Library (history and archives of British newspapers): http://www.bl.uk/collections/newspaper/newscat.html (accessed 21 September 2001).

Bromley, M. and O'Malley, T. (eds) (1997) *A Journalism Reader*. London: Routledge.

Crisell, A. (1997) *An Introductory History of British Broadcasting*. London: Routledge.

Crook, T. (1998) *International Radio Journalism*. London: Routledge.

Curran, J. and Seaton, J. (1997) *Power Without Responsibility – the press and broadcasting in Britain*. London: Routledge.

Day, R. (1989) *Sir Robin Day – grand inquisitor*. London: Weidenfeld and Nicolson.

Foden, G. (ed.) (1999) *The Guardian Century*. London: *The Guardian*.

Glover, S. (ed.) (2000) *The Penguin Book of Journalism – secrets of the press*. London: Penguin.

Goddard, P., Corner, J. and Richardson, K. (2001) 'The formation of *World In Action* – a case study in the history of current affairs journalism'. *Journalism – Theory, Practice and Criticism*, 2(1): 73–90.

Habermas, J. (1989) *The Structural Transformation of the Public Sphere*. (Trans. Thomas Burger). Cambridge: Polity Press.

Hall, J. (2001) *Online Journalism – a critical primer*. London: Pluto Press.

Langley, A. (2001) *Rupert Murdoch*. Oxford: Heinemann Library.

Luckhurst, T. (2001) *This is Today . . . a biography of the* Today *programme*. London: Aurum Press.

McNair, B. (1999) *News and Journalism in the UK* (3rd edition). London: Routledge.

Porter, R. (2000) *Enlightenment – Britain and the creation of the modern world*. London: Penguin.

Scannell, P. (1996) *Radio, Television & Modern Life*. Oxford: Blackwell.

Seymour-Ure, C. (1996) *The British Press and Broadcasting Since 1945* (2nd edition). Oxford: Blackwell.

Tunstall, J. (1996) *Newspaper Power*. Oxford: Oxford University Press.

Watkins, A. (2000) *A Short Walk Down Fleet Street*. London: Duckworth.

3 Researching and recording information

- Introduction
- Primary sources
- Secondary sources
- Obtaining and recording information
- Suggested activities
- Sources and resources

Introduction

There is a wide diversity of journalistic practice, from local and regional newspapers to national titles, from 'fanzine' magazines to specialist publications, from campus radio stations to local and national radio stations and from community television stations to national and satellite broadcasters. Therefore the following information, whilst reflecting this diversity, is primarily aimed at the aspiring or working journalist in local and regional newspapers, magazines, radio and television, but not strictly to the exclusion of other areas of journalistic interest.

Sources of information are the lifeblood of journalists whether working in print or broadcast industries. As such they provide the essential basic information for further development as news stories, radio features and television news packages. Some people contend that to distinguish between primary and secondary sources in this context is largely academic. Indeed, is a video news clip of a witness describing an event secondary because it is on tape or primary because of the first-hand information being imparted by the person? Many journalists still consider that there is a dividing line between primary and secondary sources of information. In simplistic terms a primary source may be defined as one that is personally researched by the journalist in terms of face-to-face interviews, visits, observation and first-hand experience; secondary research may be defined as using any existing material, whether it is written, stored on electronic data bases, audio/video recorded on different formats or indeed found on the Internet. Whilst appreciating the fine nuances in interpreting the differences between primary and secondary sources the following have been divided for ease of use into two categories.

Primary sources

Contacts

Contacts are people who, over a number of months or years, have provided valuable information to a journalist. They may be the local pub owner, a member of a community or voluntary organization or a traffic warden who will be trusted to provide accurate information on a breaking story. The essential tool for all journalists is their 'contacts book', which will contain the names, addresses, telephone numbers, e-mail addresses and other details of people they can contact for information. Even with the advent of mobile phones and personal organizers it is advisable to keep a written contacts book and possibly a duplicate in case of theft or loss of the original. Some journalists investigating sensitive areas tend to use code in their jottings or, in extreme circumstances, memorize the information.

Tip-offs

Tip-offs, either from freelances or members of the public, are another source of news especially for broadcasters. Some information may be valid and useful but it is well worth checking the accuracy of the information as it may be completely inaccurate, a hoax, the work of a crank or of someone with a grievance.

Freelances

Freelances, also known as 'stringers' or correspondents, are normally experienced reporters who may work part-time for a newspaper, radio or television station. They will sell their information to the relevant organization either individually or as part of a local news agency. In terms of radio they are cost effective in that they are only paid if their report is broadcast but sometimes their newspaper copy may be a little 'colourful' in order to sell the copy. However, for hard-pressed newsrooms they are a valuable source of material.

Routine calls

Routine calls or 'check calls' are an essential source of information and are made on a daily or hourly basis as a matter of course, normally by junior members of staff. Calls are regularly made to the emergency services such as police, fire, ambulance, hospitals and coastguards. Sometimes the services will reveal basic information but it may be necessary to combine information from some or all of them to build up a more detailed picture of an incident (a little like the 'jigsaw effect' in court reporting). Some press output from emergency services is taped and the quality of information may be variable in terms of depth of information and immediacy. Similarly it is very important to contact the most suitable and authorized person from which to request the information. Routine calls may also be made to ministers of religion, MPs, leaders of local councils, community and voluntary groups, press secretaries, undertakers, motoring organizations, health authorities, etc.

Pressure groups

Pressure groups are a good source of news but obviously in the majority of cases have a vested interest in seeking publicity for their cause. Freedom of access is desirable, tempered with a realistic and accurate approach, for groups such as trades unions, environmentalists, charities and welfare organizations. Caution is advised when dealing with unrepresentative groups of activists.

Courts and tribunals

Court reporting is an essential and daily aspect of a reporter's job. Assignments may range from youth and magistrates' courts to crown courts, coroners' courts and tribunals. Accuracy and clarity are the keynotes of using such information whilst attempting to capture the imagination of the reader without infringing the rights and restrictions of journalists.

Local government

Local government, from the parish council to unitary authority, provides a useful source of information for journalists. The press and public can attend all council meetings unless business is deemed confidential or exempt and basic facilities must be provided for reporters. Often seen as a chore by young reporters, reporting council meetings can be a rich source of information for follow up and investigative stories.

Community affairs

Community affairs offer a wealth of source material for a reporter. Clubs and societies exist in all communities. Arts and leisure organizations, schools and churches are always keen to gain publicity on local radio and television and in the local or regional press. Other easily accessible sources are voluntary organizations, resident's associations, trades unions, local councillors and politicians, local 'celebrities' or 'people in the know', as well as local employers.

News conferences

News or press conferences can provide invaluable official and unofficial material for a journalist. Most conferences involve the setting up of television recording equipment whilst the radio journalist will depend on a hand-held mike and a press journalist on a jottings pad and dictaphone. Sometimes only pre-arranged questions are allowed but if these relate to areas as opposed to specifics, further in-depth follow-up questions may elicit the required information.

Secondary sources

Letters

Letters to the editor or news desk often lead to good stories and reports, particularly in relation to community issues, planning decisions, central government policies and environmental and heritage issues. However, permission must be obtained from the writer to use the material and the content must be checked for accuracy and libellous statements.

Classified ads

Classified ads, especially the Births, Deaths and Marriages section, can lead to the development of human interest stories and features suitable for print and broadcast.

News releases

News releases and handouts are constantly sent to news rooms by public relations officers from commercial, voluntary, public or official organizations. Most are filed in the WPB (waste-paper bin) as being merely advertising for the particular organization. Indeed, for broadcast journalists, the person who sent the release may not be the most suitable or well informed person to be interviewed on a radio or television programme. The majority of news releases will carry an embargo, which has no legal weight, but which requests that information contained in the release is not published until a certain date and time.

Other news media

Other news media such as newspapers, magazines, radio and television are fruitful sources of news and ideas for further investigation and possible new angles. It is important not to overlook local, ethnic, international, specialist and even the journalist's own publication in seeking out stories that can be developed for print and broadcast. Remember the Law of Copyright does not extend to 'ideas'.

Syndicated tapes

Syndicated tapes are often recorded interviews, announcements or indeed complete programmes sent free of charge and unrequested to radio and television stations.

They are invariably from PR organizations seeking free publicity or a puff on the air-waves and often feature advertising. It is normally necessary to check the tapes for content and technical quality before even considering using the material.

Press agencies

Press or news agencies source news items and sell them to the print and broadcast media. There are numerous international, national and regional agencies and the following is a small selection of the main players in this field.

- *Reuters* – provides from a network of over 100 bureaux around the world a speedy and reliable news service for broadcast and print media. The World News Service (WNS) provides 24-hour news feed, news flashes, live coverage and in-depth features via satellite as well as similar online services via the World Wide Web.
- *United Press International* (UPI) – technology-driven news service offering breaking news stories, real time audio broadcasts and news photos. It covers especially the Middle East, business, sport, features, news and political events.
- *Agence France Presse* (AFP) – large French news agency that distributes news feeds in multiple languages. Supplies international news and picture services to the UK media and collects UK material for distribution internationally.
- *Associated Press* (AP) – claims to be the world's largest news agency and is co-operatively owned by US media companies. Supplies international news and picture services to the UK Media and collects UK material for American and other clients. AP Digital is the company's Web arm supplying text, audio, video, graphics and multimedia services including custom content categories to meet the information needs of a particular audience.
- *Press Association* (PA) – national news agency of the UK and Ireland delivering a continuous stream of stories, pictures, alerts and data to newsrooms of newspapers, broadcasters and electronic publishers using the latest satellite and computer technology. Covers foreign news, sport, entertainment, health and technology, in-depth coverage of parliament and politics as well as business and financial news and weather outlooks. Its three companies are PA News, PA Sport and PA Data Design, with subsidiaries Tellex Monitors, which monitors and reports on news and current affairs on radio and TV, and Two-Ten Communications, which provides customers with comprehensive marketing support services.
- *UK News* – founded in 1993 by Westminster Press and Northcliffe Newspapers it provides national and international news, sport and pictures to regional newspapers as well as having a number of lobby journalists at the House of Commons.

Press cuttings agencies

The Newspaper Licensing Agency (NLA) gathers copyright revenue from organizations that carry out large-scale photocopying of newspaper articles including the BBC and the House of Commons. Schools and charities are exempted from charges. It was launched in 1996 by a number of national newspapers and it represents a wide cross-section of the national, regional and local press. NLA-licensed cuttings agencies include Press Select, Tellex Monitors, The Press Data Bureau, etc.

Picture agencies

The British Association of Picture Libraries (BAPLA) is the key source of information on picture agencies, publishing an annual directory of over 300 members including British Library Reproductions, Camera Press, British Film Institute, Hulton-Getty, Action Images, Comstock, etc.

Pictures on the Web

The Cyberpix Guide is a comprehensive reference book on the best photo-sample sources on the Web. It includes Corbis, George Eastman House – International Museum of Photography and Film, Kodak, PhotoDisc, Publisher's Depot – PNI, etc.

News organizations

- *Independent Radio News* (IRN) – the main UK radio news agency, working in conjunction with ITN, supplying bulletins and other services to the majority of commercial radio stations. It is a commissioning agency owned by the major radio broadcasting consortia.
- *Independent Television News* (ITN) – provides national and international news to ITV, Channel 4 and Channel 5, and IRN. It is owned by a consortium of leading cross-media organizations.
- *CNN International* – Cable News Network International, a wholly owned subsidiary of Time Warner Inc., is a unique global network that distributes 24-hour news via satellite to more than 200 countries.
- *Worldwide Television News* (WTN) – provides a 24-hour satellite news service to broadcasters throughout the world as well as owning a wide-ranging film and video archive collection.
- *Reuters Television* – renamed after buying out Visnews, the international television news supplier in 1992, it has expanded its multimedia operations.
- *Parliamentary Channel* – provides live coverage of the daily proceedings in the House of Commons and recorded coverage of the House of Lords,

Question Time, the European Union, business statements and Parliamentary Committees.

● *ABC*, *NBC* and *CBS* – are all American news networks with offices in London supplying American and international news.

Local government

The leading annual directory and review of local government is the *Municipal Year Book*, which gives details of councillors and officers. If this is too dry then The Local Government Information Unit produces useful publications from a less official perspective with informed debates on local issues. Other titles that may be consulted are *Abstract of Accounts* and *Report on the Census*.

Central government

The journalist seeking information on Parliament has a number of established publications for reference including *Hansard* – the verbatim account of speeches in Parliament published daily, *Whitaker's Almanack*, *Vacher's Parliamentary Companion*, *Who's Who*, *Burke's Peerage*, *Dod's Parliamentary Companion*, *Keesing's Contemporary Archives*, *Civil Service Yearbook*, *Britain: An Official Guide* and other statistical data from the Central Office of Information (COI), the Office of National Statistics (ONS) and Her Majesty's Stationery Office (HMSO). In addition, useful information can be obtained from press releases from individual government departments as well as from the Internet.

Audience research bodies

Audience research bodies are extremely useful in highlighting short- and long-term audience viewing, listening and reading figures in broadcast and print industries and provide a journalist with up-to-date and accurate information. The four main bodies are:

● *Audit Bureau of Circulations* (ABC) – audits how many copies of a newspaper or magazine have been sold in a given period. It aims to provide buyers of advertising with a benchmark to help them choose between competing publications and to provide media owners with a promotional tool.

● *National Readership Survey* (NRS) – offers a reliable source of audience information for nearly 300 publications along with key marketing information. Unlike ABC it does not concentrate on circulation data but on the readership profiles of the audience in terms of demographics such as age, sex, education, employment, income and social status.

● *Broadcasters Audience Research Board* (BARB) – provides information on all aspects of the television industry and is the primary source of television audience data in the UK. It produces statistical information on audience viewing that is vital to both broadcasters and the advertising industry. It also provides an audience reaction service that produces qualitative data on appreciation of television programmes that is confidential to subscribing broadcasters.

● *Radio Joint Audience Research* (RAJAR) – a joint body involving the BBC and commercial radio that carries out detailed audience research that involves listeners completing detailed listening diaries over a stipulated period. The information includes details of listening patterns, age, sex, finance, area of transmission, etc. and provides advertisers and programme controllers with details of audience preferences, thus enabling selective programming and advertising.

Media directories

Media directories are an excellent source of information for print and broadcast journalists, providing up-to-date information on all areas and aspects of media. In addition to the titles mentioned previously in the section on central government, *Willings Press Guide* provides a comprehensive guide to newspapers, magazines, TV, radio, business and specialist publications in both the UK and worldwide. *BENNS Media* offers a similar directory, covering all sectors of the UK media industry as well as European and World editions. *BRAD* (*British Rate and Data*) is a monthly classified directory of media in the UK and the Republic of Ireland that carry advertising. Media are broken down into: national and regional newspapers, consumer press, business press, new and electronic media, television, radio, cinema and posters and outdoor. *BRADnet* and *BRADbase* are also available through subscription. *The Media Guide* covers most media sectors in the UK with a section for the Republic of Ireland. The *UK Press Directory* provides a complete overview of the newspaper industry, whilst *Media UK Internet Directory* gives a complete listing of online media in the UK to include newspapers, radio, television and magazines. *Kemp's Film, TV and Video Yearbook* is an important directory of international film and television production and *The Blue Book of British Broadcasting* is an excellent reference source for contacts in TV, radio and satellite broadcasting. *The Radio Authority Pocket Guide* and *The Radio Listener's Guide* are ideal reference material for radio journalists. *The Radio Academy Yearbook* is the directory of the leading professional society for the radio industry and, similarly, *The Royal Television Society Handbook* is a guide and directory for its members.

The Internet

The Internet has revolutionized the ability to research information and at the touch of a keypad provides interminable knowledge to all. Journalists are now able to access instantly all types of news and information.

Many of the sources above have Internet sites and provide an unending stream of information in text, graphic and moving image format. A few Internet sites have been mentioned but it is difficult to provide a conclusive listing; suffice to say that the Internet is a major and excellent addition to journalistic research but as such should be treated with caution and respect in terms of accuracy of information and self-interest. By all means 'surf the Web' for information but use it as a 'tool not a master'. There is a tendency to use the information as supplied, as opposed to using a different angle to create an informative, investigative and specific news piece in print and broadcast. The Internet provides immediate access to a plethora of information that, in meeting a deadline, may hinder rather than aid a journalist and traditional sources of information may, ironically, be less time-consuming in the daily journalistic routine. Ultimately the Internet can be a superb source of information for print and broadcast journalists if used selectively and with discretion.

Obtaining and recording information

Once sources of information have been identified, the next stage is to carry out research using a variety of methods and approaches and to record the information obtained in a clear, accurate and established format. This section will adopt a generic approach to methods of obtaining and recording information and more specific guidance will be given in the relevant chapters for radio, print and television journalism.

Interviews

Interviewing, either face-to-face or by telephone, is a major means of obtaining information. The interview may be an informal conversation in a shopping precinct, a pre-arranged formality with a local dignitary, a chance chat with a caller to a radio station, a follow-up telephone call or a location interview for a television report. Whatever form the interview takes the prime aim of the journalist is to elicit information such as facts and opinions about a certain issue, situation or the person themselves. Interviews can be used purely for gaining information on the facts about a particular incident or to seek an insight into the personality of a person for a human interest angle. Sometimes the interview may be strongly investigative and lead to a confrontational situation. At all interviews, care should be taken to establish that the information being given is accurate and truthful and that the interviewee for whatever reason is not withholding facts, deliberately giving misinformation or using the opportunity for propaganda purposes. Preparation is an essential element of interviewing and a journalist should be aware of the background information and the purpose of the interview before meeting the interviewee. Some journalists write down the main questions to be asked, others, particularly on radio, decide on the first and last questions and allow the interview to flow as the facts and opinions emerge. Whichever method is used the journalist should always remember that it is the interviewee's opinions that matter and not their comments.

Telephone interviews are the quickest way of obtaining information from an interviewee but can be less rewarding than face-to-face encounters: there is no eye contact or assessment of body language, the line may be of poor quality and reporters have to use precise questions when gleaning essential information as time is at a premium. However, if no one is available at short notice to visit a location a telephone interview may be seen as at least a holding device until on the spot information and actuality can be obtained.

Another form of interview is the 'grabbed' or 'quickie', which by definition is very short and may consist of one or two questions being shouted at a reluctant subject who invariably will reply with 'No comment'. This type of 'interview' will normally take place in the presence of rival journalists, news crews and reporters, all hoping to get a reaction on a major or controversial issue – a non-reaction can be as telling as an answer, especially if filmed.

'Vox pop' or voice of the people is a means of interviewing whereby a reporter can obtain a snapshot of opinion on a topical issue from members of the public. One or two identical questions are asked of a random selection of the public, often in busy town centres, and these short quotations can be used as soundbites in television and radio features and reports or as snippets in a print feature, often adding a colourful and interesting aspect to an otherwise bland piece of reporting.

The means of recording interviews varies according to the medium. Print journalists will normally use shorthand or speed writing to log the comments and essential facts and figures in a notebook; a dictaphone may also be used as an 'aide memoire' if approved by the interviewee. Radio journalists will use portable recording equipment and a notebook and a TV reporter a notebook and a

Figure 3.1 On the job

cameraperson. Obviously, with multi-skilling, some journalists will operate in more than one medium and one interview will be used for a variety of purposes and in different formats. Whatever format is used all information should be well documented, accurate and kept in a safe environment for future reference.

The art of interviewing for different media is discussed in the relevant chapters later in the book.

Visits

Visits, whether as part of routine such as court reporting, council meetings and press conferences, or to special events are a valuable means of obtaining up to the minute information and yet more and more journalists spend time in the office using electronic sources of news. However, the public still expect that there will be a journalist at a cricket match, theatrical performance, pop concert and other live events in order that they may read or listen to an account of the event from someone who was actually there and thus able to give first-hand information. Similarly a journalist sent to cover a breaking news story is much more likely to obtain crucial information by speaking with witnesses and observing the situation at the scene. In the case of a major ongoing story a reporter may have to stay at the scene of the incident for hours or even days in the hope of being the first to obtain the most recent information and reaction. The information gained may be recorded on printed, audio, video and still-image format or sent immediately by telephone to base.

Acquiring secondary material

Reading reference material is part of the essential research required in order to check background information about a subject that may form part or the whole of a radio, print or television report. Routine tasks involve reading handouts, PR material, letters to the editor, other newspapers and magazines, council meeting minutes and court reports. A cuttings file should be used to record and store this material in a logical and easily accessible manner once the validity of the information has been checked. Standard works of reference including dictionaries and media directories, such as those previously mentioned, may be found within the work place, if not the local library should hold major publications in this field as well as invaluable local information in the form of local archives and guide books. Investigative journalism may involve seeking out industrial, governmental, subject-specific and sensitive findings and reports from specialist libraries and organizations. Film, television and radio archives can be valuable sources of secondary information and clips from previous recordings can be obtained, often at a price. The Internet is, of course, a major source of information and is increasingly being used as an international reference library from which specific information can be obtained and recorded on differing storage formats as well as in hard copy. The future is indeed digital as more and more sources of information become available in the public domain and this has revolutionized the research patterns for journalists working in all media sectors.

Suggested activities

1 Using a note book with alphabetical tabs begin compiling a 'contacts book' of sources of information. Devise your own method of recording the information but ensure that names, addresses, telephone numbers and e-mail information are clearly displayed and annotated.

2 In your locality carry out individual primary research using first-hand methods such as face-to-face and telephone interviews and personal investigation on location to record the following in your contacts book:

   a The name and telephone number of the official contact or spokesperson for

   (i)   Police
   (ii)   Fire
   (iii)   Ambulance
   (iv)   Hospital
   (v)   Coastguard

   b The name, address and telephone number for

   (i)   Community, charity and voluntary organizations
   (ii)   Doctors and animal welfare organizations
   (iii)   Pressure groups
   (iv)   Arts and leisure organizations
   (v)   Schools, colleges and universities
   (vi)   Newspapers, magazines, radio and television stations
   (vii)   Religious organizations
   (viii) Courts
   (ix)   Local councillors and Members of Parliament for the constituency.

3 Using secondary sources such as the Internet, libraries, data bases and archives find out the names, addresses, telephone numbers and e-mail addresses of the following:

   a Central government departments and agencies
   b Local government departments and agencies
   c Taxation departments and agencies
   d Multimedia organizations
   e Media audience research bodies.

4 You have been asked to write a magazine feature on the use of GM crops in food production. Make a list of possible sources that would be useful in obtaining

information on the subject and evaluate the potential value of each when planning the feature.

5 Use the Internet to find information on the number and type of local independent radio stations in the UK.

6 Describe the methods you might use to carry out research for a four-minute radio feature on entertainment in your area.

7 Choose two main stories from your local evening newspaper and make a list of the possible sources and methods that the reporter might have used to write the story.

8 Your college is interested in setting up a Restricted Service Licence (RSL) radio station. Individually or in a small group investigate the feasibility of this venture by carrying out primary and secondary research and recording your findings.

9 You have been asked to write a sports story for your college/community newsletter. Decide on the content and angle of the story, which should be of immediate interest to the intended readership. Carry out primary research and make a list of the methods used, the contacts made and the information obtained.

10 Using a still camera take 12 pictures of your local area, some of which you could use later to illustrate a feature on the unique aspects of your locality.

Sources and resources

1991 Census General Report Great Britain (1995). London: The Stationery Office.

Abstract of Accounts (annually). London: The Stationery Office.

Berger, A. (1991) *Media Research Techniques*. London: Sage.

Boyd, A. (2001) *Broadcast Journalism – techniques of radio and television news* (5th edition). Oxford: Focal Press.

Chater, K. (2001) *Research for Media Production*. Oxford: Focal Press.

Harris, G. and Spark, D. (1997) *Practical Newspaper Reporting* (3rd edition). Oxford: Focal Press.

Hennessy, B. (1995) *Journalism Workbook: a manual of tasks, projects and resources*. Oxford: Focal Press.

Hoffman, A. (1986) *Research for Writers*. A.C. Black.

Keeble, R. (1998) *The Newspapers Handbook* (2nd edition). London: Routledge.

Mishler, E. (1986) *Research Interviewing*. Harvard University Press.

Peak, S. and Fisher, P. (eds) (2002) *The Guardian Media Guide 2002* (10th edition). London: Atlantic Books.

Spack, D. (1996) *A Journalist's Guide to Sources*. Oxford: Focal Press.

The Municipal Year Book (annually). London: The Stationery Office.

4 Newspapers and magazines

- Introduction
- Interviewing
- Copy presentation
- Hard news
- Softer news
- Features
- Reviews
- A brief overview of Leader, Diary, Sport and Fanzines
- Suggested activities
- Sources and resources

Introduction

The range and types of writing within newspapers and magazines is vast and varied to suit differing contexts, readership, specialisms, commercial factors, editorial control, ownership, etc. One way of categorizing writing activities within the newspaper and magazine industries is by differentiating between diary and off-diary events. Diary events for newspaper reporters include attending press conferences, the courts, local authority meetings, inquests, tribunals, local elections, community and sporting events and cultural activities. Off-diary events or 'breaking stories' include accidents, crime, demonstrations and emergencies. Diary events for magazine journalists include attending press conferences, exhibitions, fashion shows and launches for new products.

Another way of differentiating between writing for magazines and newspapers is by readership patterns. A newspaper aims at a large circulation of general readers and is primarily a vehicle for topical news and information. A magazine in weekly, monthly or quarterly guise is aimed at a specific readership that may be defined by location, specialist interest, community, gender, ethnicity, etc. Yet, whatever the categorization, there is an increasing demand for innovation coupled with fierce commercial pressure on newspaper and magazine owners to compete with rival publications. Indeed there has been an unprecedented upsurge in demand for specialist magazines in recent years. This has resulted in weaker publications that do not keep abreast of the market having to cease publication. The demise of some men's magazine titles in 2001 highlighted this issue.

At the risk of generalization, newspapers will normally contain a mixture of hard news and features including sport, finance, foreign affairs, opinion, analysis, reviews, leaders, etc. Magazines, whether general or specialist, will contain much of the above, apart from breaking news, with a tendency towards photo-features, product reviews, horoscopes, advice, competitions and advertising features. Also there is a general difference in emphasis between writing subjectively for a magazine and writing more objectively for a newspaper. Sue Green, the tutor on the National Council for the Training of Journalists (NCTJ) course at the City of Wolverhampton College has worked in both sectors and offered the opinion that:

> Writing for newspapers is more urgent than writing for magazines, which are usually produced weekly, fortnightly, monthly or quarterly. Newspapers are also more tightly constrained by space whereas magazines allow for more in-depth, descriptive and timeless pieces.

Thus, allowing for the plethora of styles of writing to suit differing readerships and contexts this chapter will consider a cross-section of types of writing that a trainee journalist may be expected to produce. It will concentrate on providing guidelines for writing hard news stories, softer news stories, features and reviews with a brief overview of writing leaders, sports and diary items. However, before considering the above in detail it would be fair to say that all writing depends on carrying out adequate research and a key method in gleaning information is by conducting interviews.

Interviewing

As mentioned in the previous chapter, interviews are a major part of the everyday role of journalists and broadcasters and can vary from simple one-question 'quickies' or 'vox pops' to planned, longer interviews with a pre-determined brief and purpose. This section describes in more detail the essential elements and professional practice when carrying out planned face-to-face and telephone interviews for writing copy for newspapers and magazines.

The face-to-face interview

Adequate preparation is vital in carrying out a successful interview and the first step is to ensure that the brief is fully understood in terms of:

● is this the most suitable person to be interviewing for this particular subject?
● what kind of story and angle is required?
● who are the target audience?

● what is the intended optimum length of the piece?
● what is the deadline?

Once these basic facts have been established more detailed planning can begin.

The second step is to arrange the interview with the designated person. Always ensure that the person you are intending to interview is the one who can give you the most accurate information on the chosen topic. Obviously if the interview is intended as a profile of the person the latter does not apply but it is frustrating and time consuming to arrive at an interview only to discover that the interviewee is not the most suitable person or indeed the official spokesperson on the topic. Most official organizations such as trades unions, NHS trusts, the emergency services and arts councils have public relations officers who may be able to either give interviews themselves or refer you to certain specialists within the organization who may give more informative interviews. It is advantageous to make an appointment for the interview either directly with the person involved or their secretary or personal assistant. When you telephone adopt a polite yet professional approach, state your name, position and the publication you are working for and explain the nature of your call in terms of the reason for requesting an interview, the particular topic and the probable time needed for the interview. If a preliminary agreement is reached ensure that the time and place are mutually acceptable, whether it be at the newspaper office, which may be rather distracting or even daunting for the interviewee, at the person's office or home, or in a relaxed atmosphere such as a restaurant or bar. The time and proposed length of the interview are very important if the interviewee has a hectic work schedule so it is wise to negotiate this in the initial request. If time allows, a formal letter confirming the arrangements should be sent to the interviewee.

It is obviously good practice to have some knowledge of the background of the interviewee and the particular topic for the interview. If time allows, then, thorough research should be undertaken about the person and the topic and the interviewee will certainly be more receptive if they believe that the reporter 'knows what they are talking about'. Specific areas such as investigations into accidents or incidents at nuclear power plants, malpractice in financial institutions, discrimination in the workplace or lack of care facilities in hospitals will require careful research into the background of the situation. Research can be as fundamental as asking a colleague for information. There may have been previous contact with the prospective interviewee by other staff on the newspaper and the information gleaned, particularly regarding the willingness of the interviewee to give information and possible pitfalls, can be invaluable. Other sources could be cuttings files, local library, government reports and even *Who's Who* if a celebrity is the intended subject of a profile interview.

It is advisable to consider your approach to the interview particularly as regards preparing suitable questions. Some journalists argue that writing down all questions ensures that you do not forget essential details. However, this may lead to a stilted approach especially if your fumbling with a notebook distracts the interviewee. Certainly it is advisable to consider the type and depth of the questions beforehand and these may be initially written down to clarify your mind as to the logical progression of the interview. The next step is to transform these questions into bullet points that will determine the rough outline of the interview. However, once the interview has begun it may take quite an unusual twist so it is imperative to keep an open mind and follow your train of thought as the interview progresses rather than stick rigidly to a formulaic approach.

Practical considerations should be the next stage in the process. This will involve checking on the mode and routes of transport particularly where difficulties may arise in city centres, in rush hours, where road works are in place, when using public transport and in unfamiliar locations. The practical advice is to make sure you allow adequate time for the journey so as to be punctual for the interview – lateness will suggest a less than professional attitude. Similarly make sure you inform the editor of the time, place and date of the interview, especially if you are going alone to an unknown location. Dress appropriately for the occasion but remember that casual smart is not scruffy and with the demise in the sales of ties it is not *de rigueur* to wear one. Commonsense dictates that first impressions count and you should dress accordingly to gain the confidence of the interviewee. Remember to take with you your notebook, writing tools and spares, a small tape-recorder if sanctioned by the interviewee, money or credit cards, your business card and a mobile phone in case of emergencies.

At the interview the initial pleasantries serve a more serious purpose. To this end you should adopt a professional approach by introducing yourself and the publication you represent and state the purpose of your visit and who you wish to meet to the secretary/receptionist/security officer at work places. Note that the interviewee may be expecting quite a number of visitors in any one day and some will arrive at unexpected and unplanned times of the day. In any case, confirm that the person you wish to meet is the one you planned for. In cases of meetings at the home of the interviewee the latter still applies. Meetings in informal locations such as restaurants and bars can be fraught with difficulties so establish basic details such as meeting them in reception or the lounge area, with a brief description of yourself and the interviewee to aid recognition. Red carnations may still apply!

Whatever and wherever the initial contact takes place be pleasant but not overfamiliar (avoid first names at the outset unless encouraged by the inter-viewee) and adopt a professional stance and demeanour. If time is at a premium there is little point in 'beating around the bush' so remind the interviewee of the purpose of the interview but attempt to establish a rapport with them by making them feel at ease, showing interest in their response, establishing eye contact and generally leading them from one aspect to the next. The standard use of the 'five Ws and H' – Who, What, Where, Why, When and How – apply to most interviews in print and broadcasting and can be a valuable framework for an interview but you need not stick sequentially to this formula if other avenues suddenly arise. You should ask 'open' rather than 'closed' questions. 'Yes' and 'No' answers will reveal little. Similarly, negative questions will elicit a negative response. Also it is advisable to avoid questions that require more than one answer. By the time the interviewee has answered the first part of the question they have forgotten the second part. The same applies to rhetorical questions, which can only lead to a short response as you are putting words in the interviewee's mouth.

One of the main problems in interviewing is if the journalist is not prepared to either listen or let the interviewee speak at length. By all means intervene if the interviewee digresses but important information and quotations can be obtained by keeping quiet at appropriate moments. In fact, the use of pre-written questions often leads the journalist to concentrate on these to the detriment of actually hearing what the interviewee is saying and thus progressing the interview. It is acceptable practice to leave deeper or more contentious questions until later in the interview and never to reveal your own ethical, political or social bias. Some interviewees may be difficult in that they are reluctant to answer certain questions or adopt a hostile approach; others prevaricate at length or maintain a stony silence. Be aware of these situations and adapt your questioning accordingly, possibly returning later in the interview to the specific area of contention. It is normal practice to end the interview by asking the interviewee whether there is any other information they may wish to give on the particular issue; it may lead to information you had completely overlooked in your preparation.

The accepted way of recording information at a one-to-one interview for newspapers is by notebook using shorthand or speed writing, unless the interviewee sanctions the use of a tape recorder. It is worth noting that the NCTJ still requires trainees to achieve 100 words per minute in shorthand, which is essential for court and council meeting reporting, although many journalists within the industry have not gained this certificate and rely on their own form of shorthand. It is advisable to use a notebook carefully so as not to antagonize the interviewee or indeed distract yourself from maintaining an interest in the conversation. However, it is essential to note down important facts and verbatim quotations and, before leaving, to re-check with the interviewee that the information you have recorded is accurate, especially as regards legal and ethical issues. At the end of the interview it is of paramount importance to thank the interviewee, however dire the information you have obtained. Leave your card or at least your telephone number or e-mail address. And finally a follow-up 'thank you' letter may not go amiss as you may need to contact the person again at a future date.

The telephone interview

As with the face-to-face interview it is vital to ensure that the brief is clearly understood, although in most instances it will not be written owing to the informal nature and work pressures in busy newsrooms. Within a training situation the brief will be fairly well documented with information as to deadlines, mode of presentation and style of copy required. The preparations for a telephone interview are very much the same as for a face-to-face interview in terms of research and planning. However, certain difficulties can arise in carrying out the interview. Obviously, a face-to-face interview, as the term suggests, means you can judge the reaction of the interviewee from posture, facial expressions, reactions and gestures. This is not possible on the telephone as the intonation and delivery of the voice and possibly long silences or faltering by the interviewee are in some situations the only clues to eliciting further information. Invariably you should attempt to contact the person at an appropriate time of day; in essence not too early in the morning or too late in the afternoon, especially if you know from your prior research that the interviewee has a hectic schedule in the workplace. For example, if you wished to contact a schoolteacher about an educational matter it would be sensible to find out the times of breaks in between lessons from, say, the school secretary and try and contact the person at those times. Similarly, unless permission has been given, it is inadvisable to contact someone very late in the evening. One final point as regards preparation is that because the interview needs to be fairly concise and precise it is useful to carefully prepare the questions and possibly write them down in a logical order (again the 'five Ws and H' apply). This does not mean that you should stick rigidly to this once the conversation begins but it should help refresh your memory as the interview proceeds and provide a check list as the interview comes to a close.

It is essential to state your name, your organization and the purpose of the interview clearly and politely before you launch into the first question. Thereafter ask logical and enquiring questions to obtain the required information. If certain answers seem rather vague try and tease out the information by adopting a less direct approach or returning later to that point when the interviewee may have relaxed and adjusted to your voice and style of questioning. However, be wary of making flippant remarks or misunderstanding a seemingly off-the-cuff comment from the person that may be deliberately misleading or not meant as intended. As mentioned previously, you cannot see the person's reaction so try and judge the response from the register and intonation of their voice and adjust your tone and delivery to overcome the impersonality of the situation. Remember, some people are reticent on the telephone especially if the caller is unknown to them so adopt an attitude that puts them at ease whilst still maintaining an inquisitive manner. As with presenting on radio, standing up, making gestures and facial expressions can all aid the communication process. Whatever stance you adopt it is essential that you speak clearly and logically; waffling on or skirting the subject will soon antagonize the interviewee. Similarly, unless the office is equipped with telephone headsets, make sure you concentrate on speaking into the mouthpiece even though you may be keying the answers into the computer or taking notes. Towards the end of the interview check all the information for accuracy, including spellings, and ask the interviewee whether you can contact them again if you need further information. Always thank them for their time.

Copy presentation

Whatever the type of writing required trainees should be aware of the need to establish a clear copy presentation style for their work. In the modern newsroom copy will be keyed directly into a computer and sent down the line to the sub-editors, so it is a moot point as to whether existing copy presentation rules apply. As a general rule journalists will input copy with their by-line whether it is subsequently used or not. Catchlines are still required: an item numbered '43' has no relevance to the editor, an item with the catchline 'Road death' certainly has. The terms 'm/f' and 'ends' are not used as the editor can clearly see where the story continues and ends. Much depends on the house style and working practices within an organization. However, it is still desirable, especially in training situations where hard copy may be needed for assessment purposes, to follow the basic rules that the industry, and training and qualification bodies accept. In a training situation the following guidelines apply:

- use one side of an A4 white sheet only
- word process the copy with double spacing
- leave a margin of about 3.5–4.5 cm to both left and right of the copy
- on the first folio identify the writer, the name of the publication, the date of the publication and the numbered one- or two-word catchline that clearly identifies the story, e.g.

    Barry Evans   Haven Times   21 July 2001   Arena demolition

    the catchline should be specific to the story and generic single words such as 'fire', 'accident', 'crime' and even 'splash', should be avoided
- the catchline is then repeated on each succeeding folio with a consecutive number
- each folio except the last should have 'more' or 'more follows' (m/f) centred at the bottom
- the last folio should have 'ends' centred at the bottom and the total number of words of the story
- if there is more copy to follow at a later stage, as with a running story, the last folio should have 'more follows later' (mfl) centred at the bottom

- if some more recent and important material emerges the reporter can 're-nose' the story by writing a new introductory section. The numbered catchline of this material should be preceded by the words 'new lead'
- in the case of names that have similar spellings such as 'Jayne' and 'Jane', in order to aid the sub-editor put 'correct' in brackets after the name to indicate that you have checked that this is the correct spelling
- paragraphs should not be indented, be clearly delineated by additional white space and not run over folios.

Hard news

Most diary events such as reporting courts, council meetings, tribunals, community events can be classified as providing hard news stories. Similarly accidents, crime and emergencies provide immediate and topical information for hard news. Whatever the source the journalist must take into account the angle of the story to best portray the facts to the intended readership. News is about people and the human angle is often the best way to introduce the story. If there has been a major fire at a local school the first thought of readers will be whether there have been any injuries to pupils and staff and not the state of the school buildings. To that end the reporter would probably begin the story with

> *Two teachers and five pupils were seriously injured in a fire at Eaststoke School early today . . .*

The fact that two classrooms and the refectory were gutted by the fire is of secondary importance.

Once the angle has been established the reporter can then concentrate on constructing the story. Most readers briefly scan pages and therefore it is paramount that the opening paragraph grabs the attention of the readers so that they wish to read on. The following basic guidelines apply to writing most intros:

Do

- keep the length to about 30 – 40 words. Try splitting the intro into two sentences to aid clarity and impact
- use vigorous and direct language to emphasize the urgency and to catch the interest of the reader
- give a precise, clear and accurate summary of the most important points; a basic test is to ask whether it could be used in the 'news in brief' section as a self-contained piece
- use positive rather than negative statements.

Don't

- begin with a quotation unless the speaker is well known, e.g., the Prime Minister
- begin with a figure/numeral – spell out the number
- use boring phrases such as 'There was' and 'There is'.

The majority of news stories use the standard formula of the 'five Ws and H' (Who, What, Where, When, Why and How) but it is not always feasible or desirable to try to include all of these elements in the intro as readers may become confused if too much information and background is given in the first sentence. The following intro illustrates this point

> *Robbers stole a charity collection box from St. Jude's Church, Westport at the weekend.*

This only answers the questions who, what, where and when but provides enough information to encourage further reading of the story to establish how and possibly why the incident occurred. In this example the naming of the church and town would be especially important for a local readership. However, the following, although attracting the reader with colourful language, is not as precise as the above and requires further explanation:

> *A baker came to the rescue when a drunken yob caused havoc on a cross-channel ferry yesterday.*

A good intro will clarify the thoughts of a reporter into making a news judgement about the most important and striking facts. Thereafter the rest of the story should follow a logical and flowing pattern. The ordering of information in a news story has traditionally conformed to what is known as the Inverted Pyramid/Triangle

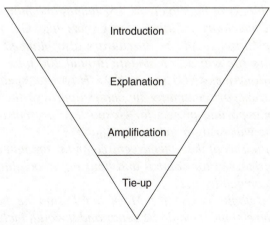

Figure 4.1 Inverted Pyramid/Triangle Model

Model, where the most important points in the story, taking into account the writer's angle, are at the beginning with gradually decreasing importance of information in subsequent paragraphs. This allows the sub-editor to 'cut' the story from the bottom if space is tight but still retain the most important facts.

Thus the basic construction of a news story would be:

- *Introduction* – a summary of the main points of the story.
- *Explanation* – following on from the summary in the intro and giving more detailed information on the participants, description of the circumstances surrounding the story, local angle, etc.
- *Amplification* – elaborating each of the points given in the first two sections with background information, quotations, eye-witness accounts, etc.
- *Conclusion* – tying-up the loose ends of the story.

The following example of a hard news story from a provincial newspaper reflects this basic structure:

by Steve Bone

The News

A MAJOR jobs boost is on the way after plans for a scheme to inject new life into a former Ministry of Defence plot were given the green light. Fairview New Homes won approval from councillors for its £10m scheme to transform St George Barracks South in Gosport. But there was opposition from Labour councillors who said the town could be getting a better deal.

Fairview hopes to start work before Christmas on a two-year programme to preserve and convert listed buildings on the barracks site and build new blocks of flats to create 167 homes and more than 2000 sq. ft of offices. Community buildings for groups like Gosport Voluntary Action and the Citizens' Advice Bureau are also planned and the new-look town centre site will accommodate around 200 jobs.

Tory councillor Aleck<NO1>corr<NO> Hayward, speaking after the planning and transport committee he chairs approved the scheme, said: 'This is a very important project for Gosport. At present it's a dead site but this scheme will bring in people and jobs'.

Labour's criticisms of the scheme centred on the amount of the housing that will be earmarked for council and housing association tenants and the space for community use.

Town ward Labour councillor Mark Smith said he had hoped the design of the development would be better and it would include a doctors' surgery and more social housing. But Conservative councillors said they

*had pushed the developers as far as possible and Liberal Democrats
voted with them to see through the plans.*

*Gavin Maber, project co-ordinator for Fairview, said after the meeting:
'I'm delighted this has been approved and we're looking forward to
pressing on. Had it been turned down, I would have appealed
immediately and would have been confident of winning'.*

*Buildings to be retained include the barrack block and hospital for
housing and the gym, sergeant's mess and chapel for office and
community use, with the possibility of leisure facilities.*

There can be variations on this structure but as a straightforward local news story
with appropriate background information and quotations the above formula works
well. Note also the check on the correct spelling of the Tory councillor's
name.

The structure of a news story is important but many other factors, including style
of language and journalistic conventions, are equally important in producing a
readable, compelling, effective and accurate account. Be aware of the following
guidelines:

Do

- keep the story as concise as possible whilst including all the main facts. The
  length of the story should be appropriate to the brief, the readership, the deadline,
  the available space in the publication, etc.
- write concisely – use one word instead of two or more – for example, 'late' is
  preferred to 'behind schedule'; 'many' to 'a large proportion of'; 'since' to 'in
  view of the fact that', etc.
- write clearly and avoid ambiguity
- keep paragraphs short – a maximum of 45–50 words is ample
- maintain a logical order and progression by linking the various elements with
  transitional words such as 'however', 'although', 'but', etc., as opposed to using
  stand alone sentences that lack any connection with the previous or following
  sentence. Try and maintain a rhythm throughout the piece
- check the correct word and spelling when using similar sounding words that
  have different meanings, such as 'complement' and 'compliment'; 'principle'
  and 'principal'; 'affect' and 'effect'; 'allusion' and 'illusion', etc.
- use quotations to reinforce facts and add ' colour' to the story – they may be
  direct, indirect or attributed quotations. In the sample story above a direct
  quotation reads:

  *Gavin Maber, project co-ordinator for Fairview, said after the meeting
  'I'm delighted this has been approved and we're looking forward to
  pressing on. Had it been turned down, I would have appealed
  immediately and would have been confident of winning'.*

In the same story the indirect quotation reads:

> *Town ward Labour councillor Mark Smith said he had hoped the design*
> *of the development would be better and it would include a doctor's*
> *surgery and more social housing.*

Other alternatives to 'said' could have been 'remarked', 'stated', 'stressed', etc.
Attributed quotations reflecting the opinion of the speaker are sometimes used in
the intro to a story as in the following example:

> *'British schoolchildren obsessed with surfing the net or playing computer*
> *games lack basic physical fitness', Mike Smith, Head of P.E. at Westport*
> *Secondary School said yesterday.*

Don't

- write long and unwieldy sentences – readers will quickly lose interest if there are
  too many subordinate clauses in a sentence
- use jargon, especially specialist terminology of one particular profession or
  occupation, such as 'woofers' and 'tweeters' in sound engineering. The non-
  technical reader will need an explanation of these terms in the text
- use clichés if at all possible – although newspapers thrive on them particularly
  when reporting sports, war, politics, etc. they quickly date and can appear
  hackneyed in the extreme, e.g., 'window of opportunity', 'broke the back of the
  net', 'the ship of state', etc.
- use unnecessary and overused adjectives such as 'horrendous', 'tragic', 'unique',
  'miraculous', etc.

Once the story has been written or 'keyed in' it is important to read through and
thoroughly check the structure, content and style of the piece. Ask the following
questions:

Structure

1 Does the intro give the main points of the news and if so could it be published
  alone as a 'news in brief' item?
2 Has the intro given the most important or most interesting part of the story so as
  to attract the reader's attention?
3 Does the main body of the story amplify and explain the main points of the intro
  in order of importance?
4 Has the story answered the 5 Ws and H?
5 Have all the loose ends been tied up?
6 Have both sides of a potentially contentious issue been given in an objective
  manner?
7 Does the piece meet the necessary word count as specified in the brief?

Content and style

1 Is the content factually correct with close attention to detail?
2 Is the content legally 'safe'? (Refer to Chapter 13 on Journalism law.)
3 Does the content and style address the target audience and establish a relationship with the potential reader?
4 Is the writing taut and crisp with a maximum of facts and the minimum of extraneous material?
5 Is the language clear and unambiguous with little use of slang, jargon and clichés?
6 If quotations are used are they accurate, correctly attributed and pertinent to the story?
7 Has the spelling, punctuation and grammar been checked and corrected?
8 Does the content have ethical, political or social undertones that may 'slant ' the piece?

Softer news

It could be argued that all news stories are about people yet in this context human interest or 'soft news' stories can be defined as the people behind the news. Human interest stories in the tabloids often revolve around the scandals and outrageous behaviour of celebrities but there are many 'heartwarming' stories to be found in local newspapers. These might involve accounts of triumph over personal adversity, a profile of a person raising money for charitable causes, investigating the changes in the lifestyle of local National Lottery winners, reporting on an animal sanctuary that is in need of financial aid, taking part in an army training course, describing the day-to-day existence of a sheep farmer in the Welsh hillsides, etc. Most human interest stories will arise from a news event but give the opportunity for further investigation and opinion with an emphasis on quotations from the participants. The following is typical of this type of story.

by Steve Bone

The News

FOR sailor Tonya Howard the atmosphere of a farmyard is a world away from her normal life at sea on board the mighty battleship USS Winston S Churchill. But now the American, from Ohio, has been adopted as mascot for Felicia Park urban farm in Gosport.

Sue Hitchman, who runs Felicia Park, responded to a story in The News ahead of the International Festival of the Sea in which the crew of the USS Winston S Churchill appealed for local people to show them around. Sue issued an invite to a sailor with an interest in animals to

*visit her farm – and was delighted when 19-year-old Tonya Howard
arrived.*

*Tonya, an electronic warfare technician on board the Churchill, rode
Felicia Park's horses and met the staff – and told them about the ranch
her parents run back home in London, Ohio. Sue said: 'She thought
Felicia Park was beautiful and said there was nothing really like it in
America. She is a big horse lover and was quite at home here. She has
grown up with horses and knows how to treat them. I introduced her to
the rest of my four-legged family too'.*

*Tonya, who has invited Sue back to her parents' stables, told The News
her trip to the sanctuary had helped make her stay in the area during
festival weekend extra-special. She said: 'We had a list of people from out
in the town that wanted to adopt a sailor for a day. I noticed that she had
horses so I thought I would give it a try. The people there were very nice.
I enjoyed it, mainly because I was around horses and other animals. It
was a relaxing place to be'.*

*Now Sue and Tonya have met, both hope their friendship will become
permanent – and they may visit one another's centres when time and
money allow.*

*Tonya, who also commented that she and her 350 fellow shipmates had
enjoyed the International Festival of the Sea experience, said: 'I would
love to come back and even bring my parents and friends. Everyone is
welcome at my family's farm any time'.*

Features

Feature writing is often seen by the aspiring journalist as a release from the
structural and stylistic restrictions of hard news by allowing much more creativity
of thought and opinions. However, it is important that a journalist understands the
fundamentals of hard news writing before moving on to writing features, which
still require a keen observation and circumspect use of facts coupled with in
depth research. Many trainees consider that by increasing the length of the piece
they will construct a good feature. This is often not the case and overwriting can
lead to vague and muddled features that confuse the reader and ultimately lose
their interest. In some ways the differences between writing hard news and news
features are not so great. Indeed one of the main differences is a matter of
urgency. Generally features are categorized as being either topical or entertaining.
The former is linked to a news event and provides further information or
explanation as background. The latter include travel, sport, hobbies, general or
specific interests, profiles, etc. As mentioned previously hard news is normally
scanned quickly by the reader hence the need for a clear and concise introduction

that gives most of the important facts. A feature allows for a more leisurely perusal after all the other short news items have been quickly assimilated. This section will explore the content and style of a cross-section of different types of features seen in newspapers and magazines but first a few thoughts on the structure of a feature.

Structure

In many ways a news feature will follow quite closely the conventions used when writing a news story with a concise and precise intro followed by explanation and elaboration. Thus to some extent the Inverted Triangle/Pyramid model can be successfully used for the development of the main themes within the piece. Where they differ is that a feature can contain background knowledge, comment and opinion and the opportunity for the writer to further explore in a creative and imaginative way the issues raised by the initial news story. Also, the telling point of a news feature may appear in the final paragraph, contradicting the idea of the editor cutting from the bottom. Entertainment features will not normally follow the hard news formula but should have a beginning, middle and end that combine to create a logical flow of information, comment, illustration and reference so as to maintain the interest of the reader. However, the beginning or intro of a feature should immediately capture the attention of the reader with creative and forceful language using a variety of techniques. These techniques include using a news/ topical peg that relates the article to a recent event; beginning with a striking quotation from a person in authority or an expert in a particular field; giving a personal observation on a topic, person or place; creating an atmosphere surrounding a place, person or situation; posing a question of the reader; deliberately being provocative to arouse the reader's feelings and sensitivities; using facts and figures to startle or astonish the reader. The main body should contain amplification, a summary of facts and figures, background information, subjective opinion, discussion, debate and quotations. Also, conclusions may be drawn as the piece progresses and not left until the end. The style of writing should reflect the nature of the topic and the readership but must be coherent, free flowing with a logical progression that leads the reader through the various twists and turns of the narrative but that does not confuse or overburden them with too many detailed facts and figures that will detract from the overall purpose of the piece. As noted in the section on hard news it is important to link paragraphs with suitable words or phrases in order to maintain continuity of thought and ideas. The concluding paragraph(s) should tie in effectively the entire piece but, contrary to that of a news story, it can be as significant as the intro. It is important to end on a high note and give the impression to the reader that the article has been worthwhile, has achieved its purpose and in some ways inspired a course of action or response. Traditional methods of concluding a feature include summarizing the main points of the piece so as to clarify the issues for the readers; provoking a reaction by stating a controversial opinion or using a strong quotation; looking to the future; leaving the situation fluid by posing an open question that encourages further debate and hypothesis. Whatever method is used the ending should leave the reader feeling satisfied that the purpose, content and style of the entire piece was worth the read.

News features

A news feature, by its very nature, must be topical and relate to some aspect of current or recent news. It should provide further background information by expanding on the main issues, satisfy the curiosity of the reader, provide an assessment of conflicting issues and allow opinions to be expressed. News features tend to be concerned with the economy, politics, social and environmental issues and are often closely related to current events. Background features are not always related to breaking news but rather are concerned with ongoing issues and people: the financial state of a NHS Trust, the decline in railway standards, the dangers of long-distance air travel. Whatever the topic it is essential to find the very latest facts and figures before voicing controversial or critical opinions.

Investigative features

An investigative feature seeks to find information about a news event that may not be apparent to the public but that may lead to revelations that the organization or people involved may not wish to be put in the public domain. As such it gives a further insight into news and is often linked to campaigns by the newspaper for better protection of the rights of people from individuals, organizations or authorities. A typical example would be a campaign for compensation for ex-dockyard workers suffering from the effects of asbestosis that they had contracted when repairing ships' boilers. The authorities may have covered up the situation for a number of years but a probing investigation by the newspaper might have found damning evidence of neglect that would then be published in support of the victims. With this type of feature writing it is essential to verify that all the facts, interviews and eye-witness accounts are accurate and available. Similarly, always differentiate between fact and opinion and attribute opinions to the people who expressed them. If allegations are made against a person or organization it is only fair to allow them the right of reply. Ultimately the decision to publish a feature will rest with the editor who must weigh up the value of the investigation against possible legal action from the person or organization. The primary aim is to produce a fair, accurate, well balanced, impartial and informative feature that is in the public interest.

Personal features

News is mainly about people and personal features or profiles of celebrities capture the imagination of the readership. Readers are fascinated by the personality behind the public image. Why is Cher obsessed with plastic surgery? What prompts David Beckham to have tattoos on most of his body? Was Margaret Thatcher really the 'Iron Lady'? Of course, profiles are not confined to national celebrities. A profile of a shopkeeper who has owned the village stores for 50 years or a student from the area who intends to hitch hike around the world would be of great interest to readers of a provincial newspaper. Profiles use diverse formats. One format is the straightforward interview in which the subject might reveal previously unknown facts about their character and beliefs. Similarly if they support a certain environmental or social cause the interview gives them a chance to air their views as to why they support the particular campaign and their contribution towards it. Sometimes the profile might concentrate on a little-known aspect of their life such as the development of a sunken garden at their home or their love of collecting shoes. Increasingly profiles of celebrities seek to give an insight into their private lives, often highlighting unsavoury or sexual proclivities; but sex sells and a half-page colour photo and splash on the front of a newspaper certainly encourages readers to buy and read the 'full story'. More in-depth and longer profiles attempt to give an overall view and may involve detailed facts and figures, extensive quotations, a 'potted' life history and a considered assessment of the work and achievements of the person. Of course, in some instances the personal feature may be written by the journalist themselves reflecting on various aspects of their own life such as the traumas of moving house, the influence of in-laws, buying a wreck of a car or other similar whimsical topics. The actress and writer Maureen Lipman has written many such pieces to the delight of readers. Whatever the style and content, personal features are increasingly a major part of modern newspapers and magazines.

Travel features

The ever-increasing demand for foreign holidays, especially to more remote locations, has led to a plethora of travel articles and reports in newspapers, supplements, magazines and on radio and television. So much so that there is a danger of overkill with numerous writers describing the same locations 'ad nauseum'. Indeed, with the public's attitude of 'been there, seen it, done it' it is increasingly difficult for a journalist to write an innovative piece. The skill is to try to find and develop a new angle that may be born out of personal hardship, unusual methods of travel, dangerous situations, nostalgia, etc. Obviously, established travel features in weekend supplements tend to follow an established pattern, with a general introduction to a country followed by information on different resorts and areas with details of landmarks to visit, state of the beaches, accessibility, transportation and inevitably the cost of food, accommodation and entertainment. Such features are easily recognizable to readers and provide a useful overall description and insight into a particular style of holiday. However, more in-depth features on travel to remote locations using basic transportation will appeal to a more discerning readership who although never intending to undertake such a journey are nevertheless fascinated by such a concept. The art of writing this type of feature is to use evocative language using sight, sound and smell. Compare the following opening paragraphs:

> *Tunis, the capital of Tunisia, is situated in the northeast corner of the country and is a bustling and modern city.*

> *The aroma of exotic spices – cardamom, ginger, coriander – mingle with the heady scent of jasmine, musk, rose and sandalwood. The incessant noise of heckling and haggling, buying and selling, complement the vivid colours of purple, gold and red of the clothes and wares on sale. There is a sense of frisson and intrigue in the brightly lit narrow streets, which lead to smaller and darker side alleys. This is the Medina in Tunis, capital of Tunisia.*

The first intro is in hard news style and would fail to capture the readers attention. The second example, using a personal angle, attempts to portray the atmosphere of the Medina so that the reader wishes to read on and explore the article. The reader has been lured into the piece by the creative use of language. Details such as accommodation, rates of monetary exchange and public transport can come later. The aspiring travel writer should always keep a diary when on vacation, take photographs, make audio and video recordings of people, conversations and places and, above all, 'feel' the atmosphere of the location. Thorough research from libraries, guidebooks, the Internet and official publications will provide the necessary facts and figures to underpin the creativity of the writing.

Illustrative features

The impact of pictures on the minds of readers cannot be underestimated. The dramatic and shocking images of the terrorist attack on the World Trade Center, New York, in September 2001 were far more influential in shaping public opinion than any number of words. Subsequent illustrative features used various pictures of the moment of impact, the collapse of the two towers, the ensuing chaos and the rescue attempts allied to the written words of eye-witness accounts, details of casualties, interviews with the emergency services and government officials, and world reaction. Indeed pictures often shape the content and style of news features. Similarly the majority of general interest and specialized magazines rely on illustrations to complement the written word and sell the publication. Sports and fitness, cookery, gardening, DIY and travel magazines all use illustrative features to good effect. The term 'illustrations' also applies to graphs, maps and charts that are used to explain and 'colour' statistical or background information. Illustrations are either obtained from picture agencies, produced in-house, commissioned from freelances or obtained as 'freebies' from commercial companies, government departments and agencies or individuals. Of course, some writers are competent in taking their own photographs and if these are of printable quality they provide a ready source of first-hand material. The maxim for all would-be feature writers is to always have a camera to hand when carrying out research for an article.

Advertising features

Advertising features or 'advertorials' are a common sight in magazines and newspapers, especially free sheets as well as in special or seasonal supplements with titles such as 'Easter Weddings', 'Eating Out' or 'Back to School'. They can be defined as a piece of writing combining the editorial style of feature writing with the purpose of promoting products, places or events. To that end the piece should be devised in journalistic style but with the underlying notion that it is for publicity purposes. Indeed the PR agency or client will either pay for the piece or at least for the accompanying display advertisement. This can sometimes lead to conflict between the editorial and advertising departments as to who actually writes the piece. Sometimes the piece is written by the advertising agency, specialist PR writers or the advertising department in the newspaper or magazine; this is especially true in larger publications. Often in local magazines, newspapers and free sheets, a journalist would be expected to write them. Whatever the formula it should be stressed that the editor takes ultimate responsibility for the inclusion of the piece in the relevant publication. The content of an advertorial will always highlight the positive elements of the product, place or event. It will seek to attract the reader with a vigorous intro using effusive language before amplifying and explaining the benefits of the particular product, place or event. The piece should also contain sufficient and accurate information as regards price, availability, location, dates, times, etc. Often with restaurant advertorials the journalist will give a first hand account of a visit to the establishment commenting on the location, ambience, decor, quality of food, breadth of the menu, service and value for money. There is normally an accompanying picture of either the interior or exterior of the restaurant allied to a boxed advertisement giving details such as opening times, telephone numbers, special deals, etc. One of the difficulties for readers is to differentiate between this type of feature and a critical restaurant review. To this end the advertorial should have a 'strapline' stating either 'Advertisement Feature', 'Advertiser's Announcement' or simply 'Advertisement'. If in small point size this heading can often be missed by the casual reader.

Reviews

Reviewing is often referred to as criticism but this definition can be misleading as in many cases the purpose of the review is to give praise when things go right and provide constructive advice when things go wrong. At the risk of generalization it could be said that reviewing in a local paper or a local magazine with a small circulation is mainly concerned with the day-to-day activities of local theatrical, orchestral, choral, community, school and other special interest groups, as well as gigs by local bands and artistes. Artistic criticism tends to refer to reviews in national newspapers and specialist arts magazines that relate to major performance events, national and international artistes, artistic exhibitions, new book launches, etc. Many reviewers such as Brian Sewell, the art critic on the *London Evening Standard*, A.A. Gill, the television and restaurant critic on the *Sunday Times* and Jaqui Stephens, the soap critic on the *Daily Mail* have gained celebrity status or notoriety, depending on one's viewpoint for national columns. This is not to say that a local paper will not include reviews of national television or radio programmes and other major national events but the emphasis will be on the local scene. Many local newspapers, free newspapers, weekly and monthly magazines both paid for and free do not have full-time specialist reviewers but use part-time writers who may have considerable experience of the artistic topic or their own general reporters who may have a special talent or interest in a particular area of the arts. A few provincial newspapers with large circulations covering several professional theatres, multiplex cinemas, large art galleries, museums and concert halls may have a full-time specialist but economic pressure precludes this on many local papers. The following guidelines for trainees concentrate on writing reviews for local newspapers and magazines as opposed to writing for national weekly newspapers and weekly, monthly or quarterly specialist arts magazines.

The first thing to establish is the brief, including the target readership, the purpose of the review and the deadline. In the simplest format a review can provide basic information about an artistic activity thus keeping readers up-to-date with current events and views, even though they were unable to be at the event themselves. Secondly, readers read reviews to try to match their own opinions to that of the reviewer about a certain play, film, concert, TV show, etc. This gives the newspaper or magazine valuable reader participation that indeed may result in letters to the editor offering a different perspective on the event. Thirdly, especially as regards amateur or community groups, the review of a local event strengthens the ties between newspaper and readers. In this sense the newspaper has a part to play in the artistic life of the community by publicizing local events and groups in the review column. This is none more so apparent when reviewing local theatrical and musical events, which would be the starting point for trainee reporters.

Local artistic events

Most communities in this country have a diverse range of local amateur dramatic groups, choral societies, guilds, orchestras, brass bands, ensembles, school and college societies, poetry reading groups and popular bands. These may be formal or informal, part of drama and music festivals, seasonal, temporary or permanent but as such contribute to the leisure and artistic life of the community. In an age of digital wizardry many communities still hold fast to the traditional values of the Christmas pantomime, the summer arts festival, the Battle of the Bands, the poetry and reading week. And the local newspaper, free sheet or community magazine will be expected to feature and record some or all of these with accompanying photographs for posterity. It is in this world that the trainee reviewer will be expected to 'cut their teeth'.

Unsurprisingly many newcomers find the task quite daunting in that although they may enjoy the particular play or style of music they find it difficult to successfully analyse or criticize the events, especially as they will need to distinguish between truly amateur efforts and semi-professional local groups. The matter is further complicated if a performance is for charity, involves children, minority or underprivileged groups. How far can a reviewer criticize such activities at the risk of alienating both the groups themselves and the readership? The simple answer might be to treat all groups the same in the desire for honesty or to be sycophantic and write overtly favourable reviews *per se*. One could argue that if payment for entrance is required then the group would be expected to provide semi-professional entertainment and be suitably criticized. But if that entrance fee is simply a token and is intended for a charitable cause the issue once again becomes clouded. In the final analysis the editorial policy of the newspaper or magazine will decide the issue but it is generally accepted that the end-of-term revue, the firm's pantomime, the nativity play and the school concert should be treated as events to give information as to who appeared, what happened and why as opposed to fierce criticism.

The difficulty arises when, as in many areas, a local theatrical, musical, dance, orchestral or choral group achieves such a reputation as to become semi-professional. One such group on the south coast regularly perform West End and Broadway musicals at a regional theatre to audiences of thousands in a weekly run. Similarly, many large local choirs take part in national and international tours and festivals, produce commercial recordings and perform major choral works throughout the year. A local popular music group may have released a debut album but still play in various venues within the area. In these cases it is desirable that the groups are judged by professional standards and indeed many, proud of their abilities, would be offended if this were not so. In these cases a review should be balanced between summary and criticism. Take for example a review of a local dramatic production.

The first question to consider is whether the reviewer should do any research on the play or playwright before attending the performance? This of course depends on the time and resources available to the reviewer, their own expertise and interest and whether it is desirable to watch the production simply as an 'average' member of the audience or as an 'expert'. Certainly the readers will expect an informed review, so some basic background information is helpful to the reviewer. Of course reporters can depend on the ubiquitous programme synopsis of plot and characters to aid them on the night and many use this to the detriment of a worthwhile and analytical review. There is an apocryphal story of an established reviewer of local 'am-drams' who would attend a production on the first night, be offered copious amounts of hospitality, watch the first act and then disappear back to the local newspaper with the programme to write up the review for the 10 p.m. deadline for the morning edition. One night this reviewer, true to form, left after Act One and his review in the morning edition concluded that the finale of the piece was both 'moving and ethereal'. Yet the front page splash proclaimed that fire had broken out in the foyer of the village hall during Act Two and the play had been abandoned for the evening! This is an extreme example but certainly a cautionary tale. What is certain is that there are basic details that should be given when reviewing a play such as:

● the full name of the play, the playwright and the venue
● the name of the performance company and the director
● the dates, times and 'run' of the production
● ticket prices if applicable.

As and when the above is included the reviewer should then address the content and structure of the play and the actual performance. The reader who is unfamiliar with the play will need some information as to the plot and characterization to whet their appetite to read on or indeed to attend a performance. It is advisable to give just enough of the story line to intrigue but leave the interesting twists and turns and the 'tying of the knot' open to encourage the readers to see for themselves. Obviously readers familiar with a well known and often-performed play know the ending anyway. In any case the majority of local amateur dramatic groups will tend to perform standard classics to attract revenue. The rest of the review should attempt to describe and comment on the various elements within the production such as the direction, the interpretation of the playwright's intention and purpose, the pace, the casting, the acting, the scenery, the props, the costumes, the lighting, the difficulties encountered and overcome, the overall impression on and reaction of the audience. Comparisons could be made between this and previous productions by the same group or questions could be raised as to the suitability of the production for the target audience or the expertise of the cast and the availability of resources for a successful outcome. Whatever angle develops certain basic guidelines should be followed.

Do

- acknowledge the 'genre' of the play to make the potential audience aware of the nature of the production
- give a basic outline of the story without revealing all
- comment on the performance of the cast if there is something worthwhile to say (either good or bad)
- justify your point of view by referring to specific aspects of a performer's portrayal of a character
- mention technical items such as sets, lighting, costumes, special effects and sound if they enhance or detract from the performance
- give constructive, fair and balanced criticism supported by tangible examples
- refer to other works by the playwright or other performances of this work as a means of comparison
- attempt to give an overall impression of the play by referring to the original playwright's intention and the director's interpretation, which may involve an innovative approach
- assess the audience's response to the production
- write for the non-specialist level of readership but do not 'talk down' to the readership or adopt a 'lofty' style for effect – allow readers some latitude to make up their own minds.

Don't

- assume readers are *au fait* with the play so no explanation is necessary as to the storyline and plot
- overuse such words as 'superb', 'convincing', 'marvellous' unless justified by illustration
- limit comment to one adjective per cast member but instead attempt to define how each performer portrayed the part in terms of realistic characterization, movement, gesture, voice and empathy with the audience
- even mention performers if there is nothing worthwhile to say about them
- use patronizing expressions such as 'is to be congratulated', 'was well supported by' or 'it is gratifying to note that'
- be afraid to give constructive criticism where due and that can be substantiated.

Much of the above will also relate to a musical stage production. However, other factors may be involved with a musical review of, say, a performance by a local orchestra, choir, ensemble, brass band or popular music group. These could present a considerable challenge to a trainee journalist weaned on 'rap', 'hip-hop', 'garage', 'indie' or 'sca'. The thought of having to sit through, never mind review, the annual performance of Handel's 'Messiah' could cause apoplexy to the uninitiated. Similarly the part-time reviewer of classical music might be equally appalled by the thought of having to review a local band's heavy metal gig at the local hostelry.

Normally common sense prevails and editors would tend to send younger reporters to such a venue, knowing that a more informed review might result. As with reviewing dramatic productions, the accurate information of name, date, time and place of the gig, concert, recital or performance is important. One notable example of the need for accuracy occurred some years ago when, because of misinformation, a concert by the popular group 'The Police' was confused with one by the local police male voice choir. Other factors to consider when writing music reviews are:

- obtain some background information on the style of music and/or the performers either by listening to recordings, reading a press release, looking in the 'cuttings file' or asking the organizer of the event for information. If it is a local group there may be reviews of previous performances that can shed some light on what is to be expected
- if at the event the music is unfamiliar, attempt to describe the atmosphere of the overall evening rather than second guessing at the technical merits or otherwise of the music. Use the audience as a sounding board
- mention any outstanding contributors to the evening such as the soloist, lead singer, backing group, musical director, sound engineer, etc.
- mention any detrimental aspects of a performance such as inadequate staging, lighting, seating and sight lines; lack of adequate ventilation; poor acoustics and acoustic feedback; all of which could affect both the performers as well as the audience
- if, as can be the case with amateur and children's choirs, the singing is off-key, voice projection is non-existent, words are forgotten and the accompanist lacks a sense of timing, it is sensible to mention this gently in passing, but try to pinpoint where and when it happened rather than severely criticizing the overall performance. However, if the choir or group is semi-professional, then stronger words should be used especially if the audience has paid for entry. Thankfully many groups and societies rehearse meticulously to avoid such incidents
- use appropriate language to describe different types of musical performances. The 'underground' language of 'garage' or 'trance' has its own argot and will be understood and expected by devotees. Similarly, lovers of classical music will readily understand the specialized terminology of their chosen genre
- try and create an overall impression of the ambience of the performance, the style of music, the venue and the audience reaction to convey to the reader a sense of the occasion by highlighting the memorable moments to the detriment of the mundane ones.

Films

The type of publication often determines the style, structure and content of a film review. Writing a film review for a specialist magazine such as *Sight and Sound* or

Empire is very different from writing one for the entertainment's page of a local newspaper. The former will demand specialist in-depth analysis of the stylistic elements of the film, mise en scene, genre and production techniques; the latter will demand a brief synopsis of the film in terms of plot, narrative, characters, effects and entertainment value. Many journalists feel comfortable with reviewing films and develop excellent background knowledge of the stars, the directors, the film companies and the distributors. Often a journalist will attend a press showing of a forthcoming film at the local cinema and compile a short review using an accompanying press release from the distributors that will give most of the relevant information on the film including cast, directors, production crew, technical details. As with other forms of entertainment it is important to give basic information such as the venues and dates of showing of the film but also the classification of the film is of prime importance to the readership. In many ways film reviews in entertainment guides are previews that allow the film goer to decide on whether to see the film or not. More detailed reviews appear in arts supplements of local and national newspapers and in arts magazines and often contain analytical and critical comment in addition to basic information. Whichever type of film review is contemplated it is useful to consider the following questions when structuring the piece:

- does the film adhere to a particular genre such as Western, Musical, Thriller, Sci-Fi or is there a mixture of genres?
- which type of film goer is the film targeting? Is the film mainly for adults, family, children, specific cultures or a combination of some or all of these?
- what is the underlying theme of the film? Love, courage, suspicion, etc.
- what is the film about and what kind of reaction is it hoping to stir in the audience? As with theatrical reviews it is sensible to describe some of the plot to interest the reader but it is not advisable to reveal all
- is the script convincing, original, witty, overbearing, mundane, based on a novel or real event?
- how effective is the casting and performance of the actors/actresses?
- if there is a musical score does it add to or detract from the dialogue?
- are special effects used and to what purpose and extent?
- is the photography memorable?
- is it a high- or low-budget production and how has this affected the outcome?
- is the direction appropriate to the theme and, if by a well known director, how does it compare and contrast with previous films?
- finally, would you recommend it to the readership?

Books

The style and content of a book review depends largely on the type of publication for which it is written. In a local newspaper the review may be quite short with the minimum of detail. In a literary supplement or specialist magazine there will be much more in-depth description, analysis and comment. However, in either format basic information such as the name of the author, the title, the publishers and the price of the book should be given. References may also be made to previous works by the same author or other authors with a similar style or persuasion. Background research is essential in reviewing books and the trainee journalist would be well advised to read as many different kinds of books as possible, whether fact or fiction. In reviewing fiction the following guidelines may prove useful:

- state the genre of the book – is it a crime story, a love story, an adventure?
- describe the underlying theme(s) of the story – is it concerned with betrayal, loyalty, ambition, love, morality or fear?
- give enough of the plot to interest the reader but no more than is necessary and do not reveal the 'denouement'
- comment on the style of language – is it concise, evocative, descriptive, metaphorical or bland?
- comment on the characters – do they 'leap off the page' and grab the attention of the reader; are they believable or far-fetched; are they well delineated in the narrative?
- attempt to describe the 'feel' of the locations, settings and time scales
- give examples of striking passages that caught your eye and explain their impact and significance
- at the end give an overall opinion of the book – will it interest the average reader; is it worth the monetary outlay; would you recommend it as a good read?

Factual books include auto-biographies, travel, political commentaries, leisure, local histories. etc. When reviewing such books it is essential to check the accuracy of the information supplied before forming and writing an opinion. Other pointers are:

- carry out background research from archives, libraries, the Internet, other books on the subject to gain a basic knowledge that may inform the content of the review
- if the book is about some aspect of local history or written by a local author visit the location or try to interview the author to find the motive behind and the reasons for writing the book; an accompanying photograph of the author would also add authenticity to the review; there may be an additional bonus in that a feature article in the form of a profile of the author could be developed for a subsequent issue
- compare and contrast this book with others of a similar genre or by other authors

- give sufficient facts to interest the reader but do not overburden them with endless statistical data to the detriment of informed comment and opinion allied to relevant illustration and quotation
- at the end give your own fair, honest and balanced evaluation of the book taking into account its content and style, accuracy of information, readership appeal and value for money.

A brief overview of . . .
Leader

The leader column is a regular feature in national, provincial and local newspapers as well as in specialist magazines. Often referred to as the 'voice of the paper', leaders in newspapers are unlikely to be written by trainee or junior reporters. Nor in many cases are they written by the editor but often by a senior and experienced reporter with an eye for writing from a pre-determined viewpoint; there is no value in commenting on a topical issue unless the writer, after arguing the case, summing up alternatives and providing accurate information, takes a definite stance. Of course this stance is frequently influenced by the ownership and political allegiance of the newspaper. Yet whatever the political, ethical or social considerations of the newspaper the leader, to be of any relevance, should refer to topical issues and invariably news stories within that edition. The language should be vigorous, precise and clear with well expressed opinion that seeks to stimulate the reader. The opening line should be incisive to capture the attention of the reader and the conclusion should leave the reader in no doubt as to the viewpoint being expressed. Comment should be made in good faith, be supported by accurate information and be in the public interest. The laws of libel hang heavily over leader writing.

Diary

Much of what has been stated above refers to diary pages that provide lively and opinionated columns on social, economic, political, moral and ethical issues from an individual viewpoint. Many diarists such as Nigel Dempster, Katherine Whitehorn, Julie Burchill and Lynda Lee-Potter have devoted readers and provide an insight into the lives of the rich and famous, albeit at a 'gossipy' level. But this is exactly what the readership demands – an escape from their mundane world into the realms of fantasy. Of course some diary pages can be very scathing and, as with leaders, awareness of the legal position is paramount. Yet the majority of diary columns whether in national or local newspapers provide a refreshing change from objective front page news and encourage readers to write in with their own observations on an issue or person. As with leaders the trainee journalist should be aware of the conventions and gain experience by writing such a column for a small independent magazine, community newspaper or fanzine.

Sport

The number of trainee journalists wishing to write sports reports and features is legion. Yet, in many ways, sports reporting of actual events is very similar to hard news as regards attention to detail, accuracy and meeting deadlines. The main difference is that some form of comment or opinion is allowed and may involve partisanship, interviews with players, coaches and managers, comparison with earlier encounters, fans reactions. It is also worth noting that sports stories can also include personal profiles, investigative features, humorous pieces and commentary. It is important to keep a good contacts book, a diary of forthcoming events, a file containing up-to-date statistics and clippings from other publications. Regular visits to official and unofficial club Internet sites can provide excellent and sometimes controversial material. As regards the language, try to avoid hyperbole but do use language that invokes the passions of the readers, whether it be for the local junior soccer team or the national rugby squad.

Fanzines

Fanzines have played an important role in the development of alternative commentary writing, particularly as regards sci-fi, pop culture and football. Although fanzines had been established in the USA by sci-fi devotees in the early 1950s they appeared in the UK only in the mid-1970s with the advent of punk music and a perceived feeling of alienation by 'youth' against more established popular music forms of the time. This theme was then adopted by football fans in the mid-1980s. Former journalist, Colin Farmery, Head of Media at St Vincent College, Gosport, and now a successful author and publisher of three professional football Web sites has strong views on the reasons for the development.

> Cornered by a real, if media-hyped, hooligan presence in and around football stadia, an unsympathetic government bent on introducing draconian policing measures such as membership schemes and manage-ment hierarchies at clubs who regarded fans as little more then turnstile fodder, proved to be the perfect environment for an 'alternative press' to thrive.

With low production values, yet often witty and incisive insights into football culture, fanzines took off. They were sold outside grounds, offering fans a more 'realistic' perspective on their favourite club than the often anodyne and patronizing comments of the official sources such as the official match day programme or the local newspaper. Colin Farmery was involved with the production of the fanzine for supporters of Portsmouth Football Club in the 1980s and 1990s. The message was more important than the presentation and Figure 4.2 illustrates the basic nature of the magazine using word processing packages and paste up techniques.

The Pompey fanzine that's not afraid to chime in!

January 3, '88

(Look it up in the Rothmans!) August 1995 £1

WE CAN STILL MAKE THE PLAY-OFFS!

	P	W	D	L	F	A	Pts
Barnsley	0	0	0	0	0	0	0
Birmingham	0	0	0	0	0	0	0
Charlton	0	0	0	0	0	0	0
Crystal Palace	0	0	0	0	0	0	0
Derby	0	0	0	0	0	0	0
Grimsby	0	0	0	0	0	0	0
Huddersfield	0	0	0	0	0	0	0
Ipswich	0	0	0	0	0	0	0
Leicester	0	0	0	0	0	0	0
Luton	0	0	0	0	0	0	0
Millwall	0	0	0	0	0	0	0
Norwich	0	0	0	0	0	0	0
Oldham	0	0	0	0	0	0	0
PORTSMOUTH	0	0	0	0	0	0	0
Port Vale	0	0	0	0	0	0	0
Reading	0	0	0	0	0	0	0
Sheff Utd	0	0	0	0	0	0	0
Southend	0	0	0	0	0	0	0
Stoke	0	0	0	0	0	0	0
Sunderland	0	0	0	0	0	0	0
Tranmere	0	0	0	0	0	0	0
Watford	0	0	0	0	0	0	0
West Brom	0	0	0	0	0	0	0
Wolves	0	0	0	0	0	0	0

It's in our own hands, says Fenwick.

Inside: A-Z of Southampton FC, Seasons to be Cheerful, Bone of Contention, The Bard of E18, Style of the 70s, Odds & Ends South Stand Scribble, Guest Who?, and much, much more!

Figure 4.2 Fanzine front cover

Football fanzine culture probably peaked in the early 1990s and the advent of professional DTP computer software resulted in increasingly sophisticated production values. Indeed some, such as the general title *When Saturday Comes*, have successfully established themselves as a niche publication within the mainstream football magazine market. With improvements in safety and comfort for football fans since the Hillsborough disaster there has been a decline in published titles, although there is an increasing tendency for titles to re-invent themselves as Web sites. The phenomenal success of fan-based networks such as Rivals.net indicates that the market for an alternative voice remains intact. The Web site shown in Figure 4.3 is the modern version of the paper-based fanzine shown in Figure 4.2.

Suggested activities

1 Plan a face-to-face interview with another class member you have not known previously. Discuss the basic structure of the interview, which should attempt to find out the views of the person on a particular topic as opposed to a general chat.

Rivals Home AFL Cricket Cycling Football Golf Motorsports R League R Union Other Bet Shop Mobiles

Rivals.net > pompey-fans.com Home

Pompey Menu

Message Board
Chat
Membership
Just In
League Table
Fixtures/Results

Club Info
Statistics
History
Pompey FAQs
Away Fan Zone
Memory Match
Pompey Web Sites
Ground Gallery Index
About Our Site
Set As Home Page
Story Index
More Links

Site Services

Free Newsletter
Mobile Phones
Casino
TOTOPOOLS
Shopping
Portsmouth Auctions

Hirschfeld not troubled as Vine nets winner

Hirschfeld

By Chris Gibbs at Fratton Park

Canadian international triallist Lars Hirschfeld looked competent enough against Reading reserves as Rowan Vine's goal sealed a low-key encounter at Fratton Park.

More...

Latest Headlines

Goods Yard billboard fuels ground speculation
A billboard outside the goods yard shows a new Pompey ground at the heart of the development - see our exclusive picture

Pompey will be made to Svet over Todorov
Pompey's bid to sign Bulgarian international Svetoslav Todorov from West Ham could be de-railed by work permit problems

Pompey look set to pip Forest to Todorov signing
Pompey are believed to be close to signing West Ham's Bulgarian striker Svetoslav Todorov in a surprise £750,000 deal

Goods Yard Picture Index February 2002
Goods Yard Redevelopment - Pictures taken in February 2002

Millers Crossing at the Anorak Arms
Things are getting tense in the old Anorak Arms. Opinion getting polarised, beer getting spilt, that kind of thing.....

Rix disappointed as another win eludes Blues
Pressure is mounting on Graham Rix as another win eludes Pompey - not helped a late decision most think was a bad call

Harper sees red as Millers hold Pompey
Pompey failed to break down Rotherham and had Kevin Harper sent off for diving when many thought he should have won a penalty

More Stories...

Featured Stories

Duggie Reid: A loyal servant on and off the field - Duggie Reid Pompey's championship forward and former groundsman died on February 7, aged 84

The new kit: Why choice isn't always a good thing - In a new edition of the Pompey fanzine January 3, '88, Steve Bone decides where to put his X in the big 'new kit' vote.

Have we a film star in our midst? Er, no... - Steve Woodhead gets carried away (at least, he should be) by the presence of a famous name in his interviewee's chair

Figure 4.3 A fanzine on the Web. Reproduced with the permission of Rivals Europe Limited and Pompey-Fans.com

Carry out the interview and write a 250-word profile in acceptable copy style. (You can then reverse the roles and become the interviewee.)

2 Select three stories from your local newspaper and photocopy them. Using the '5 Ws and H' formula decide whether the chosen stories satisfy this criteria. Write down your observations and use these notes as a basis for discussion with your tutor and fellow trainees. Discuss whether the structure of a selected story is logical. Does the intro give the main points of the story? Could the intro stand alone? Is there a logical theme running through the story? Is there enough or too much background information given? If quotations are used do they enlighten the reader? Does the ending tie up all the loose ends and round off the piece? Is the story 'readable'?

3 You are asked to write a hard news story on the increased use of speed cameras on major roads in your local area. In order to find out the latest information, telephone your local police station and arrange a time and date to ring back and carry out a telephone interview with the appropriate spokesperson. On the arranged day interview the person on the telephone and take notes of the information given. Use this and other information to write a hard news story of 300–350 words in acceptable copy style.

4 Watch a documentary on television and write a review for a weekend arts supplement in your local newspaper. Use the guidelines given in this chapter. Your review in copy style should be 500–550 words in length.

5 Look at features in a number of magazines of different genres and note the content and styles of writing. Decide on a particular genre of magazine and the topic for a feature, which is a free choice. Carry out research for the feature using a variety of sources. Write the feature of approximately 1000 words in copy style. Suggest or attach pictures/graphics that may be used to illustrate the piece.

6 Obtain recent copies of a national tabloid, a national broadsheet and a local newspaper. Each of these will contain a leader page. Read the leaders and write a brief description of how they differ in content, length and style of writing. Using these observations:

   (i) write a 150-word leader on a recent event in the style and language of a national tabloid
   (ii) write a 350-word leader on the *same* event in the style and language of a national broadsheet
   (iii) write a 200-word leader on an important local issue for your local newspaper.

   Present all three in acceptable copy style and compose a headline for each.

7 Find examples of advertorials/advertisement features in either newspapers and magazines and note the style and content. Using the guidelines given in this chapter write in copy style an advertorial of 500 words that highlights the benefits of a particular product, facility or venture of your choice. Select suitable pictures to accompany the article.

8 Imagine you are a trainee reporter on a local newspaper, *The Haven Times*. The notes below were obtained by you from various sources on a major fire at a local hotel this morning and are in no particular order of importance. Using some or all of the information including quotations decide on an angle and write a 200-word structured hard news story to accepted conventions for the evening edition of the paper.

- Four people taken to St Mary's Hospital, Eastport by ambulance.
- Fire started at 07.45 this morning in The Seagull Hotel, The Parade, Eastport.
- Woman and man with serious burns rescued by firemen.
- Fire started in main kitchen and spread rapidly via the 'dumb waiter' lift shaft.
- Flames seen at coastguard station 2 miles away at Westport.
- First ambulance took the commis chef Alan Edwards to hospital.
- Second contained hotel owner Alan Laing, his wife and a guest Miss Irene Smollett from Axebridge.
- Mrs Laing treated for shock and smoke inhalation and released later.
- Alan Edwards detained in hospital with burns to hands, upper body and face.
- Miss Smollett and Mr Laing dead on arrival.
- Chief Fire Officer David Granville said 'Leading fireman George Stephens found Mr Laing and the woman at the far end of the fourth floor corridor. He got them out just before the ceiling collapsed. There was no hope of saving the building as the lift shaft acted as a natural conductor of the flames'.
- Hotel receptionist Karen Broughton said: 'Alan was working in the kitchen when the deep fat fryer caught alight. He tried to put it out but was driven back by the ferocity of the blaze. He staggered out to reception and I rang the fire brigade before running around the hotel to warn the guests. We had a roll call on the lawn and it was discovered that Miss Smollett was missing. Mr Laing ran back into the hotel which was well alight by then. A few moments later the fire brigade arrived'.
- Background: The Seagull Hotel was built in 1921. The Laing family had run the hotel for the past 30 years. Alan Laing is 63 years old. His wife Amy is 58. They have two children who do not live in the area. The age of Miss Smollet a regular guest is unknown. Chef Alan Edwards is 27 years old and lives at 8 Walpole Place, Eastport. He is unmarried.

9 Select and read a book of your choice making notes as you go. Write a 650–850 word book review in copy style for publication in an arts supplement in a national Sunday newspaper.

10 Choose a suitable topic for a human interest story in your college or community. Carry out primary and secondary research. Write a 500-word story for inclusion in a campus or community magazine.

11 Attend a local sporting event, take notes and write a report of the event. The report should be about 350–400 words in copy style. Attach pictures if available and write a headline for the story.

12 From your reading of national newspapers and magazines select a columnist/ diaryist whose work you either admire or detest. Read their column in a number of editions and make notes on their points of view, use of language, structure, style, etc. Using this information write an analytical and critical review of the writer illustrating the piece with relevant quotations or examples of their work. The review in copy style should be 750–1000 words.

13 You have been asked to contribute an article to a popular music fanzine. Choose a suitable topic and write a polemic of 350–500 words on a controversial aspect of the current music scene.

14 Attend a local artistic event such as a play, concert, poetry reading or gig and write a 500-word review of the event in copy style for a local free arts magazine. Attach pictures if available.

Sources and resources

Harris, G. and Spark, D. (1997) *Practical Newspaper Reporting* (3rd edition). Oxford: Focal Press.

Hennessy, B. (1996) *Writing Feature Articles* (3rd edition). Oxford: Focal Press.

Hennessy, B. and Hodgson, F.W. (1995) *Journalism Workbook: a manual of tasks, projects and resources*. Oxford: Focal Press.

Hines, J. (1987) *The Way to Write Magazine Articles*. Hamish Hamilton.

Hodgson, F.W. (1996) *Modern Newspaper Practice* (4th edition). Oxford: Focal Press.

Keeble, R. (1998) *The Newspapers Handbook* (2nd edition). London: Routledge.

Spark, D. (1999) *Investigative Reporting. A study in technique*. Oxford: Focal Press.

Wells, G. (1997) *The Craft of Writing Articles* (2nd edition). Allison and Busby.

5 Print layout and production

- Introduction
- The main elements of print layout
- The stages in the production of a basic print product
- Suggested activities
- Sources and resources

Introduction

Modern newspaper and magazine design can be regarded as a form of packaging by which the contents are commended to the reader. The design must successfully project the sort of content in which the newspaper or magazine specializes to the sort of market it seeks. In essence, content governs projection so the design must look to the content and readership market for its inspiration. In the newspaper field what works for a popular tabloid would be unsuitable for a town evening paper with its many neighbourhood editions, although some local papers are increasingly adopting a tabloid approach to the front page. Similarly what works for *The Financial Times* with its simple authority would be unsuitable for *The Sunday Times* with its numerous colour supplements. Magazines, either consumer or business and professional titles, are even more so designed to reflect the readership and specific interests of different segments and life-style of the population. The need to produce eye-catching designs using illustrative material, different fonts, boxes, colour, bold headlines, etc., has seen a revolution in what the readership now expects as the norm and is due in no small part to the use of digital technology.

The impact of this technology and the change in working practices in the newspaper and magazine industries is clearly evident in the use of computers and associated software packages in producing newspapers and magazines. Today most journalists will key copy into the publication's computer system, which will then be used to handle the design, layout and automated printing process of the publication. Yet other journalists working on smaller publications will also be expected to design and layout an entire page, particularly if they are the sole author of that page, which may contain features on travel, entertainment, sport or motoring. An example of the latter is the experience of a former journalist on a provincial newspaper who began by simply writing a weekly review of a new car model but towards the end of his career was planning, designing and laying out all eight pages of the motoring supplement. Obviously methods vary from publication to publication but national and international publishing groups certainly still employ specialist graphic designers because of the nature and diversity of their products. Smaller community newsletters and magazines, specialist free magazines and fanzines are frequently the work of one or two people using simple Desk Top Publishing (DTP) packages such as Microsoft Publisher or Claris Works. In fact the fanzine shown in Figure 4.2 in the last chapter was produced on a simple word processing system and then cut and pasted ready for printing.

In this context the two leading professional DTP packages are Quark XPress and Adobe Pagemaker. It is not the intention here to compare and contrast the two systems as each have their own merits but Quark is very much the industry standard within publishing. However, many students and trainees who only have access to Pagemaker are still able to produce professional publications, especially if the college or training centre has peripheral hardware such as scanners and printers. The later example in this chapter proves what can be produced using this software.

With this in mind it is not the intention of this chapter to instruct trainee journalists in all the intricacies and specialist skills of the graphic designer but with the ever-increasing need to become multi-skilled it is prudent that a trainee newspaper or magazine journalist should have a basic knowledge of the purpose and techniques of page design, print layout and production. Unfortunately too many students and trainees, when faced with the prospect of having to design a multi-grid newspaper page, eagerly grab the opportunity to use as many different typographical devices as possible and the final product becomes a mismatch of text and graphics that is unintelligible and jarring to the reader. Similarly no amount of fancy fonts and text boxes will hide a piece of journalism that is poor in the first place. Conversely, a good piece of journalism will lose its appeal if poorly presented. The design of such a page must give an impression of 'busyness' with pictures that connect the reader, adequate space for the main and subsidiary news covering a range of topics, a choice of informative headlines and a familiarity to the readership. Natural reading patterns measured by eye flow and eye dwell often influence page design. For example, when scanning a page the eye normally begins by focusing on the optical centre of the page, which is fractionally above and to the left of the mechanical centre. The eye flow will then sweep from left to right and down the page in a lazy Z pattern. Often a strong visual is placed at the bottom right-hand corner of the page to anchor the eye to the page. In many publications this is the prized area for an advertiser. Eye dwell indicates the proportionate amount of time the eye dwells on a particular area of a page. If the page were to be divided into four quadrants the eye will normally dwell for 60 per cent in the top two quadrants and 40 per cent in the bottom two. Indeed, changes from a vertical to a horizontal style of layout by the tabloids influenced designers of broadsheet newspapers who adopted the adage of 'strength below the fold' and recognized that the bottom of the page was as important as the top. Thus modern techniques such as the use of cross-column headlines lower down the page catch the reader's eye and maintain their interest to the end of the page.

The main elements of print layout

The main aims of print layout are to:

● attract the attention of the potential reader by creating an attractive visual pattern
● signpost the various items and signal their relative importance
● establish a recognizable visual character.

Of course, many elements such as typography, pictures, colour, white space, text boxes, headlines contribute to the make up of a multi-grid page layout. The following is a brief description of these essential elements.

1 Typefaces

A dictionary definition of typography is 'the art and style of printing', which includes the design and selection of typefaces. There are myriad different typefaces and each has its own characteristic styles and sizes, called fonts. In fact the word 'font' has effectively replaced the term typeface in word processing and DTP packages. Whichever term is used each font is defined as either serif or sans serif. Serif fonts have cross stokes that embellish the beginning and end of each letter, as in Times New Roman. Sans serif fonts such as Arial do not have any embellishment and are frequently used to suggest a more modern approach in a piece of text. Compare the following intro in Times New Roman:

> It's an explosive place at the best of times – so it's fitting that the Explosion! museum will be the venue for a huge fireworks display.

in Arial:

> It's an explosive place at the best of times – so it's fitting that the Explosion! museum will be the venue for a huge fireworks display.

and even in Frankenstein:

> **It's an explosive place at the best of times - so it's fitting that the Explosion! museum will be the venue for a huge fireworks display.**

Of course many publications mix and match serif and san serif fonts. For example, sometimes the main headline of a newspaper is set in sans serif whereas the body text is in serif but it really does depend on the purpose, content and readership of a publication as to what style is used. Magazines use a wide range of typefaces to create the necessary visual effect to capture the reader's attention. Readers have come to recognize particular styles and are comfortable with them and the whole point of type is that it is primarily there to be read. Fonts can also be re-sized to suit differing situations. The standard Anglo-American system of type measurement uses the 'point' system, where each point measures 0.01383 inch with approximately 72 points to the inch. Incidentally, at the risk of becoming too technical, the Apple Mac software follows the standard system but one point measures 0.013889 inch and 72 points is exactly equal to one inch. Whatever the exactitude of the point size all type is measured from the top of the 'ascender' to the bottom of the 'descender' with the 'x-height' being the distance between the 'baseline' and the 'mean line' as shown in Figure 5.1.

Figure 5.1 Elements of a typeface

Text can be upper or lower case, regular or **bold** or *regular italic* or ***bold italic*** to create an effect or emphasize the importance of the words as in a headline. A common feature in magazines, supplements and newspapers is the use of a dropped capital, by which the first letter of the first word in a paragraph is lowered, enlarged and emboldened to attract the attention of the reader.

> Pe/ople are being asked to lend their support to a museum – and get free admission to the tourist attraction.
> The Friends of Explosion! is being launched to back the efforts of staff at the museum of the same name at Priddy's Hard.

Figure 5.2 Use of a dropped capital

Various other textual effects can be achieved by using the software of the DTP packages. Text can be underlined, have shadow effects and outline applied or be shaped into different styles on wavy and curving lines. It is worth experimenting with the various tools available within the packages but remember that in many cases 'less is more', so choose with care. Many trainees use effects too frequently and the constant use of these can irritate the reader. The main emphasis should be that the text is easy on the eye. To aid this most DTP packages have automatic 'kerning' and 'leading' facilities. Kerning controls the amount of spacing between each word and letter and normally the computer settings are adequate – if not there is a manual override facility so the spacing can be altered. Leading refers to the amount of white space or vertical distance between lines of type. It prevents the fusion of descenders and ascenders and thus aids the reading process. Again most software packages have automatic settings but can be overridden as required.

2 Text boxes and justification

DTP packages invariably use text boxes to place copy into a publication. These are invaluable and simple devices that allow the positioning of text within a document. The alignment of the text within these boxes is also crucial. Many students and trainees, to their detriment, imagine that all text should be centred and, whilst this may be true of film credits or some magazine features, symmetrical text can appear static and over formal. Apart from centred text there are three other means of alignment:

- right – the right-hand side of the text is aligned on the right-hand margin
- left – the left-hand side of the text is aligned on the left-hand margin
- fully justified – text is aligned on the left- and right-hand margins.

People are being asked to lend their support to a museum – and get free admission to the tourist attraction. The Friends of Explosion! is being launched to back the efforts of staff at the museum of the same name at Priddy's Hard.

Centre alignment

People are being asked to lend their support to a museum – and get free admission to the tourist attraction. The Friends of Explosion! is being launched to back the efforts of staff at the museum of the same name at Priddy's Hard.

Right alignment

People are being asked to lend their support to a museum – and get free admission to the tourist attraction. The Friends of Explosion! is being launched to back the efforts of staff at the museum of the same name at Priddy's Hard.

Left alignment

People are being asked to lend their support to a museum – and get free admission to the tourist attraction. The Friends of Explosion! is being launched to back the efforts of staff at the museum of the same name at Priddy's Hard.

Justified

Figure 5.3 Common text alignments

3 White space

Framing pages with white space strengthens the message by focusing the readers attention on words and ideas. Equally, the amount of white between and around paragraphs of text facilitates easy reading and can emphasize the importance of the text. As previously noted, leading is an important part of textual layout. Different publications require different amounts of white space and certainly magazines have proportionately more than newspapers. It should be noted that too little white space will result in a cluttered appearance especially if clashing styles, sizes and weights of fonts are used. Conversely, too much white space can detract from the textual message and make it appear lightweight.

4 Colour

The judicious use of colour can reflect the message that is being communicated. Bright colours indicate excitement whereas subdued colours add dignity. However, try to overcome the tendency to use too many colours on one page. Boxes filled with colour as a background to the text can be very eye catching and, whilst this is common in magazines, there is an increasing use of this technique in newspapers. Of course, white text on a black background is equally effective if used sparingly.

5 Pictures

The reader who is first attracted to a page by a picture may, if time is short, scan only the main items. With time the reader may read the whole page. A picture with a suitable caption acts as a teaser so that the reader is drawn in to read the juxtaposed text to gain further insight into the story. Other pictures may be stand-alone and contain in the caption a brief explanation of the image. Colour pictures are now prevalent in all newspapers and magazines and these draw potential readers to magazine and newspaper racks at retail outlets; if the face on the cover is instantly recognizable, the bait is taken. Who can forget the images of the terrorist attack on New York in September 2001, the plight of refugees in Third World Countries, Diana Princess of Wales, the Hillsborough soccer disaster; all powerful reminders of the power of the picture. Photographs can be cropped, scaled and re-touched for a variety of reasons but their use in any publication adds another dimension to the textual message. For trainees, digital technology has revolutionized the acquisition of images either from camera, scanner or the Internet, and the manipulation of those images for inclusion in hard copy or Web-based publications.

6 Headlines

Headlines signify the importance of the text to which they relate and the order in which they appear on the page and their size have a message for the reader. Headlines fall into the following categories:

Banner

This is the big and bold headline for the front page splash that will sell the newspaper. Tabloids with large one- or two-word banner headlines leap out from news stands and command the attention of the passing public. There is no upper limit to the size of the banner and in practice some are set at 60 points but the lower limit should not be less than 12 point to contrast with the average body text size of 8 to 10 points. Most banner headlines are emboldened for emphasis and can be justified as detailed above to suit the style and purpose of the publication. Some banner headlines are in upper case throughout as in:

AMERICAN FORCES ENTER AFGHANISTAN

others use upper and lower case:

American forces enter Afghanistan

What should be avoided is starting every word in upper case, as in

American Forces Enter Afghanistan

Strap line

Used in conjunction with the banner headline or other main headings the single line strap runs above or below the banner and provides a short subsidiary summary, thought or angle on the main headline and story. They are normally set in a smaller point size and often in a different typeface to the banner as in

Helicopters drop specialist troops in dawn raid on Kabul
American forces enter Afghanistan

Tag line

A tag line is used below the main headline to signify either the place, type of story or source as in 'Reuters' or 'Court story'.

Sub-headings

Sub-headings can either be 'side heads' or 'crossheads' and are important in relating the headline to the body text. Side heads, as the term implies, are set flush left to the margin and are more common in magazines than newspapers. They may be accompanied by asterisks or bullet points for added emphasis. Crossheads are widely used in newspapers and magazines as a means of breaking up the monotony of large chunks of text and maintaining the interest of the reader. This is of particular importance in long feature articles. They are centred in the column of text and frequently emboldened. The number and placing of these depends on the style and content of the article; too many will irritate the reader, too few will make the reader lose interest; and placing a crosshead two lines from the end of an article is nonsensical. Some are placed in visible text boxes and others are underlined for emphasis. The crosshead may be a direct quotation from the text or a one- or two-word signpost of the main points within the ensuing paragraph or paragraphs.

By-lines and date lines

It is every journalist's dream to get their first by-line – their name above the story. The relative anonymity of the titles 'Correspondent' or 'Staff reporter' is replaced by the actual name and sometimes the role of the author of the piece. Thus by-lines such as 'John Smith, Court reporter' or 'Alan Brown, Chief football writer' give due attribution to the writer. Indeed many national newspapers and magazines also print e-mail addresses of the writer at the bottom of articles. Frequently, as with a magazine article, the photographer as well as the writer will be named in the by-line as in:

Report by David Johnson. Photographs by Bill Kenyon

Similarly the by-line may contain a gist of the story as in:

John Hill reports on the intrigue at the International Wine Convention in Bordeaux

In textual terms the by-line should be set in the same or smaller point size as the body text and preferably be in a different font. The writer's name is normally emboldened.

Date lines are an important component of breaking or running news stories as they identify the urgency of the piece and in magazines they may relate to seasonal activities. They are often combined with the by-line to clarify the time and place as in:

Julia Henderson reports on millennium festivities in Sydney. 1 January 2000

Identical textual considerations apply as for by-lines.

The masthead

The masthead or flag, although not strictly a headline, is one of the most important characteristics of a newspaper or magazine. The masthead can also be termed the title and is the defining feature for recognition by the target readership. In recent years *The Guardian* has twice changed the textual style of its masthead to reflect the old and the new by using serif and sans serif in the title. Conversely the

Daily Telegraph has maintained its original masthead. In essence, the masthead and accompanying logo identify the publication and reinforce its distinctive image and style – especially true of glossy up-market magazines. The potential or regular reader of a magazine or newspaper will be drawn to the periodicals and newspaper display by the title of the publication. Hence the masthead should be composed in suitable size and type of font to attract the intended readership. In the previous chapter the masthead of the now defunct fanzine for supporters of Portsmouth Football Club reads:

January 3, '88

This means nothing to the general reader but to 'Pompey' fans this is the defining moment for the club as it is the date on which they beat their arch rivals Southampton Football Club away from home. Ultimately, whatever the style and composition of the masthead in newspapers and magazines, it should not detract from the main headlines and should be appropriate to the style and image of the publication.

7 Captions

Captions are used to link visual images with the text and should provide short yet additional information. A caption under a picture of a person that accompanies a story may just state the name of the person. A caption placed under a picture that is located some way from the story should give a brief resume of what the picture is about and its links to the story but it should not tell the whole story so as to tease the reader into reading the story. Sometimes a single word in upper case and emboldened is used followed by a short phrase in regular lower case. Thirdly, pictures that stand alone by not being linked to a story have longer captions of say 20–30 words that act as a mini report of what is happening, where it is happening and why.

The stages in the production of a basic print product

Stage 1. Assuming that all stories, graphics and photographs have been obtained a decision must be taken on the design of the product to suit the content and the target readership. Once this has been ascertained a grid will need to be constructed. Grids for magazines tend to be more complex than those for newsletters, which simply consist of columns.

Broadsheet newspapers normally use seven or eight columns whereas a community newspaper may use three or four. DTP packages have easy column setting controls that automatically or manually set the parameters. It is advisable at this stage to draw in the column outlines to facilitate the next stage.

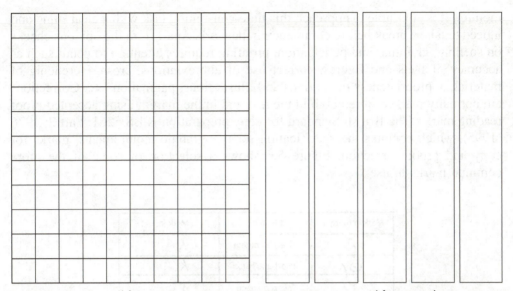

Figure 5.4 Layout grid for a magazine   **Figure 5.5** Layout grid for a newsletter

Stage 2. The resulting page grid should be printed out and a 'dummy' page outline manually drawn up with pen or preferably pencil. This should contain a rough or 'thumbnail' sketch of the proposed page and include positions of advertisements, graphics, pictures, headlines, text boxes, body text accompanied by details such as point sizes, weight, use of colour, etc. The exact execution of these guidelines may change as the process progresses but the 'rough' is an invaluable part of the pre-production process.

Stage 3. With the design having been set the next stage is to open a new file on the computer and set the required columns. As these will be the basis of the final page they must not be drawn in and therefore will not appear on the printed copy.

Stage 4. A suitable masthead and logo will have been chosen and this should be placed into the designated area on the page. Other features such as advertisements should be entered at this point.

Stage 5. The body text from a file or floppy disc is then placed in the relevant columns, facilitated either by the use of 'auto-flow' or manual input in the software package. Similarly, illustrative material will be cropped and scaled and inserted into selected areas with appropriate captions. Appropriately weighted banner, side head and crosshead headlines will then be added. A variety of textual and visual effects may also be used at this stage.

Stage 6. The page is printed out either on a laser or ink-jet printer and the copy proofread. It is far easier to proofread hard copy than the image on the computer monitor. It is advisable to approach this time-consuming task with a clear mind and indeed to take a break before commencing the work. Apart from the obvious checks on spelling, grammar and punctuation, proofing requires attention to detail such as accuracy of facts and figures, correct use of abbreviations, cross-referencing of material, appropriateness of captions and illustrations, pagination, etc. Corrections are normally marked in red both in the text and in the margin using accepted proof reading marks. The British Standard for copy preparation is BS 5261: Part 2: 1976 (1995), which contains the specification for typographic requirements, marks for copy and proof correction. Figure 5.6 shows a selection of some of the more common marks in use.

Mark in margin	Meaning	Mark in text
, ⅄	insert a comma	⅄
⊙⅄	insert a full stop	⅄
Y⅄	insert a space	Y
⌒/	close up space	⌒
⊘/	delete	/
⊂⅄ ⊃⅄	insert parentheses	⅄ ⅄
⊢⅄	insert hyphen	⅄
⊙⅄	insert colon	⅄
;⅄	insert semi-colon	⅄
⅃	insert apostrophe	⅄
'⅃ '⅃	insert single quotation marks	⅄ ⅄
''⅃ ''⅃	insert double quotation marks	⅄ ⅄
⌐⅂/	transpose elements	⌐⅂
~~/	change to bold type	~~~~
⊔⊔/	change to italic	——
≢/	change to lower case	○
⟨underline⟩	underline word	——
≡/	change to capital letters	≡
⟨stet⟩ or ⟨✓⟩	leave as printed	- - - - -

Figure 5.6 Example of proofreading marks

Stage 7. Changes may be needed at this stage to correct and improve certain aspects that have not been overtly apparent on the computer monitor. However, once the changes have been made the document should be saved and printed. (Note with the vagaries of computer technology it is advisable to save the document at frequent intervals in the production process.)

Footnote

As part of the City and Guilds Diploma in Media Techniques: Journalism and Radio students and trainees are required to produce a simple four-page newsletter using a DTP package, which must include material from their journalistic portfolios. Shaun Allaway was a young trainee journalist on this course at St Vincent College, Gosport, Hampshire in 2001. The illustrations on pp. 90 and 91 are taken from his newsletter assignment on the course and demonstrate the technological advances that have been made in enabling trainees to produce publishable work.

Suggested activities

1 Select a tabloid and a broadsheet newspaper published on the same day and compare and contrast the layout of the front pages in terms of headlines, stories, pictures, typography, use of white space, use of colour, etc. Write an analysis on the differences in layout and the possible impact on readers. Discuss your findings with your tutor and other trainees.
2 Select a popular national magazine title and analyse the proportion of editorial and advertorial in the publication, the content, the use of different typography, the use of colour, the amount of white space, the readability, the suitability of the overall package for the target audience, etc. Write an analysis and discuss your opinions with your tutor and other trainees.
3 Access a desk top publishing package on a computer and select the range of fonts available. Enter the words 'Deadline today' on screen and experiment by using

   ● different typefaces
   ● different point sizes
   ● upper and lower case
   ● regular and bold
   ● serif and sans serif
   ● italics
   ● special effects such as shadow, underline, strike through and drop capitals.

   Print out the results, annotate them and keep them in your folder for future reference.

THE GOSPORT GAZETTE

BRINGING YOU UP TO DATE

30p   Friday May 4, 2001

FIRST BUS LEAVES STUDENTS STRANDED

CROWDED: Students say buses like this one aren't big enough

■Plans to withdraw the local fleet of double deckers have left Gosport's students seething.

By Shaun Allaway

First Provincial have revealed plans to phase out their fleet of double-deckers, leaving St Vincent students facing overcrowded journeys home.

The move is part of the company's vision of the future which includes new 'mega-deckers' to serve the Fareham and Gosport region.

First Provincial currently has five double-deckers in its fleet and these will not be replaced at the end of their lifespans. The company say that double-deckers are no longer an attractive form of bus travel.

"It's a case of the industry having to face up to what the passenger wants," said Area Director Mike Smith.

However, the plans have angered students at the college, who are already unhappy at the overcrowding on college bus services.

Nineteen-year-old Ben Salmon, a science student at St Vincent, is particularly angry about the 72A service covering Locks Heath, Titchfield, Stubbington and Lee-on-the-Solent.

"They (First Provincial) already have our money from our bus passes. They don't care how we get home," he said.

But Mr Smith defended the company's plans.

"Students have to rely on the commercial side of our service," he said.

"It isn't always what they want, but the service has to be within what we can afford to run as a business.

"There can be overcrowding but what we look to do is to bring in larger and longer vehicles. The new 'mega-deckers' can hold the same number of people as a double decker, but on one level," he added.

Mr Smith also had a message for members of the public unhappy at sharing their buses with St Vincent students.

"We're living in a society where we should learn to live with each other. There has to be tolerance on both sides."

Children say pants to poverty

By Shaun Allaway

Children from Stubbington went out onto the streets yesterday to raise money for charity – by exposing their underwear to the public!

The children, all pupils at Crofton Anne Dale Junior School, collected money from shoppers in the Village Green area of Stubbington in aid of the BBC's Comic Relief appeal.

"Comic Relief were using the 'Say Pants to Poverty' idea, so we thought we'd use it too," explains Mark Allaway, 11. "We all wore a pair of pants over the top of our other clothes, which were red," he added.

The fundraisers spent about an hour collecting loose change after school, and collected almost £20 in total. But as Mark points out, every penny counts.

"That money can now help poor children in places like Africa, so it was definitely worth it, even if we did freeze!"

Jesus Christ Superstar hits Mayflower Theatre

Jesus Christ Superstar takes centre stage at the Mayflower Theatre, Southampton this week as part of a nationwide tour by the Really Useful Theatre Company.

The production uses the original score written by Andrew Lloyd Webber and lyricist Tim Rice, and runs until Friday.

Theatre-goers are advised to book early to avoid disappointment as the show is expected to be almost as popular as the original West End production.

REVIEW: PAGE 2

Figure 5.7 Front page of a newsletter

Gazette Sport
FOLLOWING THE BLUES!

POMPEY CREW

By Shaun Allaway
Chief sports
correspondent

DEFEAT ALEXANDRA

■Controversy dogs Fratton Park clash as Ref awards two penalties and shows the red card

Portsmouth 2-1 Crewe

Portsmouth fans watching the match at Fratton Park last night will be relieved that their side came away with all three points from this scruffy encounter with Crewe.

Pompey had the better efforts on goal in a dreary first half with Mike Panopoulos going close on the half-hour.

This was as good as it got in a half that saw three yellow cards. Crewe's Paul Tait was booked after illegally challenging Russell Hoult and Steve Claridge followed later

for dissent.

Pompey controlled the second half but it was Crewe who took the lead on the hour when Shaun Smith converted an undeserved penalty.

Crewe were hampered when Paul Tait received his marching orders after raising an arm.

A Pompey equaliser then seemed inevitable and duly arrived through Thomas Thogersen's shot from the edge of the box.

The Pompey winner arrived after Justin Edinburgh was brought down in the box and

Steve Claridge tucked away the penalty.

The attendance of 14,621 was above average for a midweek fixture due to the club's offer of discounted tickets for students, who were admitted for just £2.

Overall Portsmouth deserved the win even though it was messy at times. The top half of the table now beckons for this improving Pompey side.

BATTLE FIELD: Mike Panopoulos (right) competes for the ball last night

Pompey Line-up and ratings:

Russell Hoult (6.5):
Calm and reliable when called upon to make a save, but was rarely tested.

Linvoy Primus (7):
Strong at the back and was rarely beaten. Nullified the Crewe threat.

Justin Edinburgh (6.5):
Had a quiet game. Responsible for winning late penalty, though.

Shaun Derry (8.5):
Man-of-the-match. Typical strong and combative display. Passed the ball effectively.

Darren Moore (7):
As usual a defensive rock, although many of his clearances fell to the opposition (Replaced by David Waterman, 66).

Mike Panopoulos (7):
A good game in his first start since January. Worked hard and had a hand in the equaliser.

Steve Claridge (8):
Held the ball up well and link-up play with Panopoulos was excellent. Another vital goal, too.

Lee Bradbury (7):
He just needs a goal or two to restore some confidence (Replaced by Luke Nightingale, 90).

Nigel Quashie (8):
Went close and passed the ball well. A better goal return will make him a coveted player.

Thomas Thogersen (7):
Bad error when his attempted volley missed the ball. Redeemed himself with the equaliser.

Scott Hiley (7):
An inspired decision to bring him back into the frame. Played well in both defense and attack.

Referee: Mr SG Tomlin (5):
Annoyed both sets of supporters with awarding of needless free kicks.

Super gran has the Wright stuff

By Shaun Allaway

Running a marathon would be a daunting prospect for most people, but Fareham pensioner Shirley Wright can't get enough of them!

Shirley, a semi-retired health visitor, has taken part in the London Marathon five times in the last ten years, and says she has enjoyed every minute of it.

"I've always liked London due to the crowd's support," said Shirley, of Fisher Close, Stubbington.

Support, claims 64-year-old Shirley, was a key factor in her achievement of finishing in all five attempts, with her best effort breaking the five hour barrier by eight minutes.

Indeed, Shirley believes it may be harder to support than it is to run!

"Last time I ran my husband Frank was cycling around London to give me drinks and support. He helps me with my training

Shirley Wright

programme too and also runs with me sometimes."

Shirley began running in the late 1980s after her daughter Rosemary prompted a fitness drive. Shirley joined local club Stubbington Green Runners shortly after, when she decided

to attempt her first marathon.

"I thought my husband would think I was crazy the first time. I'd never run anything like marathon distance and I was 54 years old!" she laughed.

Super gran Shirley has also raised money for charities such as the Imperial Cancer Research Fund and the St. John's Ambulance group, but remains undecided about adding to her total of eight marathons.

Last night's results

FA Carling Premiership

Arsenal 5-0 Soton
Aston Villa 0-2 M'boro
Everton 1-3 Liverpool
Leicester 1-1 Bradford
Man Utd 2-3 Leeds Utd
Newcastle 2-0 Man City

Nationwide Lge Div 1

Barnsley 1-1 Stockport
Birmingham 3-1 Wolves
Blackburn 1-1 Sheff Utd
Bolton 2-1 Wimbledon
Norwich 1-0 Grimsby
Notts Forest 2-0 QPR
Portsmouth 2-1 Crewe
Preston 1-1 Gillingham
West Brom 2-2 Watford
Huddersfield 1-1 Tranmere
Sheff Weds 1-1 Burnley

FA Cup 2nd Rnd Replay

Kidderminster 2-1 Yeovil

Figure 5.8 Back page of the same publication

4 Write the introduction to a fashion article and devise a suitable headline. Experiment with different type faces, point sizes, colour and effects for the headline. Print out a selection and evaluate the fitness for purpose of each of them.

5 Select two different pictures to illustrate a review of a popular concert held in a park. Write a caption for one of the pictures that will be placed alongside the main headline. Write another caption for the other picture that will be a stand alone on another page.

6 In a DTP package explore different page layout sizes, margin tolerances, page orientation, column guides, etc., to familiarize yourself with the available layout options for producing print products.

7 Key into the computer a 75-word piece of text that you intend using for a brief news item on the second page of a newsletter. Align the text to the left, to the right, centred and fully justified. Print out your results and decide which type of alignment is best suited to the task in hand. Log the copies in your folder for future reference.

8 Draw up a 'dummy' of the front page of a community newsletter using guidelines in this chapter.

9 Plan and produce a double-page spread feature for a popular teenage magazine. Choose and research a topic. Write the feature. Select self-generated or acquired pictures and graphics. Design the layout and draw up a 'dummy' of the two-page spread. Produce the layout on a computer and print out the finished product.

10 Plan and produce the front cover and a contents page for a community arts and crafts magazine.

11 Design and produce a four-page newsletter using appropriate DTP software. You can include copy produced from the activities section of the previous chapter.

12 Devise and produce the front and back covers of a popular music or sports fanzine.

Sources and resources

British Standards Institution. BS 5261: Part 2: 1976 (1995). Available at: http://www.bsi.co.uk (accessed 20 September 2001).

Butcher, J. (1992) *Copy Editing* (3rd edition). Cambridge: Cambridge University Press.

Collier, D. and Cotton, B. (1989) *Design for Desktop Publishing*. London: Headline.

Dimbleby, N., Dimbleby, D. and Whittington, K. (1994) *Practical Media. A guide to production techniques*. London: Hodder and Stoughton.

Evans, H. (1974) *Handling Newspaper Text*. Oxford: Heinemann.

Genette, G. (1997) *Paratext*. Cambridge: Cambridge University Press.

Giles, V. and Hodgson, F.W. (1996) *Creative Newspaper Design* (2nd edition). Oxford: Focal Press.

Hodgson, F.W. (1993) *Subediting*. Oxford: Focal Press.

McLean, R. (1980) *The Thames and Hudson Manual of Typography*. London: Thames and Hudson.

6 Online journalism

- Introduction
- A bluffer's guide to Web design
- It's the words, stupid!
- Case study: Trinity Digital Media
- Summary of online journalism do's and don'ts
- Suggested activities
- Sources and resources

Introduction

The Internet and World Wide Web have been a significant part of journalism since at least 1994 when, as we saw in Chapter 1, the *Daily Telegraph* became the first UK national newspaper to make its content available online. Several billion web pages are available to the public (Quinn, 2001: 156), which can be found through commercial 'search' engines, such as *Google*. Each page is given a separate, unique 'address' called a Unique Resource Locator (URL).

Although the nature of the Internet means that precise figures are unavailable it seems likely that a substantial minority of these – perhaps 10 per cent – have a broadly journalistic content. Hall (2001: 2) notes that Reuters routinely serves 27 000 pages of data every second of every day to a potential market of over 200 million regular Web users. Certainly news and information is one of the main reasons people use the Internet, with one survey showing that 40 per cent used the medium to give them more background on a story than had been available through press or broadcasting outlets (*ibid*: 36).

Unfortunately even the largest Web server cannot cope with demand for news on the Internet when a major story breaks. This happened on the day of the terrorist attacks in the USA in September 2001. Clearly most people will not have access to a radio or TV at work so the Internet becomes the most accessible medium.

Internet usage at home is also expanding rapidly in the UK. According to a survey carried out for the telecommunications regulator Oftel, by May 2001 about 40 per cent of all households had Internet access – an increase of 4 million in just 12 months – and people were spending over 7 hours a week 'surfing' the Internet from home (Oftel, 2001). Furthermore, most of those who had recently taken up the

Internet had opted for an unlimited access scheme – which means they can stay online for as long as they want without incurring extra charges. It is hardly surprising then that most major organizations involved in journalism are dedicating increasing amounts of money and staff to their Internet services.

But how should journalism be presented on the Internet? Is it simply a case of transferring material from print copies or broadcast material to the new medium, sometimes referred to pejoratively as 'shovelware', or should the Internet be regarded as a completely new medium, demanding new and different conventions and approaches from its older brethren?

Although there has undoubtedly been much hype surrounding the Internet and news provision, the new medium does fundamentally alter the relationship between journalist, news source and news consumer.

First, there is the question of interaction required: in contrast with especially the broadcast medium, web news user, cannot be passive – they are required to make decisions and choices all the time they are surfing. This is even greater than is required for the print medium – when the consumer has to decide (usually) what to purchase, then what to read, when to read it and in what order. But, unlike the print medium, the Web news consumer is not limited to viewing only what is in the contents of that product. One of the most obvious differences is that the Web user can see the primary sources of journalism. Facilities that were previously only available to subscribing news rooms and a few hotels and businesses are now available to all: news can be viewed 'as it happens' – errors, inaccuracies and all.

But other primary sources are available too – government press releases, official reports, etc. As we shall see in the case study, this is regarded as a major 'plus' factor by journalism organizations. This should, in theory, increase the honesty of journalism – if the ordinary consumer can see the 'truth' they might become more resistant to spin, propaganda and bias. And yet one of the fundamental changes engendered by the Internet is that the traditional role of journalists – to act as gate-keepers, to assess sources and information for their credibility, to filter and check for accuracy before dissemination, is blown apart. The unique aspect of the Internet is that the cranky, scurrilous and irresponsible are allowed the same place in the system as the sane, measured and responsible. But some of the more organized of the non-mainstream news providers – such as the *Drudge Report* – can be likened to the underground press of the 1960s or the radical press of a century before: they put into the public domain gossip, scandal and speculation that no one else dares to print. But some of these stories are picked up, checked out and, if found to have substance, legitimized and published/broadcast by the established media – an example being the claims of President Clinton's sexual adventures.

The established media can provide links to such sources from their main news pages – whilst warning that they are not responsible for the content of such external sites. Thus, a story about environmental protestors can include the filtered, 'reasoned' and 'responsible' material whilst linking to pressure/protest groups and the like. A story about a political party can link to those parties' official Web sites. News consumers – especially the committed – can link to what 'their' side is saying on a controversy – pure public sphere (see Chapter 1).

Furthermore, the consumer can personalize and select their news coverage, by subject and other typologies, even creating their own 'virtual' newspaper or newscast. The danger is that in doing so news consumers may expose themselves to a more limited range of material than if they had used traditional news media and may in fact miss something that would have interested them. Rather than spread understanding and tolerance, the Web can therefore reinforce prejudice.

More positively, the Web user can personalize the news to see what it means for them – how does the budget affect my family income? What effect is the new education standards policy having on the test results of my children's school? What footpaths in my area have been closed as a result of Foot and Mouth Disease?

The Internet provides new outlets for journalists to market and present their 'own' work, rather than rely on existing organizations. For commercial organiza-tions there is the major question of how to make the Internet provision return a profit, or at the very least pay its way. Furthermore, if everything is going to be made available for free then why should the public spend money on buying that same material in another form: e.g., paid-for newspapers and magazines?

Having considered some of the main issues surrounding online journalism, this chapter will concentrate on the practical aspects of the medium – the techniques and conventions that have been applied to the new medium. As an example of how a conventional media group has adapted and developed its material from the more 'traditional' forms of journalism in a paid-for and free newspapers, we will look at a case study of *Trinity Mirror Digital*. We shall see in the case study that most journalists do not need to know a great deal about the mechanics of designing pages for online/Web use. The various techniques known collectively as authoring are now usually created by the software and templates used in the newsroom. Gone are the days when anyone wishing to be involved in the brave new online world had to know the intricacies of Hyper Text Markup Language (HTML) and the like.

Nevertheless, this chapter will first briefly consider some of the main software programmes and techniques that are used to create Web pages, if only so that the journalist will not have to look blank when faced with jargon from a know it all techie! If you like we can call this 'a bluffer's guide to Web design'.

A bluffer's guide to Web design

To view Web pages, the consumer needs a piece of software on their computer called a browser, the most popular of these being *Internet Explorer*™ and *Netscape*™ – one or both of these are now invariably 'bundled' free with each personal computer sold. The format, or protocol, developed by the team that initiated the World Wide Web that allows information of all kinds to be distributed on the Internet, is called HTML. This common standard ensures that the page created on one computer looks exactly the same on the receiving or downloading – What You See is What You Get (WYSIWYG) – or perhaps in this case it would be better described as What You See Is What *Someone Else* Gets! Without HTML there would be a succession of words without breaks, punctuation and formatting, let alone frames (boxes) charts, tables, etc. The basic unit of HTML that can produce a result of its own is called a lexia.

HTML is divided up into a number of tags that describe the type of text or other elements in that line of the Web page and they always appear between angle brackets (< >). The tag name is usually an abbreviation of its function, which makes it fairly simple to learn – if you really want to! For example, if you wanted to write out an accurate description of this book in HTML language you would write:

    This is a <I>wonderful</I>book

where I stands for italicized. The forward slash (/) shows the italicization is to end after that word.

Some tags contain attributes that give more information about the tag's action, for example where it is to be placed on that page. HTML can also specify the colour of text or other material, using the colour standard RGB – Reds Greens Blues – which are then translated to a hexadecimal number, although fortunately, colours can also be described by name!

Other important elements of HTML are links. These are tags that show the relationship between the current document and another. Meta tags are also important as they provide keywords that are used by search engines – very important in bringing other Web surfers to the information present on your page.

XML is a development of HTML that is often used by journalism Web pages and special types developed for news publication on browsers include *NewsML* and *NITF* (News Industry Text Format). For the increasingly ubiquitous WAP (Wireless Application Protocol) mobile phones there is a format called WML – Wireless Markup Language.

Although this chapter emphasizes the importance of words or text in online journalism, undoubtedly something other than straightforward text is desirable in most Web pages if they are both to attract and even inspire or entertain the reader. One of the beauties of digitization is that once information is transferred into sequences of 0s and 1s there is no bar on the type of information transmitted – it could be text, pictures (still and moving) graphics, audio, or a combination of any of these. All that is necessary is developing the programs, hardware and software to digitize these forms from their original formats or indeed to originate them in digital codes.

For more elaborate effects than are provided by HTML there is a programming language called *Javascript*™, which can allow simple graphics and interactivity. *Java* is a separate programming tool that is written in the form of applets – small, stand-alone applications.

One of the commonest ways of distributing graphics on the Web is through the Graphic Interchange Format – GIF. One of the reasons for this program's popularity is that it can be created on any platform – IBM PC, Apple Mac – and viewed on any of these. GIF files can contain up to 256 colours. These files are compressed and so, although the decompressed image (downloaded by the consumer) does involve some loss of quality, for most people it is a pretty good match – even though, to appear correctly sized on the screen, the resolution will have to be reduced. GIF is better for crisp line drawings or logos and, unlike JPEG, can be animated.

One of the best-known and most widely used piece of software for creating GIF Files is *Adobe Photoshop*™.

Probably the most common file format used for publishing a photograph on the Web is JPEG – so called because it was developed by the Joint Photographic Experts Group. Images created through this file system contain up to 24-bit colour information using RGB and can also carry greyscale images. This results in very high quality images. The compression scheme means that some information is discarded during the compression process but this is undetectable to human eyes. JPEGs need to be decompressed before they can be displayed and the consumer's browser will take longer to download a JPEG image. All of these are supported on browsers by the HTML system. Most browsers also support another format called PNG (Portable Network Graphics).

The next step up from straightforward graphics, photographs, etc., is to have animated displays. The most widely used of these are those developed by *Macromedia*™, which uses compressed files that can be delivered relatively quickly over the Web. To create these files you need to purchase the *Macromedia* software and the consumer will need to have the relevant players installed on their machine.

The really ambitious Web page will carry audio and video files for full multimedia presentations. Nearly all computers sold now have the basic *Real Player*™ or *Windows Media Player*™ already installed, so most surfers will be able to view and or listen to such files. To create such files, though, you would need to purchase software such as a *Real Producer*™. There are two main types of multimedia files sent over the Internet – streaming and non-streaming. Streaming means that the consumer views the file 'live' – it is being continuously produced from its source – although there is some buffering to ensure that the file will run and flow as well as possible even if there is some interruption to the stream. The file can start to be viewed/listened to shortly after it begins (before the file has been downloaded in its entirety). However, the computer does not store the file. Broadcasts can have live streaming – typically the Web surfer sees/hears the news broadcast, etc., about a minute after it has been transmitted over radio/TV transmitters. Thousands of radio stations are available this way over the Internet creating a global community of radio listeners. Sites such as that for the BBC's rolling news/sport network *Radio 5 Live* offer a mixture of these techniques – the most recent sports and news bulletins are 'streamed', there are links to the main

BBC news pages for individual audio and video reports, and the output of the station is continuously 'live streamed'. At the local level, BBC Radio Lancashire has been widely praised for both the wealth of content and interactivity to its site, in bringing the Internet 'to the people' both through an Open Centre at its studio base in Blackburn and a bus that tours outlying towns and villages.

Non-streaming audio/video on the other hand allows the material to be stored as a file but has to be downloaded in its entirety first. The most common file standard for this is the WAVE (.wav) type. This does not require special software for the originator but the files can take a long time to download. A better solution is the MPEG standard – so called because it originated from the Moving Pictures Expert Group – which can be either streaming or non-streaming. MPEG files maintain excellent sound quality by using a very high compression rate. There are numerous devices which utilise the MP(3) format, such as The Psion *Wavefinder*™, which receives high-quality digital radio (DAB) output and can record it in MP3 straight onto the hard disc.

Clearly, the consumer is going to be very irritated by files that take a long time to download and as ever there has to be a compromise between high quality results and speed of downloading. This is mostly determined by the bit and sampling rates. Both need to be higher for music and high-quality speech files.

One of the most critically acclaimed software packages for creating and editing video – on both Mac and PCs – is *AfterEffects*™ from Adobe. *QuickTime*™ – which can also be on both Apple Macs and PCs – is a long-established multimedia tool.

In addition to *Real Player* and *Windows Media Player*, the consumer can use audio/video through *Quicktime Movie*™. Audio file sizes are so great that compression is essential and all systems used Codecs – compression/decompression algorithms. Video files are even larger and consequently these can take longer to download. Again, the bit rate is crucial, as is colour bit depth, frame rate and frame size. Most experts agree that it is inadvisable to produce full-screen video as the amount of data required for images of that size is extremely high. As with audio, the length of the piece is a major factor.

It's the words, stupid!

Surprisingly, for what has always been thought of as a visual medium, numerous surveys and studies have confirmed that most people using the Internet have the greatest interest in the written word. This must be good news for journalists! In a period when there has been so much concentration on the visual media it is reassuring to know that words still matter!

The Stanford–Poynter Project – so called because it was a survey organized jointly by Stanford University and the Poynter Institute in the USA – is one of the most fascinating surveys carried out in this area. The survey suggested that, compared with a similar survey carried out four years previously (1996), overall their sample had reduced consumption of TV news, newspapers and magazines, although they continued to listen to radio news. But most significantly the news services on the Internet had: 'brought them back to the news reading fold' (Stanford–Poynter, 2000).

But the most innovative, original part of the research, was into exactly how people used Internet news services. The researchers attached special video recording devices to the heads of their sample readers to track not only which pages they looked at and for how long but precisely where their eyes went to on the pages, and for how long. The results of this survey are (naturally!) available online (see Sources and resources at the end of this chapter) but here are a couple of the most significant conclusions:

1 after taking in the page overall, eyes turn first not to pictures or graphics but to text
2 most photos are looked at – but only for about one and a quarter seconds!
3 online readers read widely but superficially – *but* looked at favoured articles in depth.

This survey backed up previous studies into Internet usage that indicate most people tend to scan a page for words and phrases that interest them and then either go back to read in more detail the surrounding text, or click on a (HyperText) link that provides more detailed information and comment on those topics that most interest them. From this it follows that material written for online journalism should be in short, easily digestible chunks, with blocks of headings to break up the text. Of course, print journalists and sub-editors in the traditional media tend to do this anyway with cross headings. So, again, it is a case of 'tweaking' the normal style rather than inventing a completely new one.

The length of the text presented on the screen though should be kept to a maximum of perhaps 250 words and it may need cutting from the original (print) version. Rather than simply 'cutting from the bottom' as often happens in (sub-) editing for the print media, the online journalist should make sure that all essential information is present on the first page. So what should go? It is of course only possible to give general advice on this but one of the most positive features of the Internet for journalists is that the Web user can click on links to find out background information that they need, either to make sense of it or to provide further details on certain aspects of the story. This of course is in sharp contrast to the traditional media where journalists have to make certain assumptions about the likely level of knowledge of the consumer. They usually have to compromise between providing all the background necessary for someone who is new to the story and irritating those who are familiar with the background by putting in a lot of information that they already know. The online journalist has few of these worries – the main information can be presented and those wishing to know further details or background can click on links to take them to further pages. This challenges the well established form of the pyramid structure of news writing: with small pieces of information gradually being expanded into more detail.

Care still needs to be exercised with this because surveys have shown that web users become very frustrated – indeed are likely to give up – if the information they require is more than three clicks away. Direct quotes should certainly be kept to a minimum unless they are absolutely essential to the understanding of the story. Another good reason for concentrating on text rather than on elaborate pictures and other possible presentation gimmicks is that the latter tend to slow down the time it takes for the consumer to download the page.

It should be remembered that most surfers will be using a modem with a maximum speed of 56 kilobytes per second (kbps). Note that is a maximum; in reality most will have connection speeds somewhere between 35 and 45 kbps. Indeed, many of the most popular sites base their download speed on 28 kbps – half the potential of most modems used at the beginning of the twenty-first century. A page, therefore, may be beautifully designed and contain lots of highly creative material but surfers tend to be very impatient when using the Internet and are likely to give up if the page takes more than 15–30 seconds to download. Clearly if this happens then all that effort has been wasted.

This is not to argue that Web pages should be straightforward text with no embellishments. Some simple, but eye-catching graphics and thumbnails of pictures (which the consumer can seek in 'full' mode should they wish) are to be encouraged. As with the printed page there should be plenty of 'white space' to enable the consumer to scan through the information simply and easily. For broadcasters and even for some predominantly print-based media groups there is the potential for making audio and video reports available through links on the screen. The best example of this is probably the BBC's news Website which at any one time will contain dozens of stories divided into different sections – politics, sport, entertainment, etc. – but with a 'front page' displaying the main stories of the moment. Broadcasters also have the potential to 'live stream' their radio and television output. There are copyright implications for all of this of course. Some sites, including those for some of the BBC's local radio stations, compromise by making their most recent news bulletin available and providing easy links to the main national/international BBC news sites. Both software and hardware for producing such material and downloading it to a Web server has dramatically reduced in price in the last few years.

The *Telegraph* group is naturally proud of its ground-breaking Web site. It radically overhauled its Web presence in 2001 and shares its experience with its online readers (*Telegraph*, 2001). The main features that they believe have been the most significant developments are:

1 Providing extensive links within every report to both its own archive and to relevant external sites.

2 Providing in-depth content such as fact-files on topical issues, and developing interactive features such as reader polls.

3 Using the company's huge archive resource to create a context for contemporary events – the 1998 World Cup mini-site, for example, contained reports from every tournament since the event's inception.

4 The most obvious change from the user's viewpoint is that the home page has evolved from the online equivalent of a newspaper front page into a gateway – or directory – to what has become a vast network of information and entertainment resources that have been organized into a series of subject-specific channels.

5 Pull-down menus at the top right of every page to make it easy to move between channels.

6 Using the gateway page to offer one-click access to every level of all the channels. Making the depth and breadth of content as accessible as possible has been a major factor in the changes in navigation.

7 Ability of user to personalize the pages to their own needs. For example, users can select to view weather reports from any of the 3500 on the weather database, which are automatically displayed on the telegraph.co.uk home page when they log in.

But how much material should be made available on the Web? Much of this will depend of course on available resources and policies vary enormously from the entire contents of a newspaper, including the crossword, cartoons, etc., to just a few of the top stories of the day. What is clear is that any material used for the Web must be adapted for the medium and not simply transferred from another source. Ideally this should also include some original (Web-only) material – what might be called Added Web Value.

Case study: Trinity Digital Media

Background

Trinity Mirror is Britain's biggest publishing group, the second largest in Europe and easily the biggest publisher of provincial newspapers in the UK – its total weekly circulation of nearly 18 million is 75 per cent higher than its nearest competitor, Newsquest (Peak and Fisher, 2001: p. 19). Some of the best known titles are: *Western Mail* (Cardiff), *The Journal* (Newcastle-upon-Tyne) and the *Evening Mail* (Birmingham). In 1999 it formed a £1.5 billion merger with the famous Mirror Group of national newspapers, which include the *Scottish Daily Record*, *Sunday Mail* and the *Racing Post*. It owns what is claimed to be the longest-surviving English-language newspaper in the world – the *Belfast News-letter*, which was founded in 1737. It also has interests in cable TV and its own well-established journalists' training scheme. Therefore this would seem to be a

Figure 6.1 Trinity Mirror Digital uses computer software to adapt the main stories and features from the 'hard copy' edition of its newspapers for the company's Web sites. Photo, Robin Collins

good company to investigate how they are developing their Web sites in conjunction with the traditional 'hard copy' free and paid-for local and regional newspapers. How does the oldest journalistic medium co-exist with the newest?

In its original base in Liverpool, Trinity Mirror has two daily (Monday–Saturday) well established and successful newspapers – the morning *Daily Post* and the evening *Liverpool Echo*. It owns a range of both paid-for and free local newspapers throughout the region and the Liverpool-based cable *Channel One* television.

Why go online?

Steve Harrison, content manager for the *ic north-west* Trinity Mirror Digital (TMD) brand says the primary motivation for the company to originally invest in online media was defensive. 'If we didn't protect our advertiser base we would get people coming in to take it and our advertisers may decide to migrate to online. If we didn't have an online platform then they might not advertise any more in, say, the *Echo*.'

Kath Evans, Development Manager for *icnorth-west* added: 'The other main reason was to use the existing resources. Without doing any extra news-gathering you got an extra use out of it'.

Steve explained that until the beginning of 2001 each newspaper had its own Web site and there was no consistency in structure, identity or content. The company decided it made no commercial sense to have different brands across the country, so decided to roll out its already established ic brand – *icLiverpool*, *icNorth Wales*, etc.

Those working for digital content were brought together under a single subsidiary, TMD, at the beginning of 2001. One of the advantages of this was to ensure there were common tools to create Web sites. In TMD's case this is called Content Management System (CMS), which, amongst other things, creates the templates for the Web design. As well as producing an identifiably similar look, the main advantage of this system is that the journalists do not need to learn new Web authoring skills in order to operate it. Kathy says: 'It's very straightforward – you can literally be using it on your first day at work'. She points out that all journalists have to be IT-literate these days so it isn't usually a great culture shock to work on the Web sites.

Steve says there was some suspicion and resistance from some journalists at the beginning but these are gradually being broken down: the journalists realize that by developing online sites the company is developing its business – and protecting their jobs. There is no compulsion or pressure for journalists to switch to the online service.

There are about 50 people working on the digital sites in the northwest region as a whole (about half of these are in Liverpool), including those involved in development of the content, advertising, sales, etc. Significantly, the company does not distinguish between journalists and others who work on the Web sites – they are all labelled Content Developers. 'Some do have a journalistic background, some are fully qualified journalists, others have done journalism courses or journalism modules at university or college. Some don't have a background in journalism at all but are very good writers and can generate content. So it's not exclusively people moving from print journalism – it's quite a mixture of backgrounds', says Steve.

This might lead to problems if those without journalistic training were allowed to create stories about court cases and so on. But Steve says they make sure that there is a sub-editor to check and revise copy created by all but the most experienced journalists.

Those involved in creating the news content as such for the Web tended to spend about half their day revising material originally produced for the print versions of the newspapers and the other half creating original content. At the time of writing this chapter in the summer of 2001 the technology was not sufficiently developed to allow every part of the printed newspapers to be reproduced on the Web sites – even if this were desirable. Transferring copy, graphics and pictures over to the CMS was, to use Steve's word, 'clunky'. Normally only 40–50 news stories each day from the *Liverpool Echo* and *Daily Post* newspapers are put on the Web. Therefore, editorial decisions on what to include from the newspapers have to be made on a day-to-day, or even hour-by-hour basis.

Steve says that their research shows quite clearly that the most popular stories – those that receive the largest number of page impressions or 'hits' – are (perhaps not surprisingly in the soccer-mad region) those concerning Liverpool and Everton FCs. Steve would like to put the Births, Marriages and Deaths (BMD) columns on the site – there is particular demand for this from the 'ex pat' community who log onto the site from around the world.

In the summer of 2001 the company was about to launch its North Wales site and had carried out research on what their audience would most like to see – jobs and entertainment came tops. The company part-owns (with three other newspaper groups) the *fish4*™ sites, so its jobs, homes and classified ads are powered by a link through to the *fish4* sites. Such features increase what is known in the jargon as 'stickiness'-pages, which are returned to frequently and at length for updated, detailed, information.

Print versus online

Steve doesn't believe there's a big difference between writing for the newspapers and for online. 'People say that text for the Web should be kept short and snappy but text written for the *Echo* is short, snappy and brief. You rarely find articles of more than 300 words, except for features.'

So far as news is concerned Steve reckons that it's a straightforward decision putting on the main stories that day for Liverpool and the northwest – by and large the page leads. Neither does Steve agree that only short pieces can be used online. 'If an article is interesting – and some interesting ones tend to be quite long – we don't keep it to three or four paragraphs. What we try and do is break a story up so you don't get screeds of words; we'll break it after seven or eight paragraphs, which might be on three screens of text.'

So how elaborate are the Web sites? Does Steve agree that the most important thing is text? 'If I had my way it would be all text – but it looks so dull! I compromise by having smallish thumbnails to make it look attractive – but when you go to the main article by and large the individual articles don't carry images.'

He worries that multiple and large images will take too long to download and the surfer will give up. It is possible for surfers to switch off images on their individual web browsers but Steve would not want them to do that – because then they would not see the advertisements!

Steve says one of the most valuable aspects of the Web is that detailed reports produced by official bodies can be linked to the Web reports. Late-breaking stories that will not make that night's edition are also put on the site and, if it is known that the story will break in the late afternoon and so too late for the newspaper version, the paper will carry a pre-determined Web address.

However, unlike some newspapers in the USA, Steve does not think that his company's Web pages will carry journalistic content that has been squeezed out of the newspaper version because of lack of space. 'Usually the journalist hasn't got a 5000-word backgrounder because he hasn't had time to write it.'

The Web sites also carry original reviews for theatre, etc., which are often on the Web site before appearing in any of the newspaper outlets. They are offered to the newspapers who sometimes print them – with a credit to the online source. Another idea is to use the facilities of the Trinity-owned cable TV channel – *Channel One* – to produce special video reports for the Web. In addition, there are plans to use packages produced by the television company – especially from its sports programme – to be made available through the Web. In the past it has carried match reports from *Radio Merseyside* but the BBC station, as with other local radio stations, is developing its own Web content and so has reclaimed the material for its own online service.

Steve admits that the sites are not making a profit at the moment. Most income comes from banner advertising. The Web sites also produce extra subscriptions from around the globe to the official magazine of Everton FC, which is owned by the group and to which there are links from the main pages. Naturally in such a soccer-mad city the company also produces an (unofficial) magazine for Liverpool FC!

Bearing in mind that the company runs a parallel series of free (purely advertising-funded) local newspapers alongside its paid-for daily titles, there might be some suspicion that the Web sites would in effect be glorified advertorial – advertising thinly disguised as news – rather than 'proper' journalistic content. But for anyone concerned that journalistic integrity may be undermined by the demands of the Web and the changing patterns of news consumption, Steve has some reassuring words.

> What works on the Internet is quality content and that is what you're going to find in the paid-for newspapers. If we just put advertorial it would be the kiss of death . . . people would just go somewhere else. I still believe in the criteria of editorial independence. We keep telling our sales people 'we've got to have credible content otherwise it would be no use to advertisers because people wouldn't come to us'. The criteria for editorial independence, which we hope we teach each trainee journalist, is exactly the same for online journalism. There is not such a difference there.

Summary of online journalism do's and don'ts

- Keep text simple and broken up into small sections
- make sure there are (hypertext) links for background and archive pages but:
- remember the 'three click' rule so that surfers don't become frustrated
- divide longer stories/features onto several pages
- make sure that each page has some graphics or other visuals – but keep most photos to thumbnail images

- test the download times on a typical modem/connection speed (approximately 45 kbps)
- divide the pages into clearly designated and easily navigable sections
- ensure everything is welcoming, friendly and easy to use.

Suggested activities

1 Compare the 'hard copy' of a newspaper with its online version. How in general does the writing, editing and presentation compare?
2 Pick one story covered in both media; do a word count; compare the language, use of cross-headings, etc.
3 What are the main similarities and differences? Why do you think they are different?
4 How are (hypertext) links used? Why do you think these links were used?
5 In a small group design a template for a Web page. Show the different sections. Be ready to explain and justify your decisions.
6 Download some suitable software and create your own Web newspaper. Think about who the 'readership' would be.

Sources and resources

Devx.com (2000) HTML Web Tips – *a quick guide to great Website design*. http://www.projectcool.com/developer/tips/design01_tips/index.html (accessed 6 July 2001).

Hall, J. (2001) *Online Journalism – a critical primer*. London: Pluto Press.

Newsport. 10 Points to Web Design. http://www.newsport.org/syllabus/10_points_to_web_design.htm (accessed 5 July 2001).

Niederst, J. (1999) *Web Design in a Nutshell*. Cambridge: O'Reilly.

Oftel (2001) *Consumers' Use of Internet: Oftel residential survey Q5 May 2001* http://www.oftel.org/publications/research/2001 (accessed 24 February 2002).

Peak, S. (ed.) (2002) *The Guardian Media Guide 2003*. London: Atlantic Books.

Quinn, S. (2001) *Digital Sub-editing & Design*. Oxford: Focal Press.

Rawlinson, A. (2001) CAR park UK. http://www.rawlinson.co.uk (accessed 29 September 2001).

Stanford-Poynter (2000) *Stanford-Poynter Project-Eye Tracking Online News*. www.poynter.org/eyetrack2000/ (accessed 8 July 2001).

Scott, K. (2001) *The Internet Writer's Handbook*. London: Allison & Busby.

Telegraph (2001) Site Index. http://www.portal.telegraph.co.uk/portal/main.jhtml?menuId=732&menuItemId=-1&view=SITEINDEX&grid=P9&target Rule= (accessed 23 September 2001).

Ward, M. (2002) *Journalism Online*. Oxford: Focal Press.

7 Radio

- Introduction
- Types of radio journalism
- Writing for radio
- Writing cues
- News reading/presenting
- In the studio
- The news bulletin
- Interviews
- Editing
- The feature/package
- The news programme
- Trails/promotions
- Activities
- Sources and resources

Introduction

The basic principles of good radio journalism are similar to those in the print and other media. This chapter will therefore concentrate on aspects of journalism that are specific to the radio medium and should be read in conjunction with chapters and sections on research and reporting, as well as on the cultural and historic background of radio journalism in Chapters 1 and 2, on regulation in Chapter 14 and legal matters discussed in Chapter 13.

Types of radio journalism

Radio journalism comes in many different forms. It is important to be able to identify the different types and their suitability for different occasions, as well as understand the jargon used in radio newsrooms. The table in Figure 7.1 describes these different forms.

No.	Type	Description
1	'Breaking' news	Used when first information on what appears to be a major story is available. May be included at the 'top' of a news bulletin or programme or, if very significant, it may interrupt normal programmes
2	News headlines/ Summary	A round-up of the main stories at that time – usually a one- or two-sentence summary
3	News bulletin	The regular round-up of the main news stories that hour; placed at regular and consistent times (usually 'on the hour'). Depending on the format and target audience of the station will normally consist of between four and six stories, several of them accompanied by audio (reports, interview clips, etc.)
4	News programme	A longer form than a news bulletin – typically 15 or 30 minutes. Usually broadcast at lunch-time and early evening. Consists of longer reports, features and interviews, along with slots for other types of radio journalism including sport, financial news, etc.
5	Copy only	Read by the presenter of the news bulletin or programme. Could be the full story or a short form of full story used in news headlines/summary. Used in bulletins or programmes for the less important stories or for those where there has been no significant recent development, or simply where there is no available audio. Should be kept short (maximum around 20 seconds)
6	Voice report – 'voicer'	Spoken by a different journalist from the presenter of the news bulletin or programme. Can be from the studio or location. Most suitable when there is more information on the story or is more important than the copy stories and/or when a journalist has been at the scene of the story and can provide first-hand description
7	Voicer 'wrap' ('mini wrap')	Voice report that contains short clips of audio – usually clips from interviews
8	Two-way – or Q(uestion) and A(nswer)	Between main (usually studio-based) presenter and another journalist who has been assigned to cover the story and who may be at the studio or (more usually) at the location of the story and provides first-hand/eye-witness information. Often includes audio clips
9	Interview	Between a news presenter and a non-journalist ('expert', celebrity, politician, etc., or 'member of the public'). Can be from the studio or on location, may be live or recorded. Should elicit comment, reaction, emotion – not purely information.
10	'Clips'/'cuts'	Usually generated from 9 and used in 3, 7, 8 and 12
11	Vox pops – voice of the people	Series of short, tightly edited comments from the general public on current issue or topic. Should be a variety of ages, backgrounds, etc., represented in the clips but (unlike print media) names of participants are not given.
12	Package (feature)	Multi-dimensional report with variety of voices (interviewees), reportage, description, actuality ('real sound' recorded on location) and music. Normally used in 3
13	Round table discussion/DISCO	Discussion on issue/topic, chaired by journalist with several participants who have different perspectives/views on the story
14	Personal commentary/talk	Provides journalist with scope to give more description, background and context than in 'straight' reports and is much more subjective. Usually concentrates on human interest angles. Now regarded as rather 'old fashioned' and there are legal and ethical problems with this lack of objectivity

Further details on numbers 2–12 are given later in this chapter.

Figure 7.1

Writing for radio

It seems ironic that in this chapter we should devote a major section about radio journalism – which necessarily involves the *spoken* word – with a section on the *written* word. But the fact is that most radio journalism is written before it is broadcast. Of course, some radio journalism is 'off the cuff' – or, more usually, spoken from notes – but it is still fair to say that with the exception of interviews (see below) most radio journalism originates and is based on the written word.

The number of words available to tell a story is far fewer than that generally used in the print media – certainly in broadsheet, or quality, newspapers. The main principles of good radio news writing are that it should:

● *Be concise* – the number of words available to tell a story is far fewer than that generally used in the print media so every word must convey maximum impact.
● *Play on the listener's imagination* – to paint pictures so that the listener can 'see' what is being talked about. All of our imaginations contain thousands of images that the good radio news writer can utilize. This is particularly true when trying to describe the size of something and to make figures – which should always be used very sparingly on radio – 'real'. For example, instead of writing/saying something is so many square metres, say it is 'the size of a football pitch', or 'as tall as the Empire State Building'. Most people find large figures, such as those for public spending, are meaningless out of context, so always translate this sort of information into something concrete, such as: 'that's equivalent to 20 new hospitals; 5000 new nurses', etc. (see below on how to show figures in radio copy).
● *Be written to be read out loud.* We tend to use less formal language when speaking compared with when we write, so radio writing needs to reflect the difference in styles. The language used can be more informal than that for the print media. For example, contractions, such as can't, won't and don't, are not only acceptable but necessary. It is not always necessary to stick with the strict rules of grammar and syntax (sentence structure). Writing that would look very 'ignorant' in print and would certainly appal a sub-editor in the print media, can be perfectly acceptable in radio. The main rule is: 'if it sounds OK, it probably *is* OK'. However, this is not to give a 'green light' to the general abandonment of good English. Certainly, clauses, tenses and singular/plurals should always match. Journalists are always urged to avoid jargon but this is especially so when writing for radio. Radio journalism is also notorious for being ridden with clichés: try to avoid these like the plague! Do avoid sequences of words that are difficult to say ('tongue twisters') or words with different meanings that sound similar or are just confusing or silly! For example: *police at the scene say they've seen two men acting obscenely.*

- *Be simple, clear and unambiguous*. This does not mean that the writing should be simplistic or patronizing – listeners will certainly not want to feel that they are being talked down to. But the radio journalist must always bear in mind that the radio listener *has only one chance* to understand what is being said. The listener cannot play back the words used in the way that they can re-read text. The main fault of radio news writing is the use of unnecessarily complicated sentences. Each sentence should have only one clause or subject and the radio news writer must avoid the type of sentence inversion that is common in the print media.
- *Use linear style*. The print journalist can afford to write: *Spending on schools will increase by 20 per cent in the coming year, according to the Prime Minister* as the reader can take in the whole sentence. But the listener can only take in the information as it is given to them. So a radio journalist should write: *The Prime Minister says spending on schools will increase . . . .* In this way the listener immediately knows *who* is making the claim that follows and is therefore able to understand and put the information into context. Similarly, radio journalists should avoid starting their copy with direct speech (quotes) – indeed, as we shall see, the use of direct speech must be strictly limited – unless we can hear the person speaking. Another important detail is that the ages of people in stories should be given before their name, rather than after it. So, whilst the print journalist usually writes: *Mrs Jennie Newsome (57) said that . . .*, the radio journalist would write: *57-year-old Jennie Newsome said that. . . .* One of the reasons for this is that the radio journalist cannot put in audible brackets (parentheses). Indeed, as we shall see, brackets are used in radio copy to denote instruction or advice which is *not* to be read out on air.
- *Use active and current tenses* (rather than passive, past tenses). The print journalist can write: *Anytown Council launched its new park and ride scheme on Monday morning.* If the item is being broadcast at breakfast-time on Monday, the radio journalist would write: *Anytown Council is launching its new park and ride scheme this morning. The council hopes . . .*
- *Use a personal, one-to-one approach*. Listeners should not be addressed as an anonymous group. Always try to write as if you are addressing a single person – 'you' is much better than 'listeners' or 'people'. Again, this often means extensive rewriting of the prose contained in press releases and the like. Always try to imagine that that you are writing that story or cue (introduction to story – see below) for someone who you know reasonably well but is not perhaps your best friend or close relation.

In short, anything that gets in the way of verbal communication must be changed or eradicated. The simplest and most obvious technique to achieve this is to read all work out loud before presenting it to be read on air.

Let's see now how these approaches and techniques could be used to cover the same, but developing, story on a single day. Let's imagine that just as a breakfast time news programme gets underway at 6.30 a.m. one morning, there is a gas explosion at a local school, which is in a residential area. The duty news editor writes up a copy only story for the 7.00 a.m. bulletin. It would read something like Figure 7.2.

EXPLOSION   **0700/11.5.01**   **DAVIES**   **COPY ONLY**

[19″]

There's been an explosion near the centre of Netherfield.

Emergency services are at the scene – but it's not known if anyone has been hurt.

Residents say they heard a loud bang coming from the Saint Christopher's Primary School in Swainburn [**SWIN-BURN**] Avenue just after half-past six this morning.

We'll bring you more news as we get it.

Figure 7.2

Note that at the top of the cue before the report copy itself there are some instructions set out in capitals and bold type. These are very similar to the headings of copy for the print journalist. Starting at the left, there is the catch line: a unique description of the report, usually of one or two words. Then there is the *date* of the copy and, crucially for radio – especially in a breaking or fast developing news story that is likely to be up-dated many times – the *time* of the bulletin for which it was first produced. Then there is the *surname* of the writer. Finally, on the far right, there is information that tells at a glance whether this is a 'stand-alone' piece of copy, or whether there is audio to go with it. In this case, as the story has just broken, there is no audio, so the writer puts 'Copy only'.

Under this information, centred on the next line, there is a *timing* for the piece. But how do we know how long it will take for the presenter to read the copy? Here again, computers come to the rescue! Most computer-based news systems will automatically time the length of cues by adding up the words and dividing by three – to get to the average reading speed of three words per second. But if you don't

---

Note: This is an entirely fictitious scenario and 'cast' created for this book; the 'Central Radio' and personnel referred to in this context have also been created for this chapter. Any similarity to real places, people and events is entirely coincidental.

have such a system or programme, then at least a word processor will – if you highlight/select the text of the cue (just the part that is to be read out) – count the words for you (this facility is usually under 'Tools' and called 'Word Count'!). You then have to use your maths to divide by three. In this example the number of words in the cue is 58 (the program has cleverly ignored the word in the pronunciation guide as it was in square brackets). Divide that by three and it comes to 19.333 seconds. Round any fractions up or down.

In this case you will notice though that any instructions – words that are *not* to be read on air – should always be clearly distinguished from the words to be broadcast by either putting them in brackets and/or in capitals/bold type – preferably all three! In radio copy you should never use any of these options for words that are to be read on air; in this way there can never be any confusion between what is to be read out and what is by way of information or instruction for the news presenter.

Any copy, cue or script, whether displayed on screen or printed out on paper ('hard' copy) *must* be double-spaced. This both makes it easier to read than would be the case for single or even 1.5 line spacing and, if on 'hard' copy, allows for corrections and alterations to be made.

If you think there is likely to be any doubt or hesitancy over a pronunciation, a guide should be included in cues/scripts. This applies even when the name is well known – the brain has an unfortunate habit of 'freezing' in a 'live' studio and it is just not worth risking embarrassment or humiliation. You will see in this example that the street where the explosion took place, although spelt 'Swainburn', is pronounced locally as 'Swinburn'. Local stations *must* always pronounce local place-names correctly – to do otherwise is really unforgivable and can fatally undermine the credibility of the whole news service.

Note that the pronunciation guide is put in square brackets and in capitals in bold type after the 'normal' spelling. This is to make sure the newsreader doesn't read the name twice. Phonetic spelling is a skill in itself, but fortunately it is not necessary for the radio journalist to learn this art; just to use common sense and follow the basic rules of replacing the 'real' letters with the letters as they should sound in the name. Break up words into single syllables along with dashes to show where the stress should fall in the words. Figures over three numerals in total should be written out – especially if they include decimal points and/or currency symbols. The motto should be: *if in doubt, write it out*!

Let's move on to the next likely development in the reporting by the local radio station of the gas explosion in Netherfield. There is a slot at 7.15 a.m. for news headlines and clearly something on the explosion needs to be included in this. In fact 'headlines' is a misnomer in radio. Too often trainees take the term to mean the same as it does in newspaper – a short, pithy and sometimes humorous but ungrammatical string of words. What is almost always meant in radio by 'headlines' are 'one or two sentence summaries of the main news stories'.

About 60 people who live in this busy street have been evacuated from their homes and are now standing around – many in their nightclothes – and there's a mixture of shock, excitement and worry. It's not yet clear whether anyone has been hurt. The blast is believed to have happened just after the early morning cleaner entered Saint Christopher's Primary School, the front of which is now a mass of fallen masonry and broken glass. Although the cause of the blast isn't yet clear at least one local resident has told us he smelt gas shortly before the bang. It's thought a spark from the circuits in the alarm system may have ignited the gas. The whole street has been cordoned off by the Police who fear there could be another explosion.

Sally Makegood, Central Radio, Netherfield

Figure 7.3

Next, there is the first voice report – or voicer – to be written and recorded by the journalist sent to the scene. The reporter, Sally Makegood, would either handwrite the copy for this in a notebook or write it out on her laptop computer. She has to get the main facts and developments into a report of 30–40 seconds and make it sound interesting. Figure 7.3 shows the copy for her voicer.

Note that the last words in the report take the form of a Standard Out Cue (SOC). Each station will have a standard format or style but in this case is *Sally Makegood, Central Radio, Netherfield*. That is: the name of the reporter, followed by the name of the station and finally the location from where the report was sent. Some stations don't use SOCs – or only use them in certain circumstances, for example in 'live' reports – so otherwise the 'out' words would be the last ones on the report (see below). To introduce this report, there will have to be a cue.

Writing cues

A cue has three main functions.

1 It must *grab the listener's attention*. This does not mean that it must be 'hyped', sensationalized or use tabloid newspaper-style headline journalese. But it must strive to persuade the listener that it is worth listening to the item that follows.

2 It must *provide the listener with sufficient information and context* in order to make sense of the item that follows. This is perhaps one of the trickiest parts of cue writing. A large part of journalism is concerned with additional developments about stories with which the listener will already be familiar. In addition, the radio journalist has to assume that the listener knows at least some of the main political and other public figures.

EXPLOSION/VOICER   **11.5.01/0730**   **MAKEGOOD/DAVIES**

An explosion has ripped through the front of a primary school in Netherfield. Residents near the school – in Swainburn **[SWIN-BURN]** Avenue – say a big bang shook the entire street just after six-thirty this morning.

As Sally Makegood reports from the scene, it's thought the explosion was triggered by an alarm . . . set off when a cleaner entered the school.

[GO TO AUDIO]

EXPLOSION/FIELD -ENPS: 302

DUR: 45″

OUT: SOC

[TOTAL DUR: 1′ 04″]

Figure 7.4

3 It must *lead naturally* into the piece that follows, so that the listener is prepared for the item or the comments that follow. Care should be taken, though, to avoid using the self-same words that are used in the report or interview clip. Let's see, in Figure 7.4, how this would look in our scenario.

Note that the last sentence of the cue – the 'lead in' line – tells us who is going to give us the report and encapsulates a key fact of the story. As already discussed, we have to ensure that the listener – who is unlikely to be able to give the radio news their full attention – doesn't miss vital information. So some information is given two or more times but written in a slightly different way each time. It would be perfectly acceptable in a cue for a voice report to write: 'Sally Makegood reports . . .' but the example given also prepares the listener for what they are going to hear. It's also a bit repetitive to always introduce 'voicers' with '(Paul Smith) reports . . .'. Try '(Paul Smith) has the details . . .' or '(Paul Smith) has more . . .', '(Paul Smith) has been following the story' (if our Paul has not personally been at the scene(s) of the story; if he has, make a point of saying so: '(Paul Smith) was in court . . .', '(Paul Smith) is at the scene', etc!).

Note that the 'not broadcast' information that was given in the copy-only report in Figure 7.2 is also given at the top of the cue: catch line (or slug), date/time (the latter very important for fast-developing stories to prevent out-of-date material being inadvertently used) and reporter's name – with an additional name given, which is that of the person who wrote the cue back at the station (even though it was probably dictated by the reporter who has done the voice report). It is vital that in case of any queries or problems, all stories can be traced back to the journalists who wrote them.

The [GO TO AUDIO] after the copy is optional, although is part of the BBC's standard lay-out. It isn't really necessary as it should be obvious – thanks to the information given both at the top of the cue and the fact that there are details of the audio at the bottom – that this is a cue for a piece of audio. There is additional information at the bottom of the cue that should match exactly the text information displayed on the audio piece. Some stations insist that the 'In' or first words used in the audio are written on the cue but the four following pieces of information given in this example are essential.

To avoid any confusion *each piece of audio must have a unique catch line* that must be written in the section following the cue itself and *replicated exactly* on the piece of audio. In addition to the catch line, there is a number following the initials ENPS – this stands for Electronic News Production System, which is the general name given by the BBC to its system of distributing both text and audio around its various networks and facilities. Such systems usually produce a number, which is simply where it is in the sequence of stories filed that day or week. It is a further check that the 'right' cue goes with the 'right' piece of audio. Most importantly, it describes where the audio may be found – especially important if a station is using a number of different systems to create and play-out its audio: for example, there may well be some on the hard disc system, some on MiniDisc, and so on.

Duration (**DUR**). This is important both for the news presenter to know how long the piece is and therefore when it is going to end and for the editor/producer (if a separate person) to be able to ensure the overall bulletin or programme is of the correct length.

The **OUT**, or last words, must be included so that the presenter knows when the piece has finished and therefore when to continue with the bulletin or programme. Of course, the remaining time of audio produced in digital formats can be displayed on the screen that is usually in front of the news presenter. Nevertheless, it is good policy to always include the last words on the cue. If this is not a SOC (see above) then at least the last three or four words should be used so the presenter is clear when the report has finished – it is not necessary to include the whole sentence but one or two words is too little. Be careful if the 'out' words are also used earlier in the piece. If this is so then put (second time) after the words. For example: Out: *It is disgusting (second time)*. This is more likely to happen with interviews, clips and cuts – see below.

Total duration (**TOTAL DUR**). It is this duration – the amount of time that the story will take in total to use on air – that is crucial for the calculations of the overall timings of a bulletin where the length of the bulletin or programme has to be exactly the length – to the second – allocated to it. In this example the number of words in the cue is 58. So we add 19 seconds to the length of the audio – 45 seconds – to come up with a total duration of 1 minute and 4 seconds.

News reading/presenting

Presentation is a particular art and technique that needs careful attention and constant practice. Although there are a few journalists working on BBC network radio and for the corporation's World Service who never have to read copy or reports on air, the majority of those employed as radio journalists will be involved in reading or presenting news at some level. Even if they do not present news bulletins or programmes they will have to read their own reports or those of others, so news presentation is a vital skill for all radio journalists.

Presentation of the news is the final – and to the listener most important – link between the entire journalistic effort and its transmission through the medium, so the process and technique of achieving good news presentation should be a very high priority for broadcasting trainees/students and instructors.

The first point to make – even though it may seem a blindingly obvious one – is that: *the newsreaders or presenters must understand what it is they are reading*! If they do not understand it then they cannot possibly expect the poor listener to do so. That is why they should always read news copy before presenting it on air and ideally have the chance to rewrite (rw) it, or at the very least mark it, so that you are completely happy with it. Only then do they have a sporting chance of conveying the written word into an easy to understand and interesting vocal delivery.

But what precisely is it that makes the presentation, or delivery, of radio news clear and interesting? It can be broken into three main areas – the *three Cs*.

1 *Clarity* – the actual words being said must be understandable. This involves clear and precise enunciation of words and good breathing so that sentences do not 'tail off' at the end or are otherwise indistinct. However, be careful not to over-enunciate or your delivery will sound unnatural. The trick of good news reading is that although it involves a lot of work it should *sound natural*. The most important thing is that the listener is paying attention to what you are saying, not how you are saying it. In English, comprehension is mostly to do with consonants and so it is important that these are said clearly.

The first technique is to make sure that you *open your mouth properly*. The jaw and facial muscles must be worked hard so that the consonants are formed clearly and precisely. Make sure you have a good clear-out of your throat and sinuses before going on air – especially if you are broadcasting first thing in the morning. Singing and humming make good work-out exercises. Certainly, you should never attempt to go on air before your voice has been 'warmed up'.

The next most important thing is that you *breathe correctly*. Sound is caused by vibrations in the air. If you use a lot of breath then you're not only going to have a more resonant, rich voice but you'll also be able to get to the end of sentences without fading away or, even more disastrously, having to make an unnatural pause in a sentence and thus breaking up and destroying the meaning of it.

Breathing, like any other physical activity, is something that can be improved with practice. Take a deep breath through your nose, making sure that you do not hunch the shoulders while doing so as this restricts the diaphragm and other muscles involved in breathing. Then count out loud and see how far you get before running out of breath. If you practise this regularly then you'll find that you will be able to increase your count and thus improve your newsreading skills.

2 *Comprehension* – the meaning of those words must be clear: this involves the correct stressing or emphasis and the right phrasing of words so that the meaning is clear and unambiguous. Although we usually talk about news-*reading*, in reality a better term would be news*phrasing*. This is because the best way to put over the words on a page (or screen) is to *break them up into phrases*, each of which contains a piece of information or an idea that can be taken in easily by the listener. Earlier in this chapter, when discussing radio news writing, we saw how we do not have to stick to the sorts of sentences that would be necessary in the print medium. That is why radio scripts often contain lots of dots and dashes so that the news reader or presenter can put the story across in spoken form.

Good news presentation involves *knowing which words to emphasize*. Putting the emphasis on the wrong words can make a nonsense of even the best written copy. Try not to get into a speech rhythm or pattern – which puts THE emphasis ON all THE wrong words BY stressing A word whether IT should or should not BE stressed! This not only sounds unnatural but also takes any real meaning from what you're saying. Emphasize what you think are the key words by slightly increasing the volume or stress on those words. Do not overdo this and certainly never SHOUT!

Underline what you think are the key words. Put pauses in your news copy by inserting a single forward slash (/) for a short pause and a double forward slash (//) for longer pauses. Do this particularly when you have long sentences to read that do not have sufficient punctuation – commas and full stops. Pausing slightly before or after words also gives them extra emphasis. You should also use these extra pauses when you are reading out direct quotations – they are the audio equivalent of a speech or quotation marks.

3 *Compelling* – this involves good *modulation* or *vitality* so that what is said is interesting to listen to. One of the strange things about radio broadcasting is that despite the very sophisticated and expensive equipment used – including studio microphones – somehow the voice seems to lose a lot of its natural energy and vitality. Therefore you need to work harder than normal to sound interesting! This means that most people's natural speech patterns have to be exaggerated or somewhat overemphasized.

Try to vary the pace of what you are reading; speeding up those passages that are less important and slowing down slightly for the more important sections. Make sure that you indicate verbally when you have finished one story and started the next. This is simply done by ending one story on a lower pitch, pausing and then starting the next story at a slightly higher pitch. The normal pattern of speech is in fact to start on a slightly higher note and then drop towards the end. Do make sure that you do not drop your tone so much that this speech becomes inaudible. Use your facial muscles to help change the tone and style of your delivery. Frowning really does produce a deeper, more serious sounding voice; smiling helps to lift and make the voice 'happier'.

Make sure that you have with you in the studio some water to sip at before and during the broadcast or recording. Avoid eating sweets – even supposedly refreshing things like mints – as anything which contains sugar will thicken up the saliva and cause problems. For the same reason you should avoid any sweet drinks, as well as anything with milk in it as lactose also tends to gum up the works. Avoid anything fizzy as this can have an unfortunate effect! Still water is best.

In the studio

No matter how exciting or late breaking the news, the presenter must never run to the studio – full control of that breathing is vital! Besides if you are 'panicky' you are likely to make both presentation and technical mistakes. Most 'normal' bulletins on local and regional radio these days are 'self-drive' – the news presenter operates all the equipment.

News studios (often called booths) are kept as simple as possible – it's recognized that most journalists don't make natural technicians! However, radio journalists often have to operate more complex desks, sometimes called boards. As with portable equipment, studios can be broadly divided between analogue and digital set ups. If analogue, you are likely to be faced with a bank of controls with sliders or faders that control the volume output for each channel. Each of these channels relates to a separate sound source – microphones, disc players, etc., and are normally at their lowest level (inaudible) when down, with the volume level increasing when pushed up. However, in most BBC studios it is the reverse!

At the top of each fader there will be a number of other buttons or switches. Each channel fader should certainly have its own pre-fade level (PFL) control. If you press or switch this it allows you to listen to the sound on that channel without it going on air (or on a recording). By using the PFL you can not only listen to an item, check your own mic level, etc., before going on air, but you can also set the correct level so that when you open up the fader to put that channel to air it will be at the correct level. You do this by adjusting a separate level control – usually called gain control or trim – found at the top of each fader. But how do you know whether the channel is at the right sound level? Definitely *not* by listening through the speaker or headphone monitoring and adjusting them if the channel sounds too loud or too quiet! This is because all professional studios (and portable equipment) have separate levels for monitoring and broadcasting/ recording. The broadcaster checks and adjusts levels – which indicate the number of decibels, the standard of measuring sound – by looking at the meters. Usually these will be Peak Programme Meters (PPM)s that show a range of decibels in a 180 degree arc – of 0 to 6 and over. On more basic desks you may have VU (for Volume Unit) meters, which are voltmeters using a special scale. Radio engineers regard these types of meters as less good than PPMs – dubbing them *Virtually Useless* meters – because they show every slight variation and fluctuations in sound level, which makes the job of setting and keeping to the right level very difficult. Broadcasters are mostly concerned with adjusting the peaks – the

Figure 7.5 With seconds to go before the hourly bulletin, BBC Radio Merseyside news presenter Linda McDermott makes last-minute checks in the station's news booth. Audio clips can be selected and played from the computer. Photo, Robin Collins

maximum – of sound level so PPMs, that as the name implies show the peak volumes, are preferred.

Before going on air you should check that each item is between 4, which is 0 dB, and 6 (+8 dB) on the PPM. Indeed most speech should be between 5 and 6 (see section on 'The feature/package'). Of course there will be some fluctuation in the levels of items – that's OK so long as the levels do not fall below 4 (too quiet) or rise above 6 (too loud and will start to over-modulate or distort).

More sophisticated desks have equalization (eq) controls above each channel, which alter the tone balance by boosting or reducing certain ranges of frequencies. These are very useful if a piece sounds either too 'bright' or 'crisp', or too 'dull' or 'muffled'.

Digital desks tend to have far fewer, if any, moving parts. The most hi-tech rely on touch-screen: the news presenter chooses from menus on the screen and meters will look different and operate to a different scale. Such desks often have a form of Light Emitting Diode (LED) meters arranged. Some digital studios, though, keep the well-known features of 'traditional' desks, showing the levels either vertically or horizontally, usually with increasing amounts of green lights showing the amounts of 'safe' dB, changing to red at the point of over-modulation/distort levels. These are also partly peak readings as the highest level reached is shown by the appropriate diode staying lit for a second or two.

When you've checked every item plus your own mic you're almost ready to go. Do, though, check that your seat is adjusted to be as comfortable as possible and that you can easily operate all the equipment.

The news bulletin

The bulletin is the staple news diet of most radio stations. In the commercial sector the overall length of the bulletins and the length of copy and audio clips in them has reduced significantly in recent years. Clearly each station will have its own style and editorial policy but the following principles usually apply:

1 The news is ordered into a hierarchy – the most important first, often finishing with a 'light' story at the end.
2 The first, lead, story is normally the longest and should always contain audio (voice report or interview clip). The only exceptions to this is when a story has just 'broken'.
3 There should be a variety of story lengths and forms – this helps keep the listener's interest. For example, a story with audio could be followed with a 'copy only' piece; or if two consecutive stories with audio are used, try and have one as a 'voicer' and one as an interview clip.

Figure 7.6 shows how the running order for the 8.00 a.m. bulletin in our scenario could look.

1. News intro (4″ full level, then fades, to headlines read over music fade): 12″
2. Lead story – has explosion: cue + voice report. Total: 50″
3. Copy-only national story (political row). 20″
4. Local story on protest against new waste dump: cue plus interview clip. Total: 35″
5. Copy-only international story (Indian flood). 15″
6. Local 'and finally' story: Local publican in trouble after his parrot is taught some bad language. Cue plus 'voicer wrap' featuring clip of offending parrot with expletives bleeped out and vox pops from 'punters'. Total: 45″
7. Sport headlines (teasing full sports bulletin later in the hour): 18″
8. Weather: 15″

TOTAL: 3′30″

Figure 7.6

Interviews

A great deal of the material heard in radio journalism is generated from interviews. In the typical hourly bulletins of just a couple of minutes it is rare for this material to appear in interview form – that is to say with answers given to heard questions from a journalist. Instead, short segments of interviews – generally known in the BBC as clips, in the commercial sector as cuts, and by the lay person as 'sound bites' – are used. These may be taken from interviews that were originally broadcast 'live', or more likely from an edited version of one that was originally prepared for a longer news and magazine programme. Interviews may be carried out in a variety of circumstances – most typically: face-to-face, by telephone or via a landline to a distant studio or other place where there is ISDN (enhanced digital telephone) equipment.

Just as the print journalist wishes to include the actual words used by an interviewee in their story, so the radio journalist wants to let the listener hear not just what the interviewee has said but *how* they have said it. There is another very important difference between interviews from their radio journalists and those by his colleagues in the print medium. That is, we often hear the interview *as* an interview – a number of responses to questions, rather than just the responses, so the tone and the manner of the journalist are revealed. The listener will therefore not only be judging and assessing the responses – the answers to the questions – but the way in which the questions are put.

Although all interviews should be carried out without fear or favour, radio journalists should adapt their style of questioning according to both the person being interviewed (the interviewee and the circumstances) and the background of the interview. At one extreme are highly experienced politicians being interviewed about a controversial policy (they will have almost certainly been trained in media techniques, will have been well briefed by their civil servants and are very used to a robust style of questioning); at the other an 'ordinary' member of the public, unexpectedly caught up in a story, probably involving a tragedy of some sort. Tact and sensitivity must be allied to good journalism.

Preliminaries

For the rest of this section we'll concentrate on the techniques of recorded face-to-face interviews.

Before you agree the date and time of the interview ensure that you will be able to get there for the appointment – especially important if using public transport. Also make sure that the necessary equipment will be available at that time.

Do your preliminary research as described in Chapter 3 – you need to make sure you know everything possible about the story and the interviewee so that you can think through all the likely 'angles'.

Next, take a notebook and write down your questions, almost all of which should begin with the following words, which are to journalists/interviewers something of a mantra: *who, what, where, when, why, how.*

Prepare for the interview by noting down your questions in a logical, concise way, which gives you maximum comfort and confidence but the greatest possible flexibility in case your interviewee comes out with a statement that requires at least one supplementary! *But* – and this is the really tough bit – you should conduct your interview with only a few 'bullet points' to prompt your questions.

It is quite common for interviewees to ask for a list of questions in advance – sometimes before agreeing to do the interview at all. Both the BBC's Producer's Guidelines and the Radio Authority's news and current affairs codes (see 'Sources and resources' at the end of the chapter) are explicit about this. Interviewees should not be provided with such a list as this effectively hands over editorial control to the interviewee. Unless your interviewee is very used to being interviewed for the radio, or you are under great pressure of time, it's a good idea to get them 'warmed up' by starting with an 'easy' question – indeed it is reasonable for your interviewee to ask, and be verbally given, your first question before you start recording. This helps them to focus their mind and it is in the interests of both interviewer and interviewee that the interview flows well.

One thing you must *never* allow to happen is the interviewee reading prepared answers. Even a highly skilled actor would struggle to make this sound natural and, worst of all, the listener will notice what is happening and conclude the whole thing is a 'set up' and you will have lost all credibility.

Very often interviewees will mistakenly think that you want somewhere very quiet to record the interview – this is usually not so. One of the main reasons for going out to do the interview is that there will be some ambient sound in the background, which helps the listener 'paint the mental picture' of where you are, especially if it helps contextualize the story. In our example we might want the sound of excited hustle and bustle as people are evacuated from their homes. Of course if the sound is too loud it will distract from the interview – although this can be partially reduced by sitting or standing extra close to the interviewee (you need to be especially sure you brush your teeth and use a good deodorant on 'interview days'!).

Before the interview itself you should *always* carry out a full test and do your own visual checks of the machine. When you are ready to record for 'real' you *must* get a 'level' check from both you and your subject (interviewee). Getting the levels right on your portable recorder is extremely important. Although some adjustments can be made during the editing and mixing process, it is far better to get them right at the time of the recording, as this will save you a lot of time and aggravation later! *Don't* ask interviewees to 'just say anything' as people can never think of anything to say! The best way is to ask them to describe their journey into work or wherever that morning. This usually gives you enough speech both to take level and to do a final check on the machine/mic/tape/disc. Ask them to speak in their normal speech level and hold the microphone about 4 inches (10 cm) from their mouth but slightly 'off centre' – this to avoid mic 'popping' on their 'Ps' 'Bs', etc. Don't let them grab the microphone. Adjust the record level control so that the sound peaks just before the 'Red' or 'Over' point on the recording level meter. Then take your own level.

Clearly if you are recording your interview with one microphone then you'll probably have to remember to position the microphone at different points away from yourself and the interviewee so that there is a similar level recorded for you both. You'll have to sit or stand fairly close to the interviewee, otherwise there'll be too much back and forth with the mic. Make a joke about having to get close to them! If you're seated, try to use a table and sit at right angles to the interviewee and put your machine on the table facing you.

Play the 'test' back. This will give you another chance to check the level and make sure it 'sounds' right. Now you're ready to go.

Before you actually start the interview, though, make sure you record the interviewee's name and 'position' at the start of the recording. During the interview itself you should handle the mic carefully but firmly. Make sure you don't pull on the mic lead – as, apart from the danger of this causing a loose connection somewhere along the cable or in the plugs, it makes a 'clunking' noise. Wrap the mic lead *loosely* round your forearm so that when you pull on the lead, it is pulling against that section and not on the plug. *Don't* move your hand up and down the mic as this can cause 'clunking'. Be especially careful if you wear a ring on your 'mic hand'.

Take any headphones off and have confidence that everything is going well technically. Don't keep looking at the machine, meter, etc., or you will make the interviewee anxious and it will generally distract them. Besides, you're nodding furiously to encourage them aren't you? Perhaps allow yourself a very brief glance down every couple of minutes or so. Otherwise, if you've done your 'pre-flight' checks well you should be all right!

While you record the interview, don't forget the ultimate requirements of the piece and that you are going to have to edit it. Leave a slight pause at the end of each answer, including the end and don't interrupt. Avoid conversational 'tics', such as 'umms' and 'aahs' and leave a slight pause at the end of every answer. Don't make work for yourself by making the editing more difficult than it has to be.

Before finishing the interview take a brief glance at your 'bullet points' to make sure you have covered all the main areas you intended to ask about.

At the end of the interview *before you 'let them go'* (or before you're seen out!) play back a short section of the recording ('for a technical check'!) if possible through headphones. If there has been any technical problem most people will understand and allow you to do it again. If you only find out there's a problem later the chances of being able to do it again are remote (as well as being extremely embarrassing). It is vital though that you do not let interviewees hear this check – if they get it into their heads that they can listen back to the piece they will want to do so and this can cause all kind of problems – as well as taking up valuable time.

So, check through headphones, thank the interviewee profusely for their time, tell them it was 'just what you want' and 'really good' (even if it wasn't and it isn't!) and then make your excuses and leave. However badly it goes, remember it is *not* the interviewee's fault – they did not have to give you an interview, they have given you their time and it is not their responsibility to give a 'good' interview.

After the interview

It is a convention in radio that recorded interviews are always broadcast with the pleasantries – hello, thank you, goodbye, etc. – at either end of the interview cut out so that the edited interview always begins and ends with the voice of the interview*ee*. This reflects social convention; if you are recounting a conversation to a third party you wouldn't normally include the fact that you had first said 'hello' to them or said 'thank you/goodbye' at the end! A recorded interview is, in effect, a conversation recalled, so edited/recorded interviews just leave in the 'meat'.

The cue for an interview or interview clip has to tell the main facts of the story. The great thing about cues is that they can be easily updated as new information comes to hand – or indeed be rewritten even with the same information to keep them fresh for subsequent broadcasts – but the audio can stay the same. Interviews that last longer than about 90 seconds when broadcast should also have a Back Anno (announcement). Figure 7.7 shows what the cue for the edited interview in our scenario might look like.

Having obtained at least one interview, it would then also be possible for Sally, our reporter, to construct a new voicer, this time containing a short clip or cut from

---

HEAD/INT   **11.5.01/NAN**   **MAKEGOOD**

The headteacher of a school in Netherfield – which was severely damaged by an explosion early this morning – says it'll be months before classes get back to normal.

It's thought a gas leak triggered by an alarm . . . set off when a cleaner entered the school . . . caused what local people described as a huge bang just after six thirty. No one was hurt although the cleaner – who's not yet been named – was treated for shock.

Nearly 100 residents in Swainburn [SWIN-BURN] Avenue were evacuated from their homes and were taken to a local community centre as emergency crews feared another explosion.

Lessons for nearly 300 pupils at Saint Christopher's, aged between 7 and 11, have been cancelled for the rest of the week. Headteacher Alice Burnley told our reporter Sally Makegood that the school's been so badly damaged that teaching will have to take place in temporary classrooms until at least the end of the summer term . . .

HEAD/INT-ENPS:461

DUR: 3' 57"

OUT: . . . It's going to be extremely difficult (2nd time)

[TOTAL DUR: 1' 04"]

BACK ANNO

That was Alice Burnley, the Headteacher of Saint Christopher's School in Netherfield, talking to our reporter Sally Makegood about this morning's gas explosion.

Figure 7.7

the interview – a (voicer) wrap. Several short clips or cuts could be produced either by Sally or back at the studio, each with a separate cue. These would look very similar to the cue for the interview except that as clips/cuts should not contain the reporter's voice (asking a question or reacting in any way) the name of the reporter/ interviewer is omitted. Also, as it will be a short piece of the interview a back anno is not needed. Unlike cues for interviews, it is quite usual for the length/time of these cues to be considerably longer than the clip/cut that they introduce. This is because such cues must 'tell the story' – there is no reporter to fill in the details so all essential information has to be in the cue. The clip/cut is to provide a point of view or emotional response – *not* to provide information.

Sally might also do a 'live' update of the story in a Q and A/Two-way with the main news presenter in the studio, in which she might cue in some of the interview clips/cuts, either played in by her from the radio car or from the studio. Doing a convincing Q and A requires skill and experience. It needs to sound spontaneous rather than scripted but the reporter and presenter need to agree on the questions beforehand – or at least the broad thrust of the questions. Journalists do not appreciate being asked questions by their colleagues to which they don't know the answers!

All of these types of radio journalism involve editing the audio material. This is now almost always done either on MiniDisc machines and/or using digital computer software – which can be done on location on laptop computers.

Editing – or 'the kindest cut of all'

A fundamental question: what is editing for? Answer, to:

a Get rid of unwanted material.
b Reduce the amount of material to the broadcast time allowed.
c Rearrange material to give it a more logical and coherent structure.
d Allow more 'creative' use of the available material.

Ethical/legal considerations

However tempting it might be to edit your material so that the interviewee, etc., says something more 'interesting' or 'sensational', *don't*! However much you cut, you must always remain true to the main thrust/point of the answers given and keep faith with the context in which the comments were made.

Acceptable example of editing

(The edited sections/additions are shown in brackets)
Scenario: The MD of a rail franchise operator responds to a new report from the 'rail watchdog' that severely criticizes the company's service. The parts in parentheses show where the edits have been made.

> *I am very disappointed with this report (. . . eh, ahem), we've really (tried hard . . . I mean) tried desperately hard . . . to, (er), improve our service to passengers and we're very sorry to have let them down. We are (taking steps to improve our service by) investing over (thirteen million . . . sorry that should be) thirty million (dollars . . . I mean) pounds (. . .) to improve the state of our rolling stock. We are confident our service will make a significant improvement over the next six months (and this will be reflected in the next report coughs, clears throat . . . having said that yes,)*

> [edit in pause] *there is a question-mark over the performance of one or two of our managers. If we need to make changes* [edit in pause]*(in our management team) then we will do so, (and yes), it's possible we'll have to let one or two of them go . . . although I will say we won't be sacking anyone as such.*

This is perfectly acceptable editing because all that has happened is it has been 'tidied up'; obvious mistakes have been eliminated and the whole piece is more coherent and logical to listen to. Notice how pauses have been edited – using ambient sound or 'wild track' (see below) rather than silence, which can be generated by digital editing software but sounds peculiar and 'obvious' – so that sentences that were disconnected in the original are joined together but disguise a probable change of inflection/pace.

Unacceptable example of editing

> *We are very disappointed with this report . . . we are sacking our management team . . . there is a significant question-mark over the whole service in the next six months. We are in a desperate state. I am very sorry.*

It's a great sound bite and it is 'what he said' in the sense that he did say all those words: it's just that significant passages have been excluded and the editing has re-arranged the recording in such a way as to completely alter the meaning of the interviewee. Of course, it's possible to do exactly the same thing in the press but because we actually hear the words said by this wretched manager there is greater credibility than if we just saw the words in print.

See 'Sources and resources' at the end of the chapter for links to the BBC and commercial radio sites that provide full details and commentary on the main do's and don'ts.

How editing works

Editing works by deceiving the ear. You can, in principle, cut anywhere you like, but it's probable that the edit will be clearly audible. Although digital editing systems – which have overtaken the old system of cutting and splicing magnetic tape – sometimes look rather different, they all work in the same way. The audio is recorded onto the computer system and is then shown on the computer screen in a wave-form. The further away from the centre or bottom line on the screen, the louder or more modulated is the material. Editing is achieved by highlighting material, then deleting it, or copying and pasting it into a different section. It's very similar to manipulating text but of course in this case you have to listen to the screen representations of sound.

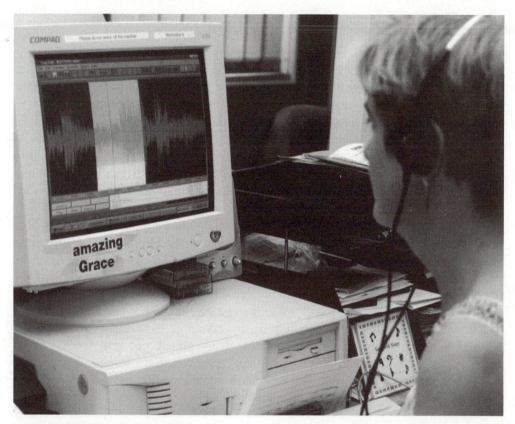

Figure 7.8 Better out than in … BBC Radio Merseyside Producer Caroline Adams edits an interview by highlighting a part of the waveform. The selected bit of audio is cut with the click of the mouse. Photo, Robin Collins

It takes most people a little time to get used to 'seeing' the sound and of course you can only become proficient at it through practice. In time, though, the beginnings and ends of words – and even different syllables – can be distinguished, especially when the words begin or end with hard consonants – p's, b's, etc. All systems allow you to magnify the section you are seeing on screen. The more you 'zoom' in the more detail is seen and the shorter the section you are listening to, enabling very precise cuts to be made.

The great thing about digital/on-screen editing is that, unlike tape, it is non-destructive: so long as you keep a copy of the 'original' material as you go along you can make as many versions of the material – and make as many mistakes! – as you like. The 'original' is still there!

Whatever system is used, though, the most important point is that the editing must not be obvious. What disguises the cut best of all is a good, sharp sound. It's a fact that some people are easier to edit than others. This has a lot to do with their speed of delivery and their enunciation. It's also possible, if you're really clever, to cut in the middle of a long sound. A good, sharp intake of breath is often a strong enough place to edit. With coughs, 'ums' and 'ers', and unwanted breaths, the same ideas always apply: look for the beginning of the sound.

One of the most common mistakes made by 'beginners' is to edit too tightly. People have to breathe, and too tight an edit sounds very unnatural! It's very important to maintain a natural 'rhythm' to speech. The other main factor that of course does not exist in editing copy, is that the intonations must 'match'. If someone is speaking with an upward inflection and you edit in the middle of it to a section with a downward inflection, it is fairly obvious an edit has been made and listeners will recognize this; whereas, if the same edit had been made and sounded natural it would almost certainly have been accepted.

There is one type of interview editing that defies most of these rules and that is the Vox Pop – short for *vox populis* – the Voice of the People. These provide a snapshot of differing opinions on a current topical question. They should never be described as a 'poll' or any suggestion that they are a representative view of the people in any area – they are not! Here, we are not concerned with trying to disguise the fact that editing has gone on – quite the reverse! Indeed, if the editing is done too smoothly it sounds most peculiar. To a very large extent, the 'rougher' the editing – cuts during intonations, breaths being edited out and, above all, a kaleidoscope of background noises 'jump cut' from one to the other – is needed to add to the impression (reality?) that you really have travelled far and wide to gain the maximum variety of people and views!

The feature/package

In many ways the feature, or package (so called because it contains lots of different elements or layers) is the summit of the radio journalist's art. The techniques encompass the sort of reportage, interviewing and actuality as described above, plus the options to include illustrative music and archive clips, together with very skilful editing and mixing. Packages or features come in various forms and lengths and indeed the techniques referred to here can be expanded to include a full-length documentary of half-an-hour or more. The point is to use all the positive features of radio journalism to their best advantage. Digital editing packages allow some very complex, sophisticated and creative packages to be put together 'in the field' by journalists comparatively quickly. Students or trainees are likely to have the luxury of more time, including time at the studio mixing desk. The main advice, though, is the same.

1 Before you start doing any recordings for the package, draw up a rough working plan. What is this story about? What is it trying to achieve? Where is it going? This will help you keep on track and make sure you don't lose sight of the story.

It should not, however, be a straitjacket: sometimes the story will 'change' in the light of information and interviews gleaned along the way. (Do make sure that if you have been sent out by an editor to do the piece or if you have been commissioned to do it that you keep the editor or producer up-to-date on developments: such people usually have a very clear idea of what they want from the piece and don't appreciate receiving something very different from their original concept!)

2 Be as inventive and creative as possible within the time and budget available. Relish the special possibilities provided by packages compared with 'straight' reports.

3 Make sure that at each location – even offices and other places with boring acoustics – you record about 30 seconds of wild track: this is ambient sound that can be used for a variety of purposes in the mixing/editing of the piece, including transitions between different locations, to cover 'dodgy' edits and to mix under your voice for voice links recorded later in the studio. (This latter technique is not cheating; you are giving the impression that you recorded the link on location but, as long as you don't actually say you recorded it then and there, it is regarded as an acceptable production technique!)

4 Try to *start packages with something other than your 'bare'/'dry' voice.* Remember that the package will be introduced by a separate news presenter, so it is not very interesting – and may even be confusing – to hear one bare or 'dry' voice followed by another. It is far better to begin the package with some of the real-life sound, or actuality, that you have recorded, or some illustrative music. This also allows the listener to take in the context of the package and to paint those mind pictures we talked about at the beginning of this chapter. The first words heard on the package should either be those of an interviewee, or your own voice presenting the first link. The links are simply ways of taking the listener from one element of the package to the next. They may either be done in the studio or – and generally this is much better – recorded on location, recorded in the studio or on the portable recorder at a later stage and mixed in with the location sound so that it appears as if they are recorded on location.

5 Try not to make straight edits or cuts from one piece of audio to another but *mix the sound under the links or actuality* so that they blend and fade more naturally into each other.

6 It is vital that at the editing or production/mixing stage, that the *sound levels are kept within a reasonably consistent range.* Speech needs to be mixed at a higher level than music because it has a lower dynamic range. Therefore, even if you wanted a 50/50 mix between speech and music you would have to set the speech higher than the music level – usually between 5 and 6 on the PPM. Most digital editing systems allow you to do pretty well everything that could be achieved in the studio on a PC or laptop computer – including multi-tracking, mixing, changing equalization, and lots of other effects such as echo/

reverb, changing the acoustic environment and even speeding up or slowing down the material.

Although there are very complex techniques used in package-making, reporters must ensure they are not too clever and end up confusing the listener. In particular, all speech, from whatever source, must be crystal clear and not be drowned out by music or other elements. Remember that although you may be mixing your package in a sophisticated multi-track studio, listening all the while over excellent studio speakers, most listeners will hear your work over very much inferior equipment and with a great deal of distracting noise. In all of this it is important to use your ears (to judge the balance and overall effect of the mixing/editing) and your eyes (to check the individual and overall sound levels).

[FAST FADE IN WT-COMMUNITY CENTRE 4" FULL LEVEL, FADE – BUT HOLD UNDER LINK 1:]

For over a hundred residents in Swinburn Avenue, the wake up call was not the alarm clock but a massive blast at Saint Christopher's School, which lies at one end of the otherwise quiet street. Shortly afterwards all the street's residents were evacuated as the authorities feared there may be another blast:

[FAST MIX TO CLIP 1-RESIDENT FOX:]

IN: It was amazing, I was just . . .

DUR: 13"

OUT; . . . just getting back to normal

[QUICK FADE OUT, MIX TO WT 2, SCHOOL. HOLD UNDER:]

LINK 2: For resident Jim Mason it was certainly a dramatic side to the day and caused some inconvenience. But for cleaner Mary Webb it could have been much worse. It's thought Mrs Webb unwittingly triggered the blast when she entered the school. Fire officers believe the tiny electric spark caused by the alarm system was enough to ignite the gas leak. Fortunately Mrs Webb only suffered from shock and was treated at nearby Hope Hospital. Divisional Fire Officer John Quincy told me Mrs Webb could have been very badly hurt . . ..

[MIX TO CLIP 2-QUINCY:]

IN: That sort of explosion could . . .

DUR: 16"

OUT: . . . much more serious.

Figure 7.9

7 The package should *maintain and develop the listener's interest in the story by including a variety of sound sources* – including where appropriate interviews, atmosphere, music, archive material, all linked by the journalist. These elements should be of various lengths and interview clips, for example, should be broken up so that we don't get great slabs of an interviewee followed by a great chunk of the reporter, etc. It's also common practice not to have two consecutive clips from the same interviewee. Be careful though not to include too many voices, especially if the interviewees sound rather similar. It is necessary for interviewees to be identified and if you go back to a clip from an interviewee after having first introduced him or her earlier in the package you may need to tell the listener again who they are. This can be a bit tedious. Above all, don't lose track of the story.

8 Before you get down to the lengthy business of editing and mixing/recording your package, draw up a rough running order or edit list. Indicate on this where all the clips that you plan to use are to be found. Write out the lengths and 'Ins' and 'Outs' of all these clips. Then script and record any voice links. Have all your material to hand before you start attempting to edit/mix on the computer or in the studio. The first part of the script/running order for the package in our scenario might look like that in Figure 7.9.

Full copyright details must be given for any music used, even if the track is listed as 'copyright free'. This information should be included with the cue and include: artist(s), composer(s), number of CD (etc.) and duration (how much music was used).

The news programme

Most local BBC stations, national network Radios 1, 4 and 5, and some of the major commercial services, have either extended news bulletins or full news programmes at least once per weekday – usually lunch time and/or early evening. These programmes allow for longer items, especially interviews and packages. In our scenario the lunch-time programme would allow for a round up of the morning's exciting events, including a news package. Such programmes often have their own editor and/or producer who can call on the full resources of the station's newsroom as well as material fed from their national/international news supplier and will sometimes have reporters working exclusively for that programme.

The aim should be to provide a comprehensive roundup of the news, sport, financial and perhaps entertainment news, so that the listener feels fully briefed. It must also be recognized, though, that many listeners – especially commuters listening in their cars on the way home from work – will not hear the whole programme, so news summaries are slotted in at several fixed points in the 'clock hour'.

Figure 7.10 The newsroom at BBC Radio Merseyside prepares for an edition of the nightly news magazine programme *Merseyside Tonight*. Although the station has use of a sophisticated computer system the journalists still use white boards to show 'at a glance' details of contacts, check calls and, most vital of all, *ideas* for news stories and programmes. Photo, Robin Collins

The editor and/or producer therefore has to ensure that the programme satisfies both the listener who listens the whole way through and the 'dip-in' listener – quite a challenge. There needs to be 'light' and 'shade' – a variety of techniques used to tell different stories – and sometimes several of the methods described in this chapter to tell the same story; e.g., a package followed by a 'live' interview, as well as items of different lengths. It is therefore as much about good radio production as good journalism.

The programme differs from the normal bulletin in that because of the complex nature of the operation the news presenters are often separated from the control room, which has the editor, producer and technical operator(s). Good communication is therefore essential. There will be talk-back (intercom) between the studio (in BBC jargon the cubicle) and those in the control area – sound-proofed glass will separate these two areas. The presenters will hear instructions over their headphones (cans). There may also be a screen on which the producer or editor can send instructions, information or suggestions for interview questions, etc. The presenters may have a green cue light, which the technical operator switches on as a 'warning' when an item is coming to an end. There will almost certainly be a red 'mic live' light both in and outside the studio so that everyone knows when the microphones are switched on and don't come barging in at the wrong time!

The whole team will be working to a running order, so called because it contains details of all the items – the order of all the items with the catch-lines and timings of all audio material. Certain items – for example the sports news, travel and weather – will be at fixed points and already inserted into the running order at the start of the day. The other stories are entered throughout the day, but often the running order is revised even while the programme is on air!

The news presenters need to give clear hand signals to the technical operator(s) – this is straightforward enough: simply point on the last word of cues so that the audio for that story can be started at the right point. The control room team then tell the presenters to 'stand by' when the item is coming to an end. A routine and discipline needs to be developed for all this so that no one gets caught out. The main concept is that communication from presenter(s) to the control room is visual, while from control room to presenter is verbal.

It is also good practice when one item is playing to double check that the next item is the 'right' one. Few things are more embarrassing or panic-inducing than a presenter to brightly introduce/cue an item only for it to be followed by silence or, even worse, the wrong piece of audio! Attention to detail and a thoroughly disciplined approach are vital if the programme is to be successful and not too stressful!

So in Figure 7.11 let's have a look at a running order for an imaginary programme – broadcast from 1.00 p.m. on the day of the gas explosion at Netherfield.

Trails/promotions

After all that effort the news team naturally wants the maximum number of people possible to listen to it. To achieve this they use the radio station to promote or trail the programme (commercial radio tends to use the term promo(s) – short for promotion(s); BBC uses 'trails'). These are effectively their own advertisements and, like all ads, they must be designed to achieve the maximum impact in the shortest amount of time. Trails/promotions come in three broad categories:

1 general, non-specific ones for regular (daily/weekly) programmes
2 specific ones for one-off or special programmes
3 a mixture of the first two: for a regular programme that has specific material relevant to that edition of the programme.

No.	TYPE	CATCH-LINE	SOURCE	DUR	RUN
1	Theme/Heads	NAA/Main Theme	MD2, T1/1B	0'50"	13.00.00
2	Pack	Explosion Pack/ Makegood	ENPS 4081	4'20"	13.00.50
3	Live 2-way	Cue from Makegood	1B/Radio Car	2'30"	13.05.20
4	News round-up	Ex newsroom	News Booth	4'00"	13.07.50
5	Live int. Counc. Dearing	Live-pres' cue	1B	3'15"	13.11.50
6	News Heads	NAA/Heads	MD2,T2/1B	1'00"	13.15.05
7	Sport	Various/sports pres'	News Booth	3'00"	13.16.05
8	Net pack'	Quake pack/Johnson	ENPS 4062	3'10"	13.19.05
9	Finance/ Geoff Newton	Live	1B/ISDN London News Centre (check)	2'30"	13.22.15
10	Rec. int.	FSB/Milligan	ENPS 5144	3'20"	13.24.45
11	Weather	Pres' cue	ISDN/Finton Weather Centre	1'00"	13.28.05
12	Closing Heads	Newsroom supply	MD2, T3/Closing Heads	0'55"	13.29.05
					13.30.00

Figure 7.11

It is the third type we will concentrate on for this section. We imagine that we are producing a trail mid-morning for that lunch-time's news programme. With digital editing this can be easily recorded, edited and mixed and prepared for transmission. The compromise is to have a standard beginning and end, with a middle or bridge section that can be changed each day. The spoken ins and outs can be the same each day – perhaps recorded by a professional voice-over. It's important there is a music 'bed' that can be at full level at the beginning and end but held (mixed) under in the middle (there are special libraries of CDs produced especially for such purposes), or you could use an instrumental section of a commercial track and edit/loop it so that it can run for an indefinite length. It's best not to choose anything too well known as the listener might pay more attention to the music than the words!

When preparing/scripting the trail put yourself in the mind of the listener: what would make me want to tune in? Try also to include as many different elements that might appeal to different sections of the audience. But be careful not to cram in too much so that sounds like a shopping list. The script for our trail would look something like Figure 7.12.

TRAIL FOR *CENTRAL REPORT*. 11/5/01

[STANDARD IN: 4" OF MUSIC FULL LEVEL, THEN HELD UNDER FOR:]

REC V/O INTRO (This lunchtime at 1, all the day's news and background to the big stories in Central Reports)

[MUSIC HELD UNDER]

V/O (PRESENTER): Today, join me Tim Speakright for a full report on the drama of this morning's gas explosion in Netherfield

CLIP OF AUDIO FROM GAS EXPLOSION (from Sally Makegood). DUR: 6"

V/O (PRESENTER) Plus. . .what now for Netherfield's soccer bad boy Wayne Carr, and why this bird might be up before the beak. . .

(CLIP: PARROT: 4")

REC V/O END: (Business news, travel and weather. Your lunch-time news digest,

Central Report, today at 1).

(ENDS 4" MUSIC FULL LEVEL)

TOTAL DUR: 44"

Figure 7.12

Suggested activities

1 Record and analyse a radio news/current affairs programme of at least half an hour. Try to classify the items according to the typology at the beginning of the chapter. Are there any items that don't seem to fit any of the categories? If so, how would you describe or classify them?
2 Take a news report from a newspaper and rewrite it in 'radio style'. Pay particular attention to the use of quotes (direct speech) and the construction of sentences.
3 In a group design a template for radio news *copy* (only) and ensure everyone has it as a file.
4 Produce a pronunciation guide for local place names in your area and one for unusual or difficult names and places nationally and internationally that are currently in the news.

5 Create a template for *cues* and share it as a file in your group.
6 Take a story from a newspaper and rewrite it for radio, imagining that it is being presented by a reporter as a 'voicer'. Write both a cue and voicer copy using the lay-outs above.
7 Mark up the 'voicer' copy, using the pause marks described above and underline key words and phrases.
8 Write the cue and copy for 'voicer' reports for two news stories, with you as the reporter. One should be rewritten from a national story reported on a Web site, and one should be a rewrite from a press release from a local authority, police, etc.
9 Record and analyse a news bulletin on a local station. Write out the running order for that bulletin – the stories, how they were dealt with (copy/voicer, etc.) and approximate durations of each item.
10 From a radio news bulletin transcribe (write out) a cue for both a voicer (report) and an interview clip/cut. How did the style vary between those two types of cue?
11 Do some breathing exercises: take a deep breath through your nose; make sure you don't hunch your shoulders while doing so. Then count out loud and see how far you get before running out of breath.
12 Prepare an interview with another member of your group. Ask them to choose as a subject a specific event in their lives that was unusual or dramatic in some way: something they can chat about for at least 5 minutes! *Don't* prepare a general 'chat' about their lives – this interview must be about a 'story'.
13 In groups of three, take it in turns to record the interviews you've prepared; with each member in turn being interviewer, interviewee and observer. Before you do this it would be useful to compile a check-list based on the do's and don't's in this chapter. Give each other feed-back after the interviews – remember next time it may be for 'real'!
14 Now edit the interview you did with another student/trainee to a duration of three minutes – you should aim to be within two seconds either side of this. Then write a cue for it.
15 Draw up a rough 'working plan' on how you would turn two features printed in a local/regional newspaper into a radio feature/package. Who would you need to interview (if you don't have actual names, write down the sorts of people you would want to interview); where would you go to record actuality; what illustrative music would you use (if any)?

Sources and resources

BBC (2000) *Producer's Guidelines* (online). Available at: http://www.bbc.co.uk/ info/editorial/prodgl/ (accessed 3 September 2001).
Boyd, A. (2001) *Broadcast Journalism – techniques of radio and television news* (5th edition). Oxford: Focal Press.

Chantler, P. and Harris, S. (1997) *Local Radio Journalism* (2nd edition). Oxford: Focal Press.

Crook, T. (1998) *International Radio Journalism*. London: Routledge.

Gage, L. (1998) *A Guide to Commercial Radio Journalism* (2nd edition) (eds L. Douglas and M. Kinsey). Oxford: Focal Press.

McLeish, R. (1999) *Radio Production* (4th edition). Oxford: Focal Press.

Radio Authority (1994) *News and Current Affairs Code* (online). Available at: http://www.radioauthority.org.uk/downloads/newscode.pdf (accessed 3 September 2001).

Reese, D. and Gross, L. (1998) *Radio Production Worktext* (3rd edition). Boston: Focal Press.

Reese, D., Beadle, M. and Stephenson, A. (2000) *Broadcast Announcing Worktext – performing for radio, television, and cable*. Boston: Focal Press.

Talbot-Smith, M. (1999) *Sound Assistance* (2nd edition). Oxford: Focal Press.

Wilby, P. and Controy, A. (1994) *The Radio Handbook*. London: Routledge.

8 Television

- Introduction
- Interviewing
- Short features
- News programmes
- Standard shots used in television reporting and production
- Suggested activities
- Sources and resources

Introduction

In the UK the average percentage of television viewers is virtually the same as that of radio listeners. However, according to official figures released by The Institute of Practitioners in Advertising (IPA) for the second quarter of the year 2001, the number of ITV viewers was down by 1.4 per cent, BBC1 down 0.3 per cent and BBC2 down 0.8 per cent on the corresponding quarter in the year 2000. Interestingly, in the second quarter of 2001 viewers on average watched BBC, ITV, Channel Four and Channel Five for just 2.72 hours per day, the lowest average figure since the first IPA research in 1985. Indeed, over a year the total number of hours spent watching television has dropped from 3.49 to 3.46 per day. However, this research also revealed that in a multi-channel household 20 per cent of viewing is now of non-terrestrial channels. The Independent Television Commission (ITC) annual report for the year 2000 stated that over 30 per cent of households have access to digital television as opposed to 60 per cent mobile phone use and 33 per cent Internet access. This review also accepted that the move by ITV to a re-scheduling of the two evening news slots from 5.40 p.m. to 6.30 p.m. and 10.00 p.m. to 11.00 p.m. had proved counter-productive, as viewing figures dropped by almost 14 per cent, especially as the BBC had re-scheduled its evening news from 9 p.m. to 10 p.m. Following a formal direction from the ITC and a judicial review ITV moved its late evening news back to 10 p.m. on Mondays to Thursdays, which resulted an increase in audience share. Whatever the machinations of the evening news debate it is certain that the majority of the population watch or listen to news programmes as a matter of course. It is interesting to note that findings by an independent research body commissioned by the ITC in 2001 revealed that people who read tabloid newspapers were more likely to watch television news, whereas people who read broadsheet newspapers were more likely to listen to radio news.

Of course there is an ongoing debate as to the presentation of news on television. Some broadcasters will maintain that a news item should be fully researched and produced to traditional standards and technical quality. Opponents will claim that the main purpose is to capture the breaking news event by whatever means possible, irrespective of technical and editorial constraints. Is it better to have shown to the world a few grainy sequences filmed by hidden cameras of the demonstrations and reprisals by the authorities in Tiananmen Square in China or waited for 'official' pictures to emerge? The increased use of videophones in reporting the war in Afghanistan in the Autumn of 2001 meant that live reports by journalists in remote areas were accessible to the news networks and ultimately viewers throughout the world.

In the demand for instant news with accompanying video images the whole concept of television news reporting has changed none more so than in the field of video-journalism. In the 1990s Associated Newspapers on their London cable Channel One employed Michael Rosenblum of Rosenblum Associates to train video-journalists to acquire news stories by using small digital cameras and then editing material on laptop computers. Exit the traditional production crew! Rosenblum fervently believed that a reporter armed with a digital camera with an in-built microphone could capture and edit news stories far quicker and produce technically superior reports to those using traditional and potentially slower methods. Indeed, an unconfirmed report in August 2001 revealed that the BBC was considering employing Rosenblum on a short-term contract to instruct regional reporters and producers on the use of digital hand-held cameras to shoot and edit news reports. Yet, whatever the debate as regards the possible changing criteria for the acquisition, scripting and editing of television news, the trainee reporter/broadcaster would be well advised to learn the basics of the job; the first of which is the art of interviewing for television.

Interviewing

The art of the interviewing for newspapers, magazines and radio has been fully described in previous chapters and much of the preparation and conventions apply equally to television, with the obvious exception that on television the interviewee is actually in vision. This therefore introduces other factors that are not common with newspaper and radio interviews. The first major factor is that often members of the public, although quite happy to give radio and newspaper interviews, become 'camera shy' and decline the invitation to be filmed, especially if caught unawares in a 'vox pops' scenario. Obviously spokespersons for the emergency services and other official bodies, press officers, politicians and celebrities are more likely to respond favourably to a filmed interview request. The second major factor is that it is almost impossible to carry out a televised interview without assistance from a production crew. Whereas the print or radio journalist can happily work as an individual the television reporter is dependent on others or at least one other person. In recent years production crews have been cut to the minimum, which may simply mean a reporter and a camera person who will also monitor sound and arrange lighting if necessary. Indeed lighting itself can be a problem. Radio and print interviews are not dependent on lighting and can be carried out in a variety of locations at any time of the day or night. Television interviews on location at night pose very different problems and editors, producers and reporters should be aware of this when arranging the time and location of a proposed interview. Another important factor in a television interview is the mode of dress of the reporter. It has been mentioned previously that print and radio reporters should dress according to the occasion, even though they will not be seen by a wider audience. It is even more important that the television reporter should dress in the appropriate manner for the situation. Indeed some reporters have adopted a style of their own in certain situations, such as Kate Adie in flak jacket for reports from war zones, Jennie Bond in smart dress for Royal reports and John Sergeant in suit and overcoat for Downing Street reports. The explosion of the so-called 'star system' in films has resulted in many reporters literally 'going over the top' when trying to interview celebrities at film premieres and galas. In practice the trainee television reporter should give some consideration to dress and presentation without either dressing up or dressing down. Jeans and tee shirt would certainly be acceptable for the Glastonbury Festival, rather less so for the Henley Regatta. Ultimately it is essential to ensure that the interviewee is comfortable in a possibly daunting situation and to dress in a manner that does not alienate them and is in keeping with the event.

Interviews broadcast on television fall into a number of general categories including:

1 News conferences

These tend to be less than satisfactory for the keen reporter intent on uncovering some in-depth information as, more often than not, they are 'stage managed' events by governments, sports clubs, financial institutions publicity agencies, etc. If the topic is of major significance the conference will be held in a large room and be attended by numerous reporters from all types of media, often with accompanying sound and camera crews and still photographers. The resultant amalgamation of shouted questions, flash bulbs and whirring camera zooms can often lead to the reporter either getting poor responses in terms of sound and picture quality or at worst not even getting the opportunity to ask a question at all. Sometimes the organization will pre-determine what questions will be allowed and from whom; a former Conservative Prime Minister was quite adept at this practice. Similarly the speaker can ameliorate a potentially damaging situation by simply avoiding a contentious question.

The normal procedure is that the spokesperson for the organization will open proceedings by delivering a carefully worded statement of the particular issue, such as a national crisis, a footballer's transfer, the resignation of a key figure in an organization or the launch of a revolutionary drug for the treatment of a previously incurable disease. Questions are then taken from the floor to clarify certain points. Following the terrorist attack on The World Trade Center, New York, in September 2001, Jack Straw, the British Foreign Secretary, attended government press conferences on the response of Britain to the attack. After an initial statement by the Foreign Secretary reporters asked pertinent questions, some of which were answered in depth, others of which were dismissed as being unanswerable at that stage. One of the main difficulties with these conferences was that as the microphones were mainly pointing towards the speaker the questions were lost in the general hubbub rendering almost intelligible the answers given. In most cases it is the sound that must take priority so the microphone must be able to clearly pick up the voice of the person even if the pictures are obscured by other people or equipment. Ultimately it is the responsibility of the reporter and crew to find the most suitable camera, microphone and seating positions in order to maximize the potential of the situation.

2 Vox pops

Guidelines on techniques for recording vox pops on radio have already been discussed in Chapter 7. Yet, as previously mentioned, the recording of vox pops for television can be more demanding if members of the general public do not wish to be seen. However, the general principle remains that vox pops attempt to gain an insight into the views of the public on a topical issue. The same one or two questions are asked and the responses recorded. As with radio the voice of the reporter is not needed and, in the case of television, neither is their picture. For this reason most vox pops are recorded by the camera person standing behind and slightly to the right or left of the reporter. This is known as an 'over the shoulder shot', which concentrates on the person being asked the question and not the reporter. Sometimes the reporter's shoulder is included in framing the shot, hence the terminology. In poor lighting conditions the camera person will often illuminate the subject with a camera-mounted battery-powered light. Of course this so-called random expression of opinions can be decidedly slanted in the editing suite to suit differing editorial viewpoints and some editors and producers question the validity of such disparate answers, although the tradition of seeking the reactions of the person in the street makes for lively television and satisfies audience expectations.

3 Eye witness

Eye witness or 'on the spot' interviews are favoured by news editors when a major incident or disaster occurs. Normally a reporter and crew will be dispatched as quickly as possible to the scene with the purpose of filming instant reactions to the event. Interviewees might be members of the emergency services, the general public, spokespersons for the organization involved or even victims of the incident. In many ways the aim is to 'colour' a news report of the event by inserting brief or 'grabbed' comments from participants and observers. As with vox pops a single over the shoulder shot of the subject is normally used. Often in the chaos of the situation the responses may be inarticulate, muffled or nonsensical as a result of the traumatic events and it is the job of the programme director to decide on the validity and effectiveness of such remarks, also taking into account legal, ethical and moral considerations. Many of these short interviews will involve emotional situations and the reporter should adopt a sensitive attitude to the type of questions asked. However, these 'sound bites' may give a 'theatricality' to such events that unfortunately viewers expect in an age when news is sometimes also seen as entertainment.

4 Door stepping

Door stepping, as the term suggests, involves the reporter and camera person waiting outside a person's house, hotel, theatre, restaurant or night club in the hope, often vain, of capturing on video a few comments from the person on a topical issue, be it an impending divorce from their partner, a fraud enquiry, a scandal, a lottery win, the result of a planning application, etc. In the case of nationally and internationally recognized public figures, some video journalists and press photographers wait for hours and even days in the hope of catching a glimpse of or comments from the person, who can be caught off guard by such attention and reply quite out of perceived character to shouted questions from a waiting reporter. George Best, the former Manchester United footballer, was frequently pursued in such a manner, as are other people in the public eye. However, standing outside a night club in Chelsea on a frosty winter's evening is not everyone's idea of broadcast journalism yet sometimes the reward of an 'off the cuff' remark provides adequate compensation.

5 The formal interview

This is also referred to in television as the 'set piece' interview in that it follows accepted conventions as regards location, camera angles, shot composition, stages in shooting and style of interviewing. The interview, which is face-to-face between two people, can be recorded in various locations such as the workplace, the home, the open air or the television studio. The latter pre-supposes the use of all studio facilities, including a set with multiple cameras, lighting, microphones, gallery with vision and sound mixing and production director and crew. This makes for ease of operation as there may be three cameras filming the interview; either boom or tie clip mics; extensive lighting and a floor person receiving instructions from the director in the gallery. Everything should run smoothly technically but live studio interviews can also take unexpected turns when contentious issues are raised by the interviewer or guests have spent too long in the Green Room prior to appearing on set; the well documented excerpts from the Michael Parkinson interviews with world heavyweight boxing champion Mohammad Ali and actor Oliver Reed are legend of what can and did go wrong. However, the aim of this section is to concentrate on the procedures and techniques for a single camera shoot of a face-to-face interview on location in daylight.

Face-to-face interview with a single camera on location

As with all interviewing research is essential for a satisfactory result but other technical factors are equally as important in this case. As the term 'set piece' suggests, the interviewee has already agreed to the topic, the location and the time and length of the interview. Normally the reporter will have outlined the brief and the issues that might be raised during the interview at an early stage in the negotiations and the interviewee would normally accept these as a broad basis for agreeing to appear. Subsequently the reporter should plan the way they are going to approach the topic, whether it be serious or light-hearted but never forgetting that it is the interviewee that is important, not themselves. Indeed it may be possible at the post-production stage to simply see and hear the interviewee if suitable leading and open questions have been posed, thus eliciting fulsome and meaningful answers. As discussed in other chapters it is not necessary or advisable to write down verbatim the questions to be asked but rather to write down the opening question and then jot down a few pointers for future questions as the interview unfolds. Some reporters may write out the last question but this is normally unnecessary as experienced reporters tend to use the standard 'Is there anything more you would wish to tell me?'.

For the purpose of this scenario it is assumed that the interview will take place on a bench in the garden of the interviewee's house at noon. Normally the reporter and interviewee would meet and have an informal chat away from the set piece, which would involve an explanation of the procedures of the shoot and a final discussion on the way the interview might be conducted. At the same time the camera person will be assessing the location for ambience, light, sound and vision and may carry out a trial recording by filming 30 seconds of 'wild track', which may be of later use to the video editor. It may be necessary at this stage to re-position the bench to avoid shooting into direct sunlight or against an unsuitable background. If it is raining or there is excessive unobtrusive noise in the locality a decision may be taken to re-locate indoors. However, if the location is suitable the participants take their positions on the bench and an audio and sound check is carried out. After confirmation that all is in order the interview commences as follows.

Stage one. The interviewer will have a hand-held microphone connected by lead to the camera and should wrap one loop of the cable around their hand to prevent cable rattle on the recording. Also, removing jewellery from this hand will stop potential metallic noise on the recording. It is essential that the interviewer holds the microphone in the same hand during all stages of the interview. Otherwise without careful editing the microphone will appear to jump from one hand to the other during the transmission.

The camera is placed at a distance behind and pointing over the shoulder of the interviewer at the interviewee. The composition of this shot should be a MCU (medium close up) or MS (mid shot).

After countdown and the 'cue' signal the reporter will begin the interview. The interviewee will answer the questions to the best of their ability and if they falter at any time the camera will keep recording whilst the particular question is either repeated as was or is re-phrased. Once all the answers are recorded the recording will be stopped and the participants asked to remain in the respective positions on the bench.

Figure 8.1 Stage one. Camera position and camera mid shot

Stage two. The camera person will move the camera to a position behind the interviewee and pointing over their shoulder at the interviewer. Again the composition of the shot should be a MCU or MS.

Figure 8.2 Stage two. Camera position and camera mid shot

In a studio situation it is possible to match the size of the image of the interviewee with that of the interviewer by superimposition, i.e., layering one image on top of the other and asking the camera person to adjust their shot composition. On location the expertise of the camera person will ensure a similar result. Once the camera person is happy with the composition the countdown and cue will be given and the interviewer will repeat the original questions asked but without reply from the interviewee. In some instances if a Production Assistant (PA) is on the shoot they will have noted the wordage of the originals; if not the reporter will have to recall them. The recording will stop after all the questions have been recorded.

Stage three. With the participants in position the camera person will compose a CU (close up) of the interviewer's face and ask the interviewee to comment quite casually about the questions previously asked. They will then record, without sound, the 'reaction shots' or 'noddies' of the interviewer. These seemingly disparate and often ludicrous reaction shots will be used as 'cutaways' in the interview to cover over 'jump cuts' or flaws in visual continuity. Invariably it is up to the editor to decide on the need for these shots and, although they have become something of an anathema, the trainee broadcaster should practise them in the event of a disjointed interview, which is often the result of poor initial preparation.

Figure 8.3 Stage three. Reaction shot

Stage four. With the participants still in their original positions the final stage is to shoot an 'establishing' or 'two-shot' of the interview. This simply involves positioning the camera directly facing and some distance away from the bench and recording a short sequence without sound of the two people talking together as though the interview was in progress. This helps establish the atmosphere, ambience and location of the interview and once again can be used by the editor to cover over lack of continuity and introduce 'wall paper' shots to vary the monotony of 'talking heads' or hide 'jump cuts'.

Figure 8.4 Stage four. Camera position and camera two-shot

Stage five. The camera person will check that the recording has been made by replaying a section of the tape. Once satisfied they will inform the participants that the interview is a 'wrap' and begin dismantling and packing the equipment. Meanwhile the interviewer should thank the interviewee for their contribution but decline to confirm whether or not the interview will be broadcast or what may be left in or taken out at the editing stage; these decisions will be taken by the producer and could be dependent on the actual footage and the way the interview has progressed. The reporter should then begin considering and writing the 'intros' and 'outros' for the interview ready for editing and ultimately transmission.

Stage six. The recording of the interview or 'rushes' will be taken to the editing suite where decisions will be taken as to what to leave in and what to leave out of the interview. It is important to note that the majority of set piece interviews on location are shot sequentially as described above in order to allow for quick and tidy editing. Once the editing is completed the interview will be inserted into the relevant programme at an appropriate time.

Short features

Short features, also known as packages or 'wraps', are frequently inserted into regional news magazine programmes. They may provide additional background to a recent hard news story, highlight a local issue or community event, or simply be a timeless 'filler' or 'fluffy bunny' story when there is little hard news available. In fact most regional magazine programmes will include a more light-hearted element as a matter of course to satisfy the 'feel good' factor of the viewers. The ideas for these packages may come from local newspapers, local radio, advertisements, community free sheets, chatting in the local pub or from stringers or contacts in the area. The trainee reporter will normally have their own 'patch' within the regional area and often it is one of their more enjoyable roles to seek out unusual stories that may provide the basis for an interesting feature.

It is common practice for students on broadcast journalism and media techniques courses to produce at least one of these packages as part of their training. The aim is to provide tuition not only in writing for television but also in learning the basic techniques of operating cameras, sound, lighting and editing equipment in order to compete successfully within an industry more and more concerned with multi-skilling. The prospective features are usually about two to five minutes duration and normally involve a reporter on location interviewing people about a particular topic or event with accompanying visual material to enhance and illustrate the narrative. They are not intended to be mini-documentaries but still require careful and detailed pre-production and planning to ensure a viewable and worthwhile final result. The following guidelines outline the main elements in planning, shooting, scripting and editing such a package and pre-suppose that the shooting will take place on one day.

Pre-production

As with all television production work good planning at an early stage should ensure a satisfactory end product. This is especially true of this type of assignment. The first task is to decide on the brief and the validity of the proposed package. Will it be of interest to the target audience? Is it of sufficient interest in itself? Do the proposed participants have a good, unusual or topical story to tell and can they articulate this in a filmed interview? Will they require payment for appearing? What is the deadline? Once the brief has been established the next stage is to carry out research on the particular topic or person. Dependent on the nature of the piece the research may be simple or in-depth. However, accurate background knowledge is essential so the reporter can interview people and construct the package in an informed manner (refer to Chapter 3). Once all the available and relevant research has been carried out the next stage is to draw up a 'treatment', which is a basic outline of how the final package might look and the possible means of achieving this outcome. Note that the treatment is not set in 'tablets of stone' and changes may occur during production because of logistics, innovative ideas, unavailability of interviewees and location environment. In general terms a treatment for a package should include:

- a working title (not necessarily the final title)
- the proposed length
- a brief synopsis of the main theme(s)
- sources of information including possible locations, interviewees, archive material, existing audio or visual material, etc.
- an outline of elements to be included such as interviews, vox pops, stills, archive footage, graphics and location shots
- duration of the shoot
- budget.

Often with news packages of topical events it is not possible or even desirable to write an in-depth treatment but the trainee should be aware of the structure and content of treatments that are always used for longer pieces such as documentaries and drama. Similarly, the next stage in a dramatic production would be to draw a storyboard. Again with short factual reports this is not necessary. Suffice to say that no great artistic skills are required for storyboarding, which is simply a pictorial representation of sequential shots and the means of transition between each. Sketches of 'stick people' in boxes with accompanying captions as regards shot

size, sound and transitions are completely adequate to give the director an outline
of the continuity and shot requirements.

The next stage in planning is to undertake a 'recce' ('reconnoitre') of the
proposed location(s). As with treatments the depth of knowledge required for such
a visit is dependent upon the type and content of the package. Often, for a simple
news package the location will be assessed on the day of filming by the single
camera person in liaison with the reporter. A more complex piece may involve the
reporter, accompanied by crew, visiting a number of sites well beforehand and
noting down various details that could influence the filming. In general terms a
'recce' involves taking into account and noting down the following as regards the
suitability of a proposed location:

- lighting conditions
- audio conditions
- shooting conditions
- provision of utilities such as mains electricity and water
- logistics for access and parking of vehicles containing equipment and crew
- location security for crew and equipment
- health and safety to include risk assessment (refer to Chapter 10: Health and
  Safety)
- amenities such as proximity of toilets and eating facilities
- contact names and telephone numbers of the nearest emergency services such as
  police, ambulance, hospitals, fire stations and coastguards
- permissions and clearances to film from authorities, landowners, police,
  organizations, etc.
- any special considerations that may apply such as obtrusive objects in view,
  traffic, time of day, hire of specialist equipment, protective clothing, etc.

Once the location(s) has been visited and selected the next stage is to draw up a
shooting schedule that contains detailed information about the filming of the
package. The following elements are essential:

- news programme title
- title of the package
- package number and tape number
- recording dates and times
- names of director, production assistant, presenter, camera person, sound recordist
  and a general assistant (if required)
- equipment
- telephone numbers of base production office, transport office, emergency
  services and location contact
- location(s), travel directions and 'pick-up' arrangements (if required), parking
  facilities

- times of crew call, recordings and wrap
- accommodation and catering arrangements (if required).

Figures 8.5 and 8.6 show an example of a shooting schedule produced by trainee journalists for a television news package on the closure of a local cinema, its impact on the public in the town and a comparison with the nearest multiplex cinema, which is seven miles away.

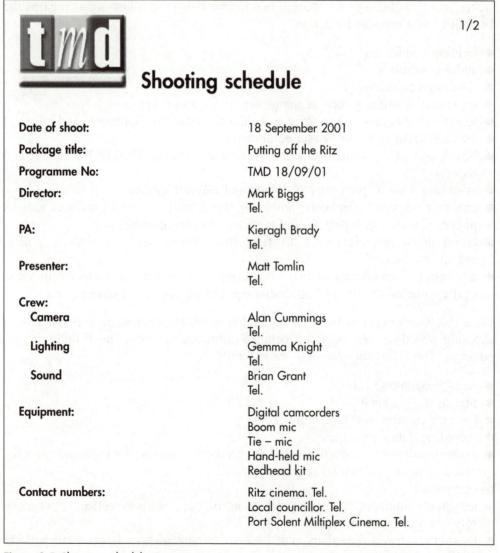

tmd   1/2

Shooting schedule

Date of shoot:	18 September 2001
Package title:	Putting off the Ritz
Programme No:	TMD 18/09/01
Director:	Mark Biggs Tel.
PA:	Kieragh Brady Tel.
Presenter:	Matt Tomlin Tel.
Crew:	
Camera	Alan Cummings Tel.
Lighting	Gemma Knight Tel.
Sound	Brian Grant Tel.
Equipment:	Digital camcorders Boom mic Tie – mic Hand-held mic Redhead kit
Contact numbers:	Ritz cinema. Tel. Local councillor. Tel. Port Solent Miltiplex Cinema. Tel.

Figure 8.5 Shooting schedule. Page one

2/2

Shooting schedule

Location 1. Ritz Cinema. Gosport

Travel Directions. Take M27 to Fareham and then A32 to Gosport town centre. Parking available in municipal car park behind main shops. Approximate travel time from studios 1hr but allow for morning rush hour and bottleneck on A32.

08:30	**RV**	Presenter, production and crew meet at Ritz Cinema
09:15	**SHOOT**	Piece to camera, interview with local councillor, vox pops and location shots
10:15	**DE-RIG**	Travel to location 2. Port Solent Multiplex Cinema. Cosham. Travel time approximately 30 minutes via A32 and A27. Free parking available on site.

Location 2: Port Solent Multiplex Cinema. Cosham

11:00	**RV**	Meet Port Solent Multiplex Cinema
11:45	**SHOOT**	Interview with cinema manager, vox pops, location shots and piece to camera.
10:15	**WRAP**	Presenter must leave at 13:45.

Facilities
Good range of restaurants available at Port Solent Marina. Hotels in immediate vicinity.

Figure 8.6 Shooting schedule. Page two

Production

When all the arrangements have been confirmed for the production crew and the participants the actual shooting can begin. As mentioned previously these guidelines relate to a one-day shoot and will typically involve a reporter, a lighting camera person and possibly a sound recordist and production assistant. However, in the era of the video-journalist the crew may be simply the reporter and a camera person and it is useful in these circumstances that the reporter has a basic understanding of video recording techniques and conventions. In such a situation the normal procedure would be for the reporter to conduct preliminary discussions with the participants and re-iterate the purpose of the recording and what is required. This may involve briefly checking that the background research is correct, explaining the mechanics of the interview, putting the interviewees at ease, verifying their names and details and informing them how long the recording will take. Whilst this is happening the camera person will be unpacking and setting up the kit to take full advantage of the location and obtain the most interesting shots. They will be assessing lighting and sound requirements, choosing suitable backgrounds for the interviews and considering the filming of additional material that will illustrate and enhance the package. If this were a complex package a shooting script listing every individual shot would have been written after the 'recce', but in most cases the camera person would be fully aware of the construction of a simple package and would work from experience. However, it is also good practice for the reporter to get a 'feel' of the atmosphere and ambience of the location, especially if they were not present at the 'recce' and contribute towards the decision making. So, even though the technical aspects are the ultimate responsibility of the camera person, there is every reason for the reporter to consider where is the most appropriate place to record the interview(s) or vox pops; the type of additional footage for the 'cutaways' and 'wallpaper' shots; the use of natural sound at the location. It is also beneficial for reporters to recognize the different types of conventional shots used in a short report and how they match together to ensure logical progression and continuity of action (refer to the illustrated glossary of shot sizes at the end of this chapter). Indeed a rudimentary understanding of the techniques of filming will help in writing the accompanying commentary and deciding the overall structure and shape of the piece. In observing and listening to a competent and experienced camera person a trainee reporter should gain an understanding of the techniques and conventions of this genre. Similarly with the increase in vocationally related courses such as the City and Guilds Diploma in Media Techniques many trainees will have gained valuable 'hands on' experience whilst at college, university or other training establishments.

The general techniques of interviewing for television have been discussed earlier in this chapter but it is worth noting a few pointers when carrying out interviews for the short topical report. In many instances all that will be required for the final piece are extracts or 'sound bites' from participants as opposed to a lengthy interview such as the set piece previously described. The following additional guidelines may be useful in this situation:

● avoid positioning the interviewee against a distracting background such as a large advertising hoarding, a company logo unless the person is from that company, one with frantic activity, movement or noise unless required for atmosphere

- conversely avoid positioning the interviewee in front of a drab brick wall
- always ask the interviewee to state their name and spell their surname whilst being recorded on camera
- sometimes it is also advisable to record on camera their title, profession and official position within an organization
- ask clear, unambiguous and 'open' questions that encourage fulsome though not rambling responses
- although your voice will not be heard on the final piece still speak clearly especially in noisy situations
- maintain eye contact with the interviewee, look interested in what they are saying, give them time to answer the question and listen to the response in order to decide on the follow-up question
- don't become involved in an argumentative situation
- as the interviewer will not be in vision it is pointless doing 'noddies'
- always remember that the interviewee is the most important person and it is their views and information that is required by the viewers, not those of the interviewer.

Paradoxically most short packages contain the ubiquitous 'stand upper' or 'piece to camera' much beloved by reporters. There is divided opinion on the value of the reporter either introducing or closing a piece in vision or both. At best it can re-assure the viewers that a familiar face, especially a regional reporter, is actually reporting from the location. It can also be used to 'fill in' for a lack of visual material; to explain certain facets of the story that may not have been apparent in the main body of the piece; to summarize and reinforce the main points within the story. As a maxim, unless the stand upper can contribute to an understanding of the story, leave it out. In most cases a Standard Out Cue (SOC) as a Voice over (VO) a closing picture is sufficient but viewers have become accustomed to seeing the reporter in vision so it is advisable for the trainee reporter contemplating presenting a piece to camera to note the following:

- ensure that the piece is delivered in front of a location background that reflects the actuality of the report and, as with the interview, does not detract from words that are spoken; by all means integrate the stand upper into the atmosphere, whether it be a noisy crowd or exciting action, but always remember that the words must be heard above all
- dress appropriately for the occasion
- adopt a confident attitude by looking directly at the camera, speaking clearly and emphasizing the key elements within the story
- ensure that the piece links to what is to follow or what has preceded it; don't just tag on the piece to 'flesh out' the report

- when delivering the stand upper either memorize the piece, use notes if unsure (although only glance at them occasionally during the recording), use a portable prompter if available, try and avoid the practice of repeating the pre-recorded previously scripted words linked to the reporter from a mini disc or cassette recorder as this can often result in a 'wooden' presentation.

Post-production

With the 'rushes' safely back at base the next stage in the production sequence is to decide how to select, edit and present the information. If the pre-production and production has been carefully planned and executed, the post-production stage will not present serious problems. Therefore if sufficient and relevant material has been acquired the task of editing should be relatively straightforward. Difficulties may arise when excess and extraneous footage has been recorded leaving the reporter, alongside the video editor, with the unenviable task of sifting through mostly unusable material in an attempt to construct a viable report for transmission. If a production assistant was at the shoot then they would have logged the footage noting at the time any usable material, any unusable material and any retakes that were necessary. The latter may include the interviewee either 'drying up', misunderstanding the question, digressing to the point of boredom or simply showing uncontrolled emotions such as crying or laughing in the middle of an answer. Equally the lone reporter should make a written note of the good or bad footage in order to refer to this in the editing suite and thus speed up the selection process. Bear in mind that a short report must have immediate impact and then retain the interest of the viewer so lengthy interviews, lingering creative sequences and padding should be avoided. The emphasis needs to be on the pace and thematic flow of the report so the viewer is left with a sense of wishing to know more about the particular event or topic. With this in mind it is important to look carefully at the rushes and decide on a probable shot list. Once this has been selected in terms of interest, information, accuracy, appropriateness, audience appeal and technical quality the reporter will begin writing the script for the commentary. It is important to refer constantly to the shot list in terms of the content and duration of each clip, which will determine the style, length and structure of the commentary. Note that timings may differ from machine to machine so the use of a stopwatch is also desirable. It is the norm to adopt the radio principle that three words of speech equals one second so the reporter should write the script to this premise bearing in mind that unlike radio there is no necessity to fill every second with speech as the pictures can speak for themselves. As a basic guide:

- use the least number of words possible to convey the message
- allow the pictures to tell the story
- adopt a conversational style

- relate the commentary to what is actually being shown on screen but don't describe in detail what the viewers can see for themselves
- above all ensure that the commentary is clear, accurate, free from ambiguity and uses language that is understandable to the general audience.

Sometimes the reporter may have to write the 'intro' and 'outro' for the package. If so, it is sensible to keep these as short as possible and to ensure that, in the case

---

1/5

Commentary script

Working title: Putting off the Ritz

Duration: 3 minutes

Introduction: Studio presenter. Inset still of Ritz Cinema.

Running order

Sequence	Dur.	Commentary
1. Matt to camera outside the Ritz	16 sec	Today witnesses the end of an era as the Ritz Cinema closes its doors for the last time. Despite a local petition the owners have decided that the cinema is no longer a viable business venture. The building will be demolished and replaced by a supermarket.
2. Archive footage with V/O	30 sec	There's great excitement as the newly built Ritz opens its doors for the first time . . . with the largest screen in the country audiences are in for a fantastic night at the pictures.
3. Matt. Interview with local councillor	25 sec	I have with me councillor John Harris who organized the petition to try and save the cinema. John, this must be a sad day for all cinemagoers in the area. Why do you think the owners have taken this decision? 'Well there are a number of factors that contributed to the demise of the cinema . . . one hopes that the supermarket will encourage people to shop in the town centre rather than at out of town outlets.'

Figure 8.7 Commentary script

of the 'intro', the final sentence leads naturally into the opening sequence of the report and the first sentence of the 'outro' or back announcement successfully ties up the report. Figure 8.7 shows part of the commentary script written to accompany the edited rushes shot according to the production schedule previously shown in this chapter.

News programmes

News bulletins, news flashes, rolling news, daily national and local news programmes, non-terrestrial news programmes, documentaries, current affairs programmes, discussions and debates are all either fully or partly involved with news that has been variously defined as 'a report on a recent event' or 'something one has not heard before'. Television news, as with radio news, has an immediacy that is not available to newspapers and magazines and there is increasing competition between terrestrial and non-terrestrial broadcasters and public service and commercial broadcasters to be at the forefront of a breaking story. The vast developments in technology have resulted in instant reports from around the world containing vivid and action-packed images that the viewer has accepted as the norm. Worldwide reports are as easily facilitated as news stories on regional television and the demand for action has led in many ways to a culture of news as entertainment as well as information. There are so many different types of television programmes that have an element of news in them that it is not feasible to discuss all of them in such a short space. This section will therefore concentrate on the requirements, production and presentation techniques for a regional television news magazine programme broadcast in the early evening.

Regional news magazine

In general the content of a regional news magazine programme follows a traditional structure in that the most important and recent news stories from the local area are placed at the top of the programme. These may then be followed by stories of lesser importance, a possible resume of national news, weather, travel, sport, entertainment, short features, interviews and a summary of the main local news to close the programme. One of the main aims of the programme is to adopt a formulaic style of content and presentation that is familiar to the viewer. It is only in cases of a major local breaking story such as a plane crash at a nearby airport or a national tragedy that the structure will be altered to include more detailed coverage such as on-the-spot reports or linking to the national news networks. In these cases there would still be a summary of the other local news of the day but less use of 'fillers' or non-essential stories that could be held back for transmission at a later date. Although there are differences between commercial and public service regional magazines as regards style, content and presentation most follow accepted conventions such as follows.

The opening sequence

The viewer has come to expect a recognizable opening sequence. This is usually in the form of a 'montage', which contains signature music, graphics, the station logo and programme title displayed at a fast-moving pace and digitally enhanced. More often than not there will be very short video clips from the news items that are to follow, voiced over by the presenter. Sometimes the presenter or, in most cases, presenters will appear in vision to highlight the main items that are to follow. As with a 'promo' on radio it will follow a standard format and use a typical phrase such as 'Coming up later in the programme' followed by 'But first the main news stories tonight'.

The setting

As with the opening sequence, the set design of the programme needs to be instantly recognizable to the viewer. There has been a significant move in recent years to create atmospheric sets for news presentation. In the past the single news desk with a MCU of the presenter sufficed and is still used when reading bulletins. However, most regional magazine programmes are presented in colourful surroundings and use a variety of lighting and digital effects for impact. The news desk may remain but is more than likely to be of a modernistic shape with the use of new materials. Large display screens are used for showing outside broadcasts (OB), live links, news packages, graphics and weather reports using 'chroma-key'. The use of separate areas on set often using casual furniture for discussions or sports coverage is favoured by many producers and adds variety to the presentation. Dramatic lighting effects projected onto a 'cyclorama' are sometimes used at the opening and closing of the programme, although the silhouetting of presenters at the beginning and the end appears to be 'passé'. Whatever methods are used the purpose is to create an atmosphere in which the news can be delivered in an up-beat style. Traditionalists feel that often the set detracts from the seriousness of the news items but the modern viewer has come to expect this type of set with all the technological wizardry it encompasses.

The presentation

In regional news magazine programmes the 'double header' format with two presenters, one male one female, is invariably used, which adds variety to the presentation. It is their role to 'anchor' the programme by reading the news, conducting live interviews either in the studio or with a reporter on location, respond to breaking news that is relayed via an ear-piece from the gallery, lead studio discussions and introduce fellow presenters such as the weather person, the sports, financial, political or entertainment correspondents, etc. Under direction from the control room and the 'floor manager' they link all the various elements together as smoothly as possible. Accurate delivery of information is an important part of the job and the presenter is aided in this by the use of an 'auto cue' or 'tele-prompter' – a device that is connected to a camera and allows the presenter to visually see the script. Early models used a strip of paper on which the script had been typed. This was fed manually through an optical reader by an operator and appeared on a screen placed under the camera lens that, by the use of a two-way mirror, reflected the image in front of the camera lens so the reader could stare directly at the lens and thus convey the impression of speaking directly to the audience. The paper-based version has long since been replaced by computerized systems that also allow the presenter to operate the speed of the scrolling via a remote control. The presenter will also have the hard copy of the script to hand just in case the prompter ceases operating. Even the most experienced presenters can easily be thrown off their stride when this occurs, often with embarrassing results. Needless to say a confident manner, good delivery and the ability to think and react positively to changing situations are essential in successfully carrying out the role of a presenter. Appearance and dress also play a significant part in the presentation of the programme and, even though there has been a relaxation in the formality of news presentation, particularly on satellite and cable channels, most presenters still dress smartly and quite formally to give authority to the message they are conveying. In the case of men this entails wearing a jacket and tie, although the latter have become quite lurid in recent years. The main aim is that the appearance of the presenter or newsreader does not distract the viewer from absorbing the information being presented.

Most presenters are journalists in their own right but some acquire a cult or celebrity status and develop an interest in other forms of television such as documentaries, travelogues and award ceremonies. The trainee broadcaster may well, in the course of training, be expected to present a news programme or, at the very least, read a news bulletin to camera that will involve using either a script alone or a script with auto cue back up. This can sometimes be a daunting experience, especially if it takes place in a fully equipped studio with a news set, multiple cameras, lights, microphones and production crew. The following is useful advice when presenting a news bulletin:

● before going on set read the script thoroughly to ensure that you understand it; to check the correct pronunciation of unusual words, foreign phrases, peoples' and place names; to ascertain the times where you will be on or off camera; to look at the duration of individual items and the entire bulletin

- if there are particular points that should be emphasized or could cause difficulty mark these on the script for later reference
- do not go into the studio whilst the crew are setting up, although you may be asked to do a voice check at some stage; sitting under intense lighting for any period of time can cause physical discomfort such as sweating, eye strain or headaches, particularly if you are also feeling the tension of the occasion
- before taking your place for the broadcast have a drink of water and check your appearance and dress, which should be suitably formal for the occasion even though it is only a training scenario; a good tutor will insist on you adopting a professional attitude at all times
- once on set make sure you are seated comfortably on a fixed, not swivel, chair; in any event assume an upright position that is of a sufficient height above the desk in front of you; avoid excessive movement caused by nervousness, which can be most distracting to the viewer especially if a chroma-key patch is being used to show images to your left or right and part of you inadvertently disappears from vision
- place the script on the desk, out of view, and look directly at the camera lens, which will display the same script as the hard copy on the auto-cue; be aware that with breaking news there may be changes made electronically to the script to bring the viewer the latest information; some tutors may deliberately change the script on the auto-cue to see how you would react in a real situation
- when using the auto-cue do not adopt a fixed stare or glazed expression and never follow the words with your eyes; occasionally glance down at the script but always look at the camera at the beginning of a new story to re-establish contact with the viewer; if you need spectacles for reading then forget vanity and wear them rather than straining to make out the words on the screen; above all try to 'love the camera' by telling the story as though to one person and displaying suitable facial expressions to reflect the tenor of the story without appearing overly dramatic
- speak clearly and at a conversational pace; breathe normally and allow natural pauses in the delivery, which should be varied in pace to reflect the type and importance of the story and keep the interest of the viewer; emphasize key words and phrases to aid understanding; do not gabble or rush through the script (many trainees are amazed to find that they have presented a 3-minute news bulletin in 2 minutes flat!)
- when ending the bulletin don't let your voice fade away on the last sentence and stay in position until the floor manager issues the instruction 'stand down studio'.

The content

Invariably the content of a regional news magazine programme will centre on news from the area, with the most important story at the beginning. Of course, editorial decisions may mean that one regional station views a certain news item as the lead where another in competition may use a different lead story and position the rival's lead story lower in their hierarchical structure. There may be good reasons for this in terms of editorial policy but it may be simply that insufficient material on the story was gathered by one channel or that the material arrived too late for editing. Whatever the lead story the news magazine programme tends to conform to a recognizable pattern of content. This might include:

1 a summary of the main news from the area presented to camera with relevant inserts;
2 short pre-recorded packages of general and timeless interest;
3 live or pre-recorded studio interviews;
4 live or pre-recorded links to a reporter on location;
5 action or still sequences with voice over;
6 local community information;
7 specialist features such as sport, entertainment, leisure, local heritage, etc.;
8 a brief resume of national news;
9 weather spot;
10 'And finally . . .'.

The production will feature music, captions, graphics and digital effects to maintain the interest of the viewer and add variety to the news provision. Finally there is obviously a fine line to be drawn between serious and casual presentation of news. It is very difficult for a viewer to watch a tragic news item and for this to be followed by a seemingly jocular exchange between the newsreader and the weather presenter.

Commercial breakfast television has tended to adopt a friendly and relaxed attitude towards the presentation of news but frequently there is a conflict of emotions for the viewer if, for example, a serious news item is followed by a lightweight item on the fashion preferences of a pop star. One may argue that doom and gloom has no place in either a breakfast show or a regional magazine but an equitable balance must be maintained between formality and informality and often the contrived chat between presenters at the end of the programme may be inappropriate to what has gone before.

Scripting a television news bulletin

As with radio, a standard format exists for writing scripts for a television news bulletin. In the case of television there is the added complication of ensuring that the script matches the pictures. The previous guidelines on writing a commentary apply equally to writing a news script. In essence keep it:

- accurate
- clear and concise
- at the correct level of understanding
- conversational
- interesting.

It is accepted practice that a television news script, unlike a film script, will be divided into two columns, with the picture information in the left-hand column and the wordage or sound in the right-hand column. The left-hand column will contain instructions for the production crew and the presenter, including shot numbers and composition, camera numbers, who is on camera at any one time (especially important when there are two presenters) and the position and duration of any Electronic News Gathering (ENG) material and captions. Figure 8.8 illustrates the main elements of a studio script that introduces the topical package previously described in this chapter. Note the use of the term BETA, which is the format on which the package has been pre-recorded. 'IN WORDS' are the first words spoken by the reporter on the pre-recorded report. 'OUT WORDS' are the last words spoken on the report and give an indication for the presenter to be ready for the next live link. 'SUPER' indicates that the captioned names of the reporter and interviewee will be superimposed live on the screen at the indicated running times. The DURATION gives the breakdown of the running time of the presenter's introduction, the running time of the pre-recorded report and the total timing of the segment.

Television studio production

It is not the purpose of this chapter to study in detail the techniques of television studio production as there are many other publications that explain these in greater detail. However, it is advantageous for the trainee broadcaster to have a basic understanding of the personnel and practices involved in producing a regional news magazine programme.

A television production team consists of a producer, director, production assistant, vision mixer, sound operator, floor manager, camera operators, lighting, sound and stage crew and a technical operations manager.

1 The producer may be an executive producer for the entire network or a producer of this particular programme but has overall control of the planning and operation of the production.
2 The director, who may also be the producer, is instrumental in reading the prepared script, relaying instructions to the studio personnel via the floor manager as to the commencement and ending of the programme, confirming the shot changes for the camera persons, informing the presenter of any probable

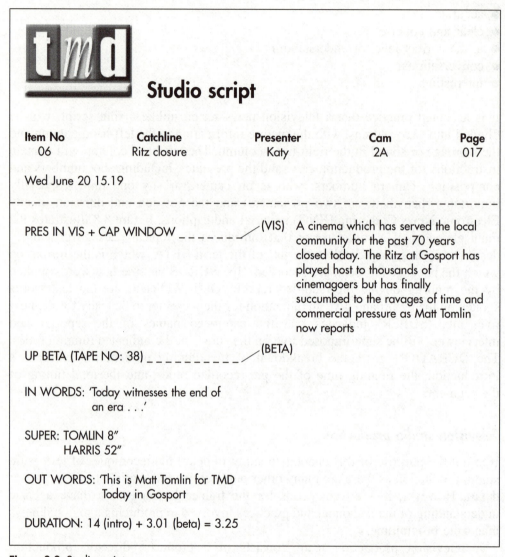

Figure 8.8 Studio script

changes in the running order resulting from breaking news and liaising with the production assistant as regards shot changes and cumulative durations of the broadcast. Standard instructions given might include 'Run VTR', 'Standby studio', 'Cue' and 'Cut'.

3 The production assistant is responsible for closely following the script, checking timings, alerting the director to the sequential shot numbers and writing up the production report at the end of the transmission.

4 The vision mixer operates the mixing desk and cuts between cameras following the director's instructions. Individual directors have their own ways of phrasing these instructions but a traditional and successful method is to first alert the vision mixer by saying 'Coming to 2' (2 being the camera number) and then at the required moment saying 'and 2'. This allows the vision mixer adequate time to set up the next shot on another 'bus bank' and avoids 'black holes' by avoiding cutting between shots on the same bank.

5 The sound operator is responsible for carrying out sound checks prior to transmission and setting levels for voice, music and effects. During transmission they cue, monitor and adjust all sound sources required for the production.

6 The floor manager is often rightly perceived as the next most important person to the director in that they have complete control of the studio floor. They are responsible for all aspects of the studio floor including set, props and the health and safety of equipment and personnel. No production will commence without a final check by the floor manager that the camera persons, sound, lighting and presenters are ready for broadcast. Once the floor manager is satisfied they will inform the director. The floor manager is also responsible for giving non-verbal cues in the form of conventional hand signals and instructions to the presenters. They relay the director's instructions to the crew and presenters and if the recording is not live, order re-takes if necessary before standing down the studio, clearing the set and writing a production report.

7 The camera operators set up the required shots according to the production script and their 'camera cards', which list the shots required by their camera. They frame their individual opening shot and then follow the script and instructions from the gallery as to subsequent shots or actions required.

8 The lighting, sound and stage crew are responsible for setting up and checking their respective areas prior to transmission with a vital emphasis on safe working practices and risk assessment.

9 The technical operations manager is responsible for the overall technical quality of the sound, lighting and visual aspects of the production including ENG, Digital Video Effects (DVE) and specific recording and transmission equipment.

Once the individual roles within the production team have been identified it is useful to consider the accepted production practices when recording a news magazine programme in a training situation. Assuming that all preliminary aspects such as set construction, rigging of lights, checking sound and vision have been successfully carried out, the sequential stages are:

1 The director checks that all stations and personnel within the control room are ready. It is customary to check each in turn and receive either an affirmative or negative answer before proceeding.

2 The director will then ask the floor manager via the talk-back system whether everyone in the floor crew and the presenters are ready.

3 The floor manager will then ask each member of the crew and the presenters whether they are ready and confirm this to the director.
4 The director will ask the technical operations manager or assistant to 'run VTR' if the programme is to be recorded. Once it is confirmed that the tape is running the director will say 'Stand by studio'.
5 At receiving this instruction the floor manager will raise their right hand to ensure absolute silence on the set.
6 The director will then say 'Fade up sound' followed by 'Fade up vision'. Note that it is an established convention that sound slightly precedes vision at the beginning of a programme. The beginning of the programme will normally be a pre-recorded opening sequence or montage as described previously. Once this is being transmitted the director will ask the production assistant to speak the 7-second audible section of the 10-second countdown for the floor manager.
7 The floor manager will audibly repeat the 7-second countdown to the floor crew and presenters and then use hand signals to denote the last three seconds before giving the inaudible 'cue' signal to the presenters by swiftly dropping their right hand. Sometimes the floor manager adopts a position nearer to the camera containing the auto-cue and places their right hand just below the eye-level lens. At the cue signal the hand is dropped and the presenter will be looking directly at the camera to introduce the programme.
8 The programme will then progress, with the director controlling the proceedings via the production script and with the help of the production crew.
9 At the end of transmission the director will announce 'Cut' and thank the floor manager and production team.
10 The floor manager will then 'stand down' the studio and thank the director, floor crew and presenters.

Note that the studio floor is the domain of the floor manager and the control room the domain of the director. It is normal practice for each to ask permission of the other to enter the respective areas.

Whilst there are variations on the above practice it is useful for the trainee broadcaster to understand and appreciate the accepted and standard procedures of studio production, which will give them good underpinning knowledge if they aspire to newsreading or presenting on television.

Standard shots used in television reporting and production

Figure 8.9 Medium long shot (MLS)

Figure 8.10 Knee shot (KS)

Figure 8.11 Mid shot (MS)

Figure 8.12 Medium close up (MCU)

Figure 8.13 Close up (CU)

Figure 8.14 Big close up (BCU)

Suggested activities

1 Book out a camcorder and tripod and, in a team of two, carry out the following basic camera techniques:

   a check that all the equipment is working and is safe to use
   b set up the camera on tripod
   c familiarize yourself with the zoom facility on the camera and the use of panning, elevating and tilting on the tripod. The in-built camera microphone will be active on recording so announce the name of each shot as you record. Ask your companion to stand against a suitable background and compose and record the following shots commonly used in television reporting and production:

   MLS – medium long shot
   KS   – knee shot
   MS   – mid shot
   MCU – medium close up
   CU   – close up
   BCU – big close up.

   Look at the previous section in this chapter to help you with the composition. Reverse roles and carry out the same exercise. Back at base play back the recording to your tutor and evaluate the results.
2 As a crew of three plan and record vox pops on location. The three roles are interviewer, camera person and production assistant, so allocate roles according to expertise. You can rotate these roles on location. Choose a topical issue and research background information on the subject. Decide on the same one or two questions you will ask people. Check all equipment is functional and safe and record 5 minutes of vox pops. Back at base make an edit decision list and edit the rushes down to 3 minutes. Evaluate the final product in terms of content, suitability for purpose and technical quality (audio as well as visuals).
3 Watch an interview on television by an established personality such as David Frost or Michael Parkinson. Make notes during the transmission and write a descriptive analysis of the content, the interview techniques used, the reaction of the interviewee, the news values and the overall style of the piece. Discuss your opinions with other members of the group and your tutor and establish guidelines for good professional practice when interviewing on television.
4 You are asked to interview the college principal or training manager about their views regarding the value of media studies courses in educational establishments. Again, as a crew of three and referring to the guidelines in this chapter, set up and record a set piece interview on location. The final edited interview should be 5 minutes' duration.

5   This exercise gives you the opportunity to face the camera. You are asked to write a 1-minute/1.30 second piece (about 180–270 words) and present it live to camera. The choice of topic is entirely yours and may be a poem, a polemic, a recollection, news bulletin, etc. You will need to work with a camera person and inform them of the shot composition you desire. You may present from a script or use an auto-cue facility. If you have both then make two recordings using both methods. You can then compare your performance on each.

6   Decide on a subject for a 1.30-minute topical television report. Research the topic and decide on images for the report. Using a still camera take the required photographs to illustrate the story. Once the pictures are ready select the most suitable ones and write a commentary to accompany the pictures. If a studio is available present the report to camera inserting the pictures at the relevant times.

7   As a group of three plan and produce a 3-minute topical package for inclusion in a campus magazine programme (see later). Decide on a topic that will complement the style of the magazine programme. Refer to the guidelines in this chapter to help you plan and produce the item. Ultimately the package must include:

● segments from at least two interviews
● vox pops
● a piece to camera
● 'wallpaper' footage.

As a group you must also produce the following written support documentation:

● a treatment
● evidence of research
● a location report and risk assessment
● a shooting schedule
● a shot list and written commentary
● a cue sheet with 'intro' and 'outro' for the studio presenter.

8   Watch a recent national television news programme and a regional news programme. Compare and contrast them in terms of:

● content
● news values
● structure
● presentation
● editorial control
● audience expectations
● technical aspects.

9 As a group plan and produce a 15–20 minute news magazine programme. Decide
   on the style and content of the programme by group negotiation. It is sensible to
   include the topical reports as mentioned in activity 7. You will be expected as a
   group to:

   ● agree a design brief and write a treatment for the magazine
   ● research, select and plan the programme content
   ● draw up a production schedule
   ● write a script and running order
   ● produce a basic studio layout
   ● present and produce the programme
   ● evaluate the success of the programme in terms of content, style, suitability for
     purpose, presentation and production, and technical aspects.

Sources and resources

Alkin, G. (1997) *Sound Recording and Reproduction* (3rd edition). Oxford: Focal
   Press.
Alkin, G. (1989) *Sound Techniques for Video and TV.* Oxford: Focal Press.
BBC (1996) *Producers' Guidelines.* London: BBC Publications.
Boyd, A. (2001) *Broadcast Journalism – techniques of radio and television news*
   (5th edition). Oxford: Focal Press.
Croton, G. (1986) *From Script to Screen.* London: BBC Television Training
   Manuals.
Fairweather, R. (1998) *Basic Studio Directing.* Oxford: Focal Press.
Grant, T. (2001) *Audio for Single Camera Operation.* Oxford: Focal Press.
Lyver, D. (2001) *Basics of the Video Production Diary.* Oxford: Focal Press.
Lyver, D. and Swainson, G. (1999) *Basics of Video Production* (2nd edition).
   Oxford: Focal Press.
Millerson, G. (1992) *Video Production Handbook.* Oxford: Focal Press.
Millerson, G. (1994) *Effective TV Production* (3rd edition). Oxford: Focal Press.
Millerson, G. (1994) *Video Camera Techniques* (2nd edition). Oxford: Focal
   Press.
Musburger, R.B. (1998) *Single Camera Video Production* (2nd edition). Oxford:
   Focal Press.
Ward, P. (2000) *TV Technical Operations. An introduction.* Oxford: Focal Press.
White, T. (2001) *Broadcast News Writing, Reporting and Producing.* Oxford: Focal
   Press.
Yorke, I. (1997) *Basic TV Reporting* (2nd edition). Oxford: Focal Press.
Yorke, I., ed., Alexander, R. (2000) *Television News* (4th edition). Oxford: Focal
   Press.

9 Freelance journalism

What is a freelance?

Freelance journalists are those who do not have staff jobs and therefore do not receive any regular income from a single employer.

It is impossible to obtain accurate figures for the numbers of journalists operating as freelances. Many belong to the main trade union, the National Union of Journalists (NUJ), who state they have over 6000 members who pay the freelance rate of contributions, but it must be assumed there are many more who do not belong to the union.

Freelance journalists can probably be divided into three broad categories:

1 The 'jack of all trades' freelance: the archetypal freelance who will 'go anywhere, report and do anything', often operating across several media but probably specializing in one.

2 The production shift worker: often working on a long-term basis in sub editing, reporting or producer shifts, or for print and publishing duties such as copy editing. May work mainly for only one or two employers – but this can cause problems with the Inland Revenue (see below).
3 The part-time freelance. Either has a main job and does a few commissions/ assignments to earn some extra money, or to 'keep their hand in', or both. Often specializing either in subject, geographic area (close to home) or media outlets, e.g., specialist magazines or other publications.

It therefore follows that the reasons, motivations and general attitudes of freelances vary enormously – as do their levels of skill and flair for the job. Of course there are enormous differences amongst staff journalists too, but there are other important differences between these two broad groups of journalists. The Inland Revenue – who collect income tax – together with their colleagues in National Insurance, treat those who will receive income from staff positions differently from those who are self-employed. There are some tax advantages to being on what is known as Schedule D – the self-employed category – as such people are able to offset some of the expenses incurred in their work against their income tax liability. This is because an employee normally use their employer's facilities and services in the course of their job – telephones, electricity, postage, etc. – whereas the self-employed have to fund these expenses from their own pocket. The tax changes brought about by self-assessment mean that some of these advantages have been eroded: tax now has to be paid within the following tax year. The Inland Revenue has also tightened up its definition of what constitutes a 'freelance' for tax purposes: for example if you are regularly doing shift work for the same employer you will not be treated under the 'Schedule D' regulations. The advantage is that due to recent changes in employment law, even if your work is irregular you will probably be entitled to paid holidays and sick leave. The tax situation is indeed a complex one and readers are advised to seek professional advice. It is worth 'shopping around' to find the most competitive fees' scale and to ask other journalists which firms they use. Fees charged will, of course, vary greatly depending on the complexity of your affairs – and how much you have done to help by keeping proper records of income, outgoings, receipts, bank statements, etc., but an annual fee in the region of £300–500 seems to be quite common. You should also seek (free) advice from the Inland Revenue who can be surprisingly helpful!

The freelance way of operating is more common in some types of journalism. It tends to suit the type of journalism that can be completed in full by one person – such as features – than, for example, TV reporting, which generally requires a crew of several people, although there are a number of freelance camera operators who sometimes work with a reporter. Others provide 'raw footage', with the accompanying report/commentary added at the main studios. Overall, there seem to be relatively few freelances operating as 'hard news' reporters, except in agencies that cover specific types of reporting, notably law courts. It is not cost effective for newspapers to 'staff' cases that may last for several weeks, so a specialist journalist or agency will provide copy for a number of outlets on a 'retainer' or piece or lineage basis. Photographers probably form the single biggest group of freelances and many staff photographers earn additional money for freelance work. Magazines provide wide scope for freelance contributions for both copy and photos. Radio work – particularly at the national level – also offers scope for features or packages.

Getting your first job in journalism is often the most difficult and, although the number of journalistic outlets has grown massively in the last couple of decades, journalism still tends to be quite a closed and incestuous world: journalists are often hired because the editor or manager has known them in a previous organization or they've been recommended by a mutual acquaintance.

For many aspiring journalists, then, the main motivation in setting up as a freelance is to gain credibility through having work broadcast or published and, most vitally of all, making those contacts in the hope that when a staff job does come along they will be in with a fighting chance. For many others, though, working in an individual capacity as a freelance – what is known as a sole trader – has some benefits way beyond the 'breaking in' level.

Our 'expert panel'

The variety of backgrounds, experiences and work of the members of our 'panel' illustrate the wide spectrum encompassed by freelance journalism. Between them our panel members have operated successfully in local, regional and national newspapers, magazines and broadcasting, and online journalism. Despite their varied backgrounds there is a great similarity in their advice – based on hard experience.

Sandy Felton: an award-winning trainer of journalists, Sandy is Head of Journalism at Liverpool Community College. She broke into freelance journalism 'by accident'. She was working as a secretary with the Lancashire Constabulary when the Chief Superintendent asked her to do an article about the history of the police station for the *Police* magazine. This encouraged her to submit pieces on local history for the local newspaper. In addition to her teaching Sandy continues to work for a variety of publications.

Mike Hally: has a degree in engineering and was an aircraft engineer for 17 years. Mike became politically active in the 1980s, realized his work was incompatible with his beliefs, and started doing press work for various voluntary groups and local authorities. He went back to college for a year to train as a journalist and did an Open University degree. He set his sights on radio freelancing and began getting shifts in local radio, which eventually led to reporting and production work for BBC network radio. He is also a professional motor sports photographer. Examples of his work and other items can be seen on his web site (http://www.mike-hally.com).

Martin Kelner: trained as a newspaper journalist through the National Council for the Training of Journalists (NCTJ) year-long pre-entry scheme, then as an indentured trainee on a local newspaper. His first radio work was through features for the Central Office of Information's (COI) radio division. This led to jobs in local radio newsrooms and thence to general radio presentation on both BBC and commercial stations, where his quirky 'off the wall' style became noticed by BBC network bosses. For several years Martin was a Radio 2 broadcaster, both 'filling in' for regular presenters and with his own Saturday afternoon slot. At the same time he developed work as a columnist and feature writer on a wide variety of topics and interests for several national newspapers. His current regular work includes *The Guardian's* back page sports column *Screen Break* and a daily phone-in show on BBC Radio Leeds. His journalistic and radio work can be 'sampled' through his web site (http://www.martinkelner.com).

Penny Kiley: her love of theatre and music (in the punk era!) inspired Penny to offer reviews and other pieces to both regional and national publications including *Melody Maker*, *Smash Hits* and *Plays and Players*. Penny gained extensive experience covering the arts for the *Liverpool Daily Post* as well as Public Relations' work for arts' organizations. Most of her work is now as a copy editor and she is publisher/editor of an online listings magazine (http://www.pool-of-life.co.uk). Her other website is (http://www.dakin-kiley.co.uk).

Is it for me?

The world of the freelance journalist is certainly not one for the faint-hearted. Although many journalists, as with other employees, may moan about their boss, their pay and the tasks they are required to do, they can at least rely on a pay-cheque at the end of the month and at least some paid holiday, along with paid and unpaid maternity and paternity leave (as appropriate!). Such 'perks' are not available to the freelance journalist. Whilst some of the minimum daily rates for freelances (see below) may seem quite reasonable when compared with the *pro rata* pay that a staffer earns, it must be remembered that employees actually work for well under two-thirds of the days of the year. They are still paid for weekends, annual and public holidays – effectively earning money for doing nothing. 'Staffers' can sit at home with their families at Christmas and other times, safe in the knowledge that their monthly salaries will still be paid into their bank accounts; the mortgage and other bills will be paid, as they will when the employee is sick. Furthermore, their employers will be paying into their pension funds, so maybe the staffer can retire when still relatively young, and write that novel (journalists are almost invariably planning to write a novel!).

Freelance journalists have none of these benefits and certainties. If they don't work they don't get paid – it's as simple as that. So freelances have to start, and pay into, their own sickness and pension schemes and organize their own tax and National Insurance payments. Nobody else is responsible for any aspect of their lives. Freelance journalists are hired guns and only receive payment for what they produce. Although it is true they are not forced to work for editors or other managers whom they do not like and may even despise, or to take on work they don't fancy, equally, and much more pertinently, no editor or manager is obliged to provide them with work.

On the positive side, many find that living on their wits, often never knowing where they might be or what they might be doing a few days ahead, is stimulating and energizing. Those who resist routine and clock-watching may find the freelance style of living highly conducive to their temperament. Many enjoy the fact that they are not tied down to one job – and one boss! Those who are 'natural' freelances – or freelances by choice – tend to be the sort who abhor routine; who like the variety and challenge that freelance work often brings; and the excitement of not knowing what their next job will be, where it will take them, who they will meet and what they will have to do.

Mike Hally says the lack of routine and no one day being the same as the next, was one of the main reasons he wanted to be a freelance:

> Part of the thing that attracted me to freelancing was that it's not that ordered. Most people don't do a 9 to 5 Monday to Friday week. I wanted to be able to pick and choose what work I did.

The unpredictable nature of freelance life might seem to work against those who have responsibilities and who need to be in certain places at the same time each day – to meet children from school, for example. But, paradoxically, Sandy Felton says freelancing can fit in with these domestic routines far better than staff jobs:

> Freelancing is very attractive to people with child-caring responsibilities who can't necessarily work from an office away from home. With the Internet freelances have virtually everything they need away from home and apart from having to go out and interview people they don't really need to leave the house.

You probably need to be even more of an extrovert if you are a freelance than if you are staff because you can't rely on contacts and invitations that will come your way as a staffer in a newsroom. Becoming a freelance requires more confidence and *chutzpah* than needed by the staffer and, as many people are freelances at the beginning of their careers – when confidence and experience is likely to be at their lowest – this can be a problem. Furthermore, confidence is not something that can be taught; it tends to come with experience and general maturity. Penny Kiley reckons that you need to be something of an extrovert to survive and thrive in reporters' jobs – and be prepared to make the most of every opportunity. She doesn't think she is a 'natural' at this and she admits that when she started it was a leap into the unknown: she didn't know how to go about 'networking':

> At the time I didn't really have a clue. I wasn't business-like at all. I didn't even have business cards. In the 1980s I went on a women's self-development course. I paid for myself and that taught me all kinds of useful things like how to present yourself, how to network. All those sorts of things that unless somebody tells you, you just don't know.
>
> You have to be a bit of an extrovert. You have to go out and meet people you don't know all the time and sell yourself and that's not always easy.

However, some freelances reckon that many of the most successful journalists are naturally introverts – somehow, though, they manage to overcome their shyness and adopt a more confident, outgoing personality when 'on the job'.

Getting started

Let's assume you've decided that freelancing is your best – or preferred – option, at least for the time being.

The first task is make a personal inventory. What skills do you have? What do you need to brush up on?

Those offering work will expect you to come with a full 'kit of parts'. If they have a training budget it will almost certainly be spent on staff development: they expect *you* to come fully trained and competent. Obviously your requirements will depend on the sort of work you intend to pitch for – and in which medium. As a bare minimum, though, you'll need some knowledge of media law (see Chapter 13). Editors are not likely to let you loose on any assignment unless they feel confident that your work won't result in a lawsuit or court appearance. Martin Kelner says that even in his radio presentation jobs – which by only a liberal interpretation could be described as 'journalism' – he has been very grateful for his training in the law:

> It's very important. At least when someone's been charged you don't say: 'oh look, there's the murderer!'. These days you might be wanting to do a variety of different shows so the journalistic background is very useful. Learning the mechanics of writing is also very useful, such as how to write intros.

There are a wide variety of options here, from full-time courses, including intensive short courses, to part-time study.

One skill that anyone interested in magazine journalism should consider is photography. Sandy Felton says that nearly all magazines expect freelances to include photos with their copy. For those returning to journalism, perhaps after a gap to raise a family, the NUJ and others run 'refresher' courses. Certainly anyone who has been 'out' for a few years will need to acquire the IT, digital editing or Desk Top Publishing skills used in today's newsrooms. This leads us on to the question of equipment needs.

What equipment do I need to set up?

So what equipment and facilities does the aspiring freelance journalist need to get going? Our team of freelances suggest the following as a minimum:

- a dedicated room that can be called an 'office',[1] including:
- a telephone and answering service/machine (can be linked to computer via a software package)
- a PC (Apple Mac preferred for print journalist) with as much RAM and hard disk space as can be afforded – especially if using multimedia software packages
- an Internet and e-mail account/address – preferably with an Internet service provider (ISP) offering unlimited 24-hour access
- a printer
- some stationery and business cards (can be produced on the PC/Mac and printer!)
- basic reference books – including a dictionary!
- subscription to key industry magazines such as the *Press Gazette* and *Writers' News*
- plus: access to a car (and have a driving licence!)

For the magazine freelance:

- a good camera – ideally both a 'traditional' and digital model
- industry standard publishing software.

For the broadcast (radio) freelance, they also suggest:

- a Mini Disc recorder with a broadcast-quality (mono) microphone
- digital editing software (computer must have a good sound card)
- ISDN line for contributions recorded or 'live' from home, together with appropriate mixer, etc.

[1] Although there can be implications in this for liability to business rates, capital gains tax, etc., if part of the house is regarded as being used exclusively for business purposes – it may be better to keep some trappings of domestic life.

In addition to the outlay for these major items you will inevitably have some general expenses. As mentioned at the beginning of the chapter, expenses that have genuinely been incurred wholly, necessarily and exclusively for your work are tax deductible. In other cases, for example telephone and car usage that may be partly for private and/or domestic use, you should claim only the percentage that has been for your work.

The situation is complicated by the fact that everyday items such as stationery, postage, phone calls, etc., are claimed as an annual cost that clearly may vary, but the tax allowance for capital items, such as computers are spread over several years. Naturally, every freelance's expenditure is going to be different, but here is an example of tax-reclaimable outgoings:

- car (claims 50 per cent usage) – £400–800
- travel (train tickets, etc.) – £150–300
- phone/Internet (claim 90 per cent of usage) – £300–500
- stationery and postage – £50–150
- newspapers, magazines, etc. – £200
- NUJ subs – £140.

Unfortunately you have to 'speculate to accumulate' – inevitably you will be spending money on setting yourself up before you start to earn anything. But try not to ensure the gap between one and the other isn't too long! Of course the tax benefits of freelancing are only of use if they can actually be offset against some earnings! The best way to start to do this is to decide where your strengths are.

What do I know about?

Most freelances start by offering material on topics on which they have special knowledge and interest. So, make a list – in what areas do you have contacts, information? Then write down all the publications and broadcasts that cover the topics you've identified as your 'specialist subjects' – the *Guardian Media Guide* lists every known outlet, along with addresses, phone numbers, etc. Then, get to know those publications, etc., inside out. Take a magazine: what is the intended audience? (A good tip is to look at the advertisements; advertisers do not waste money – they know the audience/readership.) How long are the articles? What is the style? How do they use interviews/direct quotes? Many magazines produce guidelines for freelances. Make sure you get a copy – and stick to it when pitching for work. Similarly for broadcasting: know the programmes inside out. Mike Hally says this is vital – editors are rightly contemptuous of those who approach them who do not seem to have heard the programme (some even admit they haven't!).

> They really need to be analytical about it. I am not good at that. I have to sit down with a pen and paper and force myself to analyse it. There are

simple things to look out for, for example in the *Today* programme they will never have the same person on two successive clips. You really need to be aware of that sort of thing.

How do I get the first 'job'?

This is probably the hardest one of all. It's the old story: you can't get work until you're experienced and have credibility – but how do you get that experience? You can't even join the NUJ until you've got proof that you have some earnings from journalism – although you can have a student membership if you are on an NUJ-approved course. (As mentioned above The NUJ runs a number of excellent short courses and NUJ branch meetings – called chapels – are very good places in which to make contact with other journalists.)

It's vital to make the contacts with the key person who makes the decisions at your chosen outlet. Usually this will be the news or features editor.

Penny Kiley says the aspiring freelance arts journalist should try to gain tickets to press/preview nights:

> There'll usually be about half a dozen journalists covering the show and in the interval you're huddled in a little room with a glass of wine and the press officer. Obviously then you chat about the show. I recognized a couple of the journalists from the photographs they had at the top of their columns so I just went up and introduced myself. It can be difficult but people will usually meet you half way.

Most freelances have this sort of account of how they 'got in'. Almost invariably they will then say: 'and one thing led to another'.

Getting the ideas

Ideas are the gold currency in journalism. Editors – especially those who have been working for the same outlet for some time – are often rather jaded souls who are tired of commissioning the same sorts of pieces. So if you can come up with something original you may be in luck. There are many different ways of doing this but it's a good idea to have a notebook and cuttings file where you put ideas and clippings of possible stories – especially those that appear in your local newspaper – in which national magazines and radio programmes may be interested. Most staff journalists on local newspapers are too busy to offer these stories themselves. It's a good idea to keep up this discipline of noting/filing even when the work starts coming in. There are almost certainly going to be peaks and troughs of work – or what Martin Kelner calls 'feast and famine': it's the slack periods when your notebook and cuttings file could be a life saver, as Mike Hally explains:

> The initial ideas came from things that I came across in local radio, which I knew hadn't been covered nationally and which I knew were of interest to programmes like *You and Yours*. You need to look for things that will match particular programmes that you can then target and it's almost certainly a complete waste of time to look at national papers because the programme teams will already be doing that.

The next task is certainly to approach the editorial staff of that output with some concrete suggestions. For broadcasting, Mike Hally says the secret is to build up a relationship with the producers, editors and their teams to find out what programmes and programme strands are coming up over the next few months and then start to pitch ideas at them. All our panellists agreed that when doing this it is very important not to overstate what you can produce. If you gain the commission or assignment on the basis of 'crossed fingers' that you have access to sources and contacts that you then can't deliver, you will rightly be treated as an idiot and be 'blacklisted'. Editors do not appreciate having their precious time wasted by 'dreamers'. To use the vernacular: *get real*.

Ideas for stories, features or programmes are called treatments and many 'how to' books describe how they should be laid out in some detail. The experience and advice of our panellists, though, suggest that this is not only unnecessary but may be harmful. Sandy Felton says:

> Always ring up and find out who the news editor or the features editor is and say you've got this idea – are they interested? I never do a written treatment because if you do a treatment someone else takes the idea up and uses it – unless it's people I've dealt with before, but even then it's a verbal discussion. You do need to know what each outlet wants . . . the style, length and so on. Occasionally they will take something 'off the wall'. It's 50/50.You should be finding something you know is unusual, which a magazine or a number of magazines will be ready to take up and they may not be the original magazines you thought of.

Mike Hally agrees that treatments can be too detailed:

> It can almost be very counter-productive because it's very difficult to make that look convincing unless you know the programme backwards. It's better to ring up the programme or e-mail or fax a simple crisp paragraph saying what the idea is and, if there's one or two key people that you know can contribute, say who they are and that you know they're available but, really, keep it simple. Generally these things will be commissioned on the basis of that paragraph or that phone call.

They want my piece(s), now what?

You have crossed a very important hurdle when you have had your first 'bite' – somebody actually wants your work: well done! Unfortunately your problems have only just begun. Apart from the task of producing what you've promised, you are now in the delicate (and, to many, embarrassing) position of having to agree on a price. Or should you perhaps offer the first piece for free? After all, you're trying to get established and the person commissioning you is taking something of a gamble – a leap of faith and trust. Sandy Felton strongly cautions against this 'working for free' approach:

> You can't go down that road. You have to make it clear that you are in business and you want paying. It does depend on the publication as to how much they pay and it's no good arguing with them. Sometimes when you know them well enough they'll negotiate. But they'll have these rates and they'll stick with them. If they don't know you and you say: 'Ok, now I want £190, not £150', they'll say: 'right, t'ra then!' and you lose the job. It's all very well the NUJ and others saying don't undercut but there's a fine line between earning money for a commission and not getting the commission at all. Where money's concerned a lot of people's principles will go out the window because they've got to eat.

Penny Kiley recommends taking a similarly pragmatic approach:

> You're lucky to get the going rate when you start – that's really just a guide. Basically you have to work out how much you need to live on. That's one part of the equation. You've got to balance these out.

Naturally, the NUJ is firmly against anyone working for nothing or even doing it for less than the 'going rate'. Understandably they argue that to do so undermines all journalists and plays into the hands of greedy or unscrupulous employers. Certainly if (no, *when!*) you are a well-established freelance journalist you will not appreciate others undercutting you.

The NUJ gives the minimum rate over a wide range of work and media sectors in its annual *freelance fees guide*. The figures given in Figure 9.1 have been taken from the 2001–02 guide. This summary is the responsibility of the author and the reader should check the latest information from the web site(s) – details at the end of the chapter.

The NUJ divides different media sectors into different categories, usually according to circulation/audience size. Magazine rates vary enormously, according to their advertising rates/profitability and/or type of target audience.

Note that the rates in Figure 9.1 are illustrative minimum rates and they vary considerably across titles even in the same sector. The subbing rates also vary

	Features/reports (Per 1000 words)	Subbing (Per 1000 words)
Group A – large circulation 'glossy' consumer magazines, e.g., *Marie Clare, GQ* or prestigious specialist publications, e.g., *Management Today, New Scientist*	£450	£120
Group B – consumer magazines with smaller circulations, e.g., *Time Out, The Face* or less prestigious specialist magazines, e.g., *Money Wise*	£325	£125
Group C – large circulation trade magazines and some specialist titles, e.g., *Accountancy Age, Personal Computer World*	£250	£145
Group D – small circulation trade and specialist magazines, e.g., *Nursing Times*	£180	£120

Source: NUJ.

Figure 9.1

enormously and only a rough guide is presented here. The NUJ says the daily rate for reporters should be £130.

Note, though, that sub-editing rates in the different categories seem in almost inverse proportion to those for writing.

The table in Figure 9.2 gives some examples of other recommended minimum rates in other media.

The NUJ also has some very pertinent advice about the precautions and safeguards to be taken when negotiating with editors, etc.:

1 Make sure you know the name of the person to whom you are agreeing to provide material, their position in the organization and whether they have the authority to commission you.
2 Establish the details: how many words, pictures, etc., you are agreeing to provide, the deadline and any other terms, especially *when you will get paid – and how* (author's italics). You also need to agree on additional payment for expenses and a kill fee – if, having commissioned the work, the publisher decided in the end not to use it.
3 If (time permitting) the client follows up the commission with a written contract or commissioning letter, check that everything corresponds with your understanding of what was verbally agreed. If time does not permit this, follow up your verbal agreement with a written confirmation, posted, faxed or e-mailed (with a print out of the e-mail sent by post) to the client. (NUJ, 2001a: 3, 5, 7.)

	News reporting	Features	Subbing	Production	Photography
National newspapers	£230 per 1000 words	£220–500 per 1000 words for broadsheets; tabloids may pay twice as much, but features will be shorter!	£125–270 (depending on length of shift)		£150 per day; £170 per commission
Regional newspapers	£2–3 per line (4 words) for first 10 lines; 20–30 pence per subsequent line		£100		£50 day rate – 'so low the NUJ cannot recommend that such work is undertaken'
National radio	£185 (12 hour shift)	£206 for edited package up to 7 minutes in news programmes; £178.50 for non-news		£140–150	
Local radio	From £65 per day for 'novices' to £90 for 'experienced'			As 'news reporting'	
National TV	£185 per day			£150 per day	
Regional TV	£120 per day			As 'news reporting'	
Online	£140 per day/£230 per 1000 words	As 'news reporting'	£140 per day		

Source: NUJ.

Figure 9.2

Do not be worried that this makes you look 'officious' or 'picky' – if you have a professional and thorough approach from the very start you have a better chance of being treated in a professional way and not being 'messed around'.

Even if you do everything 'by the letter' there is still a good chance that you will be left waiting for the cheque or money transfer – and you've still got to live in the meantime! So, how long should you expect to wait? The NUJ says that 'ideally' payment should be within 30 days of invoicing. Don't forget it is usually up to you to invoice them. Do not expect a payment to be triggered automatically – often called self-billing – unless this is promised, and noted, in your original agreement. Often though you will not be paid until your work is published which, in the case of magazines, may be some months after being commissioned. When this happens the NUJ recommends you try to secure payment *within a month* of the delivery of the work.

Despite being thoroughly professional in your negotiations and taking all the precautions, you may still be 'mucked about'. If you are relying on payment from the client so that you can pay your bills – and generally to live! – it can be a serious matter. If this happens you should telephone the person who com-missioned your work and follow up with a letter. If payment is still not forthcoming – or you feel you are being given the 'brush off' – you need help! Nearly all freelances have horror stories about very late or non-payment. The advice of our expert panel is unanimous: use the NUJ to take it up. They pursue cases, if necessary through the courts, as part of their service to members. Another excellent reason for joining the union as soon as possible! Some freelances have successfully pursued claims in the county court without legal representation (the county court office provides a number of excellent advice leaflets) but others have had a less satisfactory experience. Sandy Felton has a salutary tale on this – but she is also resigned to the fact that sometimes you will be 'done':

> Once I was owed £1000. I took him to the small claims court and got £25 out of him – it cost me £300 or £400 on top of that in solicitor's fees, so you will get bad debts and it's something you have to live with.

Even when you've agreed on the rate, there will still be an issue over what rights you will retain or have to give away. The section on 'Copyright' in Chapter 13 discusses the legal position on who owns what and for how long, but mainly from the perspective of the journalist using others' copyright material. Now, the boot is on the other foot, and you will almost certainly be required to give up your rights to benefit and exploit your own work. In recent years this has been particularly an issue over electronic use on the Internet/World Wide Web. Freelances will often be pressured to simply hand over all their rights to the organization that commissioned the work. The NUJ is blunt on the subject:

> Resist this. Many freelances, individually or in groups, have successfully done so. Retaining copyright is more than a principle – material may be sold on to other publications or electronic media for worthwhile fees (sometimes more than the original commission). (NUJ, 2001a: 8.)

In most cases the rates shown above are the recommended minimum and of course as you become established you may be able to negotiate a higher fee – and perhaps more lavish expenses. Some though are relatively inflexible – such as the BBC rates for features/packages and its day rates for reporting and production. These rates have been negotiated with the NUJ.

To someone starting out, who has spent perhaps several years in training or doing student or hospital/voluntary radio for nothing, the prospect of £170 for a feature seems like good money. But Mike Hally can vouch from experience that this fee is not exactly lavish when you consider that such a feature will take several days to produce: the research, interviewing/recording, scripting and editing. Mike reckons when you take all that into account it would be hard – even with regular commissions – to earn a decent living from such work alone:

> If you spend much more than a day and a half on that you start to lose out and yet really if you're just starting off you'll be lucky to do a Radio 4 feature in less than that. This is why people tend to find that they can't support themselves on features alone; either they've got a partner to support them or they're doing something else part-time.

Be humble, and gain solid experience

There may be several stages you need to fulfil before you're fit and ready to do your 'dream jobs'. Enthusiasm, persistence – and a bit of cheek – can do wonders in opening those first vital doors and gaining the first contacts. There can be little doubt that unless you are very, very lucky you will not be able to do your preferred work from the word 'go'. You'll have to do a lot of assignments that you don't particularly enjoy; that aren't fulfilling. Those hiring you are not concerned with your own fulfilment and life plan. They hire you because you've persuaded them that you can do them a job that needs doing and you're the best available person to do it. And you have to do it with a smile – even when the person in charge is a complete idiot. Martin Kelner has some blunt advice:

> You have to be extra nice as a freelance and make sure you don't burn any bridges. If you're asked to do anything which you think is beneath your dignity you do it. Even when you know it's horse s*!t and half the time you're going to be more clued up than the people asking you to do stuff. You never know when they're going to crop up in different positions.

> The humblest person asks you to do the most stupid thing, you do it and you do it with a smile because you never know where they're going to crop up again. You're a hired gun and you want to make sure you're hired again. Don't be 'cool'. You've got to be keen . . . almost embarrassingly keen and not be embarrassed to be keen. Just be a pair of hands whenever a pair of hands is needed. You've got to prostitute yourself really. It's sad but that's the way it is.

The importance of 'getting some in' (as the RAF used to say to its National Service recruits) cannot be overemphasized. In any case, you don't know whether you will like something or are good at it (usually the same thing) until you try. For example, you may fancy being a radio producer. But it's highly unlikely you'll be given work at this level straightaway. You'll probably need to establish your credibility as a reporter first. In any case, Mike Hally says that reporting skills are very useful when it comes to production work. But he recognizes that some of those attracted to more studio-based work may find reporting a painful experience:

> I strongly recommend freelances to spend their time reporting because it really helps, even if your aim is to be a producer it really helps to have done the reporting and understand that side of things. When a producer hasn't really done proper reporting work they don't always understand the possibilities and the problems in that story. For the reporting you certainly need to enjoy going out, interviewing people to get the story, including interviewing people in the street for the dreaded 'vox pops' and be willing to go to a great variety of people's homes and work-places. Some people realize early on they'd rather be office- or studio-based and concentrate on production.

The problems of success

It may seem like a long way off but with luck you'll soon be faced with more work than you can handle. For the freelance, saying 'no' is a risky business: the client may never come back to you again. On the other hand, everyone needs some time for rest and relaxation – to recharge the batteries and to get some outside stimulation, such as reading a book or going to the movies – which may in itself lead to more ideas for future projects. Sometimes a short break helps to put where you are and where you want to go next into perspective. And partners and children are entitled to some of your time! Martin Kelner admits that despite being well established in several areas he still finds it difficult to turn down work. The week in which he was interviewed for this book was particularly overflowing. By Wednesday he was worried he would 'run out of week'. This is what his list of jobs looked like:

- *Screen Break* column for Monday's *Guardian* (deadline Sunday afternoon)
- five radio phone-ins for BBC Radio Leeds
- *Radio Choice* preview for *Daily Mail* (150 words × 6)
- *Star Quest* column for Thursday's *Guardian*
- voice-over for *Close-Up North* documentary on BBC regional television
- record appearance in Leeds for *100 Greatest Sporting Moments* to be shown on BBC national television
- live appearance as 'guest pundit' on late-night *Fi Glover* programme on BBC Radio 5 Live (meant trip to and from London from his home base in Yorkshire, and overnight stay)
- phone interview on *talkSPORT* about Rugby League
- extra piece for *Guardian* on YTV Show *RL Raw* (1000 words).

You need to make sure you have enough time when you're mad busy working to line up the next project. Bear in mind that you may not see a penny of the fee for the work you've just been doing for several months – and you have to live in the meantime. Bills have to be paid, food has to be put on the table, petrol in the car. And the kids still grow out of their clothes even when you're not earning! So try and think two, three or four stages ahead. Make sure you devote some time each week to the boring but vital tasks of paper work: sending out invoices, checking up on payments (and chasing them if need be). And make sure you keep all those receipts for the taxman!

The dangers of complacency

It's easy to get into too comfortable a routine and be lulled into complacency. You have your regular clients; the work is reasonably well paid and not too anti-social. In fact, it's almost like having a proper job! Then: *crash*! Things change – sometimes literally overnight. The person who commissions you or offers you shifts leaves (resigns or is dismissed) and the new person – desperate to justify their appointment – decides you no longer 'fit': 'thank you' (if you're lucky), and 'goodbye'. The editorial policy/format changes and your skills/approach is no longer appropriate. Or the organization is taken over (and, almost inevitably, 'downsized') or simply goes bust. Or there is a downturn in revenue.

Freelances are the easiest people to get rid of because by definition the organization has no responsibilities towards you. Nearly all freelances have had these heart-stopping moments when they're told they are no longer needed: sometimes they aren't even told – the work just dries up. You are given no explanation – you aren't entitled to one and common courtesies are often not observed; phone calls don't get returned. You finally get the message.

So make sure you have a number of outlets for your work – and be flexible. It's often a case of adapt or die. Don't rely on one client. But the freelance who is multi-skilled and is adaptable is often in a better position than an employee who becomes redundant. Martin Kelner says the pluses are that when you lose one job others come along. When a new Controller took over, his Saturday programme on Radio 2 was cancelled and he was later 'given the boot' from his Jazz FM breakfast show in the northwest. In both cases: 'I didn't slit my throat because you can build things up again from a different base. The big advantage is you haven't got all your eggs in one basket'.

Where do I go from here?

As you gain in experience and increase your field of contacts lots of other doors open to you – provided you're prepared to give them a hefty kick! For example, once you become known for supplying features/packages to BBC network radio you can pitch for full programmes, a series of programmes, or programme strands, as an independent producer. This, however, is often a fraught and difficult process and only those already established have a realistic prospect of becoming acknowledged as an 'independent' and, even if you get that far, most

---

THE BBC COMMISSIONING PROCESS (factual radio programmes)

Twice a year, in the spring and autumn, there is a major commissioning round for the following year's programmes. The BBC issues a huge commissioning document giving in considerable detail how the overall schedule works and what is required for each programme slot. The process is administered by a Contract Commissioning Assistant.

Once you're on the approved list you've got a chance of getting the commissioning document. You then have a few weeks in which to get your ideas together in a specified format to match particular slots in the schedule and you're up against all the other people – there's probably ten times as many ideas as there are slots but, at the end of that, you hope to have won some commissions and go on to make some programmes.

They then give you a guide price and a tip here is that the guide price is a band, say between £6200 and £7400. Don't pitch at the minimum in the hope of getting the commission because they will choose on the idea and the treatment – put in for the maximum every time! Then if there's any reason why it could cost more, say for foreign travel, when it comes to putting in for the detailed budget put in an additional sum and a note to say why it is costing more than the guide price and almost invariably it will go through. A proposal is an idea plus the treatment. The Controller of Radio 4 has told us that one of the problems is getting proposals that are too detailed. She feels that the maximum needed for proposal plus treatment is two pages of A4.

Figure 9.3

of your ideas won't be taken up. Mike Hally says that the BBC doesn't like dealing with sole traders. It prefers to deal with small companies, at least one of whom is already established as a supplier of features to BBC networks (mostly Radios 4 and 5 Live). The trick is to get onto an approved list. Then you can pitch for work in the commissioning process. He explains how this works in Figure 9.3.

Top ten tips

Here, in summary, are the main do's and don'ts for the freelance journalist:

1 Be keen! Be ready to learn – and at first take *anything* (legal!) to get started and become established (and get your NUJ card).
2 Get (multi-) skilled – be flexible: make sure you have the full range of skills needed to do any work for which you think you might be suitable – and for things you don't fancy but may lead into interesting/profitable areas.
3 Get kitted out: you must invest in the essential equipment, software, etc., for your areas of work. In particular you must have reliable communications – phone, fax, e-mail and Internet access.
4 Don't oversell yourself or your proposals – if you let someone down you'll never be offered another job, so be realistic on content and deadlines.
5 (If at all possible) Get the going rate: don't undersell yourself – you may get one job but you'll be stuck on that rate *and* you'll be undercutting everyone else. But also be realistic.
6 Deliver! Again, if you let people down they won't give you another chance. Make sure the work is on time, as agreed.
7 Get organized: keep your paperwork up to date; keep all your receipts for your tax return (see 8). Keep your ideas files updated and make sure you've got the next job(s) set up for when the current one ends.
8 Get a good accountant/financial adviser. It's a false economy to try and DIY your tax and national insurance affairs. A good accountant will make sure you claim for everything possible and that your returns are completed correctly and on time – thus saving you from fines and even imprisonment! Pay into a pension and sickness/personal liability insurance schemes.
9 Don't rely on one client or get stuck in a rut. Spread your sources of work – and those providing it.
10 Keep your ear to the ground and your eye on the prize: spend time keeping up to date with the gossip on what's happening in the 'business'; who's up, who's down. Join the NUJ and attend chapel meetings – an excellent source of 'inside information' as well as providing mutual support with others in the same position. Keep pushing towards your ultimate goal(s).

Suggested activities

1 Make a list of the subject/specialist areas you think you know most about (and maybe have some contacts for; e.g., sport, fashion, pets.

2 Go to a major newsagents and make a list of all the magazines that seem to cover 'your' subject(s); if possible also use a reference book such as *The Guardian Media Guide* or *The Writer's Handbook*.

3 Study a selection of at least three articles in each of the magazines and make notes on their length, style, etc.

4 Try to find out whether they accept 'speculative' freelance contributions and if so, do they issue a contributors' guide/fact-sheet, etc.?

5 Listen to and study a magazine programme on BBC network radio, such as Radio 4's *You and Yours* and make notes about the length, style, etc., of pre-recorded features/packages (see Chapter 7).

6 Draw up a treatment for either: a) a magazine article from one of the publications identified after completing above, or b) a radio programme studied in 5.

7 Present your 'pitch' on the above to fellow students/trainees using both printed and verbal presentation techniques. Ask them to give you feedback on your presentation. Would they 'buy' it?

Sources and resources

Goldstruck, A. (2001) *The Freelance Journalism Page*. http://www.legends.org.za/arthur/journ.htm (accessed 30 September 2001).

Hall, C. (1999) *Writing Features and Interviews – how to build a career as a freelance journalist* (2nd edition). Oxford: How To Books.

Hold The Front Page (2001) *Regional UK journalism* http://www.holdthe-frontpage.co.uk/index.shtml (accessed 30 September 2001).

NUJ (2001a) *Freelance Fees Guide 2001–02*. London: NUJ. Also: http://www.gn.apc.org/media/feesguide/index.html (accessed 30 September 2001).

NUJ (2001b) *NUJ Freelance Directory*. http://www.freelancedirectory.org (accessed 30 September 2001).

NUJ (2001c) *NUJ Rate for the Job*. http://www.gn.apc.org/media/rates/index.html (accessed 30 September 2001).

NUJ (2001d) *London Freelance Branch*. http://www.gn.apc.org/media/lfb/index.html (accessed 30 September 2001).

Peak, S. (ed.) (2002) *The Guardian Media Guide 2003*. London: Atlantic Books.

Press Gazette. Published weekly. Croydon, Surrey: Quantum Business Media.

Rawlinson, A. (2001) *CAR park UK: Journalism Resources*. http://www.rawlinson. co.uk (accessed 30 September 2001).

Scott, K. (2001) *The Internet Writer's Handbook*. London: Allison & Busby.

Sutcliffe, P., Vaughan, J. and Macaskill, H. (eds) (2000) *Battling for Copyright – freelance journalists versus the media conglomerates*. London: NUJ.

Turner, B. (ed.) (2001) *The Writer's Handbook 2002*. Basingstoke: Pan.

Wells, G. (1999) *The Magazine Writer's Handbook*. London: Allison and Busby.

Writers' News. Published monthly. Leeds: Yorkshire Post Newspapers.

10 Health and safety

- Introduction
- Health and safety at work
- The main elements of Health and Safety Law
- A summary of additional regulations
- Health and Safety (Display Screen Equipment) Regulations 1992
- Risks when working with visual display units (VDUs)
- Reporting in hostile environments
- Reporting sports events
- Working as a freelance
- And finally . . .
- Suggested activities
- Sources and resources

Introduction

It is not feasible to address here all health and safety issues within print and broadcast industries with their wide diversity of products and personnel. Suffice to say that this chapter will concentrate on Health and Safety Law as a whole with specific sections related to the work of journalists and broadcasters. Primarily, personal safety at work involves common sense. In a newspaper or broadcasting newsroom general guidelines on house keeping should be followed such as keeping the work area tidy; regularly emptying waste bins; closing filing cabinet drawers; storing heavy objects at ground level; checking and maintaining electrical items; and keeping walkways and corridors clear of wires, cables, objects and spillages that cause slips, trips and falls at work, which account for one-third of all major injuries reported each year. The latter are also relevant in radio studio situations, either self-operated or crewed, with the additional requirements on safe use of equipment, heating, lighting and ventilation, and welfare of visitors. Television studios have similar but more complex applications in that audiences are often present and must be informed of emergency evacuation procedures, first aid arrangements, the use of hazards such as strobe lights, pyrotechnics and excessive noise. Cables must be secured and covered; gangways and steps must have adequate lighting, handrails and clear marking; seating, lighting, fittings and sets must be secure; exits must be clearly marked; ventilation must be controlled.

Recording on location involves additional issues such as time of day, weather, protective clothing, electrical safety, welfare of the public, permissions from police and other authorities, dangerous situations, safety of single camera crews, communications, etc. The use of lightweight cameras with minimal crew is the norm for gathering breaking news around the world and the risks are amplified in war zones. However, whatever the situation, the health, safety and welfare of employees at work is protected by law.

Health and safety at work

Health and Safety Regulations are a crucial element of most industries, none more so than media industries that embrace a diverse range of applications, delivery, locations, equipment, personnel and audience. The range of products is vast, including newspapers, magazines, electronic media, radio and television programmes – all, either in a full time or freelance capacity, employing numerous people, including journalists, presenters, producers, editors, technical and support staff, administrators, security and equipment suppliers. Similarly the different types of technology, which are constantly being updated, highlight the need for strict laws and guidelines regarding safety of employees and equipment in print, radio and television production.

Health and safety issues in media production are fairly specific in certain areas such as seeking permissions for filming and recording from appropriate authorities including police and owners of land, risk assessment for the public on location, precautions when undertaking studio recordings with a live audience, electrical safety, working with display screen equipment, rigging lights, working with animals in performance . . . the list is endless.

The main regulations for all industries are contained in the Health and Safety at Work Act 1974, which outlines the general duties that employers have towards employees and the public and that employees have individually and to others. The Act provides an overall framework, dealing with the majority of aspects of health and safety at work, for differing occupations and professions. However, the duties of employers and employees are qualified in the Act by inserting the phrase 'so far as is reasonably practical', which has in some instances allowed employers to contend that minor risks are not commensurate with the cost of implementing a particular safety measure. Indeed the degree of risk is often balanced against the financial implications and timescales by employers who are expected to look at the potential risks and adopt a sensible and pragmatic policy in dealing with them.

In order to further reinforce the responsibilities of employers the 1974 Act was amended by the Management of Health and Safety at Work Regulations 1992, which arose from the European Health and Safety 'Framework' Directive. Indeed, much of the UK health and safety laws are proposed by the European Commission, agreed by member states and then incorporated in domestic law. The regulations that became law in January 1993 include duties for employers and employees with an expansion of the rights of trades union safety representatives. These rights include:

- being consulted in good time by the employer on:
- any measure that substantially affects the health and safety of an employee
- the appointment of competent persons providing health and safety assistance to an employer
- the appointment of persons to oversee emergency procedures
- the planning and organization of health and safety training
- health and safety effects of new technology
- the provision of facilities and assistance that safety representatives might reasonably require to carry out their duties.

However, it is interesting to note that BECTU, the Broadcasting Entertainment Cinematographic and Theatres Union, submitted a paper in March 2000 on employment consultation and involvement in health and safety to the UK Health and Safety Commission (HSC), which expressed disappointment at the effectiveness of the role of trades union safety representatives and their acceptance by employers in some areas of the broadcast and entertainment industries.

The main elements of Health and Safety Law

The employer has a duty under law to ensure as far as is reasonably practicable the health, safety and welfare of all employees.

The employer must consult the employee or their safety representative on matters relating to health, safety and welfare of employees including:

- any changes in procedures, equipment, introduction of new technology that may affect the health and safety of the employee
- the planning of health and safety and appointment of competent people to interpret and deliver health and safety regulations
- information on possible risks arising in the work place.

In general an employer must

- ensure the workplace is safe without risks to the health of employees
- provide adequate welfare facilities
- ensure equipment and systems of work are safe

- ensure articles and substances are used, transported and stored safely and securely
- give employees information, training, instruction and supervision on health and safety issues.

In particular an employer must

- assess the risks for an employee's health and safety and make arrangements for implementing a policy for dealing with identifiable risks
- if there are *five or more* employees:
- record the significant findings of the risk assessment and arrangements for corrective measures issue and bring to the attention of employees a health and safety policy statement
- appoint a competent person to carry out health and safety duties and consult with the employee or their safety representative
- set up emergency procedures
- co-operate on health and safety with employers sharing the same work place
- ensure that the workplace satisfies health, safety and welfare requirements such as ventilation, temperature, lighting, sanitary, washing and resting facilities
- ensure that equipment is suitable for its intended use, is safe and is adequately maintained and used
- prevent or control exposure to substances that damage health and pose a danger from electrical equipment, noise, radiation and flammable and explosive materials
- avoid hazardous manual handling operations
- provide free protective clothing and equipment
- provide health surveillance as appropriate
- ensure that appropriate health and safety signs are displayed and maintained
- report injuries, diseases and dangerous occurrences to the relevant authorities within the company.

In particular an employee must

- take reasonable care for their own health and safety and that of others
- co-operate with the employer on health and safety matters
- use equipment provided by the employer in accordance with training instructions
- not interfere or misuse anything provided for their health, safety and welfare.

A summary of additional regulations

In addition to the Health and Safety at Work Act 1974 and the Management of Health and Safety at Work Regulations 1992 there are other regulations that apply to all areas of industry and some that apply only to specific industries where hazards are unique to that sector, e.g., chemicals, mining, nuclear installations. The following regulations apply in some form or another and to a lesser or greater extent in the print and broadcasting industries.

- *Workplace (Health, Safety and Welfare) Regulations 1992* covers basic issues such as ventilation, heating, lighting, workstations, seating and welfare facilities.
- *Provision and Use of Work Equipment Regulations (PUWER) 1992* requires that all equipment for use in the workplace is safe.
- *Health and Safety (First Aid) Regulations 1981* covers requirements for first aid.
- *Electricity at Work Regulations 1989* requires people who are responsible for electrical systems to ensure that they are maintained correctly and are safe to use.
- *Noise at Work Regulations 1989* requires employers to ensure that employees do not suffer hearing damage.
- *The Health and Safety Information for Employees Regulations 1989* requires employers to display and maintain posters on health and safety matters.
- *Manual Handling Operations Regulations 1992* covers the moving of objects by hand or bodily force.
- *Reporting of Injuries, Diseases and Dangerous Occurrences Regulations 1995 (RIDDOR)* requires employers to notify certain occupational diseases, injuries and dangerous events.
- *Health and Safety (Display Screen Equipment) Regulations 1992* sets out requirements for work with visual display units.

As previously mentioned, other regulations, particularly as regards hazardous substances, relate to specific industrial sectors. However, as regards print and broadcasting industries specific areas are cause for concern, including working with visual display equipment, reporting in hostile environments, broadcasting sports events and working as a freelance.

Health and Safety (Display Screen Equipment) Regulations 1992

The regulations implement a European Directive on working with display screens and require employers to minimize some of the risks outlined by ensuring that workplaces and work stations are well designed as a matter of course. The regulations affect all employed and self-employed people who daily use display screens as part of their normal job, be it by reading, inputting copy, surfing the Internet, recording and editing images and sound etc. Briefly employers must:

- analyse the environment, hardware and individual factors of people using the equipment and, after consultation with the users and safety representatives where risks are identified, take appropriate steps to reduce the risk
- ensure workstations meet minimum requirements laid down upon instalment (the term workstation means more than just a desk and can include the screen, keyboard, printer, disc drive, document holder, chair, work surface, lighting, temperature, noise and space around the display equipment)
- plan work so there are breaks or changes in activity (often impossible in a working newsroom or television studio)
- arrange eye and eyesight tests if requested by the employee and provide spectacles if special ones are needed
- provide information and health and safety training.

Note that self-employed workers (freelances) who 'habitually use display screen equipment for a significant part of their normal work' are covered by the regulations when they use a client's workstation and workers at home are covered if required by their employer to use a workstation at home.

Risks when working with visual display units (VDUs)

The use of VDUs and other display equipment in print and broadcast industries has been linked to a number of health problems, yet there is conflicting evidence on the effects of using such equipment for long periods within the working week. Possible health risks are cited as dizziness, nausea, headaches, skin diseases, RSI (Repetitive Strain Injury) or more precisely WRULDS (Work Related Upper Limb Disorders), fatigue, eye strain, stress, depression, epileptic seizures, miscarriages, Alzheimer's disease, etc. Many unions in the UK, including the NUJ and BECTU and the American Newspaper Guild, are concerned at the possible risks when using such equipment. Indeed a report in the *Daily Mail* on 14 July 1999 entitled 'Do computers make you ill?' questioned the safety of visual display units. A response statement on 16 July 1999 from The National Radiological Protection Board (NRPB), the statutory body on all radiation matters in the UK, concluded that exposure to radiation from the use of VDUs caused no significant adverse health effects. In particular it concluded that VDUs did not influence the formation of cataracts and did not appear to cause skin diseases or cause harm to a developing foetus. This reply was based on the findings of the Board's Advisory Group on Non-ionizing Radiation (AGNIR), which published its report in 1994. It concluded that most health and safety problems arising from the use of visual display systems are related to incorrect posture, working practices and environmental conditions. With this in mind the following advice is recommended when using such equipment:

- adjust your chair and VDU to obtain the most comfortable position for work, which in most cases is having your eye line the same height as the top of the monitor and also trying to keep your arms horizontal
- make sure that your feet are flat on the floor or use a footrest
- adjust the backrest of the chair so that you are sitting upright with plenty of back support
- ensure that there is enough work space for the monitor, keyboard and document holder and try different layouts to see which are more comfortable for you
- move any obstacles such as boxes or equipment from underneath the desk to allow freedom of movement of feet and legs
- avoid sitting in the same position for long periods by changing your posture or taking short breaks away from the screen. The NUJ recommends breaks of 15 minutes in every 75 minutes of continuous work but, if there are no natural breaks in the job as often occurs in a busy newsroom, the employer should plan formal rest breaks. Suffice to say that short breaks of, say, 5 minutes are preferable to fewer longer ones
- arrange the desk and screen so that bright lights are not reflected on the screen either from directly facing windows or fluorescent lights
- make sure that the image on the screen is stable and flicker free and that the characters are sharply focused for easy readability
- make sure that the screen is clean and free from finger marks, dust and grime
- adjust the brightness and contrast controls on the screen to suit differing lighting conditions
- to avoid eye strain ensure that the screen is not too close to your face and from time to time look away from the screen momentarily to give your eyes a change and a rest. Note that you are entitled to regular eye sight tests and the provision of spectacles if necessary by your employer
- adjust the keyboard to obtain a good keying position and leave a space in front of the keyboard to rest hands and wrists when not keying
- adopt good keyboard technique by keeping your wrists straight when keying, don't overstretch your fingers and keep a soft touch on the keys. Suitable rests made of foam are readily available from computer retailers and can help with correct positioning of wrists
- ensure that the environmental conditions are suitable for concentration in terms of acceptable temperature and humidity, lighting, noise and overall work space. The law recommends for sedentary workers that a temperature of at least 16°C is reasonable. The use of natural lighting, either from windows or skylights, is preferable to fluorescent or harsh lighting that may cause eye strain and headaches. Office noise levels may not necessarily be so high as to be damaging

Figure 10.1 Working at a computer terminal

to hearing but unacceptable levels may be annoying and distracting and the fitting of volume controls on telephones may be appropriate in some situations. Office areas should have sufficient height and floor area to avoid cramped and congested areas of work

● if you experience problems such as upper limb pains and discomfort, eyesight defects, fatigue and stress then report them immediately to your employer and your works safety representative.

Reporting in hostile environments

Newspaper and broadcast journalism can be a dangerous profession as evidenced by the numbers of journalists and crew who are killed or injured each year in the desire to be at the scene of the action and gain dramatic stories for newspapers, magazines, radio and television. For example, violence in war and riots, remote locations, inclement weather, unruly crowds, environmental disasters, targeted attacks by paramilitary/terrorist groups, can all pose potential risks to health and safety of reporters and acquisition crews. The demand for sensational audio/visual and written copy, often influenced by commercial competition, means that more and more full-time and part-time journalists and support crews are increasingly at risk and therefore it is important that employers and employees are fully aware of the dangers and that employees are given sufficient advice and training in order to minimize the risks involved.

Journalists regularly face violent behaviour in the form of intimidation, abuse, threats and actual bodily harm, particularly when reporting for news, current affairs programmes and documentaries. Some examples come from people who do not wish to be interviewed or recorded, people under the influence of either alcohol or drugs or indeed both, direct or indirect assault when caught in an affray, confrontational violence sometimes with weapons and public order or civil disturbances. Initially it is the person who is in charge of a radio or television production or the editor of a newspaper who must make an assessment of all the potential risks involved and, in the light of discussion with reporters and crew and sometimes authorities, decide on an appropriate course of action. This may involve deciding that the situation is too risky or putting in place accepted risk-reducing measures. For example, the BBC issues special risk assessment guidelines for those involved in short notice and unpredictable operations such as newsgathering. If the production changes after initial planning the assessment must be reviewed and if necessary amended and all personnel involved informed before production continues.

Very low risk activities such as a discussion for radio in a studio or genuine short notice assignments sometimes do not need specific risk assessment but are normally covered by a generic risk assessment. Indeed some assessments do not require a 'recce' of the location, as it is what the participants are doing that matters, but the assessment may be revised once a location is reached if circumstances have changed considerably. Trainees should, however, be aware of the need for risk assessment particularly as regards work on location. Figure 10.2 shows an example of a college-devised risk assessment form for a location television shoot for a short topical package. It is based on accepted working practices within the industry.

Most violent incidents can be avoided or diminished with appropriate planning and awareness of the possible dangers involved in an assignment but the Health and Safety Executive (HSE) has issued general guidelines and advice for journalists and support crews in the broadcasting industry in relation to the following:

Public disorder. Civil disturbance
- wherever possible find a high and safe vantage point to view the situation
- lone operators should not be used in such situations. The BBC stipulate that there must be a minimum of two people in the crew who should stick together and, if one member exercises their right to withdraw, the risk to others must be re-assessed immediately
- be aware of access and egress and transportation. The BBC asks crews to consider the advantages or disadvantages of using unmarked vehicles or ones bearing the BBC logo
- avoid conspicuous use of filming or recording equipment. The BBC asks crews to consider the advantages or disadvantages of using unmarked equipment or ones marked BBC or TV or Radio

Location risk assessment

Title of programme

Producer   **Crew**

Date(s) of recording   **Time(s) of recording**

Location(s)

**This form must be completed and approved by your tutor
before any production work is undertaken**

Hazard	Tick	Hazard	Tick	Hazard	Tick
Access and egress		Machinery		Working patterns	
Animals		Manual handling		Other (specify below)	
Asbestos		Mines/excavations, etc.			
Confined spaces		Noise			
Derelict buildings		Physical exertion			
Dangerous structures		Public			
Dangerous environment		Radiation			
Electricity		Speed			
Fire		Vehicles			
Gas		Violence/public disorder			
Glass		Water			
Heat/cold		Weather			
Hoists		Working at heights			

Give further details overleaf of all hazards ticked

Figure 10.2 Risk assessment form

- withdraw if the presence of the crew may inflame or prolong the situation or subjects begin to behave abnormally or exploit the situation because of the proximity of recording/filming equipment
- ensure there are adequate means of communication such as a mobile phone
- dress in personal protective equipment to suit the situation
- co-operate with other broadcasting news agencies.

Confrontation

If faced with the threat of violence from a person it is essential to:

- keep calm, avoid prolonged eye contact and keep a respectable distance away from and in no way attempt to touch the person
- speak slowly and quietly, avoid long sentences, listen, try and change the subject and sometimes negotiate a compromise.

Weapons

- withdraw immediately if guns are produced unexpectedly
- take defensive cover and withdraw as soon as possible if gunshots are fired
- be aware of the risk of returned fire and being in recently vacated firing positions
- remember that no programme is worth a life.

Reporting sports events

The inquiries into the disasters at Bradford and Hillsborough soccer stadia highlighted the fact that at many sporting venues there was only a single means of access to the broadcasting area, which was often difficult to negotiate. Although significant improvements have been made in recent years there are still concerns regarding the above as well as fire and other emergency situations, working at heights from temporary structures, exposure of journalists and crew to crowd disorder, personal violence, inclement weather and collisions with sports persons and equipment when recording close to the action.

Before reporting any event the broadcasting organization should have carried out a risk assessment and determined what precautionary measures were needed. Similarly, the stadium management or event organizers should have carried out a risk assessment and relayed this information to the broadcasting organization, their own staff and to the emergency and security services. The Health and Safety Executive (HSE), in conjunction with the Joint Advisory Committee for Broadcasting and Performing Arts (BJAC), has issued the following guidelines on good practice.

Access and egress routes

- access routes should be free from obstruction and debris, of sound construction, securely fixed and fitted with handrails and sufficiently illuminated even under emergency conditions
- access for equipment should include suitability of lifting equipment, competence of crew and safety of the public caused by incorrect handling and installation or defective equipment
- all obvious defects should be reported to the management of the event/stadium.

Fire and associated hazards

- reporters, broadcasters and crew should be aware of fire and emergency procedures at the venue by contacting the management of the venue to establish alarm signals, evacuation and emergency exits and assembly points
- wherever possible, a secondary means of escape from the broadcasting area should be provided such as self-lowering equipment or portable ladders.

Working at heights

- when working from temporary structures such as access towers and platforms broadcasters and crew should check that the structure is safe in terms of having boarded floors, guard rails and kickboards and is available for use.

Violence

- potential violence at sporting events can be of particular relevance to camera and sound crews at ground level and crews should ensure that they are aware of their vulnerability in these situations and establish the safest possible working conditions before the event.

Ground level cameras

- fixed cameras whenever possible should be placed behind recognized spectator barriers or adjacent to permanent hazards such as dugouts and should have suitable protective barriers attached to them in order to prevent possible injury to a performer or sports person
- mobile cameras should stay a safe distance from and not encroach upon the field of play and have a secondary operator to deal with trailing cables.

Noise

- crowd noise levels are normally very high at sporting venues so talkback between producer and presenter may be high as well. The use of sound-excluding headphones or HiFi earplugs can help reduce the noise levels reaching the ear.

Working as a freelance

As can be seen from the previous chapter there has been a huge growth in the numbers of freelances working in the print and broadcast industries and many have received little or no health and safety training, even though they may be working in unpredictable circumstances. Freelances do have health and safety responsibilities but these depend on the nature of the contractual agreement with a particular organization. Briefly, a freelance journalist or broadcaster may have either a 'contract for services' or a 'contract of service'. Freelances in the print and broadcast industries are normally self-employed and therefore work under a 'contract for services', which means that they receive their gross pay and then must make arrangements for paying their own income tax under Schedule D regulations, which also allow for expenses to be offset against the gross sum before tax is deducted. A 'contract of service' treats freelances as though they are employees of the organization, thus the employer deducts tax and National Insurance contributions at source under Schedule E or PAYE. Many jobs in broadcasting are only offered to freelances on a 'contract for services', which do not give employee status.

Normally an employer must control the risks to health and safety for employees in terms of roles, training and supervision, location of work, use and maintenance of equipment, etc. Employees also have a duty of care for themselves and others and must co-operate with the employer by adhering to health and safety practices. However, those who are self-employed must provide for their own health and safety and indeed that of anyone else who might be affected by the work, such as crew and members of the public. Freelances should also remember that if they employ others to help with work they then become an employer and should be fully aware of their health and safety responsibilities. In fact, the BBC Terms of Trade for Freelances gives any individual employee of the freelance the same obligations as the freelance. Thus the freelance should adequately supervise their employees so as not to put others at risk in a production. Yet, whilst freelances may be skilled within their own profession it does not necessarily follow that they are competent in health and safety law. Training may be required in order that they can manage others under their control, particularly if the assignment involves using unfamiliar equipment and unusual locations.

Risk assessment by employers has been mentioned previously. However, freelances must also assess risks for a particular assignment. One way is to ask the editor or producer what arrangements for risk assessments have been made. This may mean identifying problems that may arise, having contingency plans in place, deciding whether precautions to be taken are adequate, and consulting and discussing the issues at a briefing session for all concerned. Issues that may arise include:

● who has overall responsibility for the assignment in terms of risks, co-ordination and monitoring?

- on location are there potential risks regarding permissions, environmental conditions, remoteness, accessibility, disease, hazards, weather, noise and the general public?
- if working alone on location are there adequate safeguards as regards communication channels back to base, carrying out assignments late at night or on private property, wearing suitable footwear and clothes, personal safety?
- is the equipment, whether hired or personal, safe to use and familiar to the user (if not is training needed prior to the task)?
- if needed are the electrics safe to use?
- what arrangements and procedures are in place for emergencies including fire warning systems, fire-fighting and rescue equipment and accident reporting?
- what welfare facilities such as sustenance, shelter, toilets, washing facilities are available?
- what is the procedure for reporting accidents including deaths, major injuries, diseases, dangerous occurrences and injuries to members of the public?

Note that in the case of the latter if you are self-employed you must still report accidents. If you are working on someone else's premises and suffer an accident that means you cannot work for three consecutive days then they are responsible and you should report the matter to them. If, however, you are self-employed and suffer a major injury on your own premises, you or your representative should report it within 10 days to the appropriate authority, which may be the Health and Safety Executive or the local authority, depending on the situation. Advice can be obtained from the Environmental Health Department of the local council or from the nearest HSE Area Office. You should also report violent incidents, accidents as a result of hazardous or dangerous situations and most importantly when members of the public have been injured as a result of work being carried out by you. Incidentally, you should also investigate whether public liability insurance may be necessary for your particular vocation. Finally, note that normally when a freelance is employed to do work the employer should take out and maintain Employer's Liability Insurance against bodily injury and disease. There are limited exceptions and it is advisable to refer to the Employer's Liability (Compulsory Insurance) Act 1969 for clarification.

And finally . . .

In conclusion, the media industry is striving to maintain health and safety standards yet it is inevitable that because of the unpredictable nature of the job newspaper journalists, broadcasters and support staff, many of whom are self-employed, are susceptible to higher risks when gathering and producing news items. Adequate preparation by journalists before going on an assignment can alleviate some of the risks and increasing awareness by employers of the risks involved both on location and in the workplace coupled with training opportunities for staff should ensure that the industry is a safer place in which to work.

Suggested activities

1 Obtain a copy of the Health and Safety at Work Act and make notes on the sections that are relevant to your training situation.
2 Carry out a survey of your classroom or training room and make a note of possible hazards such as blocked access and egress routes, badly positioned furniture, poor lighting, dangerous electrics, etc. Write a memorandum to your tutor or training manager highlighting your concerns and suggest improvements that could be implemented. Draw up a floor plan of possible improvements to layout and attach this to the memo.
3 You are intending to carry out a location shoot in a derelict factory to be used in a short topical report on urban regeneration in your area. Visit the location and carry out a risk assessment of the area. You may wish to use the example given in this chapter or make up your own form.
4 You are working in a unfamiliar radio studio. Carry out a health and safety check on the environment. Make a note of such items as the position of emergency exits and illuminated signs, location of fire extinguishers, emergency procedure notices, fire alarms, etc. Report any possible difficulties that might arise in an emergency situation.
5 Using primary and secondary sources make a list of the most common types of fire extinguishers and their suitability for different emergency situations. Draw up a poster showing the various extinguishers and their usage and place it in a prominent position in the workplace.
6 As a group arrange a press conference in your training room with a spokesperson from the local fire brigade on fire safety in the workplace. Allocate roles in order to produce a radio item, a television report and a print feature using the information gleaned from the conference.
7 In producing a short radio news package on traffic jams in the morning rush hour you wish to record vox pops at a busy road junction. Carry out a 'recce' and make a list of the possible hazards involved in making the recording, such as risk assessment for public and yourself, permissions, environmental issues, etc.
8 As a group invite an audience to watch the studio recording of a news magazine programme. Make a comprehensive list of the health and safety regulations that must be followed in this situation. Appoint one person as floor manager to explain the procedures to the audience before the live recording begins.

9 Working at a computer terminal for long periods in an unsuitable environment can be the cause of many work-related illnesses. Using the information given in this chapter and carrying out your own research devise a four-page pamphlet that gives basic practical advice on the subject.

10 You intend filming a forthcoming demonstration for a news report. Find out which authorities must be contacted before the event and the restrictions that may be in force. Make a list of the necessary health and safety factors that might arise during the shoot and draw up a contingency plan in case of an emergency.

11 You are asked to accompany a college group on a field trip to a remote location. Your task is to act as a solo video journalist and produce a 5-minute television package on the event. Compile a list of health and safety considerations for the protection of yourself and the equipment.

Sources and resources

BBC (2001) *Guidelines on Health and Safety* (online). Available at: http://www.bbc-safety.co.uk (accessed 17 August 2001).

BBC (2001) *Public Order/Civil Disturbance* (online). Available at: http://www.bbc-safety.co.uk (accessed 17 August 2001).

BBC (2001) *Working with Lightweight Cameras* (online). Available at: http://www.bbc-safety.co.uk (accessed 17 August 2001).

BECTU (2000) *Submission on Employee Consultation and Involvement in Health and Safety to the UK Health and Safety Commission* (online). Available at: http://www.bectu.org.uk (accessed 19 August 2001).

Facts for Freelances (online). Available at: http://www.hse.gov.uk (accessed 21 August 2001).

HSE (2001) *Health and Safety Regulation* (online). Available at: http://www.hse.gov.uk (accessed 15 August 2001).

Reporting of Injuries, Diseases and Dangerous Occurrences Regulations 1996 (online). Available at: http://www.riddor.gov.uk (accessed 20 August 2001).

Safety in Broadcasting Sports Events (online). Available at: http://www.hse.gov.uk (accessed 17 August 2001).

Skillset (2001) *Health and Safety Introduction* (online). Available at: http://www.skillset.org.uk (accessed 17 August 2001).

TUC (2001) *Health and Safety Motions to the TUC Congress 2001. Motion 44 working time regulations and amendments* (online). Available at: http://www.v128.dial.pipex.com (accessed 19 August 2001).

Violence to workers in broadcasting (online). Available at: http://www.hse.gov.uk (accessed 17 August 2001).

Working with VDUs. Health and Safety Display Screen Equipment Regulations 1992 (online). Available at: http://www.hse.gov.uk (accessed 19 August 2001).

11 Central government

- The Constitution
- The Sovereign (Her Majesty Queen Elizabeth II. 'The Queen')
- The Privy Council
- The Prime Minister
- The Cabinet
- The Opposition
- Civil servants
- Parliament: key features and processes
- The House of Commons
- The legislative process
- Select committees
- House of Lords
- Governing the economy
- The election process
- Alternative electoral systems
- Political parties: an introduction
- The European Union: introduction and background
- Other international organizations to which the UK belongs
- Reporting central government
- Suggested activities
- Sources and resources

The Constitution

For many people the word 'constitution' summons up images of dusty volumes of parchment being pored over by academics. But a country's constitution is of vital importance because it determines how people are governed, what powers different levels of authority have over them – including the powers to imprison or even execute civilians, to levy taxes and to conscript into the armed services, and what the relationship is between those centres of power. In addition, in democratic countries a constitution lays out when and how elections are to be held, who can be candidates and who can vote. These are such important matters that disputes about the constitution in the UK – as with many other countries, including the

USA – have caused much bloodshed and are still controversial today. Later in this chapter we'll consider the impact on the UK's constitution of membership of the European Union. Chapter 12 considers devolution for Scotland, Wales and Northern Ireland.

It is often said that the UK does not have a constitution: this is true in the sense that, unlike the USA for example, there is no single document that lays out all the matters that affect how the country is run. If there were, it would make a chapter like this a lot simpler! The constitution of the UK is (unfortunately for those trying to get to grips with it) a complex matter, involving numerous laws, treaties, precedent (what happened before) and the subtle and ever-evolving relationship between the different power centres.

The United Kingdom of Great Britain and Northern Ireland has been formed from four previously independent nations; mainly a result of the fact that is has by far the largest part of the population in the UK, England has been the dominant nation. England, which in itself is a union of a number of kingdoms, was then joined formally and constitutionally in turn by Wales (1536), Scotland (1707) and Ireland (1801).

If an account is made of the disputes and bloodshed that led to the unions of these countries with England and the continuing disputed claims over territory, finance, etc., into the twenty-first century, then it can be seen that, broadly speaking, Wales has been the least 'problematic', followed by Scotland, with Ireland the most disputed. In fact, the Union with the island of Ireland lasted only 120 years. In 1921, following decades of political turmoil, the island was politically divided – the larger part becoming a self-governed Republic and the remainder based around the six counties of the North, into Northern Ireland, which remained part of the UK under the British Crown. Even before the 'Good Friday Agreement' (see Chapter 12) there were still a number of odd constitutional links between the Republic and the UK – for example, citizens of the Republic retained their right to be candidates for, and vote in, UK elections.

One of the most important elements of the UK's Constitution is the relationship between the Crown, personified by the Sovereign (the Queen) and Parliament.

Although the UK is often said to have a representative democracy – with power resting with the people but granted to their representatives who are chosen in elections – in fact only one of the three institutions, the House of Commons, has a democratic basis. The Sovereign is, of course, a hereditary title and members of the House of Lords are either there because they have inherited titles or have been appointed.

A highly significant change was made to the Constitution when the UK joined the then European Economic Community (now European Union – see below) in 1973. The European Communities Act, passed by Parliament the year before, meant that the British legislative and judicial system was obliged to enforce laws made by bodies from outside the country. From that point, where laws made by the UK

Parliament were in contradiction with rulings made by European courts, the latter had precedence. In the views of many, though, an even bigger change to the Constitution came with the passing of the Human Rights Act (HRA) 1998, which incorporated the European Convention on Human Rights (see below) into UK domestic law and which, moreover, established *positive rights* for citizens. The British legal system had until then only been concerned with making it unlawful to do certain things; otherwise anything was legal! It is argued that the effect of the Act is to put the decisions of the judiciary above those of Parliament and that judges (who are, of course, un-elected) are now, in effect, *making* the law – thereby demolishing the traditional claim of Parliamentary sovereignty. There is further discussion of the HRA in Chapter 13.

The main elements of the Constitution can be summarized as:

● *The Executive* – under the authority of The Crown, embodied in, and headed by, the Sovereign whose powers are invested in (her) *government*, comprising of Ministers (of the Crown), headed by a Prime Minister, answerable to Parliament.
● *The Legislature* – the law-making body – comprising both Houses of Parliament and acting, through complex and evolving processes, as a check on the powers of both Crown and Executive.
● *The Judiciary* – politically independent but empowered by laws made by Parliament and, when in doubt, making judgements by interpreting what it believes was the intention of Parliament.

Now, let's look at the major elements and offices of the modern UK government.

The Sovereign (Her Majesty Queen Elizabeth II. 'The Queen')

The Sovereign – the head of the Monarchy – is the Head of State. Although no longer directly involved in the day-to-day running of the government, the Sovereign nevertheless retains a central role in the nation's affairs and retains a great deal of theoretical power even if, in practice, power lies with Ministers and Parliament. As we shall see, it is the power that belongs to the Sovereign but that s/he transfers to Ministers using the Royal Prerogative that lies at the heart of the nation's Constitution.

The Sovereign appoints the person who seems likely to command the support of the majority of members of the House of Commons – usually the MP who is head of the political party with the greatest number of MPs in the Commons – as the Prime Minister (and First Lord of the Treasury). Prime Ministers are usually appointed after a general election – although sometimes, such as in 1990, they resign between elections. The decision as who to appoint as Prime Minister is usually straightforward as one political party wins more seats than all the other parties combined – an overall majority. However, sometimes – such as in the General Election of February 1974 – this doesn't happen and the Sovereign has greater powers of discretion as to who to appoint as Prime Minister. As we shall see, though, the Prime Minister still has to have the backing of the majority of the Commons to survive in the job.

Once appointed, ministers from the Prime Minster downwards who are known collectively – along with the civil servants and other officers of state – as Her Majesty's Government (HMG), have great powers as they formally act on behalf of the Sovereign, using the Royal Prerogative. Power formally rests with the Sovereign but it is usually delegated to the relevant minister. This is very significant because it means that ministers can – and do – make major decisions without the need to consult, or even inform, Parliament. This is particularly relevant in foreign affairs up to and including war, and in signing treaties with other countries and international organizations such as the European Union. The Sovereign maintains close contact with all aspects of government, seeing countless official and often secret documents and usually *granting an audience* with the Prime Minister once a week, as well as discussing matters of State with other ministers.

In addition to a central role in government the Sovereign is also:

- head of the armed forces – all those in the military swear an oath of allegiance to the Sovereign
- head of the Church of England (by Act of Parliament the Sovereign must be of the Protestant faith) – the 'state' or 'established' religion: a position of great historical importance
- head of the Commonwealth (see below) – a group of countries that were either former colonies (parts of the British Empire) or countries of which the Sovereign is still Head of State, e.g., Canada and New Zealand.

It is worth noting that all of those with important positions in the State – including MPs, ministers, Police officers, members of the armed forces and judges, are obliged to swear an oath of allegiance to the Sovereign (and her heirs and successors) not to the government, 'the people' or any other democratic institutions. In theory, therefore, if another major dispute arose between government and Sovereign, the King or Queen would have the necessary powers and forces to impose their will!

In addition, the Sovereign:

- formally makes most of the key appointments of the British State. Often the members of her government – notably the Prime Minister – make the recommendations. Amongst these are the Archbishop of Canterbury and other leading Church of England Bishops, the Chairman of the BBC, the Chairs of

numerous public bodies, Royal Commissions and, of course, the whole honours system – MBEs, OBEs, CBEs, Knighthoods, etc.
● with other members of the Royal Family is ceremonial head of numerous service regiments as well as having honorary roles for many charities and other public organizations.

Undoubtedly, most members of the general public primarily think of the current Sovereign, Queen Elizabeth II, in terms of her role on ceremonial and 'national' occasions, such as the Remembrance Day ceremonies in London for the country's war dead, as guest of honour at such events as the Royal Variety performance (formerly the Royal Command performance) and, perhaps most of all, for the annual television and radio Christmas message to the nation and Commonwealth. In these ways the Sovereign is seen to embody the spirit as well as the power of the State.

Although the Queen is, by any standards, an extremely wealthy woman with a large private income – since 1993 she pays income tax on this – and has many highly valuable possessions, Her Majesty is given an annual grant by Parliament for her official duties. The Civil List also includes payments to the Duke of Edinburgh and the Queen Mother. The heir to the throne – Prince Charles, the Prince of Wales – receives no public funds but instead has an income from the Duchy of Cornwall – land and properties that have been the property of the Monarchy for centuries.

The Privy Council

All Cabinet Ministers and many other leading figures – including the leaders of the main opposition parties and senior judges – are appointed by the Sovereign to be members of the Privy Council. Once appointed, membership is for life, except in the very rare occasions when a Councillor is dismissed. This ancient body of advisors to the Sovereign, now numbering over 400, still retains great power, over and above Cabinet (which has no formal basis in the Constitution) and Parliament. It can, for example, declare a state of civil emergency using powers through an Order in Council. Cabinet members often brief opposition leaders 'on a Privy Council basis' about matters of State and the background to their policies – especially if they are concerned with security or defence matters. Normally only a small proportion of Privy Councillors (the quorum is four, three of whom must be Ministers) meet with the Sovereign – sometimes with another senior member of the Royal Family – but the whole of the Privy Council meets on the death of the King or Queen to confirm the accession to the throne, or when the Sovereign wishes to marry.

The secrecy of its deliberations – some of which may never be revealed – is underlined by the oath that all Privy Councillors have to swear and which has been unchanged since about 1250.

The Privy Council also retains some other important powers; for example it decides whether to grant University status on institutions of Higher Education.

Another important function of the Privy Council is carried out by its Judicial Committee, which is the final Court of Appeal for 16 Commonwealth nations. Its deliberations have, in the recent past, been literally a matter of life or death, as a number of these countries still had the death penalty for murder and the Committee had to decide whether to grant a reprieve. The Committee also hears appeals from the Channel Islands and the Isle of Man, and the disciplinary committees of the health profession.

Finally – and something that is likely to have increasing importance in the coming years – it makes the final decision over disputes of the legal competence of decisions made by the legislature and executive of the devolved bodies in Scotland, Wales and Northern Ireland.

Members of the House of Commons who are Privy Councillors are styled 'Right Honourable', or 'Rt. Hon.' for short. They take precedence over other members when being called to speak in debates and may also speak longer than other MPs! The person responsible for organizing the business of the Privy Council is called the Lord President of the Council, who is always a member of the Cabinet and in recent years has combined the job with being Leader of the House of Commons – responsible for organizing business in that House. Thus, one person is a member of the executive body of government (the Cabinet), a member of the body that embodies the prerogative power of the Sovereign (the Privy Council) and is a member of one part of the legislature (the House of Commons) – potentially an important role for co-ordinating and influencing the course of events in the country.

The Prime Minister

The office of Prime Minister (PM) was not formally recognized and given a place in the Order of Precedence until 1905 – relatively recently in terms of the British Constitution! The Prime Minister, the Sovereign's first minister, also has the formal title of First Lord of the Treasury (the title on the plaque on the front door of the PM's official London residence, No. 10 Downing Street) and Minister for the Civil Service (it is for these offices that s/he has a salary – there is no money in being the Prime Minister as such!), is often described as 'First Among Equals' – from the Latin *Primus inter Pares*. This reflects the idea that the Prime Minister is but one of a number of ministers but is head of the executive committee – the Cabinet – of the country: a sort of 'Chairman of the Board' or 'Chief Executive'.

Once appointed, the Prime Minister decides who will be in the rest of the government and what job they will have: not only in the main executive body – the Cabinet – but around 100 Ministerial and other posts. The story of the UK

Constitution in the twentieth century was one of increased power by the Prime Minister over the rest of the executive and the executive as a whole gaining power over Parliament, so that sometimes the Prime Minister is described as acting 'Presidentially' (as a Head of State). This perception is increased when the Prime Minister appears to take on some of the role traditionally the reserve of the Sovereign, of being 'spokesman for the nation'. Equally, although it is the Sovereign who is the formal head of the armed services, in reality it is the Prime Minister who decides when and how to send troops into action and is regarded as being responsible for the success or otherwise of British military operations. Even more tellingly, it is the Prime Minister who has ultimate control over the country's nuclear weapons ('the finger on the button' – it is the Prime Minister who gives *political authority* for nuclear weapons to be launched but it would be the senior commander of the Royal Navy who would give the orders for the nuclear weapons on Trident submarines to be used).

The justification for this delegation of power from the Sovereign to a politician is that the Prime Minister is appointed through a democratic process and so has legitimate power and authority, whereas the Sovereign, owing his or her position to the hereditary process ('an accident of birth'), does not.

It should be remembered, though, that Prime Ministers are not elected directly by the people but usually derive their power from their strength as leader of the largest party in the House of Commons. If the Prime Minister loses a leadership election in their own party or, as happened to Margaret Thatcher in November 1990, is damaged by a challenge to the leadership, they are forced to resign as Prime Minister as they can no longer expect the support of their party's representatives in the House of Commons. Only the electors in the Prime Minister's constituency can vote for him or her in an election – and then only as an MP (see below). Nor does the House of Commons formally vote to appoint one of their number as the Prime Minister – as we have seen, it is the duty of the Sovereign to appoint the Prime Minister. In some respects the basis of the Prime Minister's power is a *negative* one – he or she is there until they resign, are defeated in a general election, or their support is shown to have been lost through a vote of No Confidence in the House of Commons.

Although Prime Ministers have a (relatively small) private office, their real power centre is the Cabinet Office – a group of civil servants and advisors mostly based in offices in or near 10 Downing Street. The role of advisors – un-elected 'experts' who are paid from public funds but who are not accountable to Parliament – has been, and remains, a controversial matter. Often the Prime Minister takes more notice of, and spends more time with, such advisors than ministers. This naturally leads to jealousy and tensions at the heart of government – especially when the advisors are giving different advice from that by the relevant minister! In October 1989 a long-standing Chancellor of the Exchequer, Nigel Lawson, resigned in protest at 'interference' by Alan Walters, economic advisor to Prime Minister Margaret Thatcher.

The Cabinet

The Cabinet consists of between 20 and 24 senior Ministers of the Crown. They meet as a Cabinet at least once a week, usually on a Thursday morning, to discuss the main issues and problems facing the government, to formulate policy and to decide on priorities. The chief minister of each department – normally called Secretary of State – is usually a member of the Cabinet and will also be a Privy Councillor. The Prime Minister (PM) is the Cabinet's chairperson and the style, content and even length of Cabinet meetings is, to some extent, dependent on the personality and political will of the PM. Cabinet itself has no constitutional authority – power is exercised by ministers acting in the name of the Sovereign.

The detailed work of the Cabinet is done in a number of committees, some of which are permanent and others are set up to discuss, and decide on, specific issues. Individual Cabinet Ministers have political responsibility for what happens in their departments and, until relatively recently, were expected to resign if there was a major failing in their area of responsibility, even if they could not be held personally responsible for that failing.

Members of the Cabinet are bound by what is called *collective responsibility*. This means that once a decision is made all Cabinet members are expected to support the decision or policy in public. If they feel they cannot do so they are expected to resign.

Cabinet meetings are held in secret so that ministers can speak frankly but minutes are taken and usually released into the public domain through the Public Records Office (PRO) 30 years later! However, through leaks and accounts in the published diaries and autobiographies of former ministers, it is often possible to read what happened in Cabinet some years before the minutes are officially published.

In addition to the Secretary of State, each department will also have several other ministers who also form part of the government. The next most important person in each department is normally called a Minister of State. These will usually have certain, specific, responsibilities for defined parts of the larger ministry. There are usually several other ministers below that, often called Under Secretary of State but, for shorthand, are usually referred to as 'junior ministers'. Ministers receive a salary in addition to that for being an MP; the amount depends on their seniority in government.

The lowest rung on the ladder is the Parliamentary Private Secretary (PPS) who, unlike the ministers above them, do not receive a salary for their post and, indeed, are not members of the government but are usually seen as playing a relatively minor role in helping the main ministers sort out the appointments, travel arrangements, etc.

All ministerial appointments are made by the Sovereign but in practice it is the Prime Minister who makes them, usually on the grounds of experience, capability and, not least, politics. Ministers may be taken from either House of Parliament (Commons or Lords) and, as we shall see, ministers are needed in the Lords to propose and debate government Bills. In recent years, the vast majority of the heads of the main departments have been members of the House of Commons (MPs) but as recently as the early 1980s one of the top government jobs – the Foreign Secretary – was held by a member of the House of Lords (Lord Carrington).

All ministers are bound by a Ministerial Code, which was updated by the Labour government elected in 1997. It is designed to ensure that ministers do not use their office for personal gain (beyond that of receiving a ministerial salary of course!); drawing a line between government and commercial activities – including for a period after leaving government – as well as the proper relationship with civil servants. The Code also covers the proper distinction between governmental and party duties: the taxpayer should not pay for activities such as attending party conferences and electioneering, which are carried out to benefit the minister's political party. The updating of this Code has been linked with concern over political 'sleaze' – especially the allegations of 'cash for votes' made against some MPs in the previous Parliament. There is now a Commissioner for Parliamentary Standards whose job it is to 'police' the conduct of Parliamentarians.

In addition ministers have to be wary of ensuring they act within their legal powers. In recent years there have been a number of successful challenges in the courts and the passing of the Human Rights Act is almost certain to result in further challenges.

The Opposition

Because of the very rapid transfer of power when the opposition party wins a general election, the Leader of the Opposition (LO) – the MP who represents the second largest party represented in the House of Commons – is given extensive briefings by civil servants in the months leading up to a general election. In this way the LO is prepared for power should his or her party win the election. In these sessions the LO can also inform the Civil Service of their priorities. As we have already seen, the LO and other leading members of the Shadow team of Ministers – those who sit on the opposition front bench in the House of Commons – will be aware of some of the more sensitive issues through the Privy Council. The importance of the Opposition in the Constitution is that there should always be a 'government in waiting' – a set of people who could take over the reins of government at short notice.

The office of the Leader of the Opposition attracts an additional salary and allowances and the LO is given priority for questioning the Prime Minister in Prime Minister's Questions (PMQs, see below). Opposition parties also receive additional funds through Short Money (so-called because it was introduced in 1975 by the then Leader of the House, Edward Short).

Each session of Parliament includes 20 days for Opposition motions and debates in the House of Commons. Normally 17 of these are taken up by the main opposition party.

Civil servants

Unlike ministers, civil servants are not political appointees. Their job is to give advice to ministers, to carry out research, formulate possible and alternative policies, to give advice and, most of all, to implement the policies decided by ministers. Unlike ministers, civil servants do not normally resign when there is a change of government. They are supposed to be politically impartial and not be concerned of the political colour of their ministerial masters. There is a formal career structure for civil servants and posts are filled through open and fair competition. In the past it was thought desirable that civil servants should have a good general intellectual ability rather than specialist skills and knowledge; now, however, more specific skills and experience – in business, for example – are given greater priority, although civil servants still tend to move between a number of departments during their career. Each department has its own set of civil servants, the head one called Permanent Secretary. Civil servants only rarely give interviews although they often help journalists to arrange interviews, etc., with ministers.

Civil servants do not normally speak at either the full Cabinet or in its committees, but are there to give advice when asked for and to take minutes of meetings. Civil servants have their own committees that to some extent shadow those of the Cabinet and in which they prepare advice, usually in the form of briefing papers.

Parliament: key features and processes

The maximum length of a Parliament is 5 years. Each Parliament is divided into (usually) four or five sessions, normally starting in November and lasting a year. Each session begins with the State Opening of Parliament and the Sovereign reading a speech in the House of Lords that explains what the government intends to do in the forthcoming session. Each session of Parliament ends with it being prorogued. Following changes to Parliamentary procedure agreed in 2002, any Bills that fail to complete all their stages in one session may be carried over to the next. Except for the end of the final session, MPs retain their seats and re-assemble at the start of the new session. But after a maximum of 5 years, Parliament must be prorogued for the final time and then dissolved by Royal Proclamation.

Prime Ministers have a great deal of power in deciding when general elections will take place. They may ask the Sovereign for a dissolution at any time but, if they have a working majority of MPs in the House of Commons, the generally accepted 'rule' is that an election can be called any time after the fourth anniversary of the previous general election. Earlier than four years tends to be viewed as asking for a fresh mandate too soon and looks like panic – or at least 'cashing in' while things seem to be going well – and raises suspicions in the electorate that some nasty news or development is around the corner. However, leaving the election to the last possible moment can give the impression that the government is scared to face the electors and believes it cannot win and so has decided it may as well hang on to power for as long as possible.

Since World War II only one Prime Minister – John Major – has decided to let Parliament run its maximum legal length (April 1992 to April 1997) before asking the Queen for a dissolution. After such a request the Sovereign formally consults the Privy Council before issuing the Royal Proclamation announcing the dissolution and a date is given for the general election, which is at least 17 working days later (that is, excluding Sundays and Public Holidays) and a date is also given for the summoning of the new Parliament. Until the new Parliament assembles there are no MPs – the individual seats are pending (to be filled) and if the (former) MPs are to be candidates in the forthcoming election, they must *not* be referred to as 'MP' but as a 'candidate'. However, the government, including the full range of Ministers (including the Prime Minister) continues and may be referred to as such. The UK electorate votes for a Member of Parliament, *not* a government. The government *emerges* (indeed is appointed) from, and after, this process.

At the beginning of each new session of Parliament, the MPs (from the House of Commons) are summoned to 'another place' – the House of Lords – to hear a speech from the Sovereign. The Queen's Speech is written by Ministers and outlines what 'her' government will do in the new session. The reason this is done from the Lords (apart from the fact that, constitutionally, this is still the Upper House) is that the Queen is not allowed to enter the Commons – emphasizing the independence and power of the Commons over the Sovereign and their Lordships!

The House of Commons

As we have seen, the House of Commons (HoC) is still, officially under the Constitution, the 'Lower House' in the bicameral (two part) legislature of the UK. The seating is laid out to emphasize the *adversarial* nature of British politics: unlike many other legislatures, the representatives of the government party sit on one side of the chamber, with ministers on the front bench, directly opposite their rivals in the opposition parties – with shadow cabinet members on the opposite front bench.

Ministers make their statements from the dispatch box. By tradition, the two sides are kept apart by the length of two swords, with the Mace – which represents Parliamentary authority – between them.

As we have seen, since the early part of the century the HoC has in reality gradually established itself as the more important part of Parliament: certainly it is the one with greatest *democratic legitimacy* – as all its members are elected through universal adult suffrage. This means that everyone over 18 years – aside from a relatively few and generally accepted restrictions such as the criminally insane, or those who have been convicted of a serious criminal offence – has one vote for one seat.

After a general election the newly elected MPs have to take an oath of allegiance to the Sovereign before they can formally take their seats. This oath is not seen as a trivial matter. Two Sinn Fein (Irish Republican) MPs have refused to take the oath and so, although elected, could not take their seats but following a controversial vote in Parliament, were allowed to use the MPs' facilities in the House of Commons from early 2002. A number of other MPs who object to having to take the oath have stated their objections before the 'swearing in' and – perhaps rather childishly – read the oath whilst having their fingers crossed behind their back, demonstrating that they do not believe in what they are saying!

The Speaker

The Speaker's post is one of the most ancient 'jobs' in the Commons. An MP is appointed to the post through an election by MPs as a whole (a rather complex procedure that was simplified somewhat in March 2001 following the controversial election process of electing the Speaker a few months previously). As another demonstration of the complicated relationships in the UK Constitution the Speaker has to formally petition and gain permission from the Sovereign before formally taking over the job. The Speaker then acts as the main conduit between MPs and the Sovereign.

The Speaker is the Chairperson of the Commons and has great authority over the business of the House and the conduct of its members. It is the Speaker who decides on which MPs are to speak and in what order, will rule when there is a dispute on points of procedure/order and has the power to order an MP to stop speaking, to chastise them, to order them to apologize and, ultimately, to expel them from the chamber. More positively, the Speaker is there to defend the ancient rights and privileges of MPs, most of which date from the Bill of Rights of 1689. These include the right of free speech – MPs cannot be sued for libel for anything they say in the House of Commons – as well as freedom from arrest or interference from the courts whilst they are physically present in Parliament. (It can be properly stated that Parliament is 'a law unto itself' as it has its own laws, rights and privileges that are not available to those outside Parliament.) Furthermore these privileges only apply to MPs, not to anyone else and that includes journalists! Such people are classed as Strangers and are only in the Chamber with the permission of MPs. If an MP calls 'I Spy Strangers', the Speaker is obliged to put a motion to the House that the Strangers' Galleries (which include the Press Gallery) are cleared and the Commons then meets in secret.

Each Speaker since the televising of Parliament in the late 1980s has gained international fame and both their faces and voices – especially the cry of 'Order! Order!' – are widely known. When a vote – called a Division – has been taken in the House of Commons on legislation or other matters, it is the Speaker who – after the Tellers have handed in the result of the vote – will announce the numbers of 'Ayes' and 'Nos' (for and against) and will pronounce: 'the Ayes/Nos have it!'. Speakers do not take part in debates and do not vote except when the result is a tie – by convention the Speaker then votes with the government, even if s/he is a member of another party. This emphasizes that Speakers, once they've taken over the job, should put aside party or personal considerations and be non-partisan and scrupulously fair. Many of those who believe that the UK should (again) be a Republic argue that the obvious Head of State (in place of a King or Queen) should be the Speaker of the Commons.

Backbenchers

Backbenchers are MPs who are neither members of the government nor leading members of the main opposition party (frontbenchers). They draw a salary and a pension and receive severance pay if they lose an election. To help them fund their secretarial and research needs they have an Office Costs Allowance and are also provided with free postage and free rail travel to and from their constituencies. The main roles of backbenchers are:

- to represent their constituents, bringing their concerns and interests to the attention of Parliament and government MPs, using the authority that (still!) comes with their role in taking up grievances of individual constituents, not only with government departments but other groups and individuals
- to be an advocate for their area – promoting its economic and cultural interests
- to hold the executive (government) to account by tabling (asking) questions, both in writing and orally. The first main item of business on most days when the Commons is sitting is questions (from backbenchers) to Ministers. In addition, once a week backbenchers have a chance of reaching national attention by asking questions of the Prime Minister, in Prime Minister's Questions (PMQs) – without doubt the most well known part of Parliament's procedure, even though it forms only a tiny part of the overall business and work of the HoC. By convention the first question at PMQs, is the Prime Minister's engagements that day. The MP then asks a follow up, or supplementary, question, which is of a rather more pointed

nature! The Speaker then alternately calls government and opposition members. MPs often have a pair with a member from an opposing party – this means they do not always have to be present when there is a Division (vote) – although sometimes this arrangement between parties is ended or suspended

- to debate and vote on legislation both in the chamber of the Commons and in committee (see below)
- to scrutinize the actions of government and of other public and private organizations through Select Committees (see below)
- to participate in debates of interest to his/her constituents and/or the nation as a whole and to initiate such debates by means of an Adjournment Debate (these take place in the last half hour or so of Commons' business) or an Early Day Motion
- to be a politician, nearly always as a member of a political party, and to support that party both in Parliament and in their constituency activities and to ensure so far as possible that party members and managers in their constituency are kept informed of events in Westminster and are happy about how matters are progressing. This is not a one-way communication process as it is also the job of MPs to relay the feelings – especially the discontent – of their constituents and party managers back to the party in Westminster.

In reality, it is the last function that is likely to be of most consequence most of the time!

MPs who wish to resign in between elections have to apply for one of the quaintly named, non-existent 'for profit' posts; the best known being the Chiltern Hundreds. The whips for the party represented by the MP then apply for a writ to be moved for a by-election to fill the vacancy.

The Whips

The Whips are MPs who help organize the business of government and ensure that their party's MPs are available to vote on important motions and legislation. At the beginning of every week that Parliament sits each MP receives a document from the Whips' Office that details government business that week. Important votes are underlined once, twice, or three times (the three line whip) to show their importance to the government. Any MP who fails to turn up for an important vote or, worse still, votes against the party line, is likely to be severely reprimanded. In extreme cases they may have the whip withdrawn, which means they are no longer regarded as a representative for their party in Parliament.

As MPs are elected as individuals even if they have the whip withdrawn they are still MPs – unless they decide to resign. Of course they may find it difficult to get elected as an MP at the following election unless they can persuade another party to adopt them as a candidate for a 'safe' seat.

The legislative process

One of the most important functions of the House of Commons is as part of the legislature. The majority of laws are introduced as Government (Public) Bills in the House of Commons. Sometimes before the Bill is presented to the Commons the government will have issued a Green Paper outlining what it sees as the main options for legislation followed by a White Paper, which details the government's proposals (sometimes when the government feels it is clear what it wants to do a White Paper is issued without a preceding Green Paper). To allow time for discussion and consultation before the drafting of a Bill, White Papers are usually presented in the session before the legislation is introduced. A fairly large team will usually be involved in drafting a Bill, including civil servants, ministers and legal experts – a team of some 40 lawyers is retained for this purpose. All government Bills now have to be signed by the relevant minister to confirm that the Bill is not in conflict with the Human Rights Act. Each government Bill has to complete a set number of stages. These are:

- *First Reading*: a clerk reads out the title of the Bill. No vote is taken and there is no discussion. The Bill is then published so that MPs can read the contents of the Bill: the Bills are now also published on the government's Web pages. A date is usually set for the:
- *Second Reading*: the Bill is introduced and proposed by the relevant minister – usually the Secretary of State or other member of the Cabinet. The whole House debates the principles of the Bill, usually over several days. At the end of this reading a vote is taken. If the Bill passes this stage, the Bill goes to the:
- *Committee Stage*: a committee is chosen to represent the whole House – party representation on the committee reflecting the overall balance in the House. Confusingly, although these are called Standing Committees, in fact there is nothing permanent about them – they are formed afresh to discuss each Bill but are given names from letters of the alphabet: Standing Committee A, Standing Committee B, etc., depending at what stage in the Parliamentary session the committee is formed. It is in the committee stage that MPs give detailed examination of each Bill, clause by clause. The committee can vote through amendments to the Bill, provided these amendments do not compromise the principles of the Bill, as these have already been approved by the whole House. Sometimes the committee stage is dealt with by the whole of the Commons. This happens when a Bill has great significance for the future of the nation, in particular when its passage affects the constitution. Bills that give effect to Treaties with the European Union are examples of this. When the committee has completed its deliberations there is the:
- *Report Stage*: the committee reports back to the House and notifies it of the amendments it wishes to make. The government then has to decide whether it

will accept these amendments. Sometimes the government takes exception to one or more of them and sends the Bill back to the committee. It is at this stage that there is a degree of 'horse-trading' when the political skills of the members of the government and its managers, and those of the members of the committee, come to the fore as each 'side' negotiates to get as much of what they want kept or removed from the Bill. Once this stage has been exhausted the Bill is then sent back to the whole House for its:

- *Third Reading*: the House debates the final version of the Bill and then votes to accept or reject it. Provided the government has a secure majority in the House then there is little chance of a Bill being defeated at this stage.

At any time – but usually at the second reading, committee or report stages – the government may seek to limit the time spent discussing the Bill by proposing a Time Tabling Motion, commonly called a guillotine. If passed, MPs agree to a limit on the time to be spent on any particular stage or clause in the Bill. The Speaker can also rule against MPs who s/he believes is filibustering – trying to 'talk out' a Bill by speaking for as long as possible, or raising numerous and trivial amendments and/or claimed breaches of standing orders.

The Bill is then sent to the Upper House – the House of Lords – where the process is repeated, except that the Committee stage of the Bill takes place in the main chamber with all Peers able to participate in the debate. Quite often the House of Lords will wish to make amendments to the Bill. If so, then a further committee will be formed consisting of members of both Houses of Parliament and, again, there is negotiation and 'horse trading'. If the Lords insist on amendments that the government cannot accept (or indeed if it refuses to pass the Bill at all) then the Bill fails. The government then may use the power under the Parliament Act of 1949 to re-introduce the Bill in the next session of Parliament – at least 13 months from the date the Commons voted on the second reading of the Bill – and the Lords is obliged to then accept the Bill. Since the Parliament Act of 1911 the House of Lords cannot reject or delay a Finance Bill.

A Bill may begin its passage in the House of Lords, in which case it completes the stages there before being passed to the Commons.

Although most legislation is a result of Bills introduced by the government – which controls the bulk of the time available in the House – sometimes legislation is introduced by backbenchers. At the beginning of each session MPs can propose Bills and 20 are selected by a lottery and given time to be introduced as a Private Member's Bill. Unless the government then gives up some of its time the Bill is unlikely to have the chance of proceeding but, if the MP can gain support for their Bill, the government may take note and decide to introduce a Bill of its own at a later stage. If an MP is unsuccessful in 'winning' a slot for a Bill in this way he can try to introduce a Bill under the 10-minute rule. Time is normally allowed for these Bills on Tuesdays and Wednesdays but, again, unless the government gives up some of its time these Bills have no chance of becoming law – however, they often highlight particular problems and have the effect of alerting the government to some important areas of concern. In any case a Private Member's Bill cannot go to a second reading unless the government approves any financial implications.

All of these can be classed as Public Bills – they affect the general law of the land and are capable of affecting every citizen and so are Primary Legislation: they are new and important pieces of law. When laws are additions or amendments to existing Acts of Parliament they are called Statutory Instruments. The original or enabling Act will state if further measures taken under the Bill are required to have affirmative procedure – a positive vote through a resolution in Parliament – or a negative procedure; the Statutory Instrument will take effect if no MP has objected to it within 40 days. Most EU directives are 'passed' by Parliament in the latter way. There is a Select Committee on Statutory Instruments that considers many of the proposals in detail and this function is one that the House of Lords takes seriously in its role as a *revising chamber* (see below) – there is a standing committee of the Lords to consider EU Statutory Instruments.

Another type of legislation is an Order in (Privy) Council: this is one of those areas where there is potential tension between the powers of the Sovereign, the prerogative powers granted by the Sovereign to Ministers of the Crown, and the powers of Parliament. Such Orders are normally approved by Parliament before being presented for approval by the Sovereign through the Privy Council.

The final type of legislation is Private Bills: these are measure that affect only a limited number of people or are required by public organizations or individuals in order to carry out their functions. Examples are local authority by-laws. In these cases the proposers of the Bill have to justify the necessity of the Bill at the Committee stage and may be challenged by those objecting to it. Individuals with a special financial or other interest in the Bill may be allowed to question the Bill's proposers. Sometimes a Public Bill is found to contain aspects that affect private interests or specific individuals – termed a Hybrid Bill – and the legislative process is modified to take into account both types of procedure.

After both House of have passed a Bill it is then given its Royal Assent, signed in the name of the Sovereign using Norman French, which was the language of the elite at the time Parliament developed. Whether it then becomes law immediately or on a specified date (sometimes parts of an Act come into force on separate dates) depends on what is stated in the Bill.

Select committees

These were set up to enable Parliamentarians from outside the executive to scrutinize the activities of either a whole department or a particular aspect of government business. Proceedings are almost always open to the press and public and are sometimes televised. The committees have great powers to compel ministers and others to attend, give evidence and be cross-examined. To refuse to attend or comply with demands from the committee can put the individual at risk of being in Contempt of Parliament, with potentially serious consequences. MPs with a special interest in particular areas, e.g., defence, the media (often because they were involved in these areas before entering Parliament) are usually appointed to the relevant committee. Members of these committees are selected from all political parties by what are termed the *usual channels* – effectively the party whips operating under the instructions of the executive. Committee membership does, though, have to be approved by the whole House of Commons. The Labour government had to climb down in July 2001 when the HoC rejected its decision to drop two backbenchers who had caused the government some embarrassment in the previous Parliament. Members of these committees often do not follow their party line: committee members are expected to put aside party allegiance in order to get at the 'truth' of what is happening or has happened. Reports from these committees – which, like the proceedings themselves, are privileged (see Chapter 12) so that the media can report them without fear of defamation or other legal action – are often embarrassing or 'difficult' for the government of the day.

House of Lords

This is still referred to as the 'Upper House' but increasingly is seen as less important than the House of Commons. The main functions of the House of Lords are:

- to provide a constitutional check on an otherwise potentially dangerous 'elective dictatorship'
- to reform and revise legislation from the House of Commons
- to provide a platform for the opinions of a wider section of society than is represented in the House of Commons by those who have not spent their entire working life as professional politicians
- (through the Law Lords) to act as the final and highest court of appeal in the UK in both civil and criminal cases (see Chapter 13).

The House of Lords Act 1999 was introduced as an interim measure – a half-way house between no major change and a total change involving perhaps the abolition of the Lords as such and its replacement by a partly, or wholly, elected chamber. These reforms can be summarized as follows.

- Only 92 (from 759) hereditary peers would continue to sit and vote in the House of Lords. All but two of these were elected by their fellow hereditary peers. The other peers are nominated through the Prime Minister and sit and vote in the

Lords for the rest of their life – life peers. Peers do not receive a salary but can claim an attendance allowance.

- Like the House of Commons, there are peers who support the government party and those who back opposition parties – but of course these don't change as a result of a general election. Until the 1999 reforms, whichever party was in power in government there was an inbuilt Conservative majority in the Lords, which often led to Labour and Liberal governments being frustrated by votes taken in the unelected chamber – something that came to be increasingly regarded as indefensible in a supposed democracy.

- Unlike the House of Commons there is a large number of crossbenchers: those who claim to have no party allegiance. Often these are life peers who have been appointed to the Lords because of their special experience in an important area of public policy, for example, John Birt, the former Director General of the BBC. However, the political neutrality of some of these peers has been questioned. These members can also be divided in another way – between so called 'working' and 'non-working' peers. The former category do the work of the government or opposition in the Upper House.

- As in the House of Commons there are a number of ministers and shadow ministers who speak for and against legislation and on other votes. As in the House of Commons there are government and opposition whips but, as Lords do not have to face (re)election, their powers are somewhat limited compared with those who 'control' MPs in the Commons! This fact, though, is one which is often used to support an unelected chamber. The argument goes that if people are not reliant on party patronage and elections for their livelihood and career they are more likely to speak and vote in ways that are genuinely in the interests of the nation rather than a political party or of themselves.

- The House also has 27 Law Lords and 26 Lords Spiritual – the Archbishops of Canterbury and York and other leading Bishops in the Anglican Church.

In November 2001 the government issued a White Paper outlining its proposals for the second stage of the reform of the House of Lords. Under the plans the remaining hereditary peers would have to leave; 20 per cent of the membership of the second chamber would be elected – probably through the same election system and regional constituencies as that for elections to the European Parliament (see below). 60 per cent would be political appointees and the remaining 20 per cent would be crossbenchers selected by an independent commission. The fact that only one-fifth of the chamber would be directly elected immediately drew strong criticism from the opposition and Labour parties who feared the new members would be overwhelmingly party 'hacks' and, if enacted, the proposals would result in even less scrutiny and effective opposition to the executive.

One of the most important figures in the Lords is the Lord (High) Chancellor. He has a unique – and often controversial – quadruple role as:

- Speaker of the House of Lords, similar to that of the Speaker of the House of Commons – see above (however, s/he does not have the powers of the Commons' Speaker to 'control' members – their Lordships as a whole do this for themselves!). *Unlike* the Speaker of the Commons s/he:
- is a member of the Cabinet – and therefore a *party politician* and speaks and votes in debates in the Lords
- (through the Sovereign) appoints most members of the higher judiciary (judges, QCs, JPs, etc.), advises on the procedure of the civil courts and the government minister responsible for magistrates' courts
- is the senior Lord of Appeal.

The importance of the Lord Chancellor in the Constitution can be seen that in the Order of Precedence, which determines who will be Head of State in the event of the death or indisposition of the Sovereign, the Lord Chancellor is several places above that of the Prime Minister!

Governing the economy

One of the most keenly contested areas of any government is how it manages the nation's economy. Indeed, it is common wisdom that most elections are won and lost depending on how the electorate judge the government's handling of the country's finances, especially how much it is spending (and how effectively) on public services and, perhaps most crucially, how much it is taxing and proposes to tax its citizens – making a comparison with proposals on all this made by the opposition parties.

One of the great set piece events of the parliamentary year is when the Chancellor of the Exchequer gives his budget speech. The UK is probably unique in having such a dramatic and keenly awaited revelation of its government's financial plans and in having such a well known ritual. Budget day – usually in March, so that changes can be voted on and come into effect for the new tax year at the beginning of April – is always preceded by weeks, if not months of speculation in the media. Meanwhile, while those in the know, chiefly the Chancellor, Prime Minister, Chief Secretary to the Treasury and a few other senior ministers, civil servants and political advisors, traditionally 'go into purdah' – that is they reveal nothing of the budget plans – this of course just intensifies the rumour mill! Almost every group with an interest in public spending and taxation will seek an audience with the Chancellor or his senior officials to press their case. In fact the contents of the budget statement are not quite so much of a surprise as they were before the mid-1990s as, since then, there has also been a major statement in November that outlines the general state of the country's finances and estimates public spending and tax revenues for the following three years. Nevertheless, Chancellors tend to keep something 'up their sleeve' for budget day itself: usually a tax or spending 'sweetener' of some kind that they hope will grab the headlines for the next day or so.

The government's spending and taxation plans are formulated into a Finance Bill, which has to be debated and voted on like any other Bill, except, as we have seen, the House of Lords cannot block any Finance Bill, so this is very much a House of Commons event. Furthermore, Parliamentary procedure allows some changes in indirect taxes – those on petrol, alcohol, etc. – to take place within a couple of hours of being announced, usually before the Opposition have finished their immediate responses to the budget, let alone voted on it!

The government has to gain permission in every session of Parliament to spend public money by introducing Consolidated Fund Bills. The passing of these Bills is a formality but there are adjournment debates on them – which often run into the small hours of the morning.

Like any individual or business manager, the Chancellor has to balance income – about 95 per cent of which comes from taxation – and spending. Similarly, if the government spends more than its income it has to borrow, on which, like any other kind of borrowing, it has to pay interest.

Taxation can be broadly divided into two main categories. Direct taxation is levied on income or earnings – the main examples are income tax and corporation tax (on companies' profits). Indirect Taxation is on spending – main examples are Value Added tax (VAT) and fuel duty. All employers are obliged to collect and hand on a percentage of their employees' earnings in National Insurance Contributions (NIC). Originally these were supposed to merely cover the costs of individual employees' sickness, unemployment and pensions benefits, with workers (either as employees or self-employed) getting a 'stamp' to show that they had contributed to the system and were therefore entitled to claim benefits. This money would be kept separately from other government revenue. However, it is now regarded as part of the general tax 'pot'.

Full details of forecast government income and expenditure, economic output, inflation, productivity, wage increases and much else are contained in the Treasury's Red Book. Most of the details are available from government Web sites (see end of chapter). To give some examples of spending: for the year 2001–02, spending on social security was expected to amount to nearly £110 billion, or approximately £2000 for every man, woman and child in the country; health came in at nearly £48 billion. The main sources of revenue for the government were (rounded up/down): income tax, £104 billion; VAT, £61 billion; Corporation Tax, £38 billion; fuel, £23 billion. It was estimated that there would be a surplus of income over expenditure of £5 billion – and that was after £34 billion of accumulated government borrowing/debt had been paid off.

One of the main indicators of the overall performance of the economy is the Gross Domestic Product (GDP) – the size of production or output in the economy.

Another key measure of the overall health of the economy is the inflation rate (how fast prices are increasing). The responsibility for this was (within the first few days of the 1997 Labour government taking office) taken from the Chancellor of the Exchequer and given to the Monetary Policy Committee of the Bank of England. The reason for doing this was to 'lock in' iron financial discipline for the long-term health of the economy and so that interest rates cannot be manipulated for political ends – Chancellors tended to cut rates, and thereby mortgage and other interest payments for millions of electors, just before an election or party conference! This has been blamed for helping to produce the notorious 'boom and bust' in the UK economy – cuts in taxes and/or increases in public spending producing sudden lurches in inflation, followed by drastic and often ruinous increases in interest rates and cuts in public spending.

The election process

Despite the fact that the House of Lords is still referred to as the Upper House and has, as we have seen, powers to delay or amend legislation, it is the House of Commons that in reality has the greatest power. It certainly, unlike the Lords, has *democratic legitimacy* because its members are elected. The electorate vote for a single Member of Parliament using the First Past the Post (FTTP) system to represent approximately 65 000 electors in a single defined geographical area called a Constituency. This means that a general election, in which every seat in the HoC can be contested, is in reality 659 separate contests – writs are issued by the Sovereign for each constituency – with the overall outcome ('the result') being an amalgamation of these separate contests.

Under the Registration of Political Parties Act 1998 and Political Parties, Elections and Referendums Act 2000 political parties must be registered with the new Electoral Commission. Individual candidates must either be a member of one of the registered parties, or stand as an Independent. (The Speaker stands as 'Speaker seeking re-election' and by convention is not opposed by candidates from the main parties.)

The point at which the election campaign is deemed to have begun is of crucial importance as it is from this date that the spending limits by individual candidates begin (see below). Until then, journalists should be careful to refer to them as *Prospective* Parliamentary Candidates (PPCs) and be sure they do not imply that they have begun their official campaign. For broadcast journalists the start of the 'official' campaign brings with it extra restrictions. See Chapter 13 for more on this.

Candidates for any seat do not have to be resident in that constituency but their nomination paper – which they submit to the (Acting) Returning Officer, based in the constituency's district or unitary council – needs the support of ten electors who are registered voters in that constituency. They must also (to discourage frivolous candidates) find a deposit of £500, which is returned to them if they achieve at least 5 per cent of the vote. Candidates must also appoint an agent (who should live in the constituency, even if the candidate doesn't!) to whom official correspondence is sent, who has responsibility for ensuring that spending on the election is kept within the legal limits and who has to submit a list of expenditure to the Returning Officer within 35 days of the election. For the 2001 general election, spending on each candidate was limited to £5483, plus an allowance for each elector of *6.2 p* for those in a county constituency – these are predominantly in the country areas where the population is spread out relatively thinly, making them more expensive constituencies in which to campaign – compared with 4.6 p per elector in borough constituencies, which are in the more urban areas. In addition, each candidate was allowed to spend £600 on personal expenses, such as hotel bills. Expenditure in general elections is now subject to a national limit as well as the long-standing limit for expenditure by and for candidates in individual constituencies.

Voting in Parliamentary elections takes place between 7.00 a.m. and 10.00 p.m. As well as going in person to a voting booth during these hours on the day of the election, electors can have a postal vote (this obviously has to be applied for in advance of the election but there can now be 'blanket' application for all polls), or elect a proxy (someone else on the electoral role for the same constituency) to vote on their behalf.

Whatever the method of voting, it must be remembered that this is a secret ballot. It is possible during the process of counting the votes for journalists to determine how someone has voted by noting the electoral number printed on the back of ballot papers, matching this against the names and addresses given for those numbers in the electoral roll (available for inspection and copying at public libraries) and seeing on which candidate's pile the ballot paper is placed! However, should a journalist go through this elaborate process s/he must never reveal what they have found out to anyone else. To help enforce this, journalists often have to sign a Declaration of Secrecy before being allowed into the count. It is for this possibility of matching names against votes that TV cameras are not allowed to get too close to where ballot papers are being counted – Returning Officers have threatened to bar particular organizations from counting halls for getting too close to the counting process! Journalists should also ensure that if they want to report on the count and the declaration that they (and any support/technical staff) apply for tickets from the elections office at the relevant council. If they merely turn up on the night and demand entry they may well be refused – even if they flash their press (NUJ) card! Returning Officers can, and do, exercise their right to control who is present at the count. An additional problem is that once having entered a particular count a journalist may be barred from leaving it until the result is declared (this is also to avoid information 'seeping out' of particular counts before the official declaration). This can be a problem when a town or city is divided into several constituencies and a journalist is expected to cover them all. As the author can vouch from personal experience, journalists (as well as camera operators, sound technicians, etc.) may find their exit from a counting hall barred by police officers!

See Chapter 13 for further information on restrictions on broadcast journalists of their coverage on election days.

Alternative electoral systems

As discussed above, the UK is unusual in having the First Past the Post (FPTP) or Winner Takes All (WTA) system for elections to its national Parliament (as well as local authority elections outside London and Northern Ireland). Most countries use a system in which the candidates elected match more closely the proportion of votes cast for parties at the national or regional/local level. The general name for such systems is called Proportional Representation (PR). The reason for using such systems is that it is recognized that most electors cast their votes primarily to support particular political *parties* rather than individual *candidates* and that if the overall 'result' is derived from hundreds of individual and unrelated contests it is likely to disproportionately favour one party or another. The FPTP/WTA system is very bad at ensuring that the national level of support for parties is reflected in the overall result – and the government that is formed as a consequence of this process (indeed it is a statistical fluke if it does!).

The UK system has favoured the two big parties – Labour and Conservative – which have their support concentrated in certain areas or constituencies, enabling them to get the most candidates 'First Past The Post'. As discussed below, the third or lower placed parties, even though they may have very respectable overall levels of support nationally, have not won anything like the number of seats a system of PR would have awarded them. For this reason the Liberal Democrats and others have been the most enthusiastic for a change in the voting system!

Main alternatives to FPTP used in elections in the UK

- *Additional Member System (AMS)* – used for elections to the Scottish Parliament, Welsh Assembly and Greater London Authority (except for the London Mayor – see Chapter 12). A proportion of candidates are elected in the FPTP method and represent constituencies, but those elected to a further block of seats are elected proportionately to the number of votes cast for parties, voted for on a separate list. Those elected on the 'top up' system do not represent constituencies.
- *Single Transferable Vote (STV)* – used for elections to the Northern Ireland Assembly and the three MEPs for Northern Ireland (and commonly used in trades union elections). Not, strictly speaking, a PR system. It is most suitable for multi-member constituencies. Electors list candidates in order of preference ('1', '2', '3', etc.). There is a 'winning post' or *quota* for a successful candidate.

Once a candidate has reached this number in first preference votes, the second, third, etc. preferences of that candidate's *surplus* votes (those in excess of the quota) are distributed to add to the tally of the other candidates' first preferences until all the places have been filled.

● *(Closed) Party List System* – by far the most proportional system. From 1999 used to elect Members of the European Parliament (MEPs), except those for Northern Ireland – see above. Each region is now represented by multiple members – Scotland, Wales and Northern Ireland are 'regions' for this purpose and England is divided into nine regions, electing 87 MEPs in all from the UK (see below). Political parties decide not only on who should be on each regional list, but also in which order they will be elected. Voters either put a cross against a party list, or against a non-party, independent, candidate. The first candidate elected is the one who is either at the top of the winning party list or is an independent candidate who has more votes than any other independent or party. The remainder of the seats are then filled according to the proportion of the votes their party receives; e.g., in a region electing ten MEPs, a party receiving 20 per cent of the votes would have two MEPs elected. Independent candidates are elected if they reach the minimum threshold needed for one MEP in that region – in this case approximately 10 per cent of votes. Of course, it rarely works out as neatly as this! Another important difference between MEPs elected under this system compared with that for the Westminster Parliament (or at local government elections), is that if an MEP elected on a party list dies or resigns, the seat is filled by the candidate who at the previous election was next on the party list. If an MEP elected on a party list later resigns from that party there is no requirement for s/he to resign that seat. Only if an independent candidate dies is there a by-election.

Political parties: an introduction

All MPs bar one elected in the 2001 general election are members of and representatives of a political party. In the modern British political system the larger and therefore more significant of parties are, in effect, coalitions between people with different and often competing perspectives that, because of the FPTP electoral system, have been obliged to compete for votes under the same organization. In countries with a system of Proportional Representation (see above for description of main alternative voting systems) each of the main political parties would be divided into a number of separate parties, several of which – in order to form a stable and effective government – would be obliged to forge a coalition *after* an election. In the UK the coalition takes place *in advance* of elections and is on a 'permanent' basis. Sometimes a party's internal tensions cannot be resolved, the scope for compromise is exhausted and people come out in their 'true colours'.

Journalists covering political parties need to be aware of these tensions and contradictions in political outlook and philosophy between different party members and candidates. The process of selecting party leaders and Prospective Parliamentary Candidates (PPCs – see below on how the parties do this) often produces controversy and dissent – rich pickings for any journalist! One thing is for sure: any party serious on gaining power needs to reach beyond its 'natural constituency' to the broad mass of the electorate; essentially it needs to capture the 'middle ground' of politics, and also ensure it projects a reasonably united front as well, of course, as offering attractive policies and (potential) ministers, especially a Prime Minister.

The Conservative (and Unionist) Party

This is the 'modern' version of a party that was formed out of the old Tory Party (hence the common interchange between 'Conservative' and 'Tory' today) and dates back to the Reform Act of 1832, which led to the beginning of the party and election system in operation today. The 'Unionist' part of its official title indicates the party's strong commitment to the continued union of Northern Ireland (and by extension the recently devolved nations of Wales and Scotland) with the rest of the UK. In terms of national elections it has been the most successful party in the UK including, in 1979–97, the longest unbroken period of government by one party in the twentieth century. The 1997 general election, though, resulted in the Conservatives experiencing the biggest political defeat of any party in modern times, including a wipe-out of seats in Scotland and Wales. The 2001 general election heaped further humiliation on the party, which added just one seat to its net total over the previous election.

Following the 1997 defeat the rules for electing the party leader were changed significantly and this process now involves the party membership as a whole, rather than, as previously, just Conservative MPs. It is the MPs though who have to trigger a vote of No Confidence in the leader. If this motion is supported by at least 51 per cent of the party's MPs then the leader cannot seek re-election and must resign. Candidates are then voted on by MPs in a process of elimination with the weakest candidate dropping out at each stage until two candidates are left in the race for the leadership, which is determined in a final ballot with every member of the party having one vote. The first election under this system took place in the late summer of 2001 when Iain Duncan Smith defeated his rival Kenneth Clarke by 61 per cent to 39 per cent of votes cast by party members.

The process of choosing Prospective Parliamentary Candidates (PPCs) begins with hopefuls gaining approval from Central Office to get on to the Approved List of candidates. The selection then passes to the local Constituency Association, which decides on a short-list. The process ends with a general meeting of members of the Constituency Association who vote on who they want to stand in the next election.

A significant power base in the Conservative Party is the 1922 Committee (so called because it was formed in that year!), which represents the party's backbench MPs. A new organization – the Governing Board – now represents the major sectors of the party: MPs and MEPs, Conservative Central Office (the 'professional' full-time officials and organizers), and the voluntary party workers throughout the country. Half of the membership of this Board is voted on by the Leader and Central Office, the other half by the Annual Convention, the new name for the annual party conference. Policy proposals are debated at the Convention having been developed by the Conservative Policy Forum – a 'think tank' involving all sections of the party and some from outside it.

The Labour Party

The Labour Party came about as an amalgamation of socialist societies, co-operative parties and political representatives of the trades union movement. The Labour Party has been far less successful than the Conservative Party in national government – forming administrations in only 21 of the 56 post-war years of 1945–2001. The general election of the latter year resulted in an historic full second term for the party – something it had never achieved before.

The party leader is decided by an electoral college consisting of three sections that each have one-third of the overall vote: trades unions; the Parliamentary Labour Party (MPs), and individual party members, via their Constituency Labour Party (CLP). Trades unions and CLPs have to hold ballots of their individual members before casting their votes.

Selecting PPCs usually begins with party hopefuls being nominated by a section of the party – these include trades unions and ward and branch parties – and usually getting on to the National Approved List. However, the CLP – made up of several branches, relating to the boundaries of local government wards – does not have to select its candidate from that list. Although all sitting MPs have to be formally re-selected before every general election, MPs are automatically selected if they receive the votes of 25 per cent of the nominating sections. Otherwise, the General Management Committee (GMC) then vets, interviews and short-lists candidates and the final selection is voted on by the entire CLP on the basis of One Member One Vote (OMOV). The final hurdle is for the National Executive Committee (NEC) to approve the selection.

Decisions on party policy and manifesto commitments is a complex process, including a National Policy Forum, which formulates proposals to go to the Annual Party Conference, where the trades union block vote is still a major element. Party organization is run by the NEC, which has 33 members and includes reserved places for, amongst others, trades unions, party leader and deputy leader, CLPs and local government representatives.

The Liberal Democratic Party

The Liberal Democratic Party (LDP) is the result of a coalition between two separate parties: the Liberal Party, and the Social Democratic Party (SDP), which had largely been formed from disaffected members of the Labour Party. The LDP is now generally regarded as being more radical – even more left-wing – than the 'modernized' Labour Party, with a willingness to promote extra taxation for spending on health and education, strongly 'pro-Europe' and an advocate for civil liberties.

The party Leader is selected in a straightforward system of One Member One Vote. The party has a federal structure, with separate organizations for England, Scotland and Wales, which decide on selection procedures for PPCs. A national Federal Policy Committee (FPC) formulates policy for England and Wales and includes members elected at the twice-yearly Federal Party Conference. Scottish policy is decided at a separate Scottish conference. An executive committee of the FPC is responsible for national organization.

The LDP should *not* be referred to as 'The Liberal Party' or even 'the Liberals' (a bit of 'short-hand' that is frequently used by its political competitors) as there is still a separate Liberal Party that fields its own candidates, with some success in local government and whose policies – including those on 'Europe' – are very different from those of the LDP. Journalists should either use the full title or shorten it to 'Liberal Democrats' or 'Lib Dems'.

Pressure groups

A great many organizations with very different interests seek to influence the policies of the main political parties. These range from the trades unions, business, industry and retailers, through to environmental groups, animal welfare activists, women's institutes and many, many more. A number of charities separate their fund-raising activities from their political lobbying. All of these sorts of organizations – which we can give the broad umbrella title of 'pressure groups' – are excellent sources for journalists and help to provide a range of views when discussing issues of public policy. Many have full-time, properly trained press and public relations spokespeople who give interviews, etc. The single best reference guide to them and their contacts' details is probably the *Guardian Media Handbook* (Peak and Fisher, 2002).

There is sometimes a blurring in the distinction between pressure group and political party. Normally we can say that a pressure group tries to influence the policy making of a political party, as it is through the latter that changes are made possible at central, local and international level. Clearly pressure groups spend their greatest effort on seeking to persuade the main parties of government, and they may believe that one party is likely to be more sympathetic than others. For example CND, the Campaign for Nuclear Disarmament, scored its greatest success as a pressure group in the mid-1980s when the Labour Party adopted its main policy – of the UK taking the lead in phasing out nuclear weapons. It is doubtful if CND spent much time trying to persuade the Conservative Party – then in power – of the virtues of this policy! Nevertheless, things do change and in the early to mid-1990s it is probably fair to say that the Confederation of British Industry (CBI) spent as much time in trying to influence the opposition Labour Party as it did the governing Conservative Party, which, until then, had been seen as its 'natural ally'.

The other chief distinction between pressure groups and political parties is that the former are normally seen as 'single interest groups' whereas, as we have seen, owing mainly to the FPTP election system, political parties in the UK are 'broad churches'. However, there is some blurring of these distinctions when pressure groups also put up candidates in elections. Normally such candidates have no real expectation of success but use elections to publicize and raise awareness of their point of view – the free delivery of election material for every candidate in Parliamentary elections is a very cost-effective way of getting the message across! The 'Green' or Environmental movement, in the form of the Green Party, has candidates in many Parliamentary, local and (with most success) European Parliament elections. Of course, the Green Party would say that it is not a single issue group – that the care and protection of the environment is, or should be, linked to every type of policy. Similarly, the UK Independence Party (UKIP) – which also succeeded in having candidates elected to the European Parliament in 1999 – although most obviously associated with its policy of the UK's withdrawal from the European Union, does not regard itself as a single issue group, and produces manifestos with a full range of policies.

QUANGOs

QUANGO stands for Quasi Autonomous Non Governmental Organization. Or, to put it in more everyday language, it is a body that is involved in carrying out the work of government, is ultimately answerable to government and Parliament but is not part of a government department or under the direct control of ministers. The government prefers to call most QUANGOs either Non-Departmental Public Bodies (NDPBs) or Next Steps Executive Agencies (NSEAs). Whatever you like to call them there's no doubt that there has been a huge growth of these in recent years and they absorb increasing amounts of public spending. QUANGOs can be subdivided into a number of broad categories:

● *Public bodies*, set up by Act of Parliament and usually sponsored by government departments. Examples are: Environment Agency, Arts Councils, Advisory, Conciliation and Arbitration Office (ACAS).

- *Executive agencies*, most of which used to be part of ministries but now work under a general *mission statement* and are at 'arms length' from government. Examples are: Benefits Agency, Royal Mint, Driver and Vehicle Licensing Agency (DVLA).
- *Regulatory bodies*, especially those for former public utilities that are now run by private companies but which have an effective monopoly. Their terms of reference vary somewhat; some are government departments but not under ministers and others are even more 'independent' of government. Examples are OFWAT – independent regulator of the water and sewerage companies in England and Wales; Strategic Rail Authority (SRA) and the Office of Fair Trading.
- *Commissions and advisory bodies*, set up by Parliament to advise and help formulate government policy. Examples are: English Heritage, Criminal Cases Review Commission, Food Standards Agency.

By far the largest QUANGO – or, more accurately, set of QUANGOS – is the National Health Service.

National Health Service (NHS)

The NHS is mostly funded by general taxation and National Insurance contributions and accounts for around 6 per cent of the UK's Gross Domestic Product, as well as being the country's largest employer. In England it is delivered by local NHS Trusts. They are self-governing but answerable to the Secretary of State. The controversial internal market of the NHS was abolished in April 1999. In England, GPs and community nurses work together in primary care groups, with long-term service agreements replacing annual contracts. In Scotland there are now Local Health Care Co-operatives and NHS trusts were re-organized into 13 primary care trusts and 15 acute trusts. In Wales there are Local Health Groups and Northern Ireland has 20 Health and Social Services Trusts.

In England the overall service is headed by the NHS Executive – headquartered in Leeds and formed from the eight regional offices (formerly Regional Health Authorities). Under this are 100 Health Authorities (HAs). Chairmen are appointed by the Health Secretary, and non-executive members by the relevant regional body of the NHS Executive. In Wales there are five HAs with the chairman and non-executive members chosen by the First Secretary. In Scotland there are 15 Health Boards – similar to HAs. Northern Ireland has four Health and Social Services Boards.

The European Union: introduction and background

As mentioned in the first section on the constitution, one of the greatest changes to the constitution of the UK came, when, in 1973 the country became part of what was then called the European Community, often referred to as the 'Common Market'. Ministers from the Conservative government elected in 1970 signed the Treaty of Rome and steered a highly controversial Bill through Parliament that gave legal force to the UK's membership. Although some people claim that they thought the UK was only signing up to a trading agreement, the ambitions of those behind what is now the European Union have always seen it as essentially a political arrangement. Membership of the EU has constitutional significance because, as we have seen, laws made by the EU have precedence over laws passed by the UK Parliament, and the European Court of Justice (ECJ – *not* to be confused with the European Court of Human Rights) is more powerful than even the highest court in the UK – the appeal divisions of the House of Lords. Furthermore, the EU has extended its *areas of competence* (power) into almost every major aspect of the nation's governance – including employment rights, monetary policy, justice/policing and foreign and security policy, including plans for a European Defence Force, under a separate command from NATO (see below). Large amounts of money from the UK taxpayer – mainly from VAT receipts – are sent to the EU for redistribution amongst the member states, especially in agriculture and regional development policy. These aspects would, in themselves, be almost bound to cause controversy in a country with such a long, unbroken period of self-governance. But the EU is a source of even more robust debate because of its *democratic deficit* – it is claimed that the ordinary citizen has little real ability to influence decisions made by the EU's institutions, let alone elect or remove those who make those decisions.

Economic and Monetary Union (EMU) includes the setting of a common interest rate by the European Central Bank (ECB – see below), the 'harmonization' of taxation and spending policies and the abolition of national currencies in favour of the single currency – the Euro – that, (except for the UK, Denmark and Sweden, which have been granted an *opt out* – the right to decide for themselves) all member states are obliged to join if they meet certain economic criteria. The Euro was introduced to the EMU nations in January 2002 and replaced individual national currencies a couple of months later.

Community Law – falls into three main types:

- *Regulations* – applied to all member states directly with no need for national governments or parliaments to take further action in order to implement them
- *Directives* – bind member states to enforcing the decision but leave national governments and parliaments to decide how they are to be implemented (e.g., by changing the domestic law)
- *Decisions* – binding in every detail on whom they are made; this could be member states, organizations/companies or individuals.

In addition the EU can make recommendations and give opinions – but these are not binding.

The institutions of the EU – powers and responsibilities

The Commission

This is hard to compare with any body or organization in the UK national government as it is a mixture between a civil service and executive: it proposes agreements, policies and (most controversially) directives or laws (see above), as well as administering the business of the EU. The Commission appointed in 1999 will stay in place until 2004, to coincide with the five-yearly cycle of elections of the European Parliament (see below). Until that date there are 20 Commissioners, based in Brussels, appointed by the 15 member states of the time. It therefore follows that some countries appoint more than one Commissioner: the UK, France, Germany, Italy and Spain, being the most populous countries, appoint two Commissioners each. The way that responsibilities are shared out does bear some relationship with the UK Cabinet system, as each Commissioner is responsible for a specific area of the EU's activities, called Directorates-Generals, and are expected to act in the interests of the EU as a whole rather than those of the country that appointed them. One of the Commissioners is additionally given the title of President of the Commission.

Council of the European Union or Council of Ministers (CM)

The latter name is usually used to avoid confusion with the completely separate European Council – see below. The CM consists of the ministers from the member states and its composition at any one time depends on the matter being discussed – the agriculture ministers from the national governments of the member states meet to make policy on agriculture, etc. The policy and directives of the EU emerge from the negotiations that take place at these Councils so, in most respects, it can be said that this is the most powerful body, or set of bodies, in the EU. Each member state holds the Presidency of the Union on rotation for a period of six months, embodied by that country's Head of Government. The country holding the Presidency will organize and chair the meetings of each Council and each six-month period usually includes a major Council or summit, held in the country of the current President, which often involve changes and additions to the overall treaties that govern the EU's activities – effectively its constitutional powers. The council/summit is attended by the Heads of Government in each member state, their foreign ministers, the President of the Commission and one other Commissioner.

The politicians on the Council are supported, as in the UK system, by a team of civil servants: the Committee of Permanent Representatives (COREPER). As with the Council, these civil servants will be from the relevant departments of the area under negotiation, nominated by their respective countries. To ensure continuity and experience in this rotational Presidency, there is also a further layer of civil servants that looks after the administration of the EU as a whole, nominated by the member states, called the General Secretariat.

Once firm proposals emerge from the Council of Ministers there is a formal voting process that is weighted depending on the populations represented by each member state. There is a total of 87 votes, distributed as shown in Figure 11.1.

Nation(s)	Votes
France, Germany, Italy and UK	10 each
Spain	8
Belgium, Greece, the Netherlands, Portugal	5 each
Austria, Sweden	4 each
Denmark, Finland, Ireland	3 each
Luxembourg	2

Figure 11.1

The number of votes for each state, though, is not the most controversial aspect of this system – that accolade belongs to how big a majority is needed for each issue and how that majority is made up! For most issues the proposal must gain at least 62 votes (71 per cent) to become a binding policy decision or directive. To ensure that the larger, most populous countries don't use the weighting system to push through proposals to the detriment of the small countries, in some of the most controversial areas there is Qualified Majority Voting (QMV). In these cases the *62* votes must be from at least *10* member states. For the most controversial areas of all – such as taxation – all member states must vote in favour. It is this current need for *unanimity* and proposals to abolish the requirement when new states join the Union, that is likely to provide the most controversial aspects of the EU. Many point out that when the Union comprises of 20 or more states, it will be impossible to gain unanimous approval for proposals and there will need to be an expansion of some form of majority voting.

European Parliament (EP)

The EP – which consists of 626 Members of the European Parliament (MEPs) – meets in public in either of its two Parliamentary buildings in Brussels and Strasbourg. Debates are simultaneously translated into the EU's 11 official languages. Its main role is to scrutinize, and debate decisions from the Council of Ministers, especially on budgets, and has powers to reject such decisions in a process called co-decision making. Outside its main, or plenary sessions, the EP has

20 standing committees – most of which 'shadow' the 20 areas of responsibility of the Commission – as well as numerous sub-committees.

It would be incorrect to think of it as having the equivalent powers to the UK Parliament, either in making laws and in holding the executive to account. However, it can reject the Commission's proposed budget in its entirety and dismiss the entire Commission. Its threat to do the latter in 1999 – after the so called 'wise men' found there had been widespread fraud and corruption – resulted in the resignation of the entire Commission.

The membership of the EP is weighted towards the populations of the member states. Since 1999 all EU countries have been divided into regions, which each elect a number of MEPs reflecting the region's population. The UK has a total of 87 MEPs. Unlike candidates for elections to the Westminster (national) Parliament, candidates may be members of the House of Lords and, indeed, from any country in the EU.

Each member state organizes the elections of Members of the European Parliament (MEPs) to take place across the EU every five years in the same week in June. Although, as with other elections, the UK elections take place on a Thursday, because most of the rest of the EU elects its MEPs at the weekend, the UK votes are not counted or declared until the Sunday. As noted above, the UK elects its MEPs on the British mainland through a closed regional PR (party) list, so the likelihood of a candidate being elected increases the further up the list their party places them. Individual, independent, candidates of course have to do well in their own right. Northern Ireland MEPs are elected through STV. England is divided into nine regions; Scotland, Wales and Northern Ireland are each classed as a region. The number of MEPs elected by each region is as follows:

Southeast	11
London and Northwest	10 each
Scotland, Eastern and West Midlands	8 each
Southwest, Yorkshire/Humberside	7 each
East Midlands	6
Wales	5
Northeast	4
Northern Ireland	3

To emphasize that it is a *European* Parliament, rather than just an amalgamation of separate nation-states, MEPs sit and vote in Europe-wide political groupings, the largest of these being the Group of the Party of European Socialists (PES) and the Group of the European People's Party (EPP).

As can be seen, the process of decision-making is very complex, to get an overall grasp of the subject, it can be simplified as follows:

> The Commission *proposes*; the (Council of) Ministers *decide*; the (European) Parliament *ratifies*.

But this is not the end of the story! The other main bodies in the EU are the:

- *European Court of Justice* (ECJ). Based in Luxembourg, this has 15 judges and nine advocates-general drawn from the member states. Depending on the importance or complexity of the issue (which may be about the conduct of a member state as a whole, or certain aspects such as trade), the ECJ either sits as a body – a plenary – or in chambers of three to five judges. As mentioned above, the importance of the ECJ is its powers to change the laws and constitution of the member states. It should not be viewed as a court that is impartial in the way we think of UK courts but as an advocate of the political and economic development of the EU. Its rulings are binding on member states, individuals, companies and organizations and there is no appeal.
- *European Central Bank* (ECB). Based in Frankfurt, set up in 1998 to be responsible for Economic and Monetary Union (EMU), including the operation of the single currency, the Euro (€), which amongst other things involves the setting of a common interest rate across the 'Euro zone'.
- *European Investment Bank* (EIB). Based in Luxembourg, provides long-term loans for capital investment in aid of economic development and the industrial competitiveness of the EU as a whole.

The main policy and spending areas of the EU

Some of the most important (and controversial) policies and which take up the majority of the EU's budget are:

- *Common Agricultural Policy* (CAP) – sets production 'quotas' for almost all food stuffs and provides subsidies
- *Common Fisheries Policy* (CFP) – sets quotas for the catching of all main sea-water fish and limits the fleets of each nation and decides where they may operate.
- *Structural Fund* – About one-third of the EU's total budget goes into this area. This is distributed to each member state depending on its wealth and economic activity, in order to 'level out' or 'harmonize' the economies of all parts of the EU. The poorest areas/regions – such as Merseyside in England – are granted Objective One status. The Structural Fund is divided into different areas of

activity and concern. For the UK the most significant are: the European Regional Development Fund (ERDF), which provides funds for various infrastructure and industrial development projects, and the European Social Fund (ESF), which is mostly concerned with supporting education and training. All such policies have to be sent for consultation to the Committee of the Regions, which is tasked with making good what is supposed to be one of the abiding principles of the EU – that of subsidiarity: that decisions should be made at the lowest (most local) appropriate level. In most cases the Structural Fund provides only part of the funds for any project; the member state provides the rest: matching funds. This is a hugely controversial area and the journalist should be aware of the rows between politicians at the national/local/devolved area of government over many of these projects!

Other international organizations to which the UK belongs

There follows a brief summary of some of the other main organizations that have significant effect on the governance of the country.

The Council of Europe (not to be confused with the European Union/ Commission, etc.) – founded in 1949, with the aim of promoting European social, political, economic and cultural progress amongst its members. There is a committee of ministers, consisting of the foreign ministers of member countries who meet twice a year and a Parliamentary Assembly of 291 representatives. One of the Council of Europe's main achievements made in its earliest days, and in the aftermath of World War II, was the European Convention on European Rights of 1950, leading to the Strasbourg-based Court of Human Rights, whose decisions are binding on UK courts and government. As we have seen, the Convention has now been incorporated into UK domestic law through the Human Rights Act 1998, so UK citizens no longer have to go to Strasbourg to argue their case.

World Trade Organization (WTO) – the successor to the General Agreement on Tariffs and Trade (GATT). Its main purpose is to promote 'free trade' by breaking down restrictive trade agreements and practices within and between nations. The underlying philosophy behind the organization is that unfettered market capitalism will increase the economic wealth of the world in general as well as each individual nation. The main meetings of the WTO are now routinely accompanied by huge, and often violent, anti-capitalist demonstrations by those who believe the decisions made by the WTO in fact increase the divide between rich and poor nations and peoples.

(British) Commonwealth (of Nations) – a group of 54 independent nation-states and dependencies of the UK. All were formerly part of the British Empire and/or League of Nations. As we have seen, the organization is headed by the UK Sovereign (the Queen). The original idea of a *commonwealth* – of preferential and united trading between the member countries – has been largely overtaken and neutered by the development and increasing importance of the European Union and World Trade Organization and now is mostly concerned with political influence rather than raw economic or trading arrangements.

G8 (formerly G7) – since 1975 the heads of state or government of the major industrialized democracies have met annually to debate the major economic and political questions of the time. What is now the G8 began with six countries: France, USA, UK, Germany, Japan and Italy. They were joined by Canada for the second summit. The 1998 summit in Birmingham, UK, saw the full involvement of Russia for the first time – making the G8. Thousands of journalists attend each meeting and the annual summits are now one of the major events in the international political calendar.

North Atlantic Treaty Organisation (NATO) – formed in 1949 and now consists of 17 European countries, plus (crucially) the USA, and Canada. It is designed to provide the common defence of the member nations. Article 5 of its constitution, which in essence states that *an attack on one is an attack on all* was invoked for the first time in September 2001 in response to the terrorist attacks in the USA. The North Atlantic Council, chaired by the Secretary-General, is the highest authority in the alliance and is made up of permanent representatives of the 19 member states.

United Nations – was established shortly after World War II by 51 countries with the main purpose of preventing another world conflict – and the circumstances that lead to war. Today, nearly every nation in the world belongs to the UN: membership now totals 189 countries.

When states become members of the United Nations, they agree to accept the obligations of the UN Charter, an international treaty that sets out basic principles of international relations. According to the Charter, the UN has four purposes: to maintain international peace and security, to develop friendly relations among nations, to co-operate in solving international problems and in promoting respect for human rights, and to be a centre for harmonizing the actions of nations.

UN Members are sovereign countries. The United Nations is not a world government, and it does not make laws. The United Nations has six main organs. Five of them – the General Assembly, the Security Council, the Economic and Social Council, the Trusteeship Council and the Secretariat – are based at UN

Headquarters in New York. The sixth, the International Court of Justice, is located at The Hague, the Netherlands.

The UN Charter gives the Security Council primary responsibility for maintaining international peace and security. Under the Charter, all member states are obligated to carry out the Council's decisions.

There are 15 Council members, including the UK, which is also one of the five permanent members; the others are China, France, the Russian Federation and the USA. The other ten are elected by the General Assembly for two-year terms. Decisions of the Council require nine 'yes' votes. Except in votes on procedural questions, a decision cannot be taken if there is a 'no' vote, or veto, by a permanent member.

Reporting central government

It might seem from this account of central government – with the frequent mentions of 'secrecy' – that the journalist is faced with an impossible task of reporting what goes on in Whitehall and Westminster (and this task should not be thought to be just one for London-based journalists; the regional media, especially newspapers, are increasingly 'targets' for the attention of government ministers and their officials). There can be no doubt that, as argued in Chapter 1, the UK has one of the most secretive culture and workings of any in what can be termed 'Western liberal democracies'. The evolution of the Constitution has not included a substantial increase in transparency or openness at the centre of power (see Chapter 13 for a discussion of the Freedom of Information Act and other legal developments, as well as difficulties on reporting activities of QUANGOs, and Chapter 12 on how reporting of local government has become more difficult).

Reporting of the European Union is even more problematic – and if ever an organization deserved to be put under the journalistic spotlight then surely it is the EU.

Nevertheless, the persistent and diligent journalist can often find out a great deal of 'what is really going on'. For a start, of course, the proceedings of Parliament, both in the main chambers and committees of both Houses, are almost always open to the press and are often broadcast. A record of the proceedings is available through Hansard. But, of course, journalism is not only about 'straight' reporting of debates and statements, which in any case are in the public domain. Journalists want the background to issues; to fulfil the 'watchdog' and 'scrutinizing' functions outlined in Chapter 1, they need to be able to test and probe. The policies of the government and the thinking of the Prime Minister can be tested and questioned through the twice-daily briefings given to the Lobby – a group of journalists who are nominated by the main media outlets and accredited with special access to the Prime Minister's Official Spokesman (PMOS). Until 1997 these were 'off the record' – that is to say unattributable, with the person giving such briefings named simply as 'sources close to the Prime Minister'. When the Labour government came to power in May 1997 it was agreed that these comments could be attributed to PMOS, although this new openness did not extend to being able to name this person as Alastair Campbell! (Campbell stepped down from the post just before the 2001 general election to take a more 'strategic' role in government information.)

The Lobby meets PMOS, or one of his deputies, twice a day when Parliament is sitting. The first briefing takes place at 11.00 a.m. in a basement room at Number 10 Downing Street. This will normally start with PMOS describing the main events in the PM's diary and other government business. It is then up to the journalists to question and probe government policies and actions. The second lobby briefing takes place at 4.00 p.m. in the Palace of Westminster. This time the PMOS is the guest of the Lobby – the meeting takes place in 'their' room! An additional Lobby is held on Thursday afternoons, taken by the Leader of the House (of Commons), so that journalists can be briefed about government business in the following week. There is also a separate Lobby for the journalists on Sunday newspapers.

The other official route to stories on central government is via the Government Information and Communication Service (GICS), which, as the name suggests, is supposed to be concerned with providing factual information on the government, not party-political propaganda.

The government claims there is a new culture of openness and they have built on the voluntary codes that were part of the Citizen's Charter begun under the previous, Conservative, administration. The trouble with all of these developments is that they are voluntary and leave the final decision as to what should be revealed to press and public to ministers and civil servants – there is still no overall presumption that the media and public has a right to know.

Journalists should consider using the Public Records Office (PRO) based in Kew, London (which, like GICS, has a Web site – see 'Sources and resources' at the end of the chapter) for historic background to political stories. These records often have surprisingly strong relevance to today's events. For example, research into documents at the PRO into the 1967 crisis of Foot and Mouth Disease (FMD) provided a fascinating glimpse into the contrasts and similarities with the way the FMD crisis of 2001 was handled. Indeed, it was often remarked that the government would have benefited from reading those records – as well as the official report and its recommendations produced after the crisis!

The relationship between journalists and politicians is undoubtedly a complex one, with great scope for misunderstandings and grievances on both sides. Indeed, it has been likened to that between a dog and a lamp-post – but journalists and politicians cannot agree on which is which! What is clear is that they need each other. Politicians in a democratic system need journalists to enable them to communicate their 'message' in as positive a light as possible to maintain, or restore, their popularity in order to get re-elected; journalists need politicians to provide them with interesting stories to gain and maintain the interest of their readers or audiences – and of course to make sure they keep their job by impressing their editors with their ability to bring in those stories, especially if those are exclusives.

This need to outdo their rivals means that although journalists often work as a 'pack' – in the Lobby or at press conferences, for example – they also need to cultivate their own contacts to ensure they are 'fed' gossip and 'inside tips' as to what is going on behind closed doors. This means that journalists need to build up trust with certain key individuals, ensuring they spend time away from their desks for personal contact, perhaps in the bars and tea-rooms at Westminster, or for more confidential meetings at secret rendezvous, as well as ensuring they have the phone numbers of those contacts so that they can talk to them outside 'working hours'. Leaks of Cabinet meetings, briefing papers, memos and reports, as well as off-the-record briefings by ministers and officials, are an important part of the process of revealing the 'truth' behind the machinery of power.

Suggested activities

1 Find out who your MP is, what party s/he represents and what is their main political outlook (find some cuttings or press releases). Find out what committees/select committees your MP belongs to and if s/he holds any government job.
2 What was the result of the 2001 general election in your constituency?
3 Find out the membership of the current Cabinet, then study one department of state in depth and produce a list of all its ministers, their responsibilities and the name of the Permanent Secretary.
4 Follow the progress of a bill currently going through Parliament (see Web sites below). Look up one recent Act of Parliament on the Web (see below).
5 Make list of the main political controversies of the moment – what is the position of the main parties and politicians on these?
6 Find out how a pressure group is trying to influence one of these issues (press releases/Web sites, etc.).
7 Study reports of a lobby briefing and see how these compare with information on the lobby given on the official Web site (see below).
8 Find out the names of your MEPs – look on their Web sites and draw up a 'mini biography' of at least three of them, including their main interests, political affiliations, etc.

 9 Investigate a QUANGO operating in your area – what are its responsibilities? Who is on the 'board'? Are its meetings open to the press and public?
10 Find out what the main issues facing the European Union are – when is the next summit to take place? Try to find out how the EU is affecting life in your area (funding, controversies, etc.).
11 Build a profile of an international governmental organization and its recent activities.

Sources and resources

Anderson, P. and Weymouth, A. (1999) *Insulting the Public – the British press and the European Union*. London: Longman.

BBC News (1998) *A–Z of Parliament* http://news.bbc.co.uk/hi/English/uk_politics/a.z_of_parliament/default.stm (accessed 10 April 2001).

BBC News (2001) *On Your Marks, Get Set . . .* http://news.bbc.co.uk/hi/English/uk_politics/newsid_1256000/1256066.stm (accessed 5 April 2001).

Benn, T. (1996) *The Benn Diaries*. London: Arrow.

British Monarchy (2001) http://www.royal.gov.uk/index.htm (accessed 23 September 2001).

Cabinet Office (1997) *Ministerial Code*. http://www.cabinet-office.gov.uk/central/1997/mcode/foreword.htm (accessed 10 April 2001).

Cole, J. (1996) *As It Seemed To Me*. London: Phoenix.

Conservative Party (2001) http://www.conservatives.com (accessed 23 September 2001).

Curran, J. (1998) *Media, Power and Politics*. London: Routledge.

Dinan, D. (1994) *Ever Closer Union? An introduction to the European Community*. Macmillan.

Europa (2001) *The ABC of the European Union*. http://europa.eu.int/abc-en.htm (accessed 23 September 2001).

Electoral Reform Society. *Voting Systems*. http://www.electoral-reform.org.uk/sep/votingsystems/systems.htm (accessed 7 November 2000).

Fenney, R. (2000) *Central Government 2000*. London: LGC Information.

Franklin, B. (1994) *Packaging Politics – political communication in Britain's media democracy*. London: Edward Arnold.

Government Information and Communication Service (2001) http://www.gics.gov.uk (accessed 23 September 2001).

G8 Information Centre (2001) *From G7 to G8*. http://www.g7.utoronto.ca/g7/what_isg7.html (accessed 25 April 2001).

Hicks, S. (1999) *The Political System of the European Union*. Basingstoke, Hampshire: Palgrave.

House of Commons (1998) *The Committee System of the House of Commons.* http://www.parliament.uk/commons/selcom/ctteesys.htm (accessed 3 April 2001).

Jones, N. (2000) *Sultans of Spin.* London: Orion.

Jones, N. (2001) *Campaign 2001.* London: Politico's.

Jones, B., Kavanagh, D., Moran, M., *et al.* (2001) *Politics UK* (4th. edition). Harlow: Pearson Education.

Liberal Democrats (2000) *People and Party.* http://www.libdems.org.uk/index.cfm-?page=main&section=people (accessed 19 April 2001).

Labour Party (2001) http://www.labour.org.uk (accessed 23 September 2001).

McCormick, J. (1999) *Understanding the European Union – a concise introduction.* London: Macmillan.

Monbiot, G. (2000) *Captive State – the corporate takeover of Britain.* London: Macmillan.

National Statistics (2001) *Gross Domestic Product – a brief guide.* http://www.statistics.gov.uk/themes/economy/articles/briefguides/gdpbriefguide.asp (accessed 19 April 2001).

Negrine, R. (1994) *Politics and the Mass Media in Britain* (2nd edition). London: Routledge.

Oakley, R. (2001) *Inside Track.* London: Bantam Press.

Peak, S. (ed.) (2002) *The Guardian Media Guide 2003.* London: Atlantic Books.

Peele, G. (1995) *Governing the UK* (3rd edition). Oxford: Blackwell.

Public Records Office (1998) *The Public Records System and Access to Public Records.* http://www.pro.gov.uk/about/access.htm (accessed 2 February 2001).

Rawnsley, A. (2000) *Servants of the People.* London: Hamish Hamilton.

Seaton, J. (ed.) (1998) *Politics and the Media – harlots and prerogatives at the turn of the Millennium.* Oxford: Blackwell.

Sergeant, J. (2001) *Give Me Ten Seconds.* London: Macmillan.

Stationery Office (2000) *Whitaker's Concise Almanack.* London: Stationery Office.

UK Online (formerly uk open government) (2001) http://www.ukonline.gov.uk (accessed 23 September 2001).

United Nations *The UN in Brief.* http://www.un.org/Overview/brief.html (accessed 25 April 2001).

Wheeler, M. (1997) *Politics and the Mass Media.* Oxford: Blackwell.

12 Devolved and local government

- Introduction and background
- Devolution
- Local government services
- Local government structure and powers
- Policing
- Elections
- Who can become a councillor?
- What councillors do
- Payments to councillors
- Councillors and officers
- How councils operate
- New political structures in councils in England and Wales
- Scrutiny committees
- Standards committees
- A question of tax
- Council spending
- Best value
- Reporting local government
- What is a 'key decision'?
- Suggested activities
- Sources and resources

Introduction and background

For around 200 years there have been complaints that government in the UK is too centrally controlled – certainly power is far more centralized in the UK than in many other comparable countries. This centralization has been especially resented in the former sovereign nations of Wales and, particularly, Scotland, which have their own proud history, culture and legal system. This has led to a number of unresolved tensions in the Union.

The Labour government elected in May 1997 was committed to establishing devolved forms of government to Scotland and Wales. For both these nations-within-a-nation, there was a long-term commitment to 'democratize' powers exercised through the Scottish and Welsh Offices (government departments). Devolution was agreed in Northern Ireland after protracted and extremely difficult negotiations between the Unionist and Republican parties, with involvement of the government and people of the Irish Republic.

Although each of these processes resulted in different settlements, the overall effect was that powers that had been exercised by ministers and civil servants in London were transferred to the devolved nations and province, with direct democratic legitimacy through elected members of Parliament (Scotland), Assembly (Wales and Northern Ireland) and the executives appointed through them. The main areas of government transferred in each of the devolution settlements were:

- Agriculture, Fisheries and Food
- Arts, Culture and Media
- Economic Development
- Education and Training
- Environment
- Health
- Housing
- Local government
- Planning
- Social Services
- Sport and Leisure
- Tourism
- Trade and Industry
- Transport and Roads.

For Scotland there was an additional pledge over many years to restore a Parliament with limited tax-raising powers. Scotland had retained its separate legal system and judiciary and these powers were transferred to the new executive and Parliament. Secondary legislation – laws that are made with 'permission' from the original or primary legislation – were devolved.

In all cases, though, the vital powers needed for the governance of the nation-state as a whole were retained in Whitehall and Westminster. These so called reserve powers include the overall direction of the economy, including most types of taxation; social security benefits and pensions; trade and industry; and defence and foreign affairs. Furthermore, many of the other areas of government had some devolved detailed decision-making but the overall thrust and direction continues to be set by London, which crucially continues to allocate most of the finance in the form of block grants.

Despite these limitations and restrictions on full devolution – which meant that the changes stopped well short of creating a true federal structure – the devolutionary process represents the most fundamental shifts in power and constitutional change in the UK for at least two centuries.

It should also be noted that, as with local government (see below), devolution has only occurred through an Act of the UK/Westminster Parliament. None of the arrangements described below are securely rooted in the Constitution – what the UK government and Parliament has done it can undo: a point vividly made by the suspension and then reinstatement of the Northern Ireland executive between December 1999 and May 2000 and again in September 2001.

The elections to the first Parliaments and Assemblies all resulted in coalitions in the resulting executives. The voting systems used were almost bound – and in Northern Ireland's case *intended* – to prevent rule by one political party. In the long run the necessary co-operation between political parties may cause the most significant change to the political culture of the UK as a whole.

One unresolved question in the newly devolved UK relates to the continuing arrangements in the Westminster Parliament over the governance of England. This is commonly referred to as the West Lothian question – so called because it was notably raised by the MP who represented that constituency. How can it be right that whilst MPs from Scotland, Wales and Northern Ireland can vote on matters in the UK Parliament that relate only to England, English MPs cannot do the same for matters now decided in the devolved bodies of the other nations/ regions?

One option seriously canvassed was to extend powers to regions; this happened in London in 2000 and there was pressure in some other parts of England – notably the northeast – for similarly strong executive-led and devolved administrations covering a number of local authority areas. However, there was also considerable resistance to such ideas: was another layer of politicians and bureaucrats really the answer? And England did not readily or obviously divide into regions; there were few historical and cultural factors or even obvious geographical unities in politically contrived units. Indeed, parts of some of these regions have a history of enmity – Teesside and Tyneside in the northeast, and the cities of Manchester and Liverpool in the northwest, for example.

Even with devolution and with or without regional government there remained the 'problem' of what to do with local government: the hundreds of local authorities and thousands of civil servants and elected councillors providing the services that are closest to most people and about which they should feel most engaged. Nor is local government a small matter. It is responsible for a quarter of all public spending and employs more than 2 million people.

Unfortunately, local government tends to have a rather boring image, linked in most people's minds with unglamorous tasks such as refuse collection and the maintenance of local parks.

Surveys have repeatedly shown that few people are aware of who their local councillors are and, in many cases, only think about local government when their council tax bill arrives or when they see reports of some apparently petty political infighting at their town hall. This lack of engagement or interest in local government is reflected in the turnout at elections for councillors, which is frequently less than 30 per cent.

Local government in England and Wales was subject to radical change in its structure and powers in a period of about 30 years from the late 1960s but this did not prevent central government from wishing to make further major changes. Aside from the new set-up in London, this was not so much about changing the number and structure/functions of local authorities but the way those responsibilities were carried out. Local government decision-making was regarded as cumbersome, ineffective and over-bureaucratic. In particular it was the 'governance by committee' system that, although having positive democratic features in that it allowed decisions to be fully debated with every councillor allowed to state his or her opinion, was seen as ludicrously lengthy, with its sometimes interminable 'referring back' procedures. Radical options to allow decision-making to be proposed and even made by a small group of cabinet-type councillors were passed by Parliament in the Local Government Act 2000 (LGA) (see below).

At the same time an overarching requirement for councils to pursue policies for the 'economic well-being of the community' was specified. Together with this there was a new emphasis on 'best value' for services, combined with high ethical standards from councillors and officers and nationally set targets and standards. This last feature demonstrates that, for all its talk of devolved government and decisions to be made at the lowest/most local level, the trend developed by the previous Conservative administrations of local councils acting as agents and standards-enforcers for local services, rather than necessarily providing these themselves, continued and was even strengthened under New Labour. The justification for this is that if local services are subject to the whim of local councils there will be enormous differences in the standard and quantity of such services: it would become a 'postcode lottery' and subject to the prejudices and politics of local politicians. Perhaps even more pertinent is the fact that the locally raised taxes only amount to about 35 per cent of the amount spent by local government: central government argues that as it provides most of the money through central taxation, it should have a major say in how it is spent. The amount of spending by local government is so great that decisions about how much and where money is spent are bound to have a significant impact on the overall economy of the country. Central government therefore is almost bound to take a close interest in decisions at the local level.

This chapter will describe the structures and powers of devolved government and then analyse how local government operates, with special emphasis on the major reforms to decision-making in local authorities and the implications of this for journalism.

Devolution

Scotland

The Scotland Bill was passed by Parliament in 1998 and followed a strong 'yes' vote in a referendum that year. The first elections to the Scottish Parliament took place in May 1999 and the devolution arrangements became fully operational on 1 July that year. The Scottish Parliament has 129 members – MSPs – elected for four years by the Additional Member System (AMS, see Chapter 11); 73 MSPs represent the same constituencies as for the Westminster Parliament and 56 are from regional party lists. The Parliament, under the control of a Presiding Officer (equivalent to the Speaker in the Westminster Parliament), elects a First Minister who heads an Executive. As in the Westminster Parliament, a great deal of the detailed work is carried out by committees. The Parliament is funded by a block grant from the UK government but *can increase or decrease the standard rate of income tax* set by the Westminster Parliament *by up to 3 pence in the pound* and pass some forms of primary legislation. Parliament and Executive have responsibility for most areas of domestic, economic and social policy. However, the UK government and Parliament retain control of defence and foreign affairs, national security, overall economic policy as well as employment and social security.

The legislative process is quite complex: there are three types of Bill – executive, committee, or members'. Each Bill has to be accompanied by a written statement from the Presiding Officer confirming that the Bill falls within the competence of the Parliament; a financial memorandum setting out in detail the costs that would be incurred by the enactment of the Bill and an Auditor General's Report if there will be cost to the Scottish Consolidated Fund – in essence the money available to the Scottish Executive. Once it has passed these hurdles, each Bill has to pass through three stages before it becomes law:

- *Stage one* – considers the general principles, usually discussed by the Lead Committee. This is then debated by the full Parliament, which votes on whether to allow the Bill to pass to:
- *Stage two* – a clause-by-clause examination of the Bill. This may either be done by committee or by the full Parliament.
- *Stage three* – final consideration of the Bill by the full Parliament and MSPs vote on whether the Bill should be passed. If it is, up to half of the main clauses can be referred back for further consideration under the procedures in Stage two. Parliament finally decides whether to approve the Bill. If so, it is submitted by the Presiding Officer to the Sovereign for the Royal Assent – thus emphasizing again that ultimate power belongs to the Head of State for the whole of the UK.

Wales

The timetable for Welsh devolution coincided with that for Scotland – but it is worth noting that the referendum votes here was very close and only about half of the electorate participated in it, so it could be said that only about one-quarter of those in Wales positively voted for the form of devolution on offer.

The National Assembly for Wales has 60 members, again elected for four years by the system of elections known as AMS (see Chapter 11) – 40 Assembly Members (AMs) represent the same constituencies as for the Westminster Parliament and 20 are from the regional party list system. As in Scotland there is a Presiding Officer. The Assembly has no powers for tax raising or primary legislation – it considers and passes secondary or delegated legislation – and, unlike Scotland, the Westminster government and Parliament retains power for the police and legal system. The Assembly, though, can propose specific legislation for inclusion within the UK legislature at Westminster, including further delegated powers that it would like to have. Liaison over this is mainly through the Secretary of State for Wales who therefore still has considerable power and influence. The Assembly also considers and responds to consultation papers from the UK government when they affect its own responsibilities. Most importantly – and as it turned out controversially – the Assembly and Executive now have the power and responsibilities for dealing with and distributing grants from the European Union. The Executive is run on similar lines to that in Scotland, supported by a number of committees.

Northern Ireland

The Northern Ireland Assembly was elected in June 1998 using the STV system (see Chapter 11). It consists of 108 members (MLAs) – six each from the 18 constituencies in the Westminster Parliament. The Assembly resulted from the so-called Good Friday Agreement of April that year and a referendum on its proposals held the following month. The Assembly, supervised by a Presiding Officer, has legislative and executive authority in the areas previously administered by the six government departments of Northern Ireland: agriculture, economic development, education, environment, finance and personnel, health and social services. Certain issues regarded as being especially sensitive have to receive particular majorities, to ensure they have wide cross-community support. There is an Executive, with a First Minister, Deputy First Minister and up to ten other Ministers, who are appointed according to the electoral support for the parties they represent. The executive functions are supported by parallel committees, the composition of which again reflects party support.

As well as the Assembly and Executive, four other bodies were set up – mostly in an attempt to improve co-operation, trust and reconciliation between the two parts of the island of Ireland: the British-Irish Council, North/South Ministerial Council, Civic Forum and British-Irish Intergovernmental Conference.

England

In response to the trend to devolution the government has created nine Regional Development Agencies (RDAs) in regions of England – the geographic areas being identical with those for the now regionally elected Members of the European Parliament (see below) – adding to suspicions by some observers that the UK government is conniving with the European Union in creating structures that bypass, and ultimately undermine, national parliaments. (As has already been mentioned in the introduction to Chapter 11, this is one of a number of objections to the idea of regional government in England). The job of the RDAs is to co-ordinate and promote economic, industrial and employment in their areas. These have developed work already in motion through Regional Government Offices (RGOs). The makings of regional government as such have been laid with the creation of similarly located Regional Assemblies. Although membership of these bodies, like the RDAs, is currently through appointment, they are likely to be filled through elections, if voters in the regions vote for this in referenda.

Local government services

When we consider how many people are employed by local government, the range of services they provide and above all how much money is spent at the local level, it is easier to understand the concern by central government with what happens in the country's town halls. As mentioned in the introduction, local authorities in England and Wales employ well over 2 million people and spend £70 billion – that's one-quarter of all public spending and one-tenth of the country's entire domestic economic output.

In general we can say that local government has five main functions:

1 To directly provide services and facilities (see Figure 12.1). These are clearly laid out in the relevant Acts of Parliament, which state what each type of council must do – its statutory obligations; how it is to manage each of its responsibilities (e.g., education and social services); and limits to what it may do. If a council goes beyond its powers then it is acting *ultra vires* – and may be challenged in the courts – as it may if it is thought it has not followed the correct procedures. In these cases there may be reference to the Local Government Ombudsman who will decide if there has been maladministration.
2 To contract out the running and management of services and facilities using the 'best value' criteria (see below).

3 To monitor and evaluate services provided by other public/private sector organizations, especially to ensure that nationally mandated standards are achieved.
4 To provide elected representatives to local QUANGOS, thus ensuring some democratic involvement in these bodies, as well as providing members to joint boards that run services operating over several local authority areas.
5 To be proactive in promoting the area's economy, facilities and image, including the use of central and European Union funding and partnerships with the private sector.

The main services provided by – or at least *through* – local government are:

- Education (mostly in the school sector) – over one-quarter of all local government spending is taken up by this sector. Some 26 000 schools are run by Local Education Authorities (LEAs) – or education and library boards in Northern Ireland – with 8 million children taught by 360 000 full- and part-time teachers. However, under Local Management of Schools (LMS) most of the education part of the central government grant goes directly to schools and there is increasing central government control of the curriculum, linked with standards, targets and testing. There are increasing moves for secondary schools to develop specialist subject areas and, most controversially, to be able to select 10 per cent of their intake. There can be few subjects that arouse greater public interest than education and the local news media should keep a very close watch on these developments in their areas.
- *Social Services* – about £12 billion is spent on this sector, over half of which is spent on elderly residents. Some 200 000 care staff deal with such services as community care, care of children – including adoption and fostering, residential care and nursing homes, and personal social services, such as home helps.
- *Libraries* – one of the most heavily used and popular services provided by local government – and one for which there is still a considerable amount of local autonomy. Some 22 000 staff are employed in about 3000 libraries, on which is spent £800 million a year.
- *Housing* – around £12 billion a year is still spent on building, maintaining and improving public housing stock – despite the big reduction in the numbers of 'council houses' resulting from the 'right to buy' policy. Local government increasingly plays a *strategic* and *co-ordinating role* between the public and private sectors and non-profit-making bodies such as Housing Action Trusts (HAT).
- *Planning* – local authorities exercise major power in deciding on what can be built and developed in their areas and other issues of land use. Issues such as transport and economic development often come into such decisions. The major local authority in each area is responsible for drawing up a structure plan, which is supposed to provide an overall blueprint for planning in their areas. In two-tier systems both types of authority are involved in the planning process.

● *Roads and transport* – more than 96 per cent of all road miles is built, managed and maintained by local authorities and they are often subcontracted to maintain sections of motorways and other trunk roads. In addition they are responsible for traffic management, road safety and street parking. Arrangements for road maintenance are often 'swapped' between different levels of authority when there is a two-tier system (see below).

● *Fire and rescue* – about 33 000 fire-fighters based at nearly 1500 stations not only deal with fires in their areas but develop fire prevention and education initiatives, inspect premises for fire safety measures, issue certificates and deal with road traffic accidents, chemical spills and other hazardous situations.

● *Emergency planning* – local authorities co-ordinate the different emergency services to prepare for and rehearse as well as respond to emergencies such as flooding, chemical leaks/spillages, terrorist attacks and other civil defence matters.

● *Environmental health* – a wide range of services, enforcement and control, including pollution control, food safety, animal welfare, pest control, dog wardens, noise pollution, waste disposal and collection. These are some of the services that the public most readily associates with local government through 'bin days' and waste collection and recycling centres – as well as building waste disposal sites (landfill or incineration). A wide range of regulations, laws and policies from different levels of government – including the EU – overlap in these services.

● *Trading standards/consumer protection* – with a total budget of some £120 million this is one of the growth areas of local government and is aimed at protecting the interests of the consumer and local businesses; one of the many areas in which local government enforces law and prosecutes.

Local government structure and powers

There are different structures in different parts of England, and different ones again in Scotland, Wales and Northern Ireland. Outside England all local services are covered by one unitary council.

England

The situation in England is complex and varied, and London has a different system again! In some parts of England one council provides all the government services – these are called either metropolitan borough councils – so called because they are in the main urban parts of England outside London – there are 34 of these; or unitary councils, which are normally in the less urban areas and many of which were formerly part of the two-tier structure. There are 46 of these. These 'single council areas' have joint boards to cover services such as fire, waste disposal and public transport, which run across a number of authorities. The make up of such boards includes representation from each borough/district.

In other parts of England – mostly in the rural 'shire' areas – there are *two tiers* of principal authorities: a county council that provides most of the main services (those that cost the most) such as education and social services, with a number of district or borough councils below them. These are still major councils – they have important functions that are open to public scrutiny – and are responsible for issuing and collecting the council tax in their areas.

Many areas of England also have a town or parish council. Most of these are in rural areas and can be created if local residents demonstrate there is a demand for it. Such councils are involved in such things as community centres, art and leisure facilities and public conveniences. They must also be told about planning applications in their area. However, these are not classified as principal authorities and therefore are under less obligation to provide facilities and information to journalists than is the case for the principal authorities.

London

In Greater London there are 32 borough councils equivalent in powers, functions and structures to metropolitan district/borough councils in the rest of England – plus the Corporation of the City of London (see below) and the overarching Greater London Authority (GLA), which consists of a directly elected Mayor and an assembly. The main areas of responsibility of the GLA are transport, planning, the environment, health, police, fire and emergency planning, culture and housing. The GLA has a total of 25 members – 14 directly elected to serve specific areas of London comprised of two or three boroughs, and 11 additional members elected on the basis of party political support using the Additional Member System (see Chapter 11 and below).

The (directly elected) Mayor, elected for a four-year term at the same time as members of the GLA, is the head of the GLA, whose main role is to ensure that the aims of the voters as a whole are carried out in the interests of all the people. The Mayor has extensive executive decision-making powers and is responsible for strategic planning and appointments, including those for the four bodies that are under the control of his authority – the London Development Agency; Transport for London; Metropolitan Police Authority; London Fire and Emergency Planning.

But the Mayor cannot act alone. There is a requirement to consult interested parties as well as business representatives; also, most importantly, the London boroughs, and the Assembly. The Assembly's main role therefore is to scrutinize the decisions and policies of the Mayor.

The Corporation of London is the local authority for the City of London – the famous 'square mile'. It is governed by the Court of Common Council, a legislative body that consists of the Lord Mayor (not to be confused with the directly elected

Mayor of the GLA), plus two Sheriffs who are nominated each year by the City Guilds (also known as the livery companies) and elected by the Court of Aldermen; 24 additional aldermen (a title that was in widespread use in England until the 1970s) and 130 common councilmen who are elected annually from the 25 wards of the City. A unique feature of this Council is that no one stands as a representative of a political party.

Scotland

Since April 1996 local government in Scotland has consisted of 32 unitary authorities (29 on the mainland and three island councils). Each of these councils took over the functions of the previous regional and district councils on the mainland (the island councils were already unitary authorities), except for water and sewerage, which are provided by three public bodies appointed by the Scottish Executive. Legislation for local government has now been devolved to the Scottish Parliament and two working groups are developing ideas for changing the relationship between the Scottish Executive/Parliament and local councils, as well as election systems and arrangements.

There are also some 1000 community councils. However, unlike their equivalents in England and Wales, these are not local authorities as such but they must be consulted on such matters as local planning issues.

Local authority expenditure in 2001 was around £6.5 billion, with just over £1 billion of this coming from the Council Tax and £1.5 billion from the business rate pool.

Wales

There are 22 unitary authorities in Wales, which replaced the two-tier structure in operation until 1996. These councils are variously described as city, county or county borough councils but all have the same powers and functions inherited from the previous county and district councils; except for fire services, which are provided by three fire authorities with representatives of the unitary authorities in their service areas, and National Parks, which are the responsibility of three independent national parks authorities (see section below on Policing). Wales also has about 770 town and community councils, which are most often found in Mid and West Wales. They have a combined budget of almost £17 million and manage some devolved local services such as street cleansing and traffic management and work in partnership with other organizations for such services as health promotion and play activities.

Total finance for Wales' councils in 2001 was about £2.75 billion, more than £2 billion of this was from the revenue support grant and £650 million from the business rate pool (see below).

	England			London		Scotland	Wales	Northern Ireland	Joint Board
	Metro' Boroughs and non-Metro' Unitary	County	District	GLA	London Borough				
Social services	X	X			X	X	X		
Education	X	X			X	X	X		
Libraries	X	X			X	X	X		
Housing	X		X		X	X	X		
Planning – strategic	X	X		X		X	X		
Planning – local	X		X		X	X	X	X	
Local roads	X	X		X	X	X	X		
Public transport	X	X		X		X	X		X
Museums/leisure amenities	X	X		X	X	X	X	X	X
Fire and rescue		X	X	X		X		X	X
Emergency planning	X	X		X				X	X
Environmental health	X		X		X	X	X	X	
Refuse collection	X		X		X	X	X	X	
Refuse disposal	X	X			X	X	X	X	X

Figure 12.1 The responsibility for local government services by different types of authorities (*Source: various*)

Northern Ireland

There are 26 single-tier (unitary) district councils. These have three main functions:

1 *Executive* – direct responsibility for a wide range of local services including environmental health; recreational, social and cultural facilities; street cleansing; licensing and registration.
2 *Representative* – nominates representatives to sit on statutory bodies for region-wide services, including education, fire, health, personal social services, housing, drainage, libraries.
3 *Consultative* – acting as the conduit through which local voters can express their views on other regional services that are provided by the devolved government, including water/sewerage, planning and roads.

The province's local government is financed differently from England, Scotland and Wales. Unlike the rest of the UK, Northern Ireland has stuck with the rates system for both domestic and other properties: householders are charged according to a formula based on the rateable value of their property multiplied by so many pence in the pound. The rates are collected by the Rate Collection Agency – an executive agency that is part of the Department of the Environment for Northern Ireland.

Note that Northern Ireland is also unique in the UK for having a system of proportional representation (STV) for electing local councillors – see Chapter 11.

Policing

The UK does not have a national Police service. There are some national agencies for specific aspects of policing – such as the National Missing Persons Bureau and the National Crime Squad – and the Home Office in England and Wales and the devolved governments in Scotland and Northern Ireland set the overall framework and policy. Overall, though, the service is provided and supervised at a local level by separate authorities under legislation from central government. There are 52 forces throughout the UK, each of which is responsible for policing, with day-to-day operations the responsibility of a Chief Constable.

In England and Wales (outside London) each of the 43 forces is supervised by a Police Authority. Some of these are based on the shire counties; in unitary areas, forces cover several local authority areas. The Police authorities usually have nine councillors – selected from the relevant authorities covered by the force's area – who are supposed to reflect the political balance of those authorities – plus three magistrates and five independent co-opted members. The services in these nations are financed by a precept on the council tax (see below) plus an annual grant.

In London (except for the City of London, which has its own Police force) the Metropolitan Police Authority is supervised by the Greater London Authority, which has 12 members of the assembly (including the deputy mayor), four magistrates and seven independents.

In Scotland the Scottish Executive has overall control of the service throughout that nation and there are six joint police boards made up of local councils and two other authorities, which are the councils themselves.

In Northern Ireland the Secretary of State for Northern Ireland has overall responsibility for the Royal Ulster Constabulary. The Police (Northern Ireland) Act 2000 was due to result in the replacement of the Police Authority (of) Northern Ireland with the Northern Ireland Policing Board, consisting of ten members from the Northern Ireland Assembly and nine appointed by the Secretary of State for Northern Ireland. In September 2001 the 'pro (Good Friday) agreement' parties agreed to this change, with the exception of Sinn Fein – the seats allocated for that Republican party were to be taken up by other parties. The Royal Ulster Constabulary was replaced by the Police Service of Northern Ireland at the beginning of November 2001.

These apparently small changes have deep political and cultural significance and have caused enormous controversy, leading to a delay in their implementation that was originally due by the beginning of 2001. The reader should check the relevant Web sites given at the end of this chapter for up-to-date information on these developments.

Elections

Elections in England, Wales and Scotland are held on the first Thursday in May. In Northern Ireland the elections are on the third Wednesday in May. There are different voting systems in use for different types of council. Northern Ireland has long been unique in the UK in having a Single Transferable Vote (STV) system (see Chapter 11) for elections to its councils. English, Scottish and Welsh councils all use the First Past The Post (FPTP) system described in Chapter 11. London Boroughs also use the FPTP system but the Greater London Authority uses the Additional Member System (AMS) described in Chapter 11. The Mayor of London is elected using the Supplementary Vote (SV) system: electors give their first and second preferences. If no candidate receives over 50 per cent of first preferences all but the top two drop out and the second preference votes given to the surviving candidates are added to their totals. The winning candidate is the one with the greatest number of combined first and second preferences.

The electoral cycle

Unlike elections to the Westminster Parliament, which, as we saw in Chapter 11, can be held at any time up to the legal limit of the length of a Parliament, elections to local and devolved authorities are fixed – both in years and the dates in those years by the relevant Act of Parliament. In theory therefore it should be possible to see for decades to come which local authorities will have elections and when – a very welcome situation for local newsdesks! This is particularly important for broadcast journalists as there is also a fixed time when the pending period comes into operation (see Chapter 11). However, it is not as simple as that!

First, different types of council have different election arrangements and some are given the discretion as to whether they should elect all councillors in one go – the All Council system – or hold elections for a proportion of seats in most years – the By Thirds system. Furthermore there are proposals to allow councils to switch to different proportions – say half a council each year. Most significantly of all though, in Wales and Scotland the power to decide on the election arrangements for local councils has been passed to the devolved governments. This resulted in the Scottish Parliament passing a Bill at the end of 2001 which increased the cycle for local government elections from three to four years so that they coincide with elections to the Scottish Parliament. The reader should check the relevant Web sites as well as their local councils for any developments – and of course changes to election systems are likely to create controversy and debate, creating good stories for local journalists!

England

In London boroughs the whole council is elected in the year following the county council elections. Most are multi-member wards. The Greater London Authority and Mayor of London are all elected at the same time for four-year terms.

Councillors in metropolitan boroughs/districts outside London are elected By Thirds – one-third of the seats (or as close to one-third as is mathematically possible!) are elected each year; there are no elections in the fourth year, which is when county councillors are elected. Each council is divided into wards, most with three councillors, so normally one councillor is elected in each of the election years.

In the two-tier system – where there is both a county and district/borough council – the county is divided into divisions, each of which elects one councillor in the year when there are no district elections.

Unitary authorities (non-metropolitan districts) can opt to either have all seats elected in the same year: if so, most hold elections in the mid-year between the county elections, or have a third of seats elected each year except for the county council's year.

Non-metropolitan District councils (in two-tier system) can opt for the 'by thirds' system following the pattern of metropolitan/districts – with elections in three out of the four years where there is no county council elections – or have the 'all council' system in which case the elections are held in the mid-year (two years after) the county council elections.

	2002	2003	2004	2005	2006	2007	2008	2009
London Boroughs	X				X			
Greater London Authority			X				X	
English Metropolitan Borough (All BT)	X	X	X		X	X	X	
English Non-Metropolitan Unitary	BT X	AC/BT X	BT X	(AC/BT)[a] (X)	BT X	AC/BT X	BT X	(AC/BT)[a] (X)
English Counties				X				X
Scottish[b]		X				X		
Welsh[c]			X				X	
Northern Ireland				X				X
Town and Community		X				X		

Key: BT = Thirds system (where council has elections for approx. one third of council seats);
AC = All Council system where council has elections for all council seats at the same time – every 4 years)

[a] Most non-metropolitan unitary councils do not have elections in county council years; however, because their dates of creation vary, eleven councils with a mixture of All-Council and By-Third systems fell into the county council years.

[b] Under the Local Government (Timing of Elections) (Scotland) Bill, passed by the Scottish Parliament at the end of 2001, Scottish councils will be elected on the same dates as those for the Scottish Parliament, on a four-yearly cycle – with the next elections in 2003. Consequently, elections due in May 2002 were postponed and councillors' term of office extended by a year.

[c] At the time of writing the Commission on Local Government was considering electoral arrangements in Wales and due to present a report to the Assembly in June 2002.

Figure 12.2 Election cycle for councillors in local authorities (Source: various)

In general, unitary authorities and district councils in the more urban areas have adopted the one-thirds system of their often near-neighbours in metropolitan borough councils, whilst most of those in the more countryside areas have adopted the All Council system of the county councils.

Until 2002 Scottish councils were unique in that they operated on a three-year cycle. Wales and Northern Ireland councils have a four-year term but all councils outside England are elected at the same time.

Who can become a councillor?

Like elections to the Westminster Parliament candidates need the support on their nomination papers of ten electors in the area of the council in which they wish to serve. There are also spending limits and election expenses have to be declared; however, unlike contests for House of Commons' seats, this is rarely an issue! Also unlike Westminster elections they do not have to make a deposit.

The other main requirements for would-be candidates are:

1 must be at least 21 years of age
2 must be an elector or occupy a premises that have a work purpose (e.g., a shop or other business) in the area served by the council they seek to represent
3 if they are standing as a parish or town councillor must live within three miles of the council area
4 must either stand as a candidate under the name of a registered political party or as an Independent.

The main *disqualifications* to become a councillor are:

1 is a paid officer of the council they seek to be a member of
2 is a local government officer in a neighbouring authority who holds a politically restricted post – mostly chief officers and those earning above a certain salary level
3 is bankrupt
4 within five years before the election has served a prison sentence of three months or more.

To vote in council elections you must be on the electoral register for the area covered by the council, be at least 18 years of age and be an EU citizen.

What councillors do

There are nearly 23 000 councillors in principal authorities (as of May 2000) with a further 80 000 councillors serving on the town and community councils in England and Wales.

Since the 1960s there has been increased party politicization of councillors: most councillors in principal authorities represent one of the main national political parties – the FPTP system mitigates against the smaller parties and independents just as much at local as at national levels. Most councils have one political party that holds a majority of seats, similar to the situation in the House of Commons; indeed many of the features of national Parliament, including the use of Whips, can be found at Town Halls. Many aspiring politicians first stand and campaign in local elections and journalists should be on the alert to potential 'stars' of the national scene. There is little doubt that local elections are now seen as mini national contests between general elections, with the major parties anxiously watching how their council candidates fare and how many councils they win or lose control of. Many voters undoubtedly use local elections as a way of 'punishing' parties in central government and many excellent councillors who have provided first-rate public service have lost seats because they happened to represent the 'wrong' party.

Councillors elect a council leader – equivalent to a local Prime Minister as this is the leader of the majority group on the council. However, it is worth noting that, unlike the House of Commons, councils cannot be dissolved after losing a vote of confidence. Many councils in any case have No Overall Control (NOC) after elections and so the leaders of the party groups have to form coalitions or at least 'non-aggression pacts' to keep council business flowing. Thus, even the FPTP system often fails to produce a 'winner' at the local level.

The law requires that each council elects a chairman. This is usually a Mayor – a senior politician who acts as chairperson of the council and is supposed to act impartially, rather like the Speaker in the House of Commons. They tend to be elected towards the end of one council term to start their duties after elections and are often deputy mayor in the previous council. Newer councils sometimes don't have a Mayor but instead have a Council Chairman who has the same role. As well as presiding at full council meetings these figures have many ceremonial and public duties to perform and of course are often featured in local newspapers.

With the new political structures in England and Wales there is a division between executive councillors, who have the legal powers to make certain decisions without approval of a committee or the council, and non-executive councillors, who are not able to make decisions by themselves. The Local Government Information Unit (LGIU, 2001) says the functions of councillors can be divided into five categories.

1 *Resident advocate* – they work on behalf of their electorate. Numerous activities are involved here including advice surgeries, visits to electors, telephone and, increasingly, e-mail contact. If they are not able to help the residents themselves they can advise on who they should approach and help with a letter of introduction or explanation.

2 *Communities advocate* – they put forward proposals to improve the area they represent or the area of the council as a whole. They can also be proactive in bringing together a number of bodies to help resolve problems and improve life in general.

3 *Policy advocates* – they can push certain policy proposals that they feel strongly about, be it for the area or ward they represent or for the council as a whole. These may also have regional or national implications.

4 *Strategic management* – councillors with executive responsibilities must work closely with Chief Officers and other senior managers to co-ordinate, implement and monitor council policy and decisions. Overseeing budgets is a major part of this, rolled together with forward planning.

5 *Oversight and scrutiny* – a role for non-executive councillors who make sure that they monitor and question the actions and conduct of executive members of the council. They should also contribute to the process of policy and its implementation. They have a vital role in the checks and balances in the new decision-making structures.

Payments to councillors

The councillors do not receive a salary as such but receive allowances for official council work. The two main types of allowance are: basic allowances – the standard sum set locally and paid to all councillors regardless of their responsibilities; and special responsibility allowances – these are higher sums for councillors with special responsibilities, including those of leader, committee chair or cabinet member.

Another type of payment is an attendance allowance – this is not paid by all councils and is paid only for approved council duties such as attending a council meeting. Parish, town and community councillors can also claim attendance allowances for approved duties outside the area of their own council.

Most allowances are subject to income tax. In addition councillors may claim expenses that have been incurred when carrying out business on behalf of the council.

Councillors can also claim childcare costs but this allowance has to be recommended by the remuneration panel of the local authority. Councillors who need financial help to care for dependants can also claim an allowance. Plans for significant changes to the system of payments to councillors were outlined by the government in September 2001.

Councillors and officers

There has long been tension between the effective powers of councillors – the representatives who are elected by voters in specific geographical areas – and the full-time paid officials or civil servants. This tension is greater even in local government than in the House of Commons because, unlike MPs, councillors are not supposed to be full-time professional politicians. Inevitably therefore they are relying on the full-time officials for expert advice and analysis. Furthermore, in contrast with many civil servants in Whitehall, almost all local council officials are specialists – in planning, environment, etc. The paid service is normally headed by a senior grade civil servant with the title of Chief Executive (Officer). The officers are accountable in a broad sense but councillors usually argue that they do not have the same accountability as the elected members who need residents' votes to continue in office. Councillors often feel they have to justify and defend actions that in reality they had very little say in.

How councils operate

Although the structure and powers of local government have changed enormously in the last 150 years or so, the main decision-making process has 'traditionally' been through a main council consisting of all elected members that meets at set points throughout the year – often once a month – with a committee system that debates in detail specific areas of the council's responsibilities. Some of these committees have delegated powers – which means they can make decisions and inform the main council about what they have done, whereas other decisions have to be referred back to the full council for a formal vote and decision. Often there are numerous sub-committees whose work then feeds into the 'main' committees.

The system for each council is contained in its Standing Orders.

Council officers prepare for meetings by distributing minutes of previous meetings, preparing briefings and reports and offering verbal advice during meetings when invited to do so by the elected members. Some decisions can be delegated to council officers.

Nearly all council meetings are open to the press and public although some matters can be declared to be:

● *confidential* – when they are discussing a matter initiated by central government, which insists there is a requirement to treat it confidentially, or:
● *exempt* – for example if it concerns an employee or if there is commercially sensitive information, but for which a resolution must be proposed and passed before the press can be legally excluded. The types of issues that can be treated as exempt and whether a motion has to be passed before going 'behind closed doors' are listed in Acts of Parliament, see Chapter 11 for further details, and the section below on 'Reporting local government' on how new council structures are likely to affect reporting of council business.

New political structures in councils in England and Wales

The Local Government Act 2000 required new political structures in new constitutions for all councils in England and Wales.

1 *A directly elected Executive Mayor, and a Cabinet.* The most radical and therefore most controversial option. Such a mayor could be equated at the local level with that of the Prime Minister as head of the Cabinet in central government. The Mayor would head the political executive and would have a wide range of decision-making powers. Such power is justified because unlike the traditional system, where a mayor is chosen from elected councillors, the directly elected mayor would have been voted for by the electorate at large. In addition some councils cover more than one area of a Parliamentary seat so could therefore be said to have a greater mandate than an MP for that area. The Mayor would appoint a Cabinet from the council, which would then act under his direction. The council though would still have a role: they would scrutinize the work of the Mayor and the Cabinet but may propose amendments to policy and the budget. This can be equated to the role of backbench MPs in the House of Commons.

2 *A Mayor and Council Manager.* There would still be a directly elected mayor but most of the executive power would rest with the council manager – this would be a paid appointee of the council, somewhere between a civil servant in the chief executive role and a politician. Most of the policy and budgetary decisions would be taken by the council manager. This proved to be the least favoured option among councillors, many of whom have complained in the past about the power of the full-time unelected officials (see above).

3 *An Executive Leader and a Cabinet.* It is this third option that has received overwhelming support in councils across the country. Here the council – in reality it would be the major party group – elect one of its number to act as executive leader of the council, who would either select the Cabinet or this will be selected by the council as a whole. As well as providing political leadership the leader proposes the council's budget and its main policies, and takes executive decisions within this. Members of the Cabinet would have individual responsibilities that again can be equated to the Westminster model for central government. The result of this most popular option (at least among councillors!) is that there are now two tiers of councillors: Executive/Cabinet members and backbenchers.

4 EITHER (England only): *a streamlined committee system.* This can be adopted by any district council in England with a population of below 85 000. OR (Wales only): *a politically balanced board.*

Councils were required to consult with their electorate as to which model should be introduced and, if 5 per cent of local people so petitioned, a referendum must be held on introducing a directly elected executive Mayor. The wish by central government for major councils to move to such a structure suffered a major blow in September 2001: the residents of Birmingham rejected such a proposal (Britten, 2001).

Scrutiny committees

To help allay fears of an overpowerful and unaccountable executive – which in many cases would be run by a single political party – there are new scrutiny committees that are made up of councillors who are not members of the Executive or Cabinet and must reflect the political balance of the council. Councils can choose whether it has scrutiny committees for particular services, ones that cover several departments under broad areas such as education and environment or whether to have one scrutiny body that has an overview of the whole council's operations. There must be one that looks at local health services and other public services not run by the council itself. This is to ensure that there is some local accountability and democratic involvement in some of the services such as NHS trusts which, as we saw in Chapter 11, have been criticized for their lack of public scrutiny.

Standards committees

The Local Government Act 2000 introduced a new ethical framework for councillors. Each council in England and Wales must set up a Standards Committee that has at least one independent member. The council must adopt a code of conduct for its members and the Standards Committee has the power to investigate alleged breaches of this code. If the committee believes there has been a serious breach they can pass the details to the National Standards Board for England/Wales (as appropriate).

A question of tax

As mentioned in the introduction only about 35 per cent of the total cost of local government services is raised locally. Nevertheless, local tax raising for local services still involves significant sums, causes debate and controversy, and provides many good stories for journalists.

The Council Tax – which operates at all UK councils except for those in Northern Ireland (see above), is on both the *person* and the *property*. The tax is levied and collected either by the unitary/metropolitan authority or, in the two-tier structure in England, by the district/borough council, with other councils and bodies making a precept to the charging council. Unlike income tax bills the council tax demand breaks down the amount of money spent in each of the main areas as well as the amount precepted by all the other authorities or bodies.

The tax assumes there are two or more adults living in the property. As the individual side of the tax accounts for 50 per cent of the charge there is a 25 per cent reduction for single-person households. The property side of the tax depends not, as in the past, on a notional rateable (rentable) value, but on the value of the property if it were to be sold on the open market. Prices of properties were assessed on 1 April 1991 and are due to be re-valued in the first few years of the new century – this process is likely to provide much local controversy. The property values are divided into eight council tax bands and, whereas the person side of the tax does not take into account the income or wealth of the individual, the property side of the tax varies enormously. (It is of course presumed that, in general, wealthy people live in more expensive homes than the less well off, and so the tax is seen to be fairer on all sides than its two predecessors – domestic rates, which were solely on property and the Community Charge (Poll Tax), which was on the person – the elector – hence the name 'Poll Tax').

The charging council sets the tax for *band D*, which is the middle or average band, and the rate for the other bands is calculated using a formula. For example a property in band H is always at twice the tax for a property in D, and a tax for a property in band A will always be two-thirds of the tax for property in band B. In 2001–02 the average council tax in England at band D was £901, while the actual tax per dwelling was £741 (DETR, 2001).

Band	Upper limit
A	£40 000
B	£52 000
C	£68 000
D	£88 000
E	£120 000
F	£160 000
G	£320 000
H	Over £320 000

Figure 12.3 Council tax bands (*Source:* Local Government Information Unit)

The other main source of income or for local councils is the tax on the business premises, generally known as the Uniform Business Rate (UBR). This tax or rate is still based on a notional rentable value of the property – some buildings, such as those used for spiritual or charitable purposes, are exempt. This tax rate is now set nationally and once the business premises have been set a rate it is only upgraded in line with inflation and re-valued every five years – for this reason it is formally known as the National Non Domestic Rate (NNDR). The rate is based at so many pence in the pound – known as the multiplier. It was around 50 pence at the beginning of the twenty-first century, so a rough calculation can be made that if the rentable value of a property is £10 000, the rate payable would be £5 000. The revenue from the UBR is then distributed back to local councils, depending on their population. Councils can also raise money through local charges, for example on leisure centres and car parks.

Council spending

There are two broad types of spending by local councils – capital and revenue. Revenue spending is the day-to-day expenditure on such matters as salaries, electricity, repairs and maintenance. The rest of the money needed to run a council that is not raised from the council tax is funded by the Treasury using a formula known as the Standard Spending Assessment (SSA). There can be few aspects of local government that cause so much controversy and anger as the formula used to decide on the SSA for each council. Under Conservative administrations there were frequent and vociferous protests by those in the Labour-dominated urban areas that the funding formula was biased against them and that they did not receive anything like a fair share of the national 'cake'.

The SSA is supposed to take into account the broad social and economic circumstances of each area, for example the state of the housing stock, economic wealth or deprivation, the proportion of elderly and children – as we've seen, education and social services for the elderly account for a big proportion of total spending by local authorities.

Before the start of each new financial year on 1 April, the Chancellor of the Exchequer announces the amount of money to be given to local authorities, distributed to each council according to its Needs Assessment. Central government then expects councils to make up for the difference between the amount given by the Treasury through the SSA and the Uniform Business Rate and announces the expected rates of Council Tax as Council Tax at Standard Spending (CTSS).

Each council will then be told what it can expect from central government in the Revenue Support Grant – to make up the difference between what it will receive locally through the council tax, the money from the Uniform Business Rate pool and other sources of revenue (local charges). Or, to put it formulaically:

$$RSG = SSA - CTSS + UBR$$

This is the point that local journalists in particular need to beware of likely stories involving controversy about both spending and taxation levels. If councils disagree with the settlement they may raise extra funds by putting up the council tax beyond the government's hoped-for level. The previous Conservative administrations in the 1980s and 1990s enforced capping of councils – the central government grant was cut in proportion to the 'extra' levels of spending/tax so those councils had to raise even more through local taxation. This system was phased out by the Labour government but the government believes that, if the tax is seen to be excessive, voters in that area will punish councillors at the next election.

Capital spending is for long-term projects – those that will benefit the community for more than a year. This distinction is important because councils are required to fund their revenue spending from their annual income and must legally set a balanced budget to do this. Capital spending is mostly funded by borrowing. Most of this is done from central government funds but councils are also allowed to borrow money within set limits from outside sources. They may also use capital receipts, for example from the sale of land and council houses. Since 1997 central government has increasingly encouraged councils to link with the private sector in Private Finance Initiatives (PFI) or Public–Private Partnerships (PPP). This involves investment from the private companies to finance public projects – often major buildings such as schools – which are then paid a management fee plus interest payments from the public purse. Several schools are now completely managed by private companies. Such projects are often highly controversial and consequently provide good stories for local journalists.

Best value

The concept of 'best value' replaced the highly controversial Compulsive Competitive Tendering (CCT) system introduced by the previous Conservative government. That system was designed to ensure that councils squeezed the best value for every penny they spent on services by compelling local authorities to offer contracts for services such as refuse collection to outside companies.

This was a way of bringing free-market economics in to what the Conservatives regarded as the complacent, overstaffed and inefficient services provided by local authority monopolies. If the level of service offered up was broadly equal between the would-be good contractors, the council was obliged to offer it to the cheapest.

Best value, which was introduced under the Local Government Act 1999, retains some of this approach and compels each authority to review the provision of all their services under the auspices of the Audit Commission's inspection service. Each authority is required to produce a Best Value Performance Plan. This is described as the authority's annual contract with its local community. It has to report on past and current performance, identify its plans and priorities and targets for improvement, and set out the authority's programme of best value reviews.

These reviews are the authority's scrutiny of all its functions over a five-year period. There are four principles of best value: challenge, comparison, consultation and competition.

Reporting local government

Reporting on the affairs of local government has been a crucial part of the democratic process for several centuries. Journalists and some politicians had to campaign long and hard to ensure they were able to attend and report on the proceedings of local government not as a privilege but as a right. Furthermore Defamation Act(s) allowed for qualified privilege (see Chapter 13) of reports of council meetings so that journalists had some protection from reporting potentially libellous statements and accusations made in council and some other types of public meetings.

Although, as we have seen, certain matters of a confidential or personal nature could be discussed behind closed doors (using the exempt or confidential clauses of the Acts) or with the press allowed to remain but unable to report on the discussion, there was a general obligation on local authorities to allow entrance to journalists to most meetings. Councils were also obliged to provide journalists with advance copies of minutes, agendas, etc. and reporting facilities, e.g., a 'press table', telephone, etc., where practicable.

There was enormous alarm amongst the journalistic community and in many groups that campaign for greater freedom for press and broadcasters when the New Labour administration introduced its Local Government Bill in 1999. Proposals to streamline decision-making and give more powers to Executive or Cabinet style committees allowed councils to hold meetings in private.

There then followed a campaign both within and outside Parliament to introduce amendments to the Bill and it was the determination of the House of Lords to insist on such amendments that led to an 11th hour climbdown by the government – which wanted to ensure the bill completed its passage in the closing days of that Parliamentary session.

The main obligations imposed on councils are:

● councils must meet in public when discussing all voting on a key decision (see below) unless the matter is confidential or exempt, or would mean that confidential advice would have to be disclosed
● agendas and reports for any public meeting must be available at least three days beforehand
● a written record of all key decisions and other decisions by the executive must be made 'as soon as is practicable' after the meeting
● each council must publish a Forward Plan containing details of key decisions it is likely to make over the next four months

- meetings of backbench scrutiny committees (see above) will be open to press and public with agendas and papers available beforehand.

What is a 'key decision'?

The new regulations describe a key decision as belonging to one of the following categories:

- is likely to result in the council incurring expenditure or making savings that will significantly affect the authority's budget or a service or function provided by the council
- is likely to be significant in its effects on communities in areas of two or more wards or divisions.

Despite these concessions there is still enormous concern about the implications for democracy in the new decision-making structures in local authorities. At the time of this book going to press most councils have either not implemented a new structure (they have until June 2002 to do so) or the new system had not been in operation sufficiently long to judge its consequences.

As in most areas of life the first few months or years of a new set-up are crucial as it is then that precedents are set and routines are put in place. It is therefore essential that journalists insist that councils at least adhere to the very limited obligations to allow the press and public to listen to, observe, and scrutinize their decisions. Democracy that takes place behind closed doors is not democracy at all, for how is the public to assess the arguments, debates and personalities of its elected representatives? There is scope for corruption or questionable acts when the press is not able to perform its watchdog role.

In an article in the *Press Gazette* (28 January 2000) reporter Geoff Elliott told how in Newcastle on Tyne the previous October a local government officer and a councillor in a single party cabinet had decided to buy a new £40 000 Mercedes limousine for use by the Lord Mayor. The decision was made in total secrecy. It was not part of any published agenda, it was not discussed by Cabinet members and so did not form part of the minutes of the meeting. Instead it was published on a list of the council's 'delegated decisions'. As a consequence journalists could only report this use of taxpayers' money as a *fait accompli*.

Figure 12.4

Suggested activities

1 Find out who are the local councillors where you live or study.
2 Find out what type of council(s) there are in your area.
3 Find out what the current political make-up is of the council. What were the results of the last council election?
4 Obtain the council's budget statement sent out to householders with their council tax bills. What is the most money spent on?
5 Obtain minutes and agenda for the next council meeting – is the council adhering to the 'openness' clauses in the Local Government Act?
6 Study reports on that meeting in the local press or broadcast media. Do you think these reports were written by a journalist attending the meeting or written up afterwards from information supplied by the council or councillors?
7 Obtain the council's forward plan. What are the key issues coming up?
8 Attend a meeting of the council yourself and try to write up a couple of stories suitable for inclusion in a local newspaper.

Sources and resources

Britten, N. (2001) *Voters Say No to Elected Mayor.* Telegraph.co.uk (19 September 2001) http://www.portal.telegraph.co.uk/core/K2/xmlContent.jhtml?xml=/news/2001/09/19/nbrum19.xml (accessed 20 September 2001).

Byrne, T. (2000) *Local Government in Britain* (7th edition). London: Penguin.

Department of the Environment, Transport and the Regions (DETR) http://www.detr.gov.uk (accessed 29 September 2001).

DETR (2001) *News Release March 22nd, 2001.* http://www.press.detr.gov.uk/0103/0162.htm (accessed 29 September 2001).

Fenney, R. (2000) *Essential Local Government 2000* (9th edition). London: LGC Information.

Government of Northern Ireland (2001) http://www.northernireland.gov.uk (accessed 29 September 2001).

The Highland Council (2001) http://www.highland.gov.uk (accessed 29 September 2001).

Information for local government (2001) http://www.info4local.gov.uk (accessed 30 September 2001).

Jones, B., Kavanagh, D., Moran, M. *et al.* (eds) (2001) *Politics UK* (4th edition). Harlow: Pearson Education.

Llewellyn, A. (ed.) (2000) *The Guardian Local Authority Directory 2001.* Colwall, Malvern and London: Alcourt Publishing and Guardian Newspapers Limited.

Local Government Act (2000) http://www.hmso.gov.uk/acts/acts2000/00022–c.htm (accessed 2 February 2001).

Local Government Association (LGA) (2001) http://www.lga.gov.uk (accessed 29 September 2001).

Local Government Information Unit (LGIU) (2001) http://www.lgiu.gov.uk (accessed 29 September 2001).

Local Government Net (2001) http://www.local-government.net (accessed 29 September 2001).

London Government (2001) http://www.london.gov.uk (accessed 29 September 2001).

Media Lawyer (March/April 2001) Broughton-in-Furness, Cumbria: Tom Welsh (published bi-monthly) http://www.media-lawyer.co.uk (accessed 22 September 2001).

National Assembly for Wales (2001) http://www.wales.gov.uk (accessed 29 September 2001).

Northern Ireland Office online (2001) http://www.nio.gov.uk (accessed 29 September 2001).

Scottish Executive (2001) http://www.scotland.gov.uk (accessed 29 September 2001).

Scottish Parliament (2000) http://www.scottish.parliament.ukwelcoming_you/how.html (accessed 16 September 2000).

Spark, D. (1999) *Investigative Reporting – a study in technique*. Oxford: Focal Press.

Stationery Office (2000) *Whitaker's Concise Almanack*. London: Stationery Office.

UK Local Government Information (2001) http://www.gwydir.demon.co.uk/uk localgov/ (accessed 29 September 2001).

Wilson, D. and Game, C. (1998) *Local Government in the United Kingdom* (2nd edition). London: Macmillan Press.

13 Journalism law

- Introduction and background
- Types of law
- Divisions of the law
- Structure of the courts
- The legal profession
- Scotland
- Contempt of Court
- Reporting restrictions in legal cases
- When cases become 'active'
- Court reporting restrictions
- Reporting restrictions on cases involving children and young people
- Restrictions on reporting sexual offences
- Other main reporting restrictions
- Other types of legal proceedings
- A question of privilege
- Defamation
- Privilege at common law/the 'Reynolds Defence' and the emergence of a public interest defence
- Criminal libel
- Freedom of speech and privacy: a clash of rights
- Election law
- Other legal restrictions on journalism
- Laws that help journalists
- Protecting sources
- Copyright
- Suggested activities
- Sources and resources

Introduction and background

Anyone involved in any form of public communication – including journalism in its broadest sense – or presentation, production and management, needs to have a firm grasp of the relevant areas of law. Failure to comply with the law can lead to very serious consequences, including fines and even imprisonment, not to mention the damage to reputations and careers. One of the consequences of technological developments has been the reduction in the numbers of the likes of sub-editors, who traditionally checked that material was 'legally OK'. Very often even the newest and most inexperienced journalist is likely to have their work sent straight to the printing presses or broadcast transmitters.

In general the law in the UK does not recognize journalists as being in a different category from anyone else. In only a few specific instances are journalists allowed into places from where the public is barred.

On the other hand there are no special laws that restrict journalistic activity that do not apply to the general public, and in particular there is no law of privacy as such. However, some laws, such as those on Defamation, Contempt and Official Secrets, are far more likely to affect journalists than other individuals or groups. Furthermore, some laws that have apparently been passed to deal with different problems – such as harassment and trespass, see below – have (perhaps) unintended consequences in restricting journalism.

The law has developed to try to strike a balance between the public's 'right to know' and free speech, and protection for the individual and legitimate state interests.

Journalists and others involved in the media also need to understand that Codes of Practice issued by the various regulatory bodies often have a quasi-legal basis and, in the case of broadcast journalism, full legal status. Both the 'law of the land' and these regulations need to be taken together to understand the requirements and restrictions on the journalist. For example, the Independent Television Commission requires that the vulnerability of those under 18 be carefully considered before identifying them in connection with an alleged criminal offence, as either defendants or witnesses. The ITC also bans payments for interviews to criminals who have not completed their sentence. No such law applies to print or Internet journalists. Chapter 14 discusses these regulations and codes in some detail and the relevant Web sites are included at the end of this chapter.

Types of law

Many laws that are still active in England developed from the Middle Ages. The elites of the time codified many disparate and diverse rules and laws in different parts of the country by giving judgements and handing down punishment in what became known as common law. Many of these laws were based on the scriptures, particularly those against murder, other violent acts, theft and robbery. Judges noted what had been decided in courts in other parts of the country and developed the law into one cohesive body. As Parliament developed as a legislature it added to this body of law through Acts of Parliament, which are known as the statute law.

Chapter 11 describes how laws are made in the UK (Westminster) and Scottish Parliaments.

Unfortunately, as the law seeks to deal with a wide variety of human activities and frailties, it cannot deal with every possible situation and circumstance. Therefore judges are still given a large area of *discretionary power* in deciding on individual cases. In the case of statute law, however, they are obliged to consider what they believe Parliament intended to happen in those circumstances. This culmination of the decisions based on the original law is known as case law or precedent.

As we also saw in Chapter 11 there are two other sources and interpreters of law that are highly relevant to today: law emanating from the European Union and from the European Court of Human Rights, which operates under the European Convention on Human Rights, now incorporated into UK law through the Human Rights Act 1998 (HRA).

One of the most important aspects of the law for journalists – and indeed for civil liberties – is that, in adult courts, except in very rare and exceptional circumstances, all cases are heard in front of the press and public. Justice must not only be done but must be manifestly and undoubtedly seen to be done. Perhaps more than in any other aspect of life in courts of law, journalists are the eyes and ears of the public as a whole.

The legal system in England and Wales can be summarized in Figure 13.1.

Divisions of the law

Laws can be broadly categorized into two main divisions: criminal law and civil law. Criminal law deals with acts that are deemed to endanger the peace and security of the whole community – in the quaint legal phrase the *Queen's peace*

European Union	–	Commission and Court of Justice
		↑
Monarch	–	has to give assent to all Parliamentary legislation
		↑
Common Law ('law made by judges')	–	Precedent/Case Law
		↑
Executive ('government')	–	uses Royal prerogative; Statutory Instruments
		↑
Parliament	–	primary legislation has to pass through both Commons and Lords

---

Figure 13.1

(as we saw in Chapter 11, the Sovereign is supposed to embody the interests of people as a whole). Most obviously these include a murder, other physical assault, theft and robbery. It is recognized that all citizens need protection from such acts and everyone has their peace and feeling of security undermined when they take place. It is also recognized that those who undermine the peace of the individual and society should be punished, including having their liberty taken away in a term of imprisonment (and, until relatively recent times, by forfeiting their life in the most serious cases of murder and treason).

Civil law, on the other hand, deals with disputes that affect individuals, groups of individuals or organizations, but do not affect the whole of society. In civil law the state sets the rules and adjudicates how such disputes should be dealt with, and the punishment for those who are deemed to have transgressed the law is financial rather than through imprisonment.

Unfortunately, this division is not always completely clear cut. Some matters are deemed to potentially involve both civil and criminal law. For example, *negligence* could be deemed as *both* a civil and criminal matter, depending on the recklessness and irresponsibility of those found to be negligent and the extent to which the negligence could be harmful to the wider community. Another good example of cases being pursued in both civil and criminal courts includes complainants of rape suing for civil damages.

An important distinction in the way that these two broad types of proceedings are resolved is on the extent to which a case has to be 'proved': in criminal cases the burden of proof for the prosecution is that it is beyond reasonable doubt – the jury has to be *sure* the defendant is guilty of the charges. In civil cases the evidence has only to be shown to be true *on the balance of probabilities*.

Structure of the courts

Both civil and criminal cases have to be heard in the formal surroundings of a court and these are broadly divided between those dealing with civil and criminal matters (although there is a great deal of overlap) and in a *hierarchical* system: generally speaking, the further up the court system the case is being heard the more serious it is. The appeal system generally also works in this hierarchical fashion, with the next highest stage being the place of appeal for the court below it. The primary structure of the court system can be summarized in Figure 13.2.

In criminal cases in England and Wales the decision on whether to prosecute is made by an independent body, the Crown Prosecution Service (CPS). The service is headed by the Director of Public Prosecutions (DPP) under the supervision of the government's law officer, the Attorney General. Almost all criminal hearings begin

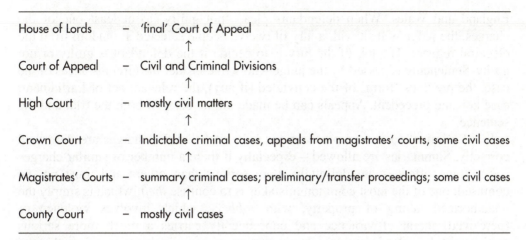

House of Lords	–	'final' Court of Appeal
Court of Appeal	–	Civil and Criminal Divisions
High Court	–	mostly civil matters
Crown Court	–	Indictable criminal cases, appeals from magistrates' courts, some civil cases
Magistrates' Courts	–	summary criminal cases; preliminary/transfer proceedings; some civil cases
County Court	–	mostly civil cases

Figure 13.2

at the Magistrates' court and most cases are heard in their entirety by lay magistrates, normally consisting of a bench of three, with the most senior as the chairman. Sometimes though, especially in the big cities, cases are heard by a single, professional lawyer, formerly known as a stipendiary magistrate but now as a district judge.

These courts are limited to imposing *maximum sentences* of *12 months in total* or *six months for any one offence* and normally a *maximum fine of £5000* (can be higher in VAT or Customs' cases).

Cases that can be dealt with entirely by Magistrates' courts are known as Summary offences, those that must be dealt with by the higher, Crown Court as Indictable offences. Some cases may be dealt with by either the magistrates or crown courts and are therefore known as tryable either way.

The right to be tried by one's peers through a jury is an ancient one and suggestions by the government that some defendants be denied the option of being tried at the Crown Court – where it is thought they have greater chance of been found not guilty – is therefore a controversial matter. In any case, if the magistrates feel that having heard all the evidence they have insufficient powers to sentence they are liable to send the case to the crown court for *sentencing*.

The other main use of the Magistrates' courts for criminal matters is to commit or transfer a case to the Crown Court – known, respectively, as committal or transfer proceedings. As we shall see, there are severe restrictions on what can be reported from these sorts of hearings. Magistrates' courts also deal with some civil matters such as applications for drinks and entertainment licences.

If the case is liable to attract the more serious sentences (should the defendant(s) be found guilty) it will be dealt with in Crown Court, in one of about 98 centres in

England and Wales. When defendants plead 'not guilty' to at least one of the charges, the judge will sit with a jury of twelve people selected at random from the electoral register. The job of the jury is to decide if the defendant is guilty or not guilty. Sentencing is passed by the judge who will consider the circumstances of the case, the previous 'form' of the convicted (if any), the relevant act of Parliament, case law and precedent. Appeals can be made on the basis of both the trial and the sentence.

In all criminal cases and prosecutions it is vital that the charges are described correctly. Summaries are allowed – especially if there a number of similar charges – but some offences are definitely more serious than others and must not be confused: one of the most common mistakes is to confuse *theft*, which is simply the unauthorized taking of property, with *robbery*, which involves violence or (perceived) threat of violence and consequently carries a much more serious punishment. It is also important when reporting on a criminal case to ensure that the circumstances and nature of the *alleged* offences are not reported as 'fact' but are attributed to counsel or a witness. For example, in a murder trial the reason for the death(s) concerned may be an issue – was it in fact murder, or could it have been manslaughter, accident or suicide? Remember that under English law everyone is innocent until proved guilty *beyond reasonable doubt* in a court of law and all reports must reflect this presumption of innocence.

Most civil cases are dealt with in their entirety by the county courts – there are about 220 of these in England and Wales, many of which are small claims (where amounts being sought by the claimant are under £5000). Claims between this figure and £15 000 are dealt with under the so called 'fast track' procedure. Others fall under the process that involves more complex and lengthy procedures. Cases are heard either by circuit or district judges.

It is very important to use the correct language in describing the very different cases in civil and criminal law. Proceedings in civil cases are begun by the claimant (the person taking action) issuing a claim form against the defendant (this term is the same in both civil and criminal cases). It is very important though that in civil courts the defendant is not said to have been 'charged' or 'prosecuted' with anything – these are terms to be used only in criminal cases. Cases are then listed for a 'hearing'.

The outcome of the case, which is usually decided by judges rather than juries (except in defamation cases, see below), the correct wording is 'the: judge (style/name, see below)/jury found for the claimant/defendant'. The words 'guilty' or 'not guilty' should *never* be used in civil cases. Similarly, people in civil cases are not 'punished' or 'sentenced' but they are often ordered to pay (costs/ damages).

Most civil cases to do with children, such as rights of access by parents, wards of court, etc., are dealt with by family courts, which are normally held in Magistrates' courts buildings.

The Supreme Court consists of a Court of Appeal, the High Court of Justice and the Crown court. The High Court of Justice is the top civil court and has three divisions: the Chancery Division, which is concerned with financial matters such as bankruptcy and probate; the Queen's Bench Division concerned with commercial law, serious personal injury and medical negligence cases; the Family Division is the final call for matters relating to the family law.

The legal profession

Aside from the police and members of the Crown Prosecution Service (CPS) most of the law professionals whom the journalist will come across, and therefore have to describe, can be classified either as judges, magistrates, barristers or solicitors. Judges and barristers – known in either singular or plural form as counsel – have very different functions in the courts but have a similar professional background. Judges have been barristers but few have been solicitors. In court, barristers wear wigs and gowns. Solicitors do not wear wigs but do wear gowns (although these are less elaborate than those of barristers) in Crown or higher courts. Experienced barristers can apply to be a Queen's Counsel (QC) – also known as 'taking silk' because their robes are lined with silk! The initials QC should always be added to the name of such judges or barristers, e.g., 'John Smith, QC'. When the Queen is succeeded by a male heir QCs will become KCs – for King's Counsel.

Most magistrates are lay people – they have not spent their whole life in the legal system and are supposed to represent the ordinary community. It is a central principle of English law and a vital protection for the ordinary citizen dating back to the Magna Carta that those charged should be judged by their peers – others like them – rather than by the elites. It is a fact that magistrates are ordinary people, which justifies their role acting as both judge and jury in the less serious, summary, cases.

Magistrates are similar to judges however in that they adjudicate, and pass punishment where appropriate, on those whose cases they hear. Barristers and solicitors are similar in that both represent clients or the state/public body and seek to prosecute or defend these in the courts. Barristers are freelances and are appointed on a case by case basis, usually being paid a fee for taking on the case, followed by refreshers for each day the case continues. Solicitors, on the other hand, are salaried professionals. Some are specialist but many deal with a wide range of civil and criminal legal matters and these are the first people who are involved in prosecuting/claiming, or defending, an individual.

It should be a matter of professional pride for journalists to ensure that they describe people correctly. The correct form of description can be summarized in Figure 13.3.

TYPE OF JUDGE	STYLE/DESCRIPTION
The Lord High Chancellor	The Rt. Hon. The Lord (Irvine of Lairg)
↑	
Court of Appeal	The Rt. Hon, Lord/Lady Justice (Smith)
↑	
High Court	The Hon. Mr/Mrs Justice (Smith)
↑	
Crown Court (Circuit)	His/Her Hon. Judge (Smith)
↑	
Judge Advocates (Courts Martials)	Judge Advocate (Smith)

'Rt. Hon.' is pronounced 'Right Honourable'; the name is given of the Lord Chancellor at the time of going to press; otherwise (Smith) is the example given for a surname which should be substituted for the actual surname. Many journalistic style guides say 'Mr Justice', 'Mrs Justice', 'Lord Justice', etc. are acceptable shortened terms. Note that women appeal court judges are still called *Lord Justice*.

Figure 13.3

Scotland

As part of the Act of Settlement, Scotland was allowed to retain a separate and different legal system from that in England and Wales (and Northern Ireland). As we saw in Chapter 12, Scotland has retained its powers in the revived Parliament to make primary legislation that applies in Scotland only. Equally, some laws that apply in the rest of the UK do not apply in Scotland. Most of this chapter deals with the system in England and Wales but the following is a summary of the main differences in Scotland.

Public prosecution is headed by the Lord Advocate who is independent of the Police – who take no part in prosecutions. Prosecutions in the High Court are led in court by an advocate-depute or solicitor advocate. In the lower courts prosecution is handled by procurators fiscal.

The court system is organized under six sherrifdoms, each of which has a number of sheriff court districts. Serious criminal cases are tried by sheriffs with a jury of 15 members. Minor (summary) cases are dealt with by district courts, administered by local authorities (see Chapter 12), which are presided over by lay justices of the peace, except in Glasgow, which has stipendiary magistrates (see above).

Appeals against decisions made by a sheriff can be made to the sheriff principal and/or the Court of Session in Edinburgh, which has an Inner and an Outer House. The High Court of Justiciary is the final court of appeal within the Scottish legal system. Appeals from the Inner House only may be made to the House of Lords. In civil cases there is a route of appeal to the House of Lords only from the Court of Session. Matters affecting the constitution which have arisen because of devolution (see Chapter 12) can be heard by the Judicial Committee of the Privy Council.

Children under 16 years are usually dealt with by an informal children's hearing consisting of three lay people.

There are no Coroners in Scotland (see below) but there is an equivalent Fatal Accident or Sudden Death Enquiry presided over by Sheriffs.

Contempt of Court

The risk – and threat – of falling foul of the Contempt of Court laws is one of the greatest affecting anyone who might describe or comment on legal cases. In everyday language 'contempt' usually describes actions that demonstrate disrespect for someone or something. Certainly, this does apply to those involved in news media – for example a journalist's mobile phone ringing in court. But the law has a more specific – and potentially more serious – meaning for the media. This involves reports or comment that could affect the legal process, especially influencing the jury. Contempt also applies when journalists attempt to find out what has gone on in the jury room or in other aspects of the case that are not presented in court, or ignore a ruling by a court, for example to delay publication of a case or not to reveal the identities of defendants or witnesses.

Contempt can be a common law offence but the Attorney General has to prove there was an intention to interfere with the administration of justice. An example would be where a journalist or news organization campaigned with great vehemence – verging on malice – on behalf of either prosecution or defence. Publication by mistake or with no intention to commit contempt is no defence and is known as Strict Liability. Under statute law (Contempt of Court Act 1981) strict liability is confined to both of the following circumstances:

- the case was active (see below)
- the report (etc.) poses a *substantial risk of seriously prejudicing the proceedings*.

Judges – and the law generally – take a very serious view of contempt and have draconian powers to punish offenders, including unlimited fines and imprisonment (including immediate imprisonment!). Clearly the most serious contempts are those that have prejudiced proceedings so much that trials have to be abandoned – at great public cost with defendants being set free, or re-trials also at great cost, and with the likelihood that the defence would successfully argue that their client(s) could not have a fair trial because of all the previous prejudicial reporting and comment.

Reporting restrictions in legal cases

The laws restricting what may or not be reported before during and after court cases – during the whole period of legal proceedings – are quite complex. This principle is that in general the news media is free to report on what happens during the legal proceedings. This is balanced with a need to protect the integrity of the legal process – to make sure that it is unaffected by reporting or, in legal language, is not prejudiced by it. The law does not recognize in general that there is any right to 'trial by media'. In court proceedings – and the period leading up to them – the media's role is to be the eyes and ears of the general public, not to influence those proceedings one way or another. This is most important when reports might affect the decision of a jury.

Another set of laws restrict the reporting of certain cases in order to protect the victims of crime – notably children and victims of sexual crimes – or those who are regarded as being young enough not to have their involvement in a crime publicized as this may harm them in adulthood. The law also allows judges some discretion to restrict or delay reporting for a variety of reasons, collectively described as being *in the interests of justice*.

A final category bars or restricts reporting in order to protect vital interests of the state, especially in defence and intelligence matters.

It should be noted that many of these powers to restrict reporting are discretionary; they may often be challenged by the news media as being unreasonable and/or unlawful.

Failure to follow the restrictions can lead journalists and/or their editors to face proceedings for defamation (see below) and/or contempt of court.

When cases become 'active'

Reporting on criminal proceedings is greatly affected by the point at which, in criminal cases, someone has been charged with an offence – or seems likely to be – or a warrant has been issued, or an inquest has opened. In civil cases it is when a matter has been set down for a hearing or fixed in the 'warned' list.

From these points the case becomes 'active' and journalists must be very careful not to publish or broadcast anything that might affect the court case. This particularly applies to any alleged evidence against the accused – which may or may not even be presented as part of the case – and any comment or allegations. Even stating the precise nature of the expected charges before the defendant(s) first appear in court is risky, as charges might be varied or dropped. In all cases the journalist should be careful not to speculate or deviate in any way from official statements issued to the media from the Police or CPS.

Difficulties often arise for journalists in cases where an incident has occurred and someone is arrested immediately or shortly afterwards. The media is usually free to report on the incident but must be very careful not to imply that anyone arrested or charged is responsible for a crime connected to that incident. Newspapers often do this by reporting the full drama of the incident on, for example, page one and a separate story about an arrest/charge on a separate page. Legally-safe terms include: 'A man has been charged in connection with . . .'.

The media should not give the name of someone who has been charged unless this is given by the Police. This can sometimes seem ludicrous if, for example, three children and their mother are found murdered, the husband is later arrested by the Police but it is merely confirmed that: 'a 42-year-old man has been charged'.

The other main dangers are confusing someone being *arrested* and being *charged* and someone being *questioned* and *charged*. The Police often interview a number of people, some of whom they suspect have committed the crime, others they do not suspect but may be important witnesses, or provide evidence. Some suspects are there voluntarily, and are free to leave at any time. Others are interrogated and released without charge (there are strict time limits between being arrested and charged and between then and the first court appearance).

Even when the Police tip-off journalists that they have 'got the guy', until it has been confirmed that someone has been charged the reporters should stick with the time-honoured phrase: 'helping police with their enquiries'.

Sloppy reporting in these areas is likely to run the risk of defamation proceedings by those who have been 'branded' a criminal or suspect – when neither or either is the case.

Similar problems arise when Police make a 'wanted' appeal, with the name and description of the person they're looking for. Sometimes it is obvious that Police think this is the person who committed the crime – they may even describe him as 'dangerous'. In these cases the media is certainly providing an invaluable public service and there do not seem to be any examples of the media facing legal difficulties for doing this. If it were otherwise programmes such as *Crimewatch* would be impossible. Nevertheless, such phrases as: 'Police would like to eliminate (x) from their enquiries' or 'would like to interview (x) in connection with' are advisable.

In all these cases – as with many others – the media will normally be protected from legal action if it sticks to official statements from the Police or other public authorities.

Photographs (etc.) are unlikely to be in contempt unless there is a dispute about the defendant's identity. Contempt at common law is possible when proceedings are not active but the prosecution has to prove the journalist intended to create prejudice.

Court reporting restrictions

All criminal cases begin with defendant(s) making their first appearance at a local Magistrates' court. In summary proceedings – where the case is to be heard in its entirety at this level – the journalist can normally report on all matters that are presented to the magistrates.

For cases at Magistrates' courts where those charged are being remanded or when magistrates are providing preliminary hearings before transfer to Crown Court – including an 'automatic' transfer, under the Magistrates Courts Act 1980 and the Crime and Disorder Act 1998, reports are restricted to the following facts:

- name of court, magistrates, counsel and solicitors
- names, addresses and occupations of those charged
- description of offences defendants have been charged with
- decision by court to send for trial, etc., and on what charges
- if proceedings are adjourned, the date, location, etc., of adjournment
- bail arrangements *but not reasons why bail was opposed or refused*
- whether legal aid is granted
- decision by court to lift reporting restrictions (normally only if *all* accused request it – if decision so made then case/evidence can be reported in full).

The Contempt of Court Act says proceedings CEASE to be active when:

- arrested person is released without being charged (except when on Police bail)
- no arrest is made within 12 months of an issue of a warrant
- the case is discontinued
- defendant is acquitted or sentenced
- defendant is found to be unfit to be tried or unfit to plead, or the court orders the charge to lie on file.

After every major trial – and especially if there is a conviction – the news media will run extensive background features to the case, including evidence from witnesses who were not included in the trial. This is perfectly acceptable as once the case has finished and sentence pronounced there is no risk of the processes of the law being prejudiced. But of course such features and documentaries are not suddenly put together at the end of the trial! Journalists are working on them from almost the time the crime was committed. The danger is that in the process they may interview witnesses who will give evidence in the trial and come across evidence that isn't presented. All of this may be said to have prejudiced the trial and so risk contempt. In any case the journalist must not offer financial inducements to those giving evidence dependant on whether the accused is found guilty or not. This is forbidden by the PCC and broadcasters' codes (see Web sites at the end of this chapter) and is certainly playing fast and loose with the contempt law.

There is a theoretical risk of contempt when a defendant is found guilty but launches an appeal on the conviction. If the appeal is allowed there is then the possibility the conviction will be quashed or even that there will be a re-trial. After the conclusion of the trial it is quite common for there to be an impromptu news conference outside the court at which relatives and/or lawyers say they intend to appeal. Journalists need not worry that this means that the case becomes active again immediately as the appeal papers have to be lodged before the case is re-activated. This usually takes several weeks and by then the media will mostly have reported the case to their hearts' content.

Even when an appeal is confirmed, the law thinks that judges are even less likely to be influenced than juries by media coverage and so there is little risk of the process of law being prejudiced in the terms of the Act. In reality there is little risk to the media if it reports that there is to be an appeal and the main reasons for it.

Reporting restrictions on cases involving children and young people

Although there are legal distinctions between children and young people, the key age at which additional reporting restrictions are lifted is when the defendant/ convicted person reaches 18 years of age. Under the Youth Justice and Criminal Evidence Act (1999) it is an offence, once Police have begun an investigation, to publish anything leading to identification of anyone under 18 years who has allegedly committed an offence. This specifically includes names, addresses, schools (etc.), workplace or any picture that might lead to identification. These restrictions can be lifted if journalists can persuade a court that a report including these details was in the public interest on the grounds the restriction(s) would impose a substantial and unreasonable restriction on the reporting of the offence. A clause that would have prevented reports containing information about *victims* of crimes or those who have witnessed one was left in reserve by Parliament after a vigorous campaign by the press and broadcasters. Such a clause would have prevented the reporting of a monstrous crime such as the shooting of school children.

Reporting cases in the Youth Courts have the same restrictions unless – under the Children and Young Persons Act 1933 – they are lifted by the Home Secretary, to avoid injustice to a youth or by the Youth Court (under the Youth Court (Crime Sentences) Act 1997) in the 'public interest'.

There is no automatic ban on identification when those under 18 years appear in an adult court but a ban may be – and often is – imposed by the Judge. This can be challenged by the media but most newspapers or broadcasters voluntarily operate a self-imposed ban on identification.

Restrictions on reporting sexual offences

In general the law gives anonymity to alleged victims of sexual attacks, but this specifically applies to rape (male and female). This includes: rape; attempted rape; aiding, abetting, counselling or procuring rape or attempted rape; incitement to rape; conspiracy to rape; burglary with intent to rape; and other serious sexual offences that do not involve actual or attempted rape. This applies as soon as an allegation of rape has been made and extends to *any information* that might identify an alleged victim of rape.

After a person has been accused/charged with rape nothing can be published that might link the accused with the alleged victim. This applies even if charges are later withdrawn but not where a complainant makes a false accusation of rape and is later convicted for wasting police time or for perjury (lying under oath). This anonymity also applies to civil proceedings but may be lifted.

For both these special categories of reporting restrictions the law is concerned with so-called jigsaw identification: this is where someone is able to work out who is being referred to by joining together bits of information in different reports, even when in different publications or broadcasts. This adds an extra burden of care to journalists in their reporting of such cases that might seem unreasonable or even impossible. As always, the inexperienced reporter should seek advice from a more experienced colleague.

Other main reporting restrictions

Divorce – no report until *all* evidence has been heard and then limited to: 'bare facts' of the parties involved; concise statement of charges, counter-charges, etc; submissions on points of law and decisions on them; judgement of court and observations by judge.

Family proceedings – under the Children Act 1989 there are restrictions similar to those relating to divorce, with the additional – and crucial – element of banning anything that could lead to the identification of those under 18 years. This also applies to reporting of the case outside the court, e.g., interviews with parents fighting a custody battle. In wards of court cases it is possible for journalists to argue for the identification ban to be lifted if the child has been involved in a news event. These types of hearings are unusual in that – together with Youth Courts – journalists are normally able to attend the courts, but the public is barred. This is because the law cannot 'trust' the public to keep what it hears private but 'knows' that the media are obliged to do so and, by allowing the media in to the courts, the principle of 'open justice' can be maintained. Journalists are often even allowed to be present when cases are heard before judges in Chambers (court rooms barred to the public), provided such reporting does not breach statutory restrictions, but discussion in Chambers cannot be published – just the decisions made. It should also be noted that any information provided by lawyers or parties present is not privileged against libel proceedings (see below). Perhaps surprisingly, despite this special 'rights of access' to both civil and criminal courts involving children and young people, the news media rarely bothers to send reporters to such hearings/cases. This is because journalists and editors find that stories that do not contain names and personal details are devoid of the vital 'human interest'. Nevertheless, journalism undoubtedly performs a public service in reporting these cases as they reveal a great deal about young people, criminality, the state of the family and how society deals with all these problems.

Other types of legal proceedings

Coroners' courts

The office of Coroner is one of the oldest in England (and Wales). Coroners have a number of duties and in many respects have even more power than 'ordinary' judges. The most likely way that journalists will report on their work is at Inquests, which are legal hearings into deaths that are unexpected or violent – except in the case of road accidents, which, sadly, are so common that inquests are rarely necessary.

Whereas court cases are based on an *adversarial process* – two sides trying to convince others of the 'rightness' of their 'side' – inquests are governed by an *inquisitorial process* – trying to find the truth about what has happened. It is generally up to the Coroner whether a jury (of between seven and eleven electors) be appointed to reach a verdict, but a jury has to be appointed when the incident leading to death is likely to be one of significance to general public safety. It is important to remember that inquests are not there to determine responsibility for the death, still less to accuse someone of a particular crime, for example murder or manslaughter. The main purpose is to establish the *identity* of the deceased and how they met their deaths. When someone has been charged with an offence relating to the death(s) it is normal for the inquest to be 'opened and adjourned'. If a subsequent court case then establishes in law the cause of death and who was responsible then the verdict of the Coroner is a formality.

The level of privilege at inquests is essentially the same as in courts of law and the media have a general right to attend. Coroners often make extremely newsworthy comments and recommendations after an inquest verdict.

Tribunals

Tribunals are legally established bodies to make legally binding judgements in a wide range of public life. There are some 80 types of tribunal and they vary widely in their processes and powers. The Council on Tribunals is a permanent body that supervises this wide range of bodies. The ones likely to be of most interest to journalists are employment tribunals, which provide many newsworthy stories about disputes between employers and employees. The Defamation Act 1996 provides for the same general level of protection of privilege for reporting in legally constituted tribunals as it does the proceedings in courts of law. This is extremely important as aggrieved employees are likely to make many damning statements and claims against their current or former employers. There is a question mark as to whether all tribunals have this level of protection and some may only have what is described below as the third level of privilege – subject to a statement by way of explanation or contradiction. In any case it is good practice to seek comments after a case has finished from, for example, an employer who is found to have unfairly dismissed a worker.

A question of privilege

A basic understanding of privilege – what it means and where it applies – is essential for anyone involved with journalism in its broadest sense. As with prejudice (see above) there is a particular legal meaning to this word. In general language, privilege refers to special advantage given to individuals or organizations. In media law it gives legal protection to the reporting of matters, statements, claims and information that otherwise could lead to legal action for defamation/libel to be taken against the journalist, editor and publisher. In general, privilege depends on where the statement (etc.) is made or published and on what sort of matter, not *who* is responsible for its publication; so there is privileged *material* but not privileged *people*.

So far so good ... but of course it isn't that simple! In some circumstances the material is described as having absolute privilege, others have qualified privilege. And, so far as the media is concerned, 'absolute' doesn't mean 'no matter what' and there are different qualifications in qualified privilege.

This section will look at the most common and significant types of privilege for journalists.

Reports of the courts in the UK do provide journalists with absolute privilege – the motivation of the journalists in these reports is not an issue (if this were not the case then a claimant could seek to stifle reports of a case by claiming the journalist 'had it in for me'; this would fatally undermine the principle of open justice). Nevertheless, the law says that to enjoy this privilege, reports must be fair, accurate and contemporaneous.

● *Fair* – gives reasonable weight to prosecution and defence (if presented) and/or any mitigating circumstances presented. It is particularly important that when a broadcaster or publisher reports one side of the case, usually the prosecution evidence and witnesses at the beginning of a trial, that it also gives due time and space to the defence case – even though from a journalist's point of view the defence case is rather dull. Fairness does not mean absolutely equal wordage or time is given to both defence or prosecution (claimant or defendant) but that a fair-minded person with no connection in the case would be given a balanced account of both sides in the dispute or prosecution. Reports of cases that have not concluded should always end with '(Proceeding)' or '(Continuing)' in the print media; broadcasters tend to use the expression: 'The case continues'. These phrases explicitly tell the news consumer that they have only heard part of the evidence/case.

- *Accurate* – although the law accepts that journalists have to condense and simplify court proceedings, reports must accurately state what was said in court, as well as when stating matters of fact such as the charges and the name, age and address of the defendant(s).
- *Contemporaneous* – the report must appear *only* in the first available edition of a publication. For broadcasters there is some latitude in that reports could appear in several bulletins/programmes the same day but should certainly not be regurgitated on the following day(s). A programme or feature at the end of a trial reflecting on the whole case can be broadcast – provided it does not undermine the decisions of the courts, e.g., implying that a defendant who was cleared of committing an offence was 'really' guilty.

The oldest form of privilege attaches to members of Parliament (Commons or Lords). Under the Bill of Rights of 1689 any statement made in either chamber or its committees, etc., is protected by absolute privilege – speakers can make any claim and attack anyone or anything in the most outrageous terms free in the knowledge that action cannot be taken against them from outside (the Bill of Rights established that Parliamentarians alone were responsible for making and enforcing their own rules). This privilege also applies to the official reports of Parliamentary proceedings in Hansard.

In reality, media *reports* on Parliament, as well as other legislatures around the world, are also covered in the UK by such a level of privilege through the Defamation Act 1996 – if this was not the case then the robust attacks and claims that make the UK Parliament such a lively institution would be impossible. Furthermore, this 'cloak of privilege' is extremely useful when journalists wish a story and a claim to be given publicity but are not confident they could justify their claims in a libel court.

However, reports on Parliament are said to carry only qualified privilege because there is a theoretical risk that legal protection could fail if the claimant could show the journalist acted with malice. There is also a general requirement that the reports be 'fair and accurate'. However, this does not mean that reports must be completely even-handed in terms of how they report on speakers from different political parties, etc. Reports should certainly not misquote or misrepresent the statements and views of speakers. Almost as importantly the privilege extends to reports and other publications produced by Parliament, including those by select committees, etc. These often deal with matters over a wide area of public life and are often very critical of named individuals and organizations. The protection extends to any other legislature in the world, to such bodies as the European Court of Justice, United Nations, etc.

It is crucial to remember though that this protection is completely lost as soon as someone steps outside the official chambers and committee rooms of Parliament, for example interviews made on College Green – the strip of grass outside Parliament where the media often congregates.

The third, and 'lowest' tier of privilege includes a qualification or requirement that the reports are: *'subject to a statement by explanation or contradiction'*. These include local authorities (councils), commissions, tribunals and inquiries, public meetings, proceedings at a general meeting of a UK public company, reports on information intended for the general public from the legislature of member states of the EU and Parliament, the government of any member state or the European Commission and any international organization, including conferences of these bodies. In a hugely important judgement in 2000, the House of Lords ruled that a press conference is a public meeting and so carries this level of protection from qualified privilege, as do press releases describing what was said at the conference.

The requirement that the privilege should be subject to this statement of explanation (etc.) is so that those who are named and possibly vilified in these meetings and reports have the chance to give their side of a story. Take the example of a council meeting when a councillor who is absent has his reputation and actions attacked by another councillor. The criticized councillor has the right to defend his reputation. Normally this would be achieved by quotes from an interview in a follow-up piece and/or in a letter from the councillor in the next edition of the newspaper. So, although in the print media there is no legal requirement to give 'a right to reply' (the law for broadcasters and regulations in effect make this a requirement), if the newspaper wishes to print allegations made at public meetings, in reports, etc., they must be aware that they need to offer this opportunity of reply if they are to avoid defamation proceedings.

It must also be emphasized that, as with Parliamentary reporting, all privilege/ protection is lost as soon as the councillor (etc.) speaks outside the council meetings for interviews, etc.

Defamation

If reports on statements, claims and accusations from a wide range of public bodies are protected through privilege, the journalist needs to be aware of what protection is offered when these are made in 'normal' life. The conflict and compromise between the right of free speech and the protection of the individual or organization from unfair attacks is enshrined in the law of defamation. The law recognizes that everyone – individuals and organizations – have the right to be protected from unfair attacks on their reputation, conduct and motives. This is almost an existential argument: the law is based on the view that we are all more than just a physical being, and can be thought of and described purely by our appearance, weight, height, etc. An essential part of our being is our character and, crucially, how other people think of us. At the same time the law recognizes that, in a free society, individuals and the media should be able to comment and criticize individuals and organizations.

Most cases of defamation, or threats of defamation proceedings, are civil claims; they will be heard in the High Court, usually with a jury – one of the few instances of civil proceedings that are routinely decided by a jury – and one for which the claimant is seeking monetary damages: in legal language, a tort.

But what is defamation? There are two broad types of defamation: libel, which is defamation in the printed or permanent form but now includes broadcasting and public performances; and slander, which is defamation in the transient form; that is, spoken.

The law says that a publication or broadcast is defamatory if has the effect on individuals or organizations of:

● exposing them to hatred, ridicule or contempt
● causing them to be shunned or avoided
● lowering them in the estimation of right-thinking members of society
● disparaging them in their trade, business, office, or profession.

It should be noted that the aggrieved party does not have to prove they have suffered damage to their reputation, let alone suffered financially from the claims and allegations, merely that the material *tended* to have that effect.

But who are these 'right-thinking members of society'? The law created this concept to ensure that people could not be successfully sued for defamation because some members of society were damaged by reports of their activities. For example, if someone involved in criminal circles was accused of being a Police informer, that would damage them in the eyes of other members of that society but not to 'right-thinking members'. But in certain legitimate but rather select groups in society the defamation may be rather greater than would be recognized by the wider community. And in multicultural Britain, different ethnic groups have different standards, especially in the area of sexual morality. For example, to imply that someone, especially a male, was not a virgin when they married would not usually be defamatory in the white, ethnic majority. Indeed, such is the revolution in sexual mores, that in twenty-first-century Britain to claim that an unmarried man had *not* lost his virginity by his early 20s could be defamatory, as it might imply that the individual was socially inept, had a personal hygiene problem or was in other ways sexually unattractive. But to make such a claim about a woman from some of the ethnic minority cultures, where virginity before marriage is still prized, could be defamatory and indeed have serious consequences for the person concerned. Juries in defamation cases are therefore instructed by judges to take account of the *actual* effect – whether intended or not – on the way the claimant is regarded by those who are likely to have heard or read the offending material.

Similar changes in attitudes apply to male homosexuality, which has lost much of the stigma that applied to it until relatively recent times (helped by the legalization of homosexual acts between consenting males and the age at which this begins). It is now unlikely that a claim that a person is 'gay' would in itself be regarded as defamatory but an action might succeed if it can be shown that the report implied the person was dishonest, hypocritical or leading a 'double life'.

It is also important to remember that the defences for a defamation action will only be concerned if it can be shown the person has been defamed in the terms of the Act(s). In extreme cases it might not matter if the offending material made statements about someone that were untrue if the persons or organizations concerned were already held in such low esteem by 'right-thinking members of society'.

To proceed with an action for defamation, the claimant must be able to prove:

● that the material is capable of having a defamatory meaning (as defined above)
● that it can reasonably be inferred to refer to the claimant
● that it has been published to a third party (except for criminal libel, see below); obviously in the case of the news media this can be assumed
● that the claimant is alive – again with the exception of criminal libel you cannot defame the dead (hence the number of 'the True Story of . . .' type of documentaries and features of dead people); although care should be taken not to defame living relatives, etc., by implication.

If that was the sum of the law it would make most journalism impossible! Fortunately there are important defences available to the journalist. A successful defence can be mounted if one of these can be proved:

● Justification – the material was true in substance and in fact. It is not necessary to prove the finest detail of every allegation or claim but anything that forms a significant part of the claimant's case must be capable of being proved on the balance of probabilities. This often presents problems for journalists; even when they 'know' something to be true and have been told it by reputable people, they have to be sure that those people are prepared to come to court and give evidence on oath. Do they have signed statements (affidavits), or other kinds of written evidence – including good short-hand notes?

● Fair comment, honestly held, without malice, on a matter of public interest. Let's unpick this test:

1 *Fair comment*. This term again shows the gap between 'normal' language and what words mean in law. Case and precedent has demonstrated beyond doubt that the law does not mean that the comment must be couched in measured terms, that it be balanced with 'on the one hand this, on the other hand, that'. On the contrary, judges in previous cases have recognized that newspapers in particular often use robust, harsh and insulting language and have a biased point of view. This is still regarded as 'fair'. However, on rare occasions newspapers have been found to have gone 'over the top' and the claimant has consequently won the case. Most notably this was due to what was deemed to be unnecessarily personal and insulting remarks about a television personality.

2 *Honestly held*. The defence will fail if the comment is shown not to be something that the writer/broadcaster actually believed in, either as 'fact' or a point of view that s/he subscribed to.

3 *Without malice*: the defence will fail if it can be shown the writer/broadcaster had a personal interest in 'doing down' the subject(s) of the piece, through a personal grudge, vendetta, etc. The law is not framed to give protection to people to pursue their private grievances through the public media.

4 *On a matter of public interest*. The defence is only valid if it is on a matter that can be defined as something that is of legitimate concern to society or a section of it. Clearly, comments on public officials, and most private and public organizations, would meet this criterion. Naturally, most media comment is about such people and organizations, as these are the ones which will interest their readers/audiences. Comments on the private life of an individual or perhaps a small, private company owned by a family, might not meet that test, even if the story is a 'juicy' one that makes 'good' copy. This is not to suggest that 'fair comment' can only apply to serious, public affairs stories: reviews of entertainment and artistic offerings are nearly always covered by this defence. The problem with comment of the sort that appears in editorial or leader pages in newspapers is that the comment is based on factual claims. For example, a local newspaper's comment column may claim that: 'Our local council is one of the worst in the country with some of the least inspiring councillors and officials in local government' (fair comment), but flesh out this statement by stating: 'The Chief Executive is clearly incompetent and some of the leading councillors have been fiddling their so-called expenses'. Clearly this would be defamatory and the newspaper might well be taken to court and required to produce evidence for these claims. In what way is the Chief Executive incompetent? How has he failed to fulfil his duties and in whose judgement? Which councillors have 'fiddled' which expenses? What, when,

where and how? The only sure way of keeping out of the libel courts is to ensure that all comment is fair and the facts on which it is based are true and can be proved; unless

The matter was privileged (see above).

Another defence is that the news organization had already come to a satisfactory agreement with the complainant to settle the dispute, for example by printing a correction and/or apology, or even paying an out-of-court settlement. This is called Accord and Satisfaction. Difficulties sometimes arise when the complainant at first agrees to the offer of amends but then consults a 'hot shot lawyer' who advises them to go ahead and sue. It is important that any agreement to resolve the claim is fully documented.

Other ways in which the media has got into trouble with defamation law is by:

- *Juxtaposition* – e.g., stories about corruption in Police placed next to photographs/pictures of identifiable police officers (a particular danger for television with its use of general 'wallpaper' or 'library' shots to illustrate specific stories).
- *Unintentional inference* – e.g., a story about unnamed teachers said to have sexually abused pupils is taken to refer to a particular teacher or school. This illustrates the importance of making sure that allegations are specific. In contrast to some wrongly held beliefs, the danger of defamation does not necessarily recede if the allegations are vague and unspecific; on the contrary it may increase the chances of innocent people feeling they have been defamed!
- *Relying on the* Have I Got News For You! *'defence'* – many people seem to have been much taken by the amusing and heavily ironic use of the word 'allegedly' attached to some clearly defamatory claim made by the team members on the satirical BBC TV news quiz *Have I Got News for You!* This 'allegedly' is often accompanied by a knowing wink or similar and produces a hearty laugh from the studio audience: everyone is meant to infer that the team member believes the allegation to be true and has said 'allegedly' as some sort of legal mantra to prevent the subject of the remark from suing. Unfortunately, anyone else who attempts to use the same 'get out' is unlikely to have had several lawyers advising on the editing of the pre-recorded programme.
- *Relying on the 'I Was Only Reading What the Paper Said' defence* – many radio presenters feature a 'review' of the newspapers – especially of the 'red-top' tabloid variety – and gain much amusement from reading out all sorts of outrageous and scandalous allegations, particularly about politicians and celebrities. The presenter will be appalled to find out that he is required to prove the truth of these allegations in court – or more likely, as of course he will not have access to the sources of the journalist who wrote the original story, he and

his station will have to settle out of court with substantial damages after the station's lawyer tells them they have been 'banged to rights'. The law says every time a libel is repeated it is a fresh libel – and claimants can successfully sue an unlimited number of different and varied outlets for repeating the 'original' libel.

Unlike most criminal cases there is no legal aid and the cost of mounting an action for defamation can be huge – often more than can be hoped to receive in damages, especially after recent trends for damages to be more modest than was the case in many spectacular awards to celebrities in the 1980s. Nevertheless, juries still have wide scope to recommend the level of damages if they find for the claimant. However, the risk of losing a claim and being faced with huge legal costs is certainly a major disincentive to many ordinary people of modest means from initiating such action. It is for this reason that libel has been described as 'a rich man's plaything', although recent trends for lawyers to offer a conditional fees arrangement – 'no win, no fee' – means that ordinary people are better able to pursue such matters in court without risking financial ruin.

Owing to the high risks for all concerned very few defamation claims reach the High Court – the vast majority are settled out of court. Most journalists and just about every editor will have the (to say the least) unsettling experience of receiving a solicitor's letter, stating that their client intends to sue for defamation. Usually the threat to go to court is reduced if the news outlet will issue a prominent and fulsome apology and/or correction. The editor would in most cases be well advised to agree to this, or to settle out of court unless s/he is absolutely certain that one of the defences given above can be used and/or that the claimant is trying to use the libel laws to stifle debate and information on a crucial matter of public interest.

If a case does reach court the media organization can make a payment into court. This is a real test of nerve for both parties: if the court finds for the claimant but makes an award either the same as or lower than the amount paid in they will be liable for the legal costs of both parties – a powerful incentive (as it is intended to be) to bring the case to a swift conclusion. Furthermore, the courts take a dim view – and are likely to substantially increase damages – if the media organization continues with the case and insists on the truth of its allegations (if its defence is justification).

All of this demonstrates that defamation is both a constant threat for journalists and a 'game' that is very imprecise and the outcome of which is impossible to predict if it ends in a court case. Furthermore, although almost every major news organization will keep lawyers on standby to give advice on stories it plans to run, such advice is likely to be couched in ambiguous language along the lines of: 'well it could be a problem but you'll probably get away with it'.

It is just another demonstration that journalism often involves strong nerves, courage and, above all, thoroughness and professionalism in ensuring that notes, interviews, statements and research are meticulously carried out and recorded so that if 'push comes to shove' journalists will be able to defend their stories in the courts.

Privilege at common law/the 'Reynolds Defence' and the emergence of a public interest defence

Most of the discussion above has been based on provisions in statute law – specifically the Defamation Acts of 1952 and 1996. However, a landmark case, when Albert Reynolds, the former Taoiseach (Prime Minister) of the Republic of Ireland sued the *Sunday Times* for defamation, led to the development of a public interest defence at common law. The importance of this case for UK journalism can hardly be overstated. The reader who is interested in delving into the background of the case is recommended to consult *McNae's Essential Law for Journalists* (Welsh and Greenwood, 2001) and other books specializing in media law (see 'Sources and resources' at the end of this chapter).

McNae's neatly sums up this public interest defence by quoting part of the judgement from Lord Chief Justice, Lord Bingham in the Court of Appeal:

> As it is the task of the news media to inform the public and engage in
> public discussion of matters of public interest, so that is to be recognised
> as its public duty (Welsh and Greenwood, 2001: 236).

In other words, the journalist might not have to be sure of proving each and every allegation made in a report if the story can be truly said to be in the public interest. However, before readers rush off to write and broadcast stories about public figures, which they 'know' but can't 'prove' to be true in a court of law, they should note that in 1999 the House of Lords, in a judgement given by Lord Nicholls, set some of the requirements that must be met for the public interest defence to be accepted. These include the seriousness of the claim – the more serious it is, the greater is the harm to those involved and so the greater is the requirement that allegations, etc., should be based on truth; the credibility of the sources of information; and whether the individual or organization was given the chance to respond to the allegations.

It should also be noted – in a rather typical quirk of law – that although the courts decided that this defence existed, the *Sunday Times* could not use it in the Reynolds case. However, *McNae's* records that the defence has been used successfully by at least one other newspaper.

Criminal libel

Prosecutions for criminal libel are – fortunately for journalists – very rare. In line with the distinction between civil and criminal cases outlined above, criminal libel must contain such strong material that is likely to result in a breach of the peace – either by the person(s), organization or groups named (for this reason there is no need to show it was communicated to a third person) or by others towards the complainant. For example, to accuse someone of being a paedophile might cause a very violent response. Similarly if outrageous claims were made about the conduct of a group in society there may be violent reaction by others in the community against a number of people. Criminal libel can even be taken on behalf of the dead if their relatives feel people will take action against them to take revenge on the dead person. The defence of justification is unlikely to help in these cases and it is the one area where the phrase 'the greater the truth, the greater the libel' is correct.

The same section of the law also deals with blasphemy, obscenity, sedition and malicious falsehood.

- *Blasphemy* – is vilifying the Christian religion only. Case law and precedent has demonstrated that blasphemy cannot be used if other religions are defamed – a quaint and, to many people, outrageous hangover from the days when the UK was almost wholly a Christian country. The official state religion is, of course, still the Church of England – a Protestant faith – and some experts hold that not even Catholicism is protected by the blasphemy law.
- *Obscenity* – the prosecution must prove that the material tends to deprave and corrupt those likely to see it.
- *Sedition* – the material is so extreme that it is likely to undermine the main institutions of society, specifically the government, Monarchy and armed forces.
- *Malicious falsehood* – sometimes used as an alternative to defamation where the offending material might not damage someone's reputation as such but it could harm the individual or organization, for example by stating that a company was no longer trading. A successful prosecution must show that the claims were untrue and that they were published maliciously.

Freedom of speech and privacy: a clash of rights

There is no specific right under British law and constitution for freedom of speech. Since the end of the 1940s the European Convention on Human Rights has contained a possibility that under Article 10 – which states there is a general right to freedom of expression and communication of opinion and ideas – the European Court of Human Rights sitting in Strasbourg (*not* to be confused with the European Court of Justice, part of the European Union structure – see Chapter 11) could help in fighting censorship of publications or broadcasts. Until October 2000 the practical difficulties and cost of fighting a case in Strasbourg, as well as the doubtful chance of success, prevented this from being a viable course of action for most journalists and others.

However, the *incorporation* of the Convention into UK *domestic law* through the Human Rights Act (1998) (HRA), which came into force two years later, has led to more feasible prospects of using the Convention to fight illegal and improper restrictions on journalism.

For journalists, though, the HRA is a double edged sword: for Article 8 also gives rights to privacy; including respect for private family life and financial and other affairs (e.g., bank statements, correspondence, etc.). There is extreme concern on the part of journalists and editors that those who are carrying out immoral or even illegal activities will use the HRA to muzzle legitimate investigative journalism. At the time this book was written several test cases were going before the courts and, as discussed in Chapter 11, this law provides enough scope for judges to effectively *make* the law. The importance of these judgements to journalism in the UK can hardly be overstated. Readers should keep up-to-date with these developments through the broadsheet press (and their Web sites) and articles in the *Press Gazette* and *Media Lawyer* (details at the end of this chapter).

Election law

There is no time when politicians, political parties and activists (and perhaps the general public) take a greater interest in journalism and the media than during election campaigns. This is when there will be maximum pressure and 'spin' to have stories angled in a way that is helpful to a party or politician, so reports will be closely scrutinized. For the print journalist there is no legal requirement to be fair or balanced in political coverage at elections any more than at any other time: newspapers and magazines can be completely biased in their reporting and are not required to give equal time/space to parties. The Political Parties, Elections and Referendums Act 2000 outlawed the publication of opinion polls *on the day of an election*.

The print journalist must though be aware that the laws affecting reporting, including defamation, Public Order, etc., are not suspended at election times – if anything they might 'apply' even more than usual – and must be careful not to publish false information about a candidate that might affect their election chances. The law is particularly tough on 'false information' at election times because a successful defamation action after the election is no compensation if, as a result of untrue allegations, a candidate lost the election.

In general, then, it is both good practice as well as legally advisable to be particularly careful about the publication of claims about the character and conduct of candidates. It is best to stick to a discussion of the issues, although of course the experience (or lack of it), and the record of candidates, are perfectly legitimate areas of public discussion.

There are particular problems with political parties whose material and statements might contravene the general law; in particular the re-emergence in the early 2000s of far-right parties, hostile to racial minorities. A discussion of some of their policies might lead to charges that the media has incited racial hatred and otherwise threatened public order. When does legitimate discussion of public issues become racist propaganda? Similar problems arise with the so-called 'right to life' parties. Here the problem is more likely to come in advertisements (or party election broadcasts). Are pictures of aborted foetuses part of information that should be in the public domain or are they obscene? The journalist, manager or advertising head has an almost impossible task to exercise judgement in these highly emotive and contentious areas. Refusal to broadcast or publish will lead to charges of 'censorship' and of being the stooge of party/government/political correctness. If publication goes ahead the media will doubtless be blamed for subsequent outbreaks of public disorder and the destruction of property and possible serious injury or even death. With power comes responsibility and in these areas at least the journalist is probably in a 'no win' situation.

In contrast to their print colleagues broadcast journalists are under a general obligation to be fair, impartial and objective, and coverage is put under the microscope (or stethoscope!) at election times to make sure that they stick to these requirements, especially on the 'time formula' for coverage of parties and candidates. Until 2000 broadcasters had special restrictions on how they reported constituency issues and interviewed candidates for those constituencies, with a veto on the whole broadcast by any candidate who did not wish to take part. The Political Parties, Elections and Referendums Act (2000) scrapped the (notorious) Section 93 of the Representation of the People Act (1983) and replaced it with a requirement for broadcasters to produce codes of practice for the inclusion of candidates in parliamentary and local government elections. The codes can be viewed online and the Web addresses are given at the end of the chapter. These codes are operational in different timescales depending on the type of election:

- *General election* – from the date of the dissolution of Parliament
- *Parliamentary by-election* – from the date of the issue of the election writ
- *Local government election* – from the last date of the publication of the notice of election (usually 5 weeks before the election).

The broadcasters and their regulators produce codes covering all aspects of election coverage and the broadcast journalist must ensure they are fully familiar with them before an election campaign. One of the curious aspects of broadcasting in elections is that on the day of the poll itself – after weeks when almost every news bulletin and current affairs programme has been dominated by the election – there must be no discussion of the issues, leaders or candidates. Broadcasters have to restrict themselves to observations about the weather and such trivia; certainly there must be no speculation or information of any kind about the likely outcome of the election. These restrictions apply until the close of the polls at 10.00 p.m. – then it's open season!

Other legal restrictions on journalism

Public order

It is an offence to publish threatening, abusive or insulting material or the intention of which, where the likely effect is to stir up hatred against any group in the community by reference to colour, race, nationality, citizenship, ethnic or national origins This may be particularly problematic in elections (see above).

Official secrets

The Official Secrets Acts are designed to prevent the publication or broadcasting of important information that it is in the public interest to keep secret, as to reveal it to the general public could imperil the security and peace of the population, usually through potentially helping those – foreign and domestic – who might wish to harm the state and its citizens. The Acts cover a wide range of material from Police operations, to secret services, to diplomatic relations. If strictly applied, it would stop the reporting of a huge range of stories that might be said to be of legitimate public interest. There have been many accusations that various authorities have used the Acts to prevent stories that would be embarrassing to those involved, or show up incompetence, or lying, by officialdom – rather than being a genuine threat to internal or external peace and security. If the law was strictly enforced it would make a mockery of the claim that the UK is a 'free' society with a 'free' press. Fortunately, prosecutions under the law are relatively rare and are only proceeded with in what the authorities regard as 'extreme' cases. To help journalists untangle this complex area of law and work out whether reports are likely to breach the Acts there is the Defence Press and Broadcasting Advisory Committee – commonly known as the 'D' notice committee. It is chaired by the Permanent Under-Secretary of State for Defence. S/he heads a committee of four senior civil servants from the relevant ministries and 13 representatives across the different sectors of journalism. There are five standing or permanent 'D' notices and these can be viewed on the Web (see end of chapter) and the committee advises on other developments and responds to specific requests from news organizations. However, the committee has no statutory basis – it can only give advice and journalists are 'free' to ignore it; equally the fact that an item was 'OK'd' by the committee won't in itself prevent a successful prosecution under the Acts.

Rehabilitation of offenders

The law is intended to protect those with relatively minor convictions to continue life without constant references to past convictions. There is a tariff of years relating to sentence imposed – after which the conviction is spent. This can affect journalists being sued for libel (see above): justification fails if the complainant can prove the journalist acted with malice when s/he revealed the 'spent' conviction. Journalists lose privilege if court reporting includes reference to a spent conviction that the judge has ruled is inadmissible evidence.

Confidentiality/injunctions

Both this chapter and Chapter 2 have stated that one of the most important aspects of a 'free press' is that there should be no pre-publication censorship. This principle is severely compromised by the use of court injunctions to stop a story – one of the most powerful devices for suppressing journalists. The most common weapon is through claiming that a story breaches confidentiality clauses in someone's employment – there is an implied duty of confidentiality between employer and employee even if this is not specified in the contract of employment. Less frequent is a claim that the material would be so defamatory that redress after publication could not possibly undo the damage caused. Very often an investigative journalist will be nervous about approaching someone who is the subject of some sort of exposé for fear that they will go to the courts to impose an 'eleventh hour' injunction by persuading the judge – often sitting late at night, in Chambers (in private) and with only the aggrieved party present (in legal language *ex parte*) – that publication would breach such confidentiality. Even if all the facts are not laid before the judge at this time (and how could they be without the journalist being present?) the judge may feel there is sufficient grounds to believe publication would infringe this confidentiality and order that publication be stopped. Sometimes papers have already been printed and have to be pulped, or broadcasts have already been scheduled and have received publicity. Sometimes, indeed, the aggrieved party may have been told of the story through the early editions and succeeds in having an order preventing further printing/editions of the story to appear. Needless to say this is a very expensive business for news organizations.

This is not to imply that such attempts at injunctions always succeed. Judges are sometimes surprisingly supportive of journalists and journalism. It is the case, though, that people and organizations whose activities the journalist has the greatest public duty to monitor are likely to be the ones who are rich enough to have expensive lawyers on permanent standby to get a judge out of bed to 'slap on an injunction'.

A further problem is that an injunction might only name one media outlet – because that is the only one the aggrieved is aware of – an injunction would also apply to any other outlets, which may coincidentally have been working on a similar story and 'target' or, more likely, has 'lifted' the story off the first editions of a newspaper and run a 'spoiler' in their own outlet. The general rule is that an injunction on one is an injunction on all.

Harassment

The Protection from Harassment Act (1997) is a classic example of a law that was supposedly brought in because of a problem in society – in this case people being 'stalked' and otherwise receiving unwelcome attentions from someone, and feeling threatened and intimated by such actions – being used in ways that Parliament almost certainly never intended. In this case the law has been used to prevent legitimate inquiries into the lives of people in the news. If the complainant can show there was 'alarm' and 'distress' there could be a criminal prosecution against the journalist/photographer. Even more worryingly for journalists is the type of case (being threatened or pursued at the time of this book's publication) that people who receive threatening letters and the like after stories have been published or broadcast about them may be able to 'blame' the journalist and news organization for this. Again, how the courts respond to these cases in the first few years of the Act's life will set the tone for many decades to come.

Trespass

Trespass can be described in summary as the *unlawful access or entry to land, property or person.* For the journalist the most usual problem area is when they enter land or property in pursuit of a story – without the owner's permission. It should be borne in mind that many places that are used by the public, including shopping centres, football stadia, theatres, etc., are private property and the owners have the right to exclude or eject anyone, including journalists, whom they do not want on the premises. This is mostly a civil matter. In the case of alleged trespass on to land there is an onus on the claimant to prove that the person against whom action is being taken has gained unlawful access to the land. This protection allows the journalist/photographer to use binoculars or cameras to record activities from public land, e.g., outside the perimeters of a house or business. There is the possibility of criminal law against journalists/photographers/camera operators, etc., if the Police believe they are blocking access or refuse to leave when told to do so, for example when covering a demonstration.

Again, the PCC and broadcasters' codes need to be taken into account, along with the civil and criminal law in these matters.

Data protection

The Data Protection Acts (1984) and (1998) are designed to protect the public from having information gathered by one source and one purpose being made available, either deliberately or by carelessness, to others and to give people the right to see large amounts of information held on them by public authorities. Unfortunately for the journalist these laws taken together provide two major problems.

1 The vital information contained in newsrooms' contact books, on central computer systems, often for years on end, could be held to be illegal. Safeguards and procedures need to be built in under the legally necessary Data Protection Officer at each organization to ensure that others cannot get hold of that information. Freelances should consider registering under the Data Protection Act.
2 The reluctance or even refusal by some authorities, especially the Police and local authorities, to release information to the press when they are fearful they may be barred from so doing under the Acts. This has been a particular problem for journalists in trying to find the names, addresses, etc., of road accident victims and the routine 'condition checks' from hospitals. If strictly applied and enforced the staple diet of information needed for much journalism would be cut off. Fortunately, after much pressure and campaigning from news organizations and others, guidance notes to the Police, law courts and other bodies have helped to ease the situation. Nevertheless journalists need to monitor and oppose over-zealous and unreasonable interpretations of the Act(s).

The Regulation of Investigatory Powers Act 2000 – another example of a law that was supposedly brought in to deal with one type of problem: the use of e-mail, phone and other forms of personal communication by criminals intent on harming individuals or society – causes problems for journalists. The difficulties arise when journalists are assuring their contacts of the confidentiality of their communications. The Act gives powers to a wide variety of public bodies and authorities to intercept communications and report on *communications data* – the numbers, addresses used, length of communications, etc., with a higher level of authorization required for covert monitoring of the content of the communications. All authorities empowered to carry out these actions are required to publish a Code of Practice. These are supposed to give protection to information given in confidence – but not to 'non-confidential' material. Journalists should therefore make sure that any communications with contacts that are of a sensitive nature should openly stress (for the benefit of anyone monitoring the communication) that it *is* confidential. Yes: one *more* thing to remember!

Laws that help journalists

Freedom of information

The UK is one of the most secretive so-called liberal democratic states in the world. Unlike some other countries, notably the USA, there is no presumption that the citizen has a right to know anything – and therefore neither is the journalist entitled to be given this information. This makes reporting on the various tiers of government and other public affairs very difficult. The Code of Practice on Access to Government Information issued in the mid-1990s provided the authorities with broad guidelines on what they should make available to the public and journalists, but there was no automatic right to such information. The commitment of the Labour government elected in 1997 to introduce a Freedom of Information Act (2000) (FIA) gave rise to great hope by journalists (and others) that at last they would have something equivalent to the rights of US journalists to information necessary to pursue stories in the public interest. Unfortunately, freedom of information seems to be something that political parties are enthusiastic about when in opposition but much less keen on when they reach office. It is a truism that knowledge is power and governments tend to want to hang onto that power and find reporting and exposure of government activities in the press rather frightening. Consequently, what became the FIA, which began to come into force in 2002, was, to say the least, something of a disappointment. Relevant Web sites and further reading on the theoretical scope of the Act are given at the end of this chapter but essentially the Act covers information on which decisions are taken in the public interest by central and local government, devolved government and most other public bodies. Unfortunately it gives ministers and others the right to block the release of information! At the time of writing it was impossible to see how the Act would be used in practice as its full implementation was delayed until 2005.

Public interest disclosure

One of the greatest problems for journalists in trying to make stories 'stand up' is the reluctance of employees to reveal information about their employment and employers through a fear of either losing their jobs, or themselves being subject to legal action through breaking the confidentiality clauses in their contracts of employment. Even information that most people would agree should be known to the public and are legitimate forms of journalistic enquiry, such as the safety of public transport systems, might, and have been, stymied by such worries. The Public Interest Disclosure Act (1998) – the so called 'whistleblowers' charter' – provides protection for employees from disciplinary procedures on breach of confidence grounds who reveal such information or worries to journalists.

Companies' Act(s)

The Companies Act(s) oblige all businesses, except sole traders, partnerships or unlimited liability companies, to lodge their accounts and a wide range of other information at Companies' House. In his book *Investigative Reporting* David Spark approvingly notes not only the wealth of information that is available to journalists but the ease of access and helpfulness of the staff there. Such information can be crucial in making stories about the activities of companies and their directors 'stand up'.

On the whole then we can see that there are laws which both help and hinder journalists. These are summarized in Figure 13.4.

Protecting sources

Sometimes courts order journalists to reveal the sources of their stories – either in terms of information or people. In the opinion of the author, and many other far more experienced practitioners and commentators, the journalist has a moral duty to protect the source of his information if he has given an undertaking to do so and/ or if to reveal the source would cause great difficulty to that person in their private and professional life and even lead to him losing his liberty through a criminal prosecution. There have been several examples of journalists being jailed for refusing to reveal their sources. Sometimes journalists have to pay a high price for producing material that they believe to be of vital public interest. Fortunately the authorities are generally loathe to take tough action against journalists – it turns the journalist into a martyr or, at the very least, a *cause célèbre* and is certain to produce a very hostile reaction in the press. If it is a government that is pressing the action then it can be sure that the political party and leaders concerned will face a very hostile press at the next election! Journalists, after all, tend to look after their own.

Copyright

It is vital that anyone practising as a journalist has a rudimentary knowledge of the law of copyright – and this chapter can only aim to provide such a rudimentary level. The 'Sources and resources' list at the end of the chapter provides recommended texts, including the NUJ's own easy-to-read guide.

Copyright exists to protect the creators of works involving time, talent and artistry, from being used and exploited by others without proper recompense or permission of the creators of the work. Since 1988 there has also been the right for the creators not to have their work given a derogatory treatment (without their consent).

Laws that are a hindrance	Laws that are a help
Defamation Act(s): Libel – 'an unwarranted and/or unreasonable attack on the reputation, conduct and character of a person or organization on matters which are not privileged'	Defamation Act(s) provide important defences if reporting is factually accurate and/or is fair comment on a matter of public interest and without malice. Reports of proceedings in Parliament, commissions, etc., appointed by Parliament and of a wide range of other public bodies are protected by varying degrees of 'privilege'
Contempt of Court Act (1981) – serious penalties for 'a serious and improper effect on the course of justice and/or unreasonable comment or actions calculated to bring the processes of justice into disrepute'	Contempt of Court Act provides privilege (protection from legal action) for fair and accurate reporting of main/final proceedings of most legal actions and for reasonable comment/campaigning on miscarriages of justice, etc.
Official Secrets Act(s) – restrictions of reporting matters concerning the military, security services, defence, foreign affairs and 'internal security' (DA Notices)	*Public Records Act(s)* – relatively easy access to wide range of official papers from the past (and see Freedom of Information Act below)
Terrorism Act (2000) – can require journalist to reveal sources and to report 'suspicions'	
Regulation of Investigatory Powers Act 2000 – can undermine confidentiality of communications with contacts	
Protection From Harassment Act (1997) – restrictions on 'door-stepping' and other 'robust' forms of journalistic enquiries on individuals	
Breach of Confidence/Injunctions: restricts ability of individuals to discuss matters of public interest	*Public Interest Disclosure Act (1998)* – to protect individuals who make disclosures of interest in the public interest ('whistleblowers'): means sources are more likely to come forward
Data Protection Act(s) – can frustrate storing of information/contacts; can be used by authorities as 'excuse' not to reveal information	*Freedom of Information Act (2000)* – very limited 'right' to see papers of government and 'public bodies', but 'presumption of secrecy' remains
Human Rights Act (1998) – Article 8 specifies 'rights' of individuals to privacy: may frustrate 'legitimate' journalistic enquiries	*Human Rights Act* – Article 10 gives right to freedom of expression that should help 'legitimate' reporting, and Section 12, which limits injunctions
Local Government Act (2000) leading to 'cabinet style' meetings being held in private and tough *public interest* tests on disclosure of information	*Local Government Act* states 'significant decisions' must be made in public; *Access to Information Act(s)* give rights of reporting in 'principal local authorities'

Figure 13.4

It is important to understand the basic principle of what is copyright(able) and what isn't. Crucially for journalists there is no copyright in news as such – the publication or broadcast that something has happened – or in information, for example the results of the National Lottery (the latter has been tested in law) or ideas (e.g., for a feature or programme).

It is how that news and information is put together and presented, specifically the skill, time and talent that makes that presentation a unique product, that is protected by copyright. The law allows the publication of extracts of material, particularly *for the purposes of criticism or review and, crucially, for the reporting of current events*. This includes (again it has been tested in law) for short sections of television coverage by another channel of a football game included in news bulletins later that day. Such extracts should be credited to the originator of the material – usually the news organization or broadcaster.

The Copyright Act(s) also contain a concept called Fair Dealing. This means that any such extracts used should not deny the originator financial rewards for their work, for example by reproducing whole chunks of material of a book that might then stop a potential buyer of that book from making the purchase, as they had seen everything they wanted 'for free'. There is no set and precise limit to the amounts that might be reproduced but certainly more than 10 per cent of a book – or a whole chapter in a book – would almost certainly be excessive and lead to a breach of copyright claim. In any case, it is good practice to seek permission from the publishers/authors of the work and to acknowledge this in the extract.

Copyright usually belongs (naturally enough) to the individual who created that work and exists in most cases for 70 years after the death of the originator, or 50 years after a broadcast. However, many employees, through their Contract of Employment, sign over the copyright of the work created for their employer on the employer's time to that employer. This will usually include the exploitation of that material in all outlets at home or overseas, including the Internet. Controversially, many news organizations have pressured freelances to hand over their rights for such exploitation for all time to the organization that first commissioned it. The NUJ has successfully fought many such 'all inclusive' contracts.

The copyright of photographs is rather more complicated than that for the written word. Photographs taken before the Copyright, Designs and Patents Act (1988) came into effect in July 1989, are the copyright of the person who commissioned them; after this Act copyright belongs to the photographer (or the employer). This can be an issue for wedding photographs, which are often used by the news media when one or both of the happy couple are killed. If the wedding took place up until 1989 the person who commissioned the wedding photographs – typically the bride's father – would own the copyright and could sue for copyright infringement if his permission is not sought and given. Crucially though, the 1988 Act still gives protection to someone who commissions a photograph for private or domestic purposes (which would clearly include wedding photos) even though he does not own the copyright of the photograph: this would belong to the photographer.

An issue sometimes arises over the copyright of a speech (made outside Parliament, councils, etc., which are exempt from copyright). The spoken word is now included even if the speaker is not using a written text, so the speaker would have a claim for copyright against the news organization that used it without his permission. However, thankfully for journalists, the law makes a special exemption for the reporting of current events. This means that almost every speech likely to be used by the news media is free of copyright, provided that the person making the speech did not clearly state in advance that the speech was not to be reported and that the speech did not contain material that was in itself subject to copyright.

This clause in the Act also safeguards the journalist from having to get release forms from people whom they interview or depict in news and current affairs stories. This is in contrast to the situation for non-news material, e.g., 'human interest' documentaries of the 'real life' or 'docu-soap' variety. The line between 'current events' and some other types of current affairs documentaries is somewhat blurred – if in any doubt the journalist is recommended to seek 'release' or 'disclaimers' using the standard forms provided by all such media organizations.

Contrary to what many people believe, there is no need for journalists and others to state the work is copyright and insert the copyright (©) symbol on every page on even the most mundane report, as novice journalists, especially freelances, are prone to do. Doing so in fact makes the writer look rather amateurish and provides no additional protection: a work is copyrighted as soon as it is created.

The 'moral rights' that were incorporated in the 1988 Act effectively prevent satirical 'takes' on work – for example poems, books or songs: this has been something of a problem for satirists!

Suggested activities

1 Note how a story involving likely criminal activity, e.g., a suspected murder, violent robbery, is covered in the local media. Did any of the reports seem to break the Contempt of Court Act?

2 Study reports of committal/transfer proceedings involving defendants in this or another story. Did the reports stay within the law?

3 Attend a court case and follow how it is reported in a newspaper. How did the journalist(s) sum up the evidence, etc.? Was anything significant that happened in court *not* included in the report(s)? If so, why do you think that was? (Suggest which laws might be relevant.)

4 Study newspaper reports of a meeting of your local authority or other public body. List some examples of material that would be subject to defamation proceedings were it not for privilege. How did the newspaper give an

'explanation or contradiction' by others named in the reports? (You may need to study several editions of the newspaper to do this.)

5 Study one edition of a newspaper, magazine or TV news broadcast. Note the number of defamatory statements/stories. How were those people/organizations defamed? Show which defences would be most likely to be used if those named tried to sue for defamation.

6 Using 'searches' of the Internet and the resources suggested below, investigate a famous libel case. How was the person's/organization's reputation, etc., said to have been damaged? Summarize both sides of the case. Why do you think the jury came to its decision?

7 Study reports of an election. Were there any apparent breaches of the election law?

8 Investigate stories involving defence or other 'secret' matters. How might the law prevent publication of important aspects of the story; which part of the 'D' notices might have been relevant?

9 Study the Freedom of Information Act and see how it might help in investigating the background of a current story involving local and/or central government.

10 Study a newspaper story that has been given an 'exclusive' tag and see if other newspapers have a similar story or information, pictures, etc. Would the original paper have claim for breach of copyright?

Sources and resources

BBC (2000) *Producer's Guidelines*. http://www.bbc.co.uk/info/editorial/prodgl/index.shtml (accessed 22 September 2001).

BBC (2001) *BBC Programme Makers' Guidelines for the General Election Campaign*. http://www.bbc.co.uk/info/genelection/index.shtml (accessed 30 March 2001).

Carey, P. (1996) *Media Law*. London: Sweet & Maxwell.

Companies House: http://www.insolvency.co.uk/credit/cohouse.htm (accessed 2 February 2001).

Crone, T. (1995) *Law and the Media*. Oxford: Focal Press.

Cornish, G. (2000) *Understanding Copyright in a Week*. London: Hodder & Stoughton.

Criminal Justice System (2001) *Overview of Criminal Justice System*. http://www.criminal-justice-system.gov.uk/citizen/overviewof_cjs.htm (accessed 24 April 2001).

Crook, T. *Radio Presentation: Theory and Practice*. Oxford: Focal Press (forthcoming).

Defence, Press and Broadcasting Advisory Committee (2001) http://www. dnotice.org.uk/agenda.htm (accessed 2 October 2001).

The Guardian Media Law page published in Media Guardian every Monday. http://www.media.guardian.co.uk (accessed 22 September 2001).

Hooper, E.S. (1995) *A Journalists' Introduction to Courts and Lawyers*. Harlow: NCTJ Training Ltd.

Her Majesty's Stationery Office. *Acts of the UK Parliament*. http://www.hmso. gov.uk/acts.htm (accessed 2 February 2001).

The Stationery Office (2000) *Whitaker's Concise Almanack 2001*. London: Stationery Office.

Home Office (2001) *The Work of the Coroner*. http://www.homeoffice.gov.uk/ccpd/coroner.htm (accessed 10 February 2001).

Home Office *Code of Practice to Government Information*. http://www.home office.gov.uk/foi/ogcode982.htm (accessed 2 February 2001).

Independent Television Commission (2000) http://www.itc.co.uk (accessed 23 September 2001).

Media Lawyer Broughton-in-Furness, Cumbria: Tom Welsh. (published bi-monthly) http://www.media-lawyer.co.uk/default.htm (accessed 22 September 2001).

Press Complaints Commission (1999) *Code of Practice*. http://www.pcc.org.uk/cop/cop.asp (accessed 22 September 2001).

Press Gazette (published weekly) http://www.pressgazette.co.uk (accessed 22 September 2001).

Radio Authority (1994) *News and Current Affairs Code*. http://www.radioauthor ity.org.uk/downloads/newscode.pdf (pdf file) (accessed 22 September 2001).

Radio Authority (2001) *Commercial Radio's Election Guidelines*. http://www. radioauthority.org.uk/downloads/pdf/ELECTION (pdf file) (accessed 22 September 2001).

Spark, D. (1999) *Investigative Reporting – a study in technique*. Oxford: Focal Press.

Welsh, T. and Greenwood, W. (2001) *McNae's Essential Law for Journalists* (16th edition). London: Butterworths.

14 Media regulatory bodies

- Introduction
- The Press Complaints Commission
- The Radio Authority
- The Independent Television Commission
- The British Broadcasting Corporation
- The Broadcasting Standards Commission
- The British Board of Film Classification
- The Advertising Standards Authority
- The Mechanical Copyright Protection Society
- The Performing Right Society
- Phonographic Performance Limited
- Suggested activities
- Sources and resources

Introduction

In the UK all aspects of newspaper and magazine journalism and production, and radio and television journalism and production are regulated and given advice by government-appointed and independent advisory bodies, which seek to ensure a balance between ethical and legal considerations and possible infringement of the right to freedom of speech in all media. Any journalist or media producer should be aware of their responsibilities either under the law or as part of self-regulation in adhering to professional attitudes and practice. The main regulatory and advisory bodies are given in this chapter.

The Press Complaints Commission (PCC)

The Press Complaints Commission, which replaced the former and largely ineffective Press Council, is an independent self-regulatory organization dealing with complaints from members of the public about the editorial content of newspapers and magazines. The majority of its 16 members should have no connection with the press, thus attempting to ensure its independence from the newspaper industry, but in 2001 six members were editors of national and regional newspapers and magazines. The independent chairman is appointed by the newspaper and magazine industry and must not have any vested interests or connections in the publishing industry. The public members are appointed by an Independent Appointments Commission and once again may not have any connections with the publishing industry, other than their work on the commission. Each of the press members must have experience at a senior editorial level. The Code of Practice, which has evolved since its introduction in 1991 to meet changing circumstances, is written by a committee of editors and ratified by the commission. As it is not a legal document it can and has been amended to reflect parliamentary comment and advice from members of the public, newspaper editors and the PCC itself. The code sets the benchmark for the press, demanding that they adhere to ethical and professional standards by protecting the rights of the individual whilst at the same time upholding the public's interest and right to know. The Code of Practice, which was ratified by the Press Complaints Commission on 1 December 1999, consists of 16 clauses, some of which may be excepted in the public interest, which includes detecting or exposing crime or a serious misdemeanour, protecting public health and safety and preventing the public from exposure to misleading statements from an individual or organization. Briefly the 16 clauses relate to:

1 Accuracy	9 Hospitals
2 Opportunity to reply	10 Reporting of crime
3 Privacy	11 Misrepresentation
4 Harassment	12 Victims of sexual assault
5 Intrusion into grief or shock	13 Discrimination
6 Children	14 Financial journalism
7 Children in sex cases	15 Confidential sources
8 Listening devices	16 Payment

The code performs a dual function in that it provides the press with a firm set of binding principles and guidelines as well as giving the commission a clear framework with which to deal with complaints from the public. Editors are asked to ensure that all staff observe the code, not only to the letter but in full spirit, and it is their responsibility to respond with alacrity to any complaints raised by the PCC on behalf of any individual, organization or group of people. Editors must print in full the adjudication and in most cases complaints are resolved by the publication of an apology or correction. The outcome of each investigated complaint is published in a regular Complaint's Report, which is circulated to all branches of media, consumer, legal and public services. Some will argue that the PCC is still largely ineffective in curbing the power of the press. However, the alternative is to impose legal and statutory controls on the industry that may conflict with the freedom of the press and the public interest.

The Radio Authority (RA)

The Radio Authority, which was created by the Broadcasting Act 1990, commenced its licensing and regulatory role in January 1991. The members of the authority are selected from a variety of backgrounds and serve for five years. Basically, the RA has three main functions: to plan frequencies; to appoint licensees with a view to broadening listener choice and also to monitoring output; and to regulate programming and advertising. It publishes regulatory and obligatory codes on engineering, sponsorship and advertising and programming.

It licenses and regulates all commercial radio services (not the BBC) including national, local, cable, satellite, national FM subcarrier and restricted services. The latter include short-term, freely radiating services such as 'special event' radio, hospital and campus radio and localized permanent stations. It also licenses both national and local digital services and derives its income solely from licence application and running fees. National licences, which last for eight years, are advertised in open competition and are awarded to the highest cash bidder following criteria set down in the Broadcasting Acts of 1990 and 1996. Three licences are in existence – one for a 'non-pop' station, one for a primarily 'speech-based' station and one for an 'all-comers' station. Local licences, also of eight years' duration, are advertised in open competition in areas that the authority considers appropriate in terms of availability of a suitable frequency, projected financial stability of the proposed station and solid evidence of a serious applicant being available. Restricted Service Licences (RSLs) are issued on a temporary basis for a period not exceeding 28 days and function on low-power transmitters to a designated area of interest or for a special event. Many colleges and other institutions apply for these licences in order to give students the opportunity to gain broadcasting experience. Long-term Restricted Service Licences (LRSLs) are intended for a single establishment such as a hospital and are often transmitted either on an induction loop or low-powered FM and AM wavebands. Cable and Satellite Licences, which are issued for a period of five years, are subject to conditions ranging from ownership, transmission details and programme content. Digital Radio Licences comprise National Multiplex, Local Multiplex and Sound Programme Services and will be awarded for periods of 12 years.

The RA's advertising and sponsorship code relates to the content and presentation of advertisements and sponsorship and follows the Advertising Standards Authority's guidelines on honesty, legality, decency and truthfulness, although sponsorship proposals do not need advance clearance. However 'special category' advertisements and national advertising campaigns broadcast on more than one station require advance clearance from the Radio Advertising Clearance Centre (RACC), a body approved by the Radio Authority. The news and current affairs code sets out rules governing the broadcasting of news and related programmes. These rules cover impartiality and accuracy, library material, phone-ins, interviews, discussions, undue editorial influence or opinion and political programming, especially at the time of elections. Finally the programme code covers such overall matters as taste and decency; portrayal of violence, sexual conduct, terrorism and anti-social behaviour; children; religion; and sensitive areas.

The authority considers complaints from the listener and, if it decides to proceed with a complaint, will request a recording of the offending output. If the station is found to be in breach of its licence agreement the RA can apply sanctions including a demand for an apology or correction to be broadcast, fines and the shortening or revocation of a licence. Findings are published in *The Radio Authority* and the *Listener*. It should be noted that technical aspects and transmission of broadcasting, including the radio spectrum, is the responsibility of The Radio Communications Agency.

The Independent Television Commission (ITC)

The Independent Television Commission, which like the Radio Authority was set up by the Broadcasting Act of 1990, replaced the Independent Broadcasting Authority (IBA) and the Cable Authority. It is the public body responsible for licensing and regulating commercial television companies broadcasting in and from the UK. These include ITV, Channels 4 and 5, public teletext and a range of cable, satellite and local delivery services. It does not regulate the BBC or S4C, the fourth channel in Wales. The Secretary of State for Culture, Media and Sport appoints the chairperson, deputy chairperson and up to a further ten members. They are supported by a full-time staff with specialist regulatory and licensing expertise as well as a range of advisors, including several specialist committees. The Central Religious Advisory Committee (CRAC) advises the ITC, the BBC and the Radio Authority on religious matters. The Medical Advisory Panel, consisting of eminent and independent consultants gives advice on medical- and health-related advertisement. The Advertising Advisory Committee (AAC), comprising of members from the advertising industry and consumers, debates sponsorship and advertising issues. The Schools Advisory Committee (SAC), with practising teachers and national educationalists as members, provides guidelines on classroom television programmes and Channel 4 service to schools. All members of the commission must abide by government guidelines on best practice for members of public bodies, which sets out their responsibilities and their relationship with the Department for Culture, Media and Sport. However, as well as the specialist advisory committees, the commission receives regular comment from 12 Viewer Consultative Panels (VCCs), nine in England and one each in Wales, Scotland and Northern Ireland. These panels consist of a wide cross-section of society, age and interest and are encouraged to discuss the content and range of programmes, particularly within each council's region.

The ITC licences set out conditions on standards of broadcasting and advertising, monitor broadcaster's performance against the requirements regarding programme content, sponsorship, advertising and technical performance. It ensures that a wide range of television services that are of good quality and appeal to a diverse audience is available in the UK and that there is fair competition in the provision of these services. It investigates complaints and publishes its findings on a regular basis in its Programme Complaints and Intervention Reports and yearly in its Annual Performance Reviews. Although the ITC does not make, broadcast or transmit programmes it regulates the standards for programme content in the ITC Programme Code, which includes guidelines on privacy, taste and decency, violence, charitable appeals, religious programmes, impartiality and commercial product placement. Minor breaches of the code will lead to advice regarding the guidelines. Serious offences will incur the issuing of a formal warning, a requirement for on-screen corrections and apologies, imposition of a fine or shortening or revocation of the licence.

It should be noted that regulation for satellite and cable programme content is different from terrestrial services in that there is no requirement for cable or satellite channels to provide a mix of education, information and entertainment. Significantly the 9.00 p.m. 'watershed' is brought forward to 8.00 p.m. for subscription and pay-per-view services protected by a pin system. However, licensed programme channels are still regulated by the ITC's Programme, Advertising and Sponsorship Codes and can be censured by the ITC for breaches of these regulations.

The British Broadcasting Corporation (BBC)

The British Broadcasting Corporation is established under successive Royal Charters (the latest expires in December 2006), which set out its public broadcasting obligations to inform, educate and entertain. BBC services are regulated by a separate agreement under the Charter, thus recognizing the BBC's editorial independence. Twelve Governors, who are part-time non-executives, are appointed by the Crown on the recommendation of ministers. They are men and women with a wide range of experience in arts, business, industry and public service and are trustees for the public interest in ensuring that the BBC is accountable to listeners and viewers, licence payers and Parliament. The Governors, who meet monthly, ensure that the BBC is directed and managed in the public interest, complies with the Charter and the law and maintains the highest standards and values expected of the nation's official broadcaster. They also appoint the Director-General and the senior management of the corporation, who run the day-to-day affairs. However, the Governors can hold management to account for their activities and are responsible for monitoring performance, setting strategies and ensuring compliance with laws, regulations and policy, which must serve audience needs and deliver good value for the licence fee. The Governors submit an Annual Report to Parliament containing their assessment of performance. They ensure that programme makers observe the Producer's Guidelines and that the BBC's commercial arm is not subsidised by licence payers. The Governors observe the Cadbury and Nolan Codes on corporate governance and standards in public life and, in deference to their responsibilities, maintain an Audit Committee, a Fair Trading Audit Committee and a Remuneration Committee.

The Governors conduct formal public consultations and seek specialist views on BBC services and programmes as part of their commitment to providing a quality service. The Governors' Programme Complaints Appeals Committee considers appeals against the findings of the BBC's Head of Programme Complaints, which in itself investigates serious complaints about BBC programmes. The Governors are assisted in their oversight and awareness of the needs of BBC listeners and viewers in Northern Ireland, Wales, Scotland and the English Regions by National Broadcasting Councils and an English National Forum. Similarly, the Governors are instrumental in safeguarding the independence of the BBC World Service and seek advice on output and audience perceptions from the World Service Consultative Group.

The Broadcasting Standards Commission (BSC)

The Broadcasting Standards Commission is the statutory body for standards and fairness in broadcasting in the UK. It is the only regulatory body that covers all commercial and public broadcasting organizations as well as cable, satellite, digital services and text. The commission consists of 13 members, representing different professional backgrounds, who are appointed by and can report directly to the Secretary of State for Culture, Media and Sport. The BSC monitors the standards of UK broadcasting and, through a programme of independent research, reports on the attitudes of the public towards issues of broadcasting standards and fairness in compliance with its published codes, which are based on research and consultation. As an alternative to a court of law it provides redress for people who believe they have been unfairly treated. Standards complaints are usually concerned with sex, taste and decency and the portrayal of violence or offensive language. Fairness complaints are usually concerned with unfair treatment, misrepresentation or infringement of privacy. In the majority of cases the BSC, after receiving a formal complaint, has the power to demand a recording of the broadcast as well as written statements, in preparation for a hearing. Decisions are published frequently and broadcasters must report any action taken as a result. Normally the broadcaster will transmit summaries of the findings on air and also publish them in a newspaper or magazine. The Commission is accountable to Parliament and publishes an annual report of its work as well as a report on its financial situation, which is scrutinized by the National Audit Office.

The British Board of Film Classification (BBFC)

The British Board of Film Classification, formerly the British Board of Film Censors, is an independent body that decides on the classification of films and video that are distributed in the UK. It has no legal status but works within the remit of established laws, particularly as regards the exploitation of children. To maintain its independence the board does not accept funding from the film industry, although it offers guidance regarding possible classification of a film in production. Funding is obtained by the fees levied for classifying films and videos. Films are classified into the following categories:

U (Universal)	suitable for all ages
PG (Parental Guidance)	general viewing but some scenes may be unsuitable for young children
12	suitable only for persons of 12 years or over
15	suitable only for persons of 15 years or over
18	suitable only for persons of 18 years or over
R18 (Restricted 18)	to be supplied only in licensed sex shops or cinema clubs to person of not less than 18 years.

The responsibility for showing a particular film in an area is the responsibility, not of the BBFC, but the local authority, although most accept the recommended classifications.

The Advertising Standards Authority (ASA)

The Advertising Standards Authority, a self-regulatory body, ensures that non-broadcast adverts appearing in the UK adhere to the rules in the British Codes of Advertising and Sales Promotion, which have been written and agreed by the industry through the Committee of Advertising Practice. The basic principles state that advertisements should be legal, decent, honest and truthful; be prepared with a sense of responsibility towards consumers and society in general; and are in line with the principles of fair competition in business. The ASA is funded by a small levy on display advertising and direct mail expenditure and thus preserves its independence from the publishing and advertising industry. All advertisements and promotions in non-broadcast media are regulated by the ASA and include the national and regional press, magazines and free sheets. The ASA also regulates outdoor advertising, direct marketing, sales promotions and cinema commercials, and advertisements in electronic media such as computer games, video, CD-ROM and the Internet.

Complaints, of around 12 000 per year, usually fall into three categories: those that need investigating under the code; those where a complainant has misunderstood the meaning and gist of an advertisement; and those, such as television commercials, which are under the jurisdiction of the Independent Television Commission. Most complaints are from members of the public but some are from consumer groups and competing companies. If an advertisement is found to break the codes then the ASA will ask the company to withdraw or change it, and most act upon this advice. However, if a company or organization refuses to comply, the ASA can apply sanctions such as asking publishers and media owners to refuse more space for the advertisement unless it is changed; withdrawing trading privileges; creating adverse publicity through the media; and in the last resort, referring a persistent offender to the Office of Fair Trading (OFT), which can seek an injunction through the courts to prevent the same or similar claims being made in future advertisements.

The Mechanical Copyright Protection Society (MCPS)

The Mechanical Copyright Protection Society is one of the world's largest royalty collection societies. It is a membership organization that represents thousands of composers, songwriters and music publishers and has reciprocal agreements with equivalent organizations throughout the world. The MCPS negotiates agreements on behalf of its members with people and organizations who wish to record music and then ensures that the copyright owners are paid for the use of their music. The society collects and then distributes the mechanical royalties that are generated by the recording of music onto many different formats such as vinyl, CD, cassette, video, broadcast programmes and multimedia.

The Performing Right Society (PRS)

The Performing Right Society collects royalties on behalf of music creators and publishers for the 'public performance' and broadcast of their copyright musical works. A licence is required to play music in public for commercial businesses, charities, clubs or music venues. However, a licence is not required for performances during divine services in places of worship, live musicals and operas and other dramatic productions. There are over 40 different PRS public performance tariffs that take into account the nature and extent of the music used and the venue. Radio stations must log the titles and duration of broadcast music in order that royalties may be collected and paid to the copyright owners.

The PRS is also a member of the British Music Rights (BMR), which works to promote the interests of UK composers, songwriters and music publishers. It also funds the Performing Right Society Foundation, which aims to encourage, promote and sustain music creation and its performance at all levels.

The Performing Right Society and The Mechanical Copyright Protection Society have formed a Music Alliance of their separate societies in the UK for the benefit of composers, authors and music publishers. PRS and MCPS remain separate societies in terms of income, constitution, membership and guardianship of different rights but the alliance combines their individual strengths to the benefit of members.

Phonographic Performance Limited (PPL)

Phonographic Performance Limited, a non-profit-making society, was set up by the record industry to grant licences for the broadcasting or playing of sound recordings in public. The licence gives permission to use any or all recordings included in the repertoire of members for the stipulated purpose, as a 'blanket licence' is simpler than obtaining individual licences from all recording companies concerned. Broadcasters licensed by PPL include the BBC and commercial radio and television. Members, which include most well known multinational and independent recording companies, assign their rights to the society so that on their behalf it collects and distributes licence fees to record companies, recording artists and musicians. Different tariffs are agreed to reflect the variety of venues and types of music being played. It should be noted that Phonographic Performance Limited is different to The Performing Right Society in that the former distributes royalties to record companies, recording artists and musicians whereas the latter distributes royalties to composers and music publishers.

Suggested activities

1 You wish to find out more information regarding the regulations for broadcasting on independent radio in the UK. Contact the Radio Authority and ask for their publications on this issue. Make a set of notes and a visual display on the main regulations and present your findings to your tutor and other members of your group.

2 The ITC is the regulatory body for independent television broadcasting in this country. Contact them and ask for information on the composition and the main roles of the commission. Make a set of notes and a visual display and present your findings to your tutor and class members.

3 Contact the Press Complaints Commission and request a copy of the Journalists' Code of Practice. Circulate the information to other members of your group.

4 As a group, select a number of stories from a tabloid newspaper and with reference to the above discuss whether any of the stories contravene the guidelines laid down in the code. Draw up a list of conclusions as a result of your discussion.

5 You intend using a segment of a pre-recorded music track from a popular singer's recent CD in a radio feature. Investigate the correct procedure needed to implement this and contact the relevant authority for permission.

6 Try to find an advertisement in a magazine or newspaper that you find offensive, inaccurate or unfair. Write a letter to the Advertising Standards Authority outlining the reasons behind your complaint. Discuss the resultant reply with your tutor and group.

7 You are holding an end-of-course party at a local hall that involves members of the public paying for admission. You intend playing pre-recorded music at the venue. Investigate whether you will need a licence to do so and contact the relevant regulatory authority for further information and advice.

8 The BBC is one of the largest broadcasting organizations in the world and as such has a responsibility via its Charter to provide informed public service broadcasting. Contact the BBC and ask for information on the future plans for the corporation in a digital age.

9 As part of your journalism course you may be asked to write a review of a new film release. This will involve an assessment of the suitability of the film for the target audience and the viewing certificate it has been given. Contact the BBFC and request the latest information on their classification systems for films and videos.

10 You are shocked by a documentary on television that contains explicit sexual behaviour and offensive language. Find out information on the regulations governing the broadcasting of such material. Decide which regulatory body is best suited to dealing with this issue and write a letter of complaint to them expressing your concerns.

11 As a group you hope to set up and run a Restricted Service Licence (RSL) radio station at your college or training centre. Contact the Radio Authority and ask for an information pack and application forms. Use the guidelines received to ascertain the feasibility of the project. Complete the necessary forms either as a training exercise or for submission to the authority.

Sources and resources

Advertising Standards Authority (2001) *British Codes of Advertising*. Available at: http://asa.org.uk (accessed 14 June 2001).

British Board of Film Classification (2001) *Annual Report 2000*. Available at: http://www.bbfc.co.uk (accessed 14 June 2001).

British Broadcasting Corporation (2001) *About the BBC*. Available at: http://www.bbc.co.uk (accessed 13 August 2001).

British Broadcasting Corporation (2001) *Governing today's BBC*. Available at: http://www.bbc.co.uk (accessed 13 August 2001).

British Broadcasting Corporation (2001) *Charter and Agreement*. Available at: http://www.bbc.co.uk (accessed 13 August 2001).

Broadcasting Complaints Commission (2001) *About the Commission*. Available at: http://www.bsc.org.uk (accessed 14 June 2001).

Broadcasting Complaints Commission (2001) *Complaints and Bulletins*. Available at: http://www.bsc.org.uk (accessed 14 June 2001).

Independent Television Commission (2001) *ITC Annual Report 2000*. Available at: http://www.itc.org.uk (accessed 27 September 2001).

Mechanical Copyright Protection Society (2001) *MCPS Media Licensing*. Available at: http://www.mcps.co.uk (accessed 19 September 2001).

Mechanical Copyright Protection Society (2001) *MCPS – PRS Alliance*. Available at: http://www.mcps-prs-alliance.co.uk (accessed 19 September 2001).

Performing Right Society (2001) *Broadcasters*. Available at: http://www.prs.co.uk (accessed 19 September 2001).

Phonographic Performance Limited (2001) *About PPL*. Available at: http://www.ppluk.com (accessed 19 September 2001).

Press Complaints Commission (2001) *About the PCC*. Available at: http://www.pcc.org.uk (accessed 13 May 2001).

Press Complaints Commission (2001) *Code of Practice*. Available at: http://www.pcc.org.uk (accessed 13 May 2001).

Radio Authority (2001) *The Radio Authority – what it is, what it does*. Available at: http://www.radioauthority.org.uk (accessed 1 October 2001).

15 Careers and training

- Introduction
- Training for newspaper journalism
- Training for magazine journalism
- Training for broadcast journalism
- Additional training providers and associations
- Suggested activities
- Sources and resources

Introduction

A career in 'the media' is eagerly sought after by an ever-increasing number of young people, none more so than in newspaper, magazine and broadcast journalism. Newspaper journalism is seen as a challenging and rewarding profession, which accounts for the numerous enquiries about careers and job vacancies that national and regional newspapers receive from budding 'writers' of all ages, backgrounds and education. Similarly, writing for a magazine is often seen as an exciting and creative job; indeed more so than working in the newspaper sector. Also since de-regulation there are ever increasing job opportunities for journalists within the broadcasting industry.

So what personal attributes do prospective employers look for in assessing the potential of a trainee journalist in newspapers, magazines and broadcast? To a greater or lesser extent many of these attributes and qualities are applicable to all three areas, especially with the increase in multi-skilling. Taking into account the specific skills in each area the main common and transferable skills for someone hoping for a career in journalism would include the following:

- have an outgoing and confident personality
- be interested in people, places and events, especially within the area of circulation and transmission
- have an up-to-date knowledge of current affairs
- possess an inquisitive and enquiring mind and demonstrate a determined and logical approach to the task in hand

- demonstrate good investigative research skills
- be able to write accurately, clearly, logically and succinctly with good spelling, punctuation and grammar
- display a confident manner with excellent written and spoken communication skills and a good microphone voice in the case of broadcast journalism
- show the ability to offer original and creative ideas and follow them through to fruition
- demonstrate proof of your desire to get into journalism and show genuine enthusiasm for your chosen area
- be prepared to accept that the job is far from 'glamorous' and involves long and irregular hours with hard and sometimes stressful work in the constant struggle to meet deadlines
- be capable of working alone or as part of a team
- follow other pursuits and hobbies outside of the job such as films, music, sports, theatre etc.
- possess IT skills
- show a willingness to adapt to changing working conditions, situations and new technology, particularly in a multi-skilling environment
- be able to seek, maintain and foster contacts within the industry
- show enthusiasm and a determination to succeed in the business
- build up portfolios of work and experience such as: for newspapers and magazines a portfolio of your writing, which may include something as simple as letters, short articles, reviews and commentary published in a local-community, free, campus or school magazine or an entire publication such as a newsletter or fanzine as well as evidence of work experience; for broadcasting, practical experience of pre-production, production and post-production on a college or university course, campus radio or television station, community radio and television, hospital radio and television or RSL with examples of selected video and audio clips and written support documentation such as cue sheets and scripts.

If you possess most of the above you are an editor or producer's dream but even with some of these attributes how do you get into the business and what training and qualifications are available? There is no finite answer to this as the diversity of the media industry dictates that there are various entry routes, training and qualifications available to suit differing circumstances. Yet in many cases the qualifications for a career in the three main areas of journalism are broadly the same except that a job in broadcast is more likely to involve more technical expertise. It is, however, accepted that the two main routes for a career in newspaper, magazine and broadcast journalism are either pre-entry training at a college, university or training agency or direct entry onto a newspaper, magazine, radio or television station. Each have their own merits and often a media organization will consider applicants from both types of entry dependent on their requirements at any given time. Opinions within the industry vary as to what is the best method: some organizations prefer direct-entry candidates who can then be trained in the house style; others consider that a pre-entry qualification in an educational establishment is desirable. The basic entry requirement for journalism is a minimum of five GCSE passes, one of which must be English Language (grades A–C) or equivalents, but most entrants have two or more A Levels and increasingly a first or second degree. In fact, over 60 per cent of entrants are graduates who either take the direct-entry route and then undertake further training either in-house or on a block release course or graduates who have already achieved a pre-entry journalism qualification at a university or college of Further Education or Higher Education. The following describes some of the main training opportunities available for the aspiring journalist in each sector.

Training for newspaper journalism

Pre-entry

This normally involves trainees attending a full-time one-year vocational course at a college or university accredited by the National Council for the Training of Journalists (NCTJ). Contact them for a list of universities and colleges who offer the qualification on http://www.nctj.com. In most cases colleges require trainees to have achieved two A Levels or equivalents such as a BTEC Diploma in Media and the City and Guilds Diploma in Media Techniques. Most colleges operate a strict application procedure that may involve a written test followed by an interview with the course manager to ascertain whether applicants have the necessary abilities to successfully complete the course and also their future potential for a job in the industry. The course itself combines practical skills in writing and shorthand with underpinning knowledge of media law and central and local government. By the end of the course trainees should have passed preliminary examinations in newspaper journalism, handout, local government, central government, law (two parts) and shorthand at 100 words per minute. However, to become a fully qualified journalist, after a period of employment and dependent on success in all the preliminary examinations, trainees sit the NCTJ National Certificate Examination (NCE). This consists of three parts: interview, speech and newspaper practice and tests communication skills, journalistic skills, underpinning knowledge and, most importantly, an accurate and proven command of the written language. The average pass mark required is 60 per cent and there is one additional mark that is provided by the trainee's newspaper editor. Concerns regarding the training for this examination and the validity of the examination itself were voiced by the industry after a very low pass rate of 35 per cent in 2000. In the Spring 2001 series there was some improvement with 47 per cent of candidates passing newspaper practice, 60 per cent passing speech and 52 per cent passing news interview. The debate is ongoing, with some trainers and editors still having concerns regarding the structure and depth of ongoing training that the candidates receive once they are in the industry as preparation for the qualifying examination. At some provincial newspapers trainees have regular training sessions with either the editor, deputy editor or news editor. These look at stories the trainees have written, highlighting strengths and weaknesses and also ensure that trainees are getting a wide range of experience in writing for the paper.

Direct entry/in-house

Newspapers recruit direct entrants either from school, which is very rare these days, or from colleges and universities. The newspaper will normally expect the entrant to sign a two-year training contract but there may be a three- to six-month probationary period written in to ascertain the person's aptitude, attitude and ability for the job. The employer will contract to train the entrant in-house as well as sending them on a block release or day NCTJ-accredited course at the nearest college offering the scheme. As with trainees on the full-time NCTJ course the direct-entry trainees must pass all subjects in the preliminary examinations. After a period of about 18 months trainees will be entered for the NCTJ National Certificate Examination and if successful will become qualified journalists.

Some regional newspaper publishers run their own in-house training schemes. One such scheme is run by Trinity-Mirror plc, the largest publisher of regional newspapers in the UK. The Editorial Training Centre, based in the offices of the *Newcastle Chronicle* and *Journal* newspapers runs Foundation Courses covering basic skills such as writing, interviewing, shorthand and newsgathering in a modern newsroom. Underpinning knowledge of law and public affairs is also taught and tested. Other schemes are offered by Midland News Association Training, Johnston Training Centre, Regional Independent Media and The Editorial Centre.

NVQs/modern apprenticeships

These schemes, which are similar to direct entry, enable trainees to undertake training leading to NVQ Level 4 qualifications in Newspaper and Periodical Journalism and Press Photography. National standards for the industry are the responsibility of the Publishing National Training Organization, which was set up in 2000 and includes representatives of the lead bodies the Newspaper Society and

Figure 15.1 Keying in copy

the Periodicals Training Council. It is a strategic body concerned with education, training, promotion and development in the publishing industry, which includes newspapers, magazines, books, journals, directory and data based interactive publishing.

Training for magazine journalism

Pre-entry

The Periodicals Training Council (PTC) is the lead body for training in the magazine industry and as such liaises with training providers to ensure that excellent standards are maintained in line with the needs of the industry. It accredits journalism courses at colleges and universities, which may lead to graduate or post-graduate qualifications. Course delivery may be full time, part time or 'fast track' in the case of independent training organizations. Some courses may not specialize exclusively in magazine journalism but also include elements such as online, newspaper and broadcast journalism. However, the main emphasis must still be on the techniques and practice of writing for magazines including interviewing, feature writing, subbing, design and layout, editorial and advertorial. Most courses also include media law and public and current affairs. For details of training providers and courses content contact the PTC on http://www.ppa.co.uk/ptc. In addition to existing newspaper journalism qualifications, in the summer of 2001 the NCTJ accredited three new magazine journalism courses that prepare trainees for the NCTJ Certificate in Magazine Journalism. Harlow College now offers a 19-week fast-track course for graduates and Brighton College offers a 20-week fast-track course for graduates as well as a 36-week part-time course for applicants with a minimum of two A levels or equivalents. Similarly, Liverpool Community College offers a magazine journalism course as well as an 18-week fast-track course provisionally accredited by the NCTJ. Further details from http://www.nctj.com.

A major independent training organization is the PMA Group. As one of the largest editorial and media training organizations within the European Union it provides workshops and short courses in writing copy, Web page design, DTP, advertising, marketing, presentation skills, etc. It is supported by The Newspaper Society and The Periodicals Training Council and is at the forefront of training for the newspaper and magazine industry. Indeed its fast-track nine-week post-graduate course in magazine journalism is highly regarded, not just for the intensive training but also for the offers of job opportunities at the end of the course.

Direct entry/in-house

Most of the large publishing groups, such as Emap and IPC Media, offer direct entry and in-house training and have their own particular entry requirements. Many require a journalistic qualification and sometimes previous work experience and there is provision for ongoing training within the organization. It is advisable to contact magazine publishers directly to ascertain job vacancies and training opportunities. The *Guardian Media Guide* (Peak and Fisher, 2002) includes listings of the main magazine companies and *Benn's Media* is the definitive guide to media organizations, publications and broadcasting stations.

NVQs/modern apprenticeships

The Publishing National Training Organization is working with awarding bodies and training providers in developing modern apprenticeship schemes to satisfy the industry's need for a well qualified workforce that is trained in innovative techniques in a new media age.

Training for broadcast journalism

Pre-entry

A degree is not a necessity for entry into the broadcasting industry but it certainly helps, as demonstrated by the number of graduates currently employed at the BBC and in the commercial sector. Many universities and colleges of higher education offer a variety of undergraduate and postgraduate courses that contain elements of the theory, practice and techniques of broadcast journalism. However, with the development of multi-skilling within the industry many courses also include television, newspaper and magazine journalism. The Broadcast Journalism Training Council (BJTC) has sought in recent years to rationalize the recognition of different types of provision. Although each individual course is granted a standard recognition the BJTC has attempted to define in general terms the main areas of provision. These are:

1 *broadcast journalism* – with the main emphasis on basic journalistic and broadcasting skills most probably in radio but with other subsidiary elements such as television, print, online and multimedia journalism being offered as an integral but non-examinable part of the course
2 *bi-media journalism* – with the main emphasis on basic journalistic skills but concentrating on two main areas of journalism for examination
3 *multimedia journalism* – with the main emphasis on offering a wide-ranging course covering all aspects of journalism including print, broadcast, online and multimedia to examination standard.

In 2000 the BBC initiated a News Sponsorship Scheme to attract potential journalists into BBC News. Successful applicants are given full funding for their postgraduate diploma in broadcast journalism as well as a subsistence allowance. Each trainee has an individual mentor who is an experienced news journalist and there is a four-week paid placement in an area of network news at the end of the course. At the other end of the spectrum the vocational courses offered by the City and Guilds, Edexcel, SCOTVEC, NCFE and OCN provide a good basic introduction to broadcasting techniques and are offered at many colleges of further education. Skillset, the National Training Organization for TV, Radio, Film, Video and Interactive Media, works closely with awarding bodies and is currently discussing the possibility of introducing Related Vocational Qualifications (RVQs) or Progression Awards within a limited number of full- and part-time courses. The aim is to allow students to gain basic skills and underpinning knowledge of the industry that are specifically related to Skillset standards and qualifications whilst pursuing academic and vocational qualifications at an educational establishment. Certainly some successful students from these types of courses who can demonstrate excellent practical skills and underpinning knowledge find their way into local radio and television stations without progressing to university.

Direct entry/in-house

Entry-level jobs require evidence of basic technical skills, a commitment to journalism, previous work experience, a tenacity to deal with the rigours of the job

and creative flair. Academic qualifications including formal journalistic qualifications are a definite advantage but experience such as previously working as a
freelance for the organization also count and, of course, having contacts within the
industry is a definite plus point, even though this is strongly denied by the industry
in support of equal opportunities policies. Whatever the entry requirements a period
of further training is often provided by the employer. One of the most sought-after
training opportunities is the BBC Broadcast Journalist Trainee Scheme, which is
offered periodically. The scheme is open to anyone and offers on and off the job
training in broadcast news, media law and current affairs. Obviously demand far
exceeds the places available and only a few talented individuals are offered
placements after undergoing a rigorous entry procedure. Initial training is at the
state of the art facilities in Bristol and then at regional newsrooms throughout the
country. Trainees receive a salary, which in 2001 was £16 000 plus a London
Weighting. No job is guaranteed at the end of the scheme although the depth and
variety of the training experience well equips trainees to gain a position as a
broadcast journalist. Some ITV companies offer technical training schemes and
infrequent yet invaluable journalism schemes within their own region as well as
links with local educational establishments by providing guest speakers, specialist
short-course tutors and work placement. As regards formal training for commercial
radio the EMAP group offers fixed six-month contracts for aspiring broadcasters.
Although the main emphasis of most commercial stations is on music output,
EMAP does offer training for news journalists with the possibility of more
permanent positions after successful completion of the course.

NVQs/modern apprenticeships

Some media companies offer modern apprenticeships for people who wish to
enter the industry without formal higher-level academic qualifications. Skillset
has pioneered, and is still developing, a system of Intermediate and Modern
Apprenticeships within the Broadcasting, Film and Video Industries. Most of
these are concerned with technical aspects and there has been much emphasis
placed on the initial and re-training of freelances within the industry. Indeed a
Freelance Training Fund (FTF) has been established under the auspices of
Skillset with monetary contributions from all major broadcasters, trade associations and advisory bodies. Encouragingly, Skillset in late 2001 also began
dialogue through QCA with the main awarding bodies as to the mapping of
existing and proposed educational vocational schemes in media to national
industrial standards with the possibility of allowing the underpinning knowledge
elements of such educational schemes to contribute towards the relevant NVQ,
particularly in areas such as researching and recording information, knowledge of
the structure and current practices within the broadcast industry, law, and central,
devolved and local government.

Additional training providers and associations

It is not possible to mention here all the public, commercial and charitable media training providers and associations. As in any field there are some who have been delivering very good industry-related media training for a number of years and there are newcomers who come and go with relative frequency. The pages of the *Media Guardian* demonstrate the latter with numerous advertisements offering 'instant' training and the promise of work at the completion of the course. Some short courses are very good and are run by ex- or existing practitioners. Others may not meet expectations and as most can be quite costly it is advisable to choose with care and ascertain exactly what the course entails and what qualification is awarded at the end.

The following organizations and associations have consistent records of either offering training themselves or providing information and support for *bona fide* training organizations.

CSV Media

As one of the largest independent media training agencies in the UK, Community Service Volunteers offers social action media services and training. It works with local media throughout the UK to encourage people to become involved with their local community and to inform them on issues such as educational opportunities, health, welfare and environment, and where to seek practical advice. Long-established Action Desks at BBC and independent local radio and television stations produce broadcasts, answer queries and give information on the above and other issues. CSV also works closely with charities, community organizations and the public sector on appeals and campaigns that seek to raise social awareness of specific issues. Training is an important aspect of the work and CSV has been delivering vocational media techniques schemes in print, radio and television offered by the City and Guilds in England, Wales and Northern Ireland for a number of years with very good outcomes as regards direct entry to the industry or as a foundation for advanced study. Contact them on http://www.csv.org.uk.

The Community Media Association

The CMA, formerly the Community Radio Association, is a membership body for community media with the aim of supporting a third sector of local television and radio services alongside mainstream BBC and commercial output. It offers training at a local level that may be free to unwaged applicants and it also encourages applications from ethnic minority groups. It provides training for managers and trainers themselves as well as actively supporting community training projects. For further information contact them on http://www.commedia.org.uk.

The Commercial Radio Companies Association

The CRCA is the non-profit-making trade body for commercial radio and its members include almost every commercial radio station in the country. It offers training workshops in a variety of broadcast areas including management, presentation skills, interviewing and strategic planning. In particular their Next Generation workshops aim to develop the skills of 'middle managers' and enhance their suitability for chief executive positions within the industry. Contact the CRCA on http://www.crca.co.uk.

The Student Radio Association

The SRA is the national representative body for student radio in the UK and as such provides a national voice for student radio as well as linking with the International Association of Student Television and Radio (ASTAR) on European issues. It is supported by the Radio Authority and organizes conferences and training events featuring leading broadcasters, provides annual awards and publishes the magazine *In Frequency* three to four times a year. Trainees on broadcast journalism courses will find it an excellent source of information. Contact for further information on http://studentradio.org.uk.

The Television and Radio Training Unit

The TRTU works in partnership with Learning Skills Councils throughout the UK to provide intensive introductory courses in television, radio and public relations. Trainers are experienced journalists and presenters from within the commercial and public service sectors and specifically tailored courses include such elements as interviewing for print and broadcast, copy writing, basic media law, etc. Further information can be obtained on http://www. peaknet.co.uk.

Other sources of information

In addition to other bodies previously mentioned in the book the following are worth contacting as regards careers and training within the industry.

- British Film Institute (BFI)
- British Interactive Multimedia Association (BIMA)
- Broadcasting, Entertainment, Cinematograph and Theatre Union (BECTU)
- Guild of Editors
- Networking. Vera Media
- National Union of Journalists (NUJ)
- Producers Alliance for Cinema and Television (PACT)
- RADAR (Royal Association for Disability and Rehabilitation)

- Radio Academy
- Royal Television Society (RTS)
- Skill: national bureaux for students with disabilities
- The Moving Image Society (BKSTS)
- Women in Film and Television
- Writers' Guild of Great Britain.

Suggested activities

1 Contact the following for information on careers and training opportunities in the print and broadcast industries:
   a The National Council for the Training of Journalists
   b The Broadcast Journalism Training Council
   c The Periodicals Training Council
   d The British Broadcasting Corporation
   Make a note of the requirements and qualifications necessary for your chosen career path.
2 Find out information on the range of college and university courses that lead to a media qualification and make a list of those that offer the training that you seek. Consult a copy of *Media Courses UK* (BFI), which is a comprehensive guide to higher and further education courses on the BFI and Skillset data base.
3 Contact Skillset, the National Training Organization for radio, television, film and video, for information on careers in these areas. Similarly contact the Publishing National Training Organization for information on careers in magazine, newspaper and photo journalism. Make a short list of possible job and training opportunities on offer.
4 Peruse a selection of specialized trade journals such as *The Press Gazette*, *Broadcast*, *ICVA Magazine*, *The Radio Magazine*. Cut out or photocopy job advertisements for future reference.
5 Contact the BBC and request details and application forms for The Broadcast Journalist Trainee Scheme. Fill in the forms as an exercise to ascertain whether you have the qualifications, knowledge and ability to submit the application for real.
6 Write to local newspapers, magazines and radio stations requesting information on possible work placement. Put this in your folder.
7 Begin assembling a portfolio of your work. This may contain audio and video tapes, print items, photographs, work published in a college or community newsletter or magazine. Organize the work in a logical order – good presentation is vital.
8 Write an up-to-date CV that can be available at a moment's notice if a job opportunity arises.

9 Try to gain work experience on a voluntary basis at a local community or hospital radio/television station. Keep copies of your input to add to your portfolio.

10 Attend as many media-related events as possible and establish contacts with people in the industry. Keep a note in your contacts book for future reference.

Sources and resources

Benns' Media (annually) London: Miller Freeman Information Services.

British Broadcasting Corporation (2001) *BBC World of Careers*. Available at: http://www.bbc.co.uk (accessed 20 August 2001).

Broadcast Journalism Training Council (2001) *Welcome to the BJTC*. Available at: http://www.bjtc.org.uk (accessed 1 October 2001).

Community Media Association (2001) *About CMA*. Available at: http://www.commedia.org.uk (accessed 1 October 2001).

Commercial Radio Companies Association (2001) *Training and Events*. Available at: http://www.crca.co.uk (accessed 23 September 2001).

Community Service Volunteers (2001) *Home Page*. Available at: http://www.csv.org.uk (accessed 4 October 2001).

Editorial Training Centre (2001) *So you want to be a journalist*. Available at: http://www.editorial-centre.co.uk (accessed 15 October 2001).

Emap UK (2001) *Jobs*. Available at: http://www.emap.com (accessed 2 October 2001).

GWR Group (2001) *BJTC and GWR Reward The Best*. Available at: http://www.gwrgroup.com (accessed 15 October 2001).

Hold the Front Page (2001) *Training – becoming a journalist*. Available at: http://www.holdthefrontpage.co.uk (accessed 1 October 2001).

Llewellyn, S. (2000) *A Career Handbook for TV, Radio, Film, Video and Interactive Media*. A.&C. Black.

National Council for the Training of Journalists (2001) *Want to be a journalist?* Available at: http://www.nctj.com (accessed 29 August 2001).

Newspaper Society (2001) *Journalism Training*. Available at: http://www.newspapersoc.org.uk (accessed 1 October 2001).

Peak, S. and Fisher, P. (2002) *The Guardian Media Guide* (10th edition). London: Atlantic Books.

Periodicals Training Council (2001) *Training Careers/Work Experience*. Available at: http://www.ppa.co.uk/ptc (accessed 2 October 2001).

PMA Group (2001) *Starting in Journalism*. Available at: http://www.pma-group.com (accessed 16 October 2001).

Publishing National Training Organization (2001) *Home Page*. Available at: http://www.publishingnto.co.uk (accessed 10 August 2001).

Radio Authority (2001) *Careers in Broadcasting*. Available at: http://www.radioauthority.org.uk (accessed 12 August 2001).

Skillset (2001) *The Skillset/BFI Course Database*. Available at: http://www.skillsformedia.com (accessed 15 October 2001).

Student Radio Association (2001) *Support and Training*. Available at: http://www.studentradio.org.uk (accessed 21 August 2001).

Television and Radio Training Unit (2001) *Why Media Training?* Available at: http://www.peaknet.co.uk (accessed 16 October 2001).

Trinity Mirror plc (2001) *Editorial Training*. Available at: http://www.trinity.plc (accessed 17 October 2001).

Index

**Focal Press**

www.focalpress.com

Join Focal Press on-line

As a member you will enjoy the following benefits:

- · an email bulletin with **information on new books**
- · a regular **Focal Press Newsletter**:
  - o featuring a selection of new titles
  - o keeps you informed of **special offers, discounts and freebies**
  - o alerts you to **Focal Press news and events** such as author signings and seminars
- · complete access to **free content** and reference material on the focalpress site, such as the focalXtra articles and commentary from our authors
- · a **Sneak Preview** of selected titles (sample chapters) *before* they publish
- · a chance to have your say on our **discussion boards** and **review books** for other Focal readers

Focal Club Members are invited to give us feedback on our products and services.
Email: worldmarketing@focalpress.com – we want to hear your views!

Membership is **FREE**. To join, visit our website and register. If you require any further information regarding the on-line club please contact:

Emma Hales, Marketing Manager
Email: emma.hales@repp.co.uk
Tel: +44 (0) 1865 314556
Fax: +44 (0)1865 314572
Address: Focal Press, Linacre House,
Jordan Hill, Oxford, UK, OX2 8DP

Catalogue

For information on all Focal Press titles, our full catalogue is available online at www.focalpress.com and all titles can be purchased here via secure online ordering, or contact us for a free printed version:

USA
Email: christine.degon@bhusa.com
Tel: +1 781 904 2607

Europe and rest of world
Email: jo.coleman@repp.co.uk
Tel: +44 (0)1865 314220

Potential authors

If you have an idea for a book, please get in touch:

USA
editors@focalpress.com

Europe and rest of world
focal.press@repp.co.uk